D1074999

Speaking of
Higher Education

Speaking of Higher Education

The Academic's Book of Quotations

ROBERT BIRNBAUM

AMERICAN COUNCIL ON EDUCATION
PRAEGER
Series on Higher Education

Library of Congress Cataloguing-in-Publication Data

Birnbaum, Robert.
    Speaking of higher education : the academic's book of quotations / Robert Birnbaum.
        p.   cm. — (ACE/Praeger series on higher education)
    Includes bibliographical references and indexes.
    ISBN 0–275–98071–5 (alk. paper)
        1. Education, Higher—Quotations, maxims, etc.   2. Universities and colleges—Quotations, maxims, etc.   I. Title.   II. American Council on Education/Praeger series on higher education.
    LB2322.2.B57   2004
    378′.008—dc22   2003059646

British Library Cataloguing in Publication Data is available.

Library of Congress Catalog Card Number: 2003059646
ISBN: 0–275–98071–5

First published in 2004

Praeger Publishers, 88 Post Road West, Westport, CT 06881
An imprint of Greenwood Publishing Group, Inc.
www.praeger.com

Printed in the United States of America

The paper used in this book complies with the
Permanent Paper Standard issued by the National
Information Standards Organization (Z39.48–1984).

10   9   8   7   6   5   4   3   2   1

Contents

Preface

In the first century B.C.E., the Roman poet Horace expressed his gratitude to Athens for enabling him to "pursue truth through all her windings in the groves of the academy." In giving us the phrase that today is rendered as "the groves of Academe," Horace became one of the first of a number of scholars and philosophers, scientists and poets, dreamers and social critics, from antiquity to the present day, who have commented about the purposes, programs, and successes—as well as the fads, foibles, and failures—of the higher learning. *Speaking of Higher Education* (*SHE*) is the first published compilation of quotations dealing exclusively with higher education.

A good quotation encapsulates an idea and, to paraphrase a famous higher education advertising slogan, "an idea is a terrible thing to waste." The best quotations are those that are likely to arouse one of two kinds of reactions in readers: either "I wish *I* had said that," or "How could anyone *say* such an outrageous thing?" In a society bombarded by media giving precedence to the novel and innovative, it is all too easy to forget the voices of the past and the ideas they represent. These ideas, whether we accept or reject them, are our cultural heritage.

In *SHE* you will find poetry, imagination, and enthusiastic statements regarding the importance of higher education to the molding of the human intellect and spirit, and its centrality to the maintenance of democracy and freedom. You will also find equally passionate voices criticizing the academic enterprise and despairing over the perceived loss of an imagined Eden of long ago. Many of the views expressed here, whether supportive or critical, are cogent, rational, and principled. Others rely on unsupported generalizations, unreasonable claims, and occasional balderdash. Readers are free to decide which is which.

Some quotations are included because they are beautiful ("The University is a Paradise, Rivers of Knowledge are there . . ."), some because they are profound ("The task of a University is the creation of the future . . ."), and some because they are well known—sometimes because of their eloquence ("It is, Sir, as I have said, a small College. And yet, there are those who love it"), and sometimes ("rising tide of mediocrity") because they have been influential, political sound bites.

The words of others provide a vocabulary for discussing important ideas and can be sources of information, inspiration, and pleasure for writers, researchers, administrators, teachers, students, politicians, and other professionals. Scholars, administrators, and writers searching for some well-remembered, but elusive comment or a telling statement that enlivens a story may use this book to trace it to its source. Students of the history or culture of higher education may find it interesting to assess changes in concepts and language over time. *SHE* should prove helpful to anyone preparing a presentation about an academic issue, or a presentation to an academic group (and particularly to one preparing an academic presentation *to* an academic group). But an equally important audience for this book is the general reader who is interested in the world of academia and finds pleasure in well-crafted language Whether *SHE* is kept on the work desk or the night table, the essential purposes remain the same: to inform and delight.

What Is Included?

Quotations have been selected that explicitly refer to higher education, or that were made in a higher-education setting (such as a commencement) so that the relevance to higher education is implied, even if not explicitly mentioned, or that were made by an author generally considered a higher educationalist even if no reference to higher education appears in the quotation. The decision not to include comments about education in general means that many memorable statements that could be applied to the higher learning, but which were not written expressly about it, have been excluded. Therefore, you will not find in *SHE* such classics as Aristotle's view that educated men were superior to the uneducated "as much as the living are to the dead," John Adams's comment in his letter to Abigail Adams that "education makes a greater difference between man and man than nature has made between man and brute," and H. G. Wells's caution that "human history becomes more and more a race between education and catastrophe." Statements that met the higher-education-specific threshold were then considered for *SHE* based on three criteria: brevity, importance, and delight.

Brevity. Many quotations in *SHE* are under 50 words, and only a handful (because they can best be appreciated by reading them in their entirety) are more than 100 words in length. For example, Mark Twain's lengthy appreciation of the pleasures of receiving honorary degrees was included because of its humor. Other longer comments, from scholars of the past such as Adam Smith, Cardinal Newman, and Thorstein Veblen, provide pleasure through their mastery of majestic language cadences of long ago. And more contemporary authors such as Clark Kerr or P. F. Kluge dazzle us with paragraphs of unusual beauty and power that trace the lineage of the university back over 500 years to its beginnings, or evoke the essence of an institution.

Importance. A quotation may be important because it provides insight into a significant or enduring issue, reflects a social or educational movement, represents a seminal idea by a key figure, exemplifies one or another position in an ongoing educational or social policy debate, or captures the essence of an historic era. Importance should not be confused with truthfulness. All truthful statements are not memorable (as evidenced by any reading of academic prose), and not all memorable statements are universally considered to be truthful. The essence of a quotable quotation is not that it is necessarily true, but rather that even readers who disagree with the author's views acknowledge that something of importance has been said in an exemplary or particularly insightful or artful way.

Delight. One person's humorous quip is another's offensive jape. And what some may see as soaring prose may be dismissed by others as maudlin claptrap. I have attempted here to include statements made by educators and others when they speak as poets as much as they do practitioners or scholars, and when they attend to style as well as substance. Delight results when a statement engages the reader because of its wit, craftsmanship, or charm.

Although readers will enjoy perusing the entries in the form presented here, I hope that at least some will be captivated enough by an author's argument, substance, or style to return to the original text to more fully understand the author's intentions and place the brief samples given here into the context of the larger work. Those readers who do may find additional gems of ideas and language that could not be included in *SHE* because of editorial production considerations or copyright law limitations. To the extent possible, sources for the quotations have been provided in enough detail to enable those who wish to read further to locate the original texts from which they come. Complete bibliographic information regarding almost all the books and journals cited in *SHE* can be found in the Library of Congress Online Catalog at <http://catalog.loc.gov/>.

The Uses of Quotations

Colleges and universities are social systems constructed by language. We come to understand what they are, and what they should be, through the language we develop to discuss them. To study, in Matthew Arnold's phrase, "the best which has been thought and said in the world" about higher education is to understand how our perceptions of these institutions, and their relationship to society, have developed, as well as how they have changed over time. Words are the building blocks of the narratives that guide our lives. A renewed awareness of words of the past may help remind us of the importance of colleges and universities, not just as an industry, but as social institutions. *SHE* has no real themes; the variety of topics and the differences in perspective are too diverse for that. But perhaps there are meta-themes that may be considered—how enduring the issues, how varied the voices, and how diverse the purposes of the uniquely American higher education enterprise.

Higher education is at the same time timeless and in constant flux. Its timelessness is best expressed in Clark Kerr's description of universities as among the few institutions to come down to us essentially unchanged since medieval times, while its flux can be seen in the dramatic changes in institutional structures, programs, and students over the past 200, 100, or for that matter, 50 years. Following the chronological presentation of quotations in *SHE* will demonstrate that arguments over such matters as the nature of the curriculum, the degree to which institutions should be held to criteria of efficiency developed in other sectors, the benefits versus the corrosive effects of intercollegiate athletics, and whether faculty involvement in research improves or worsens teaching, are much the same today as they were 100 years ago. Now as then, presidents are criticized for failing to provide leadership, institutions are criticized for mimicking business forms, faculty are criticized for failing to teach effectively, and students are criticized for educational sloth and weak preparation. The anguished cry against anonymity of the 1960s, "I am a student. Please do not fold, spindle, or mutilate" is presaged in the 1920s by the distressed student claiming "They do not know I am here." A faculty senator of 1900 brought back to life today might find the order of business, the interactions of members, and (more to the point) much of the agenda instantly recognizable.

That most issues seem never to change, and nothing is ever finally settled, should not be considered a criticism of American colleges and universities as much as it is a recognition that our higher education system accurately reflects the varied interests of a pluralistic, democratic society. Different groups create their own narratives of what institutions should do, how they should function, what should be taught, and who should participate. The growing acceptance of one group's narrative is challenged by other groups with a different story to tell. It is the bane of our higher education system, as well as its genius. The issue of what should be taught cannot—and should not—ever be settled. After all, as Frederick Rudolph pointed out, "If the world does not always make sense, why should the curriculum?"

The articulated functions of academic institutions are so diverse that quotations related to "purposes" were subdivided into eight categories to accommodate them. Here you will find, in miniature, the conflicting claims that higher education should serve the individual or serve society, strengthen democracy or strengthen the economy, develop the intellect or serve more hidden purposes related to the maintenance of the existing social order. Visionaries may believe that it is possible to create a single system, curriculum, or policy that can accommodate equally these different narratives, but that is only pleasant delusion. The only purposes about which there are likely to be some moderate consensus are those suggested in the beautiful and poetic statements that are listed in *SHE* under the subject heading "Purpose: Transcendent." They may be agreeable precisely because they are so general that while they provide inspiration they have few direct implications for policy or practice.

SHE is not an essay, but a series of disconnected comments waiting for the reader to determine how and if they may be related. To be sure, the quotations are grouped under subject headings, but they themselves are somewhat arbitrary and equivocal. Many, perhaps most, of the quotations could have been placed under a different heading depending on which of several words or ideas one wished to stress. The quotations themselves are arranged under each subject heading in temporal rather than "logical" order. A reader can select and organize any quotations in any desired way to tell a story of his or her own choosing, to support one or another position, or to defend or attack the higher education enterprise. Different readers are likely to find different quotations to be the most compelling, and you are encouraged to reform my categories into any groupings that are congenial to your own ideologies and imaginations, and to create different connections between them.

The Limitations of Quotations

SHE's avowed goal of presenting "the best" of what has been said about higher education is a scholarly conceit that must be taken figuratively rather than literally. As with any collection of quotations, only a minuscule sample of what has been written about higher education over more than two millennia—and has been translated into English and considered of enough value to have been repeated by others—could be reviewed for inclusion. And there are obvious biases that arise not just from the process of selecting the quotations, but also from the nature of the authors themselves, the topics about which they wrote, and reasons they chose to write about them. For example, you will note that some institutions (and the presidents of these institutions) are mentioned frequently, while others appear not at all. This should not be interpreted as reflecting the relative excellence of specific institutions as much as it reflects their relative social status. As suggested in the words attributed to Berton Braley in the 1930s, referring to the fact that stories of college athletics gave disproportionate attention to a small number of colleges, that "gridiron heroes exclusively hail (in stories) from Harvard, or Princeton or Yale!" had to do with their institutional cachet rather than their athletic prowess.

Just as institutions differ in the frequency with which they are represented, so some authors are more likely to be cited than others. College presidents, for example, are often quoted because they are presidents, rather than because they necessarily have more important things to say than nonpresidents. Providing quotable quotes is part of their job description; as with other aspects of the president's role, some have done it better than others.

These limitations suggest that quotations in *SHE* are best thought of as dealing with generalities rather than with specifics. That is, interesting or provocative comments made about one particular institution, one particular incident, one specific crisis, or one specific president, for example, are important mainly because they can be generalized to other schools, other incidents, other crises, or other presidents. Frank Lloyd Wright's statement that "Harvard takes perfectly good plums as students, and turns them into prunes" makes perfect sense when the names of other institutions are substituted.

Problems like these suggest that any selection of quotations is unlikely to present a balanced view of higher education. It is in the nature of things, in education as in politics, that sound bites that are strident, outrageous, or even on the fringes of lunacy are often more memorable than comments that are thoughtful, reasoned, and nuanced. Hyperbole or sarcasm may be cheap ways to make a point, but they are often effective. In general, because of the styles of writing usually employed, memorable quotations are least likely to come from works of scholarly analysis, more likely to come from works of synthesis, and most likely to come from works of opinion.

I have not included in *SHE* several charming statements either because the collections of quotations in which they are found provide no source, or I was unable to confirm that the author quoted actually ever existed. As one example, "if your professor wrote it, it's as near to truth as you ever need to get" (a brilliant insight whose validity will be affirmed by any graduate student) is attributed in several quotation collections to one John Watson of the University of Canterbury. The only person by that name at that institution has informed me that he is not the source. So was there ever such person who made such a statement? If there wasn't, there certainly should have been!

Some wonderful statements, although attributed to real people, were not included for other reasons. For example, lack of corroborating evidence led to the painful decision to omit from *SHE* the classical comments of the eponymous William Archibald Spooner (1844–1930), Warden of New College, Oxford, who is reputed to have told an undergraduate student "you have tasted your worm, you have hissed my mystery lectures, and you must leave by the first town drain." Warden Spooner is also remembered for proposing a toast to "our queer old dean." I have assuaged my guilt for omitting these delightful statements from *SHE*'s text by including them in this preface.

Quotations may morph from one variation to another, as dimly remembered phases go through successive faulty communications channels in a manner similar to children playing the game of "telephone." For example, there are at least a dozen versions of how William F. Buckley stated his preference to be governed by a group of citizens rather than by the faculty of Harvard University. Which of them is accurate, and does it matter? After all, as Shakespeare said, "if you call a rose something else, it would still smell good," or something like that. Which is exactly the point. Buckley is a masterful stylist, who obviously gives careful consideration to how he wishes to express an idea. You will find the authentic (as well as the most graceful) version of Buckley's statement in *SHE* under the subject heading "Ivory Tower."

Successive inaccurate transmissions are not the only cause of problematic attributions. For example, some quoted statements may have originally been spoken, rather than written. U.S. President James Garfield's famous comment about Mark Hopkins (the president of Williams College) and the log, was made during a dinner speech and reconstructed later (in various renditions) by those in attendance. One standard book of quotations has it as "A university is a student on one end of a pine log and Mark Hopkins on the other." Another says, "A pine bench with Mark Hopkins at one end of it and me at the other, is a good enough college for me." The version used in *SHE* is "The ideal college is Mark Hopkins at one end of a log and a student on the other." It may not necessarily be the most authentic rendition, but since it was good enough for Frederick Rudolph, the eminent academic historian and authority on Hopkins, it's a good enough quotation for me.

Other attribution problems come when it is difficult to locate any original source (for example, "University politics are vicious precisely because the stakes are so small," usually attributed to Henry Kissinger), or when a statement is included in a primary source by different authors. For example, both Alfred North Whitehead and Robert Maynard Hutchins used the phrase "a well-planned University course is a study of the wide sweep of generality . . ." in their original works; in this case, *SHE* cites the Whitehead version since it predates Hutchins by several years.

These examples suggest that it is well to be cautious about using quotations—even those that are well known—for other than literary purposes unless their provenance can be established. I have tried whenever possible to identify in *SHE* the most plausible versions of attributed quotations, recognizing that future scholars may conclude that they are partially or wholly inaccurate. Nevertheless, before you assume that a certain statement was made by a certain author, take heed of the words attributed to the esteemed quotemeister Yogi Berra: "I didn't really say everything I said."

Searching for Quotations in This Book

The body of *SHE* consists of over 1,670 quotations sorted into 13 chapters under 99 subject headings. The subject headings in each chapter are arranged in alphabetic order. Quotations within subject categories are listed chronologically so that readers can see how ideas may have changed over time (or, of equal interest, how they have not). When the exact date of a quotation is not known, it is identified as "no date." As a convention, unless there is evidence to the contrary, its place in the chronological record was calculated as 80 percent of the time between the author's birth and death.

The first step in searching for a quotation is to look under the subject heading in which it is most likely to appear. When a quotation does not appear under the expected heading, related subjects should also be checked (for example, a statement related to administration might instead appear under such headings as management, leadership, or president).

Two indices are provided at the conclusion of the quotation entries. The first is a subject heading index, in which all 99 subject headings are shown in alphabetic order. The second is an author index to assist in locating materials when the subject headings are not helpful but the author is known or suspected. Each author's name is followed by a listing of the subjects and page number(s) in which quotations appear

Each quotation entry is divided into three parts: 1) the source, 2) the quotation, and 3) the author.

Part 1. The Source (Date, Citation)

Date. The date provided indicates when the statement was made or published. When the quotation is taken from an original text, the date of the publication of that text is considered to be the date of the quotation (unless the text itself identifies the statement as having been made at another time). If a quotation is taken from a later printing of an original text, the date used is that of the original publication. If there is no way to determine when a statement was made, the notation "no date" appears. When an approximate date can be inferred, it is preceded by the abbreviation "c." (for "circa," Latin for "about").

Citation. Although there may be occasional variations, citations used in *SHE* basically take one of three forms based on the nature of the source. The three forms differ considerably in the confidence that can be expressed concerning the authenticity of the quotation. The three forms are 1) an original source, 2) a secondary source citing an original source, and 3) a secondary source without a citation. In all cases the sources are cited in enough detail to permit the reader to verify them.

1) Original source. This is a quotation in *SHE* that has been taken directly from material prepared by the author of the quotation. When the statement has been confirmed in the first edition of a book, or in a published journal article,

the page number is given. If instead the statement has been verified using an edition other than the original, or through an authoritative electronic version of a book (such as those available through Project Gutenberg and similar sources located on the Online Books Page, <http://onlinebooks.library.upenn.edu/>), identification by chapter or section may be provided since page numbers may be misleading. Quotations that are identified in *SHE* as coming from an original source may be relied on as authentic.

2) Secondary source citing an original source. This is a quotation taken from a secondary source that provides a citation to an original source. The source cited may be an obscure journal that is difficult to locate, a journal or book cited without providing specific dates or page numbers, material from a specialized library collection, or some other source that makes confirmation in the original difficult or impossible. Readers will have to use their judgment in determining whether the secondary source appears credible, and from that decide the degree to which the quotation may be accurate as presented. Experience indicates that such quotations may be moderately paraphrased, ellipses may not have been used to identify missing portions, typographical errors or sloppy scholarship may have inserted plausible (but incorrect) words into the text, and the beginnings and endings of statements may not be properly identified. Readers may rely on the source "quoted in" as being authentic (that is, it is presented in *SHE* as it appears in the secondary source), but no claim is made as to the authenticity of the statement in the primary source, or to the accuracy with which the secondary source has quoted it.

3) Secondary sources without citations. These are the quotations for which the phrase *caveat emptor* was created. They often appear in print or electronic quotation collections. They provide no citation to the source from which the quotation was taken. The fact that the wording of such a quotation is consistent across a number of different volumes or sites on the World Wide Web does not increase the probable validity of the quotation, since many sites merely copy material available (errors and all) from other sites. In other words, for the most part there is little pretense that there has been any attempt to verify these quotations through any scholarly process. Attempts to confirm the actual authors of these quotations are usually futile, and in several cases when *SHE* attempted to authenticate attributed quotations the presumed authors denied they had ever said them. Quotations in this latter category have been removed from *SHE,* although the unwary reader will still find them being presented elsewhere. Quotations in *SHE* that share this provenance are identified as "attributed in," rather than "quoted in," a secondary source. No primary source is identified, and readers should not assume without further investigation that the statement is an accurate representation of the author's words, that the words were uttered or written by the author identified, or even (without being authenticated in other ways) that the author even exists.

Part 2. The Quotation

The quotations themselves are the core of *SHE,* and every attempt has been made to present them as they were created by their authors. That means that statements taken from original sources preserve their original punctuation, spelling, and wording. When spellings appear that are archaic or based on non-

American or nonstandardized English (e.g., Peter Finley Dunne's comment by Mr. Dooley that "Ye can lade a man up to th' university, but ye can't make him think"), they are usually so obvious that no additional notation is required. Occasionally, a simple definition of an esoteric word or translation of foreign phrase (e.g., *functus officio*) is inserted in brackets so that it is not mistaken for a part of the original statement. When typographical errors appear in the original text, they are identified in *SHE* with the notation [sic], Latin for "thus," indicating that the material is presented as originally written and is not an error. A quotation that begins in the middle of a line in the original is indicated by capitalizing the first letter of the abstracted material and enclosing it in brackets. When quotations are taken from secondary sources, fidelity to the original cannot be assumed.

Portions of some of the quotations in *SHE* will be familiar because they exist in other quotation collections. They may be presented here in more complete form than elsewhere when such extension provides context, clarifies, or just adds to the pleasure of the reader. As an example, Robert Ingersoll's oft-quoted aphorism "Colleges are places where pebbles are polished and diamonds are dimmed" becomes even more delightful when the next line, which doesn't appear in other quotation collections, is included: "If Shakespeare had graduated at Oxford, he might have been a quibbling attorney, or a hypocritical parson."

For purposes of clarity, brackets are used to insert added words that do not appear in the original statement, but that would be understood by a reader of the complete work (for example, a sentence beginning "It is . . ." may be clarified by inserting in brackets words consistent with the author's clear intention so that it reads "It [the university] is. . . ."

Part 3. The Author Heading (Name, Dates, Professional Position)

Name. Usually given in the form used by the author (e.g., J. McKeen Cattell rather than James McKeen Cattell). When the author is better known by a pseudonym, the pseudonym is followed by the legal name in brackets (e.g., Mark Twain [Samuel Langhorne Clemens]).

Dates. Years of birth and death are given, when known. In some cases, dates are unknown and are indicated by "?". When the dates are questionable (e.g., Ambrose Bierce, whose year of birth is uncertain and who is alleged to have died at some point on an adventure in Mexico), the presumed years are given and followed by "?".

Professional Position. Many of the authors quoted in *SHE* have been accomplished people who have held a number of important positions. Since a complete biography cannot be provided for each of them, I have adopted a convention that, while simplifying their identification, may also at times be misleading. The convention is that an author who has been the chief executive of one or more institutions of higher education is identified in that way, even when the author is as well, or sometimes even better known for some other achievement (e.g., W. H. Cowley who is probably better known as a professor of higher education at Stanford than because of his earlier service as president of Hamilton College). With rare exceptions (for example, those who have in addition to their academic careers also served as U.S. representative or senator, or president of the United States) these other achievements are not listed. Giving precedence to academic presidencies means that, although a person who later became a president may have said something quotable, he or she may not have been president at the time the statement was made. Authors who have neither been president of a college or university, or held a comparable position of national visibility, are usually identified by their position and institution at the time the quoted statement was made, or by their present position if known.

Errors and Omissions

I have tried to make the materials in this book as accurate as possible. However, to collect quotations is to wend one's way through a minefield of dubious attributions, misidentified authors, and statements erroneously validated through repetition rather than through reference to evidence. In addition, editorial errors are inevitable in any large collection of collected materials. Admitting that there are errors is one thing; knowing what they are is quite another.

In the hope that there may be a future revision of *SHE*, I invite readers to provide scholarly assistance by informing me of sins of commission. In particular, I would welcome suggestions of original published sources for quotations that are identified here as "attributed." Comments on sins of omission are welcome as well. The statements presented in *SHE* were drawn from only a fraction of the original and secondary sources available. Please inform me of materials that do not appear in *SHE* that are as important and delightful as the best of those included here and that should be considered for future editions.

Readers can send suggestions to me by e-mail at she@ace.nche.edu or by snail mail at 8920 S. Bryerly Court, Hereford, AZ 85615. I will respond to all comments, and persons who submit suggestions that are included in any future editions of *SHE* will be acknowledged in the revised text.

Acknowledgments

A number of colleagues provided assistance by suggesting quotations for inclusion in *SHE* or by locating sources. They include Luis Angel Alejo, Estela Mara Bensimon, Matthew Birnbaum, George R. Boggs, Rita Bornstein, Richard Chait, Monique Clague, Arthur M. Cohen, Joseph Crowley, Thomas Ehrlich, Marian L. Gade, Judy Glazer-Raymo, Edmund J. Gleazer, Jr., Chanita Goodblatt, Joseph Hankin, Stanley N. Katz, Joseph F. Kauffman, David Leslie, Patricia Marin, Roger H. Martin, Christine McPhail, Michael A. Olivas, KerryAnn O'Meara, Donna Paoletti, Thomas Schaefer, Jack Schuster, Merrill P. Schwartz, Lauren Scott, Steven Selden, Mary Ann Settlemire, Patrick Terenzini, John R. Thelin, and George B. Vaughan. I am also grateful to the library staffs at the University of Arizona, the University of Maryland (and particularly Diane Harvey), the Sierra Vista Public Library, the American Council on Education's Library and Information Service, and the Association of Governing Board's Zwingle Resource Center for obtaining materials and suggesting resources. I appreciate the courtesy of Gary Rhoades and his higher education colleagues at the University of Arizona in appointing me a visiting scholar for the 2002–2003 academic year and giving me access to library materials. I wish also to acknowledge the assistance of Carl Gaither, author of a number of specialized scholarly collections of quotations, for freely sharing with me his experience and advice, and Ron Magid, University of Tennessee-Knoxville, for his collegial generosity in giving me access to his collection of quotations accumulated over a 40-year academic career.

Section One

Higher Education and Society

Chapter 1

Purpose

Purpose: Conflicting

1929, "Preface," in Howard J. Savage, *American College Athletics,* p. xviii.

The weakness of the American university as it exists to-day lies in its lack of intellectual sincerity. It stands nominally for high intellectual ideals. Its effort at intellectual leadership is diluted with many other efforts in fields wholly foreign to this primary purpose. Inter-college athletics form only one of these.

> —**Henry S. Pritchett** (1857–1939), President, Carnegie Foundation for the Advancement of Teaching

1936, *The Higher Learning in America,* p. 1.

The most striking fact about the higher learning in America is the confusion that besets it. This confusion begins in the high school and continues to the loftiest levels of the university.

> —**Robert Maynard Hutchins** (1899–1977), President, University of Chicago

1963, *The Uses of the University,* pp. 8–9.

The university is so many things to so many different people that it must, of necessity, be partially at war with itself.

> —**Clark Kerr** (1911–2003), Chancellor, University of California, Berkeley; President, University of California

1965, *The Modern University,* p. 10.

A university is only one of many kinds of educational enterprise, and it may lose its distinctive value if attempts are made to enlarge its function unduly.

> —**George Leslie Brook** (1910–1987), professor of English language and medieval English literature, Manchester University

1968, *The Academic Revolution,* pp. xx–xxi.

American educators have seldom been able to give coherent explanations for what they were doing. Even when they did have a consistent theory, it often had little or no relationship to the actual results of their actions.

—**Christopher Jencks** (1936–),
professor of social policy,
Harvard University; **David Riesman**
(1909–2002) professor of sociology,
Harvard University

1968, "First glimpses of a new world," in Norman Cousins (ed.), *What I Have Learned,* p. 178.

The most embarrassing question that can be raised in a university is, what are we trying to do?

—**Robert Maynard Hutchins**
(1899–1977), President,
University of Chicago

1972, "Four paradoxes of higher education and how to deal with them," *Chronicle of Higher Education,* 1 May, p. 8.

[O]ur goal in higher education should be . . . to reaffirm the importance to society of protecting the university as a conservator of the past against the Philistines of the left and as an oasis for dispute, discovery, and creation, protected from assault from the Philistines of the right.

—**Kingman Brewster** (1919–1988),
President, Yale University; Master,
University College, London

1973, *The Purposes and the Performance of Higher Education in the United States,* pp. 4–5.

The campus is a place for concern with values, but it is not a church; for concern with public policy issues, but it is not a political party; for concern with the environment for the developmental growth of students, but it is not a parent; for concern with effective management of its own affairs, but it is not in business to manage the affairs of others; for concern with the application of the coercive power of government, but it has neither the power nor the responsibility of government; for concern with the physical condition of life of its members, but it should not be a "company town."

—**Carnegie Commission
on Higher Education**

1974, *Leadership and Ambiguity,* p. 195.

Almost any educated person can deliver a lecture entitled "The Goals of the University." Almost no one will listen to the lecture voluntarily. For the most part, such lectures and their companion essays are well-intentioned exercises in social rhetoric, with little operational content.

—**Michael D. Cohen** (1945–), professor
of complex systems, information, and
public policy, University of Michigan;
James G. March (1928–), professor
of international management,
political science, and sociology,
Stanford University

1975, "The Little League and the imperatives of independence," *Educational Record,* Winter, p. 6.

[T]he outsiders want the students trained for that first job out of college, and the academics inside the system want the students educated for 50 years of self-fulfillment. The trouble is, the [students] want both. The ancient collision between each student's short-term and long-term goals, between "training" and "education," between "vocational" and "general," between honing the mind and nourishing the soul, divides the professional educators, divides the outside critics and supporters, and divides the students too.

—**Harlan Cleveland** (1918–), political
scientist; President, University of Hawaii

Purpose: Democratic

1786, letter to Matthew Robinson, 23 March, quoted in David McCullough, *John Adams,* 2001, p. 364.

[A] memorable change must be made in the system of education and knowledge must become so general as to raise the lower ranks of society nearer to the higher. The education of a nation instead of being confined to a few schools and universities for the instruction of the few, must become the national care for the formation of the many.

—**John Adams** (1735–1826),
President of the United States

1822, letter to W. T. Barry, 4 August, quoted in James Morton Smith (ed.), *The Republic of Letters, Volume 3,* 1995, p. 1821.

Learned Institutions ought to be the favorite objects with every free people.... What spectacle can be more edifying or more seasonable, than that of Liberty & Learning, each leaning on the other for their mutual and surest support.

—**James Madison** (1751–1836),
President of the United States

1826, letter to Thomas Jefferson, 24 February, quoted in James Morton Smith (ed.), *The Republic of Letters, Volume 3,* 1995, p. 1967.

[T]he University [is] the temple thro' which alone lies the road to that of Liberty.

—**James Madison** (1751–1836),
President of the United States

1832, Baccalaureate Address, quoted in Richard Hofstadter and Wilson Smith (eds.), *American Higher Education: A Documentary History, Volume I,* 1961, p. 377.

Wherever there is a privileged order, no matter how constituted—whether like the *patrician* of ancient, or the *ecclesiastic* of modern Rome—it will, if not fully checked and counterbalanced, in the long run, become overbearing and tyrannical. I look to the college for a seasonable supply of countervailing agents. I look to a well-educated independent yeomanry as the sheet anchor of the Republic.

—**Philip Lindsley** (1786–1855),
President, University of Nashville

1902, "The university and democracy," in *The Trend in Higher Education,* 1905, p. 12.

Democracy has been given a mission to the world.... [T]he university is the prophet of this democracy and, as well, its priest and its philosopher; ... the university is the Messiah of democracy, its to-be-expected deliverer.

—**William Rainey Harper** (1856–1906),
President, University of Chicago

1921, *The Frontier in American History,* p. 283.

Nothing in our educational history is more striking than the steady pressure of democracy upon its universities to adapt them to the requirements of all the people.

p. 288.

The light of these [state] university watch towers should flash from State to State until American democracy itself is illuminated with higher and broader ideals of what constitutes service to the State and to mankind; of what are prizes; of what is worthy of praise and reward.

—**Frederick Jackson Turner** (1861–1932), professor of history, University of Wisconsin

1932, quoted in John S. Brubacher and Willis Rudy, *Higher Education in Transition,* 1958, p. 169.

The state universities hold that there is no intellectual service too undignified for them to perform. They maintain that every time they lift the intellectual level of any class or group, they enhance the intellectual level of every class or group.

—**Lotus D. Coffman** (1875–1938), President, University of Minnesota

Purpose: Individual

c. seventeenth century, *Of Education: To Master Samuel Hartlib,* quoted in A. C. Spectorsky, *College Years,* 1958, p. 335.

I call a complete and generous education that which fits a man to perform justly, skillfully, and magnanimously all the offices both public and private of peace and war.

—**John Milton** (1608–1674), English poet

1858, *The Idea of a University,* Discourse VII.

[University training] is the education which gives a man a clear conscious view of his own opinions and judgments, a truth in developing them, an eloquence in expressing them, and a force in urging them. . . . It prepares him to fill any post with credit, and to master any subject with facility. It shows him how to accommodate himself to others, how to throw himself into their state of mind, how to bring before them his own, how to influence, how to come to an understanding with them, how to bear with them. . . . He has the repose of a mind which lives in itself, while it lives in the world, and which has resources for its happiness at home when it cannot go abroad. He has a gift which serves him in public, and supports him in retirement, without

which good fortune is but vulgar, and with which failure and disappointment have a charm.

—**John Henry (Cardinal) Newman** (1801–1890), Rector, Catholic University of Ireland

1867, "Inaugural address," in Francis W. Garforth, *John Stuart Mill on Education,* 1971, p. 215.

The proper business of a university is . . . not to tell us from authority what we ought to believe, and make us accept the belief as a duty, but to give us information and training, and help us form our own belief in a manner worthy of intelligent beings who seek for truth at all hazards and demand to know all the difficulties, in order that they may be better qualified to find, or recognize, the most satisfactory mode of resolving them.

—**John Stuart Mill** (1806–1873), Rector, St. Andrews University

1868, Charter Day Address, quoted in Arthur Levine, *Handbook of Undergraduate Curriculum,* 1978, p. 561.

[I] trust we have laid the foundation of an University—"an institution where any person can find instruction in any study."

—**Ezra Cornell** (1807–1874), U.S. financier; founder of Cornell University

1899, quoted in Waitman Barbe, *Going to College,* 1899, p. 68.

It has been well said that an educated man has a sharp axe in his hand, and an uneducated man a dull axe. I should say that the purpose of a college course is to sharpen the axe to its keenest edge.

—**Nathaniel Butler, Jr.** (1853–1927), President, Colby College

1902, "University building," *Popular Science Monthly,* August, p. 332.

Higher education has been defined as that training which demands that a man should leave home. It means a breaking of the leading strings. It means the entrance to another atmosphere.

—**David Starr Jordan** (1851–1931),
President, Stanford University

1904, notes for "Alumni Dinner, Orange, 10 November," quoted in Lawrence R. Veysey, *The Emergence of the American University,* 1965, p. 242.

[Princeton is] not a place of special but of general education, not a place where a lad finds his profession, but a place *where he finds himself.*

—**Woodrow Wilson** (1856–1924),
President, Princeton University;
President of the United States

1905, quoted in Frederick Rudolph, *Curriculum,* 1977, p. 239.

The educated man is the all-round man, the symmetrical man. The aim of a college is not to make scholars. The aim is to make broad, cultivated men, physically sound, intellectually awake, socially refined and gentlemanly, with an appreciation of art, music, literature, and with sane, simple religion, all in proportion . . . all-round men.

—**George Harris** (1844–1922),
President, Amherst College

1909, quoted in Christopher J. Lucas, *American Higher Education,* 1994, p. 201.

If young gentlemen get from their years at college only manliness, esprit de corps, a release of their social gifts, a training in give and take, a catholic taste in men, and the standards of true sportsmanship, they have gained much but they have not gained what a college should give them.

—**Woodrow Wilson** (1856–1924),
President, Princeton University;
President of the United States

1909, Inaugural address, in *At War with Academic Traditions,* 1934, p. 3

Among his other wise sayings, Aristotle remarked that man is by nature a social animal; and it is in order to develop his powers as a social being that American colleges exist. The object of the undergraduate department is not to produce hermits, each imprisoned in the cell of his own intellectual pursuits, but men fitted to take their place in the community, and live in contact with their fellow men.

—**Abbott Lawrence Lowell**
(1856–1943), President,
Harvard University

1912, in Henry Festing Jones (ed.), *The Notebooks of Samuel Butler,* p. 180.

Schools and colleges are not intended to foster genius and to bring it out. Genius is a nuisance, and it is the duty of schools and colleges to abate it by setting genius-traps in its way. They are the artificial obstructions in a hurdle race—tests of skill and endurance, but in themselves useless.

—**Samuel Butler** (1835–1902),
English novelist; scholar

1912, "The social value of the college-bred," *Memories and Studies,* p. 309.

The best claim that a college education can possibly make on your respect, the best thing it can aspire to accomplish for you, is this: that it should *help you to know a good man when you see him.*

—**William James** (1842–1910),
professor of philosophy,
Harvard University

1914, speech, Pittsburgh, 24 October, quoted in Stephen Donadio, et al. (eds.), *The New York Public Library Book of Twentieth-Century Quotes,* 1992, p. 166.

The use of a university is to make young gentlemen as unlike their fathers as possible.

—**Woodrow Wilson** (1856–1924),
President, Princeton University;
President of the United States

1914, *Report for 1913–14,* quoted in Edward C. Elliott (ed.), *The Rise of a University, Vol. II,* 1937, p. 25.

Scholarship alone is plainly useless as a guide to conduct. Science is in the same category. Literary achievement and literary reputation are no guarantee of common sense and ordinary decorum. It must be true, then, that the world-old problem remains. It is that of shaping and directing men's conduct. This is, after all, the end and aim of a university's existence and the only reason that can justify the labors and sacrifices necessary to make a university possible.

—**Nicholas Murray Butler**
(1862–1947), President,
Columbia University

1914, attributed in *The Underground Grammarian,* February, 1985.

Gentlemen, you are now about to embark on a course of studies which will occupy you for two years. Together, they form a noble adventure. But I would like to remind you of an important point. Nothing that you will learn in the course of your studies will be of the slightest possible use to you in after life, save only this, that if you work hard and intelligently you should be able to detect when a man is talking rot, and that, in my view, is the main, if not the sole, purpose of education.

—**John Alexander Smith** (1863–1939),
professor of moral and metaphysical
philosophy, University of Oxford

c. 1948, motto, cited in Frederick Rudolph, *The American College and University: A History,* 1962, p. 487.

Let each become all he is capable of being.

—**State University of New York**

1954, *Many a Good Crusade,* p. 422.

The ability to think straight, some knowledge of the past, some vision of the future, some skill to do useful service, some urge to fit that service into the well-being of the community—these are the most vital things education must try to produce.

—**Virginia Gildersleeve** (1877–1965),
Dean, Barnard College

c. 1960, attributed in Thomas Ehrlich, *The Courage to Inquire,* 1995, pp. 1–2.

A university education should equip one to entertain three things: a friend, an idea, and one's self.

—**J. E. Wallace Sterling** (1906–1985),
President, Stanford University

1962, *The American College,* p. 19.

The great problem today is not essentially different from what it has been for a long time. It is how to do better the things that colleges were intended to do; how to realize more fully, despite pressures from without and divided councils within, the aim of developing the potentialities of each student.

—**Nevitt R. Sanford** (1909–1995),
professor of psychology and education,
Stanford University

1963, "Mass society and liberal education," in *Power, Politics and People,* pp. 367–68.

The aim of the college, for the individual student, is to eliminate the need in his life for the college; the task is to help him become a self-educating man. For only that will set him free.

—**C. Wright Mills** (1916–1962),
professor of sociology,
Columbia University

1963, *Quote,* 27 January, quoted in James B. Simpson, *Simpson's Contemporary Quotations,* 1988.

The most important function of education at any level is to develop the personality of the individual and the significance of his life to himself and to others. This is the basic architecture of a life; the rest is ornamentation and decoration of the structure.

—**Grayson Kirk** (1903–1997),
President, Columbia University

1966, *The Reforming of General Education,* p. 181.

For the young student himself, it is important that the college experience be unhampered and distinctive.... [T]he college can still be one of the few places of broad intellectual adventure, the place where one can resist, momentarily, the harness that society now seeks to impose at an earlier and earlier stage on its youth.

—**Daniel Bell** (1919–), professor of sociology, Columbia University; Harvard University

no date, attributed in August Kerber, *Quotable Quotes on Education,* 1968, p. 218

Character building, like moral victory, seems to be the peculiar province of wretched colleges and losing football teams.

—**Kenneth E. Eble** (1923–1988),
professor of English, University of Utah

no date, attributed in
<www.quotationspage.com>.

In university they don't tell you that the greater part of the law is learning to tolerate fools.

—**Doris Lessing** (1919–),
English author

1971, organizational slogan, quoted in James B. Simpson, *Simpson's Contemporary Quotations,* 1988.

A mind is a terrible thing to waste.

—**United Negro College Fund**

no date, attributed in *Your Ultimate Success Quotation Library* (software program) at <http://www.cybernation. com/>.

Within the university ... you can study without waiting for any efficient or immediate result. You may search, just for the sake of searching, and try for the sake of trying. So there is a possibility of what I would call playing. It's perhaps the only place within society where play is possible to such an extent.

—**Jacques Derrida** (1930–),
French philosopher

Purpose: Instrumental

1643, *New England's First Fruits,* quoted in Richard Hofstadter and Wilson Smith (eds.), *American Higher Education: A Documentary History, Volume I,* 1961, p. 6.

After God had carried us safe to New England, and wee had builded our houses, provided necessaries for our liveli-hood, rear'd convenient places for God's worship, and setled the Civill Government: One of the next things we longed for, and looked after was to advance learning and perpetuate it to Posterity; dreading to leave an illiterate Ministery to the Churches, when our present Ministers shall lie in the dust.

—**Author Unknown**

1754, quoted in John S. Brubacher and Willis Rudy, *Higher Education in Transition,* 1958, p. 8.

Colleges are Societies of Ministers, for training up persons for the Work of the Ministry.

—**Thomas Clap** (1703–1767), President, Yale College

1764, quoted in John R. Thelin, *Higher Education and its Useful Past,* 1982, p. 61.

Institutions for liberal Education are highly beneficial to Society, by forming the rising Generation to Virtue, Knowledge, and useful literature, and thus preserving in the Community a Succession of Men duly qualified for discharging the Offices of Life with usefulness and reputation.

—**Charter of the College of Rhode Island** [later Brown University]

1780, letter to Abigail Adams, 12 May, quoted in David McCullough, *John Adams,* 2001, p. 236.

I must study politics and war that my sons may have liberty to study mathematics and philosophy. My sons ought to study mathematics and philosophy, geography, natural history, naval architecture, navigation, commerce, and agriculture in order to give their children a right to study paintings, poetry, music, architecture, statuary, tapestry, and porcelain.

—**John Adams** (1735–1826), President of the United States

1862, *Morrill Act,* quoted in Richard Hofstadter and Wilson Smith (eds.), *American Higher Education: A Documentary History, Volume I,* 1961, p. 568.

And be it further enacted, That all moneys derived from the sale of the lands aforesaid by the States . . . shall constitute a perpetual fund . . . the interest of which shall be inviolably appropriated by each State which may take and claim the benefit of this act, to the endowment, support, and maintenance of at least one college where the leading object shall be, without excluding other scientific and classical studies, and including military tactics, to teach such branches of learning as are related to agriculture and the mechanic arts, in such manner as the legislatures of the States may respectively prescribe, in order to promote the liberal and practical education of the industrial classes in the several pursuits and professions in life. . . .

—**Congress of the United States**

1922, *My Discovery of England*

Higher education in America flourished chiefly as a qualification for entrance into a moneymaking profession, and not as a thing in itself.

—**Stephen Butler Leacock** (1869–1944), professor of political economy, McGill University

1929, *The Aims of Education and Other Essays,* Chapter One.

In the conditions of modern life the rule is absolute, the race which does not value trained intelligence is doomed. Not all your heroism, not all your social charm, not all your wit, not all your victories on land or at sea, can move back the finger of fate.

> —**Alfred North Whitehead**
> (1861–1947), English philosopher and
> mathematician; professor of philosophy,
> Harvard University

1930, *Universities: American English German,* p. 131.

I am inclined to think most Americans do value education as a business asset, but not as the entrance into the joy of intellectual experience or acquaintance with the best that has been said and done in the past.

> —**Abraham Flexner** (1866–1959),
> U.S. educator

1934, Inaugural Address, *School and Society,* 20 October, p. 508.

[T]he primary purpose of a college is to produce not learned books but able men.

> —**Dixon Ryan Fox** (1887–1945),
> President, Union College

1963, *The Uses of the University,* pp. vi–vii.

The basic reality, for the university, is the wide-spread recognition that new knowledge is the most important factor in economic and social growth. We are just now perceiving that the university's invisible product, knowledge, may be the most powerful single element in our culture, affecting the rise and fall of professions and even of social classes, of regions and even of nations.

> —**Clark Kerr** (1911–2003), Chancellor,
> University of California, Berkeley;
> President, University of California

Purpose: Intellectual Development

1858, *The Idea of a University,* Preface

[A University] is a place of *teaching* universal *knowledge.* This implies that its object is, on the one hand, intellectual, not moral; and, on the other, that it is the diffusion and extension of knowledge rather than the advancement.

Discourse VI.

[J]ust as the work of a Hospital lies in healing the sick or wounded, of a Riding or Fencing School, or of a Gymnasium, in exercising the limbs, of an Almshouse, in aiding and solacing the old, of an Orphanage, in protecting innocence, of a Penitentiary, in restoring the guilty, I say, a University, taken in its bare idea . . . has this object and this mission; it contemplates neither moral impression nor mechanical production; it professes to exercise the mind neither in art nor in duty; its function is intellectual culture; here it may leave its scholars, and it has done its work when it has done as much as this. It educates the intellect to reason well in all matters, to reach out towards truth, and to grasp it.

> —**John Henry (Cardinal) Newman**
> (1801–1890), Rector,
> Catholic University of Ireland

1867, "Inaugural Address," in Francis W. Garforth, *John Stuart Mill on Education,* 1971.

An university exists for the purpose of laying open to each succeeding generation, as far as the conditions of the case admit, the accumulated treasure of the thoughts of mankind.

> —**John Stuart Mill** (1806–1873),
> Rector, St. Andrews University

1895, C. E. Norton et al., *Four American Universities: Harvard, Yale, Princeton, Columbia,* cited in Lawrence R. Veysey, *The Emergence of the American University,* 1965, pp. 186–87.

The highest end of the highest education is not anything which can be directly taught, but is the consummation of all studies. It is the final result of intellectual culture in the development of the breadth, serenity, and solidarity of mind, and in the attainment of that complete self-possession which finds expression in character.

—**Charles Eliot Norton** (1828–1908),
professor of art history,
Harvard University

1925, *Report for 1924–25,* quoted in Edward C. Elliott (ed.), *The Rise of a University, Vol. II,* 1937, p. 386.

The university is a fundamental human institution which rests upon a like basis to those which support the state and the church. Man's efforts to live happily and helpfully with his fellows in organized society gives rise to the state; man's spiritual aspiration and wish to worship are the origin of the church; man's persistent desire to know the truth which shall make him free has brought the university into being.

—**Nicholas Murray Butler**
(1862–1947), President,
Columbia University

1936, *The Higher Learning in America,* p. 66.

One purpose of education is to draw out the elements of our common human nature. These elements are the same in any time or place. The notion of educating a man to live in any particular time or place, to adjust him to any particular environment, is therefore foreign to a true conception of education. Education implies teaching. Teaching implies knowledge. Knowledge is truth. The truth is everywhere the same. Hence education should be everywhere the same.

—**Robert Maynard Hutchins**
(1899–1977), President,
University of Chicago

1937, Inaugural Address, quoted in Edgar W. Knight, *What College Presidents Say,* 1940, p. 49.

A great university should be a place in which there are relatively undisturbed opportunities to live with ideas. Much of life is otherwise engaged. But on campuses such as this thoughtful men and women, of faculty and student body alike, should be led to seek out all sorts of ideas; ideas that are deeply rooted in human experience; ideas that, like constellations in the intellectual firmament, have guided the earlier mariners of human thought; ideas that have more recently opened the doors of new knowledge of nature and of man; ideas that afford the foundation of our systems of law and order, of justice and liberty.

—**Edmund E. Day** (1883–1951),
President, Cornell University

1948, "Report of the President's Commission on Higher Education," *Educational Record,* April, p. 116.

The distinguishing mark of the educated person is intellectual power. Hence, the primary aim of higher education is the development of intellectual power

—**Robert Maynard Hutchins**
(1899–1977), President,
University of Chicago

1963, "The universities," in *Encounter,* April, p. 7.

The intellect . . . the intellect . . . the intellect. *That* is what universities exist for.

Everything else is secondary. Equality of opportunity to come to the university is secondary. The need to mix classes, nationalities and races together is secondary. The agonies and gaieties of student life are secondary. So are the rules, customs, pay and promotion of the academic staff and their debates on changing the curriculum or procuring facilities for research. Even the awakening of a sense of beauty, or the life-giving shock of new experience or the pursuit of goodness itself—all these are secondary to the cultivation, training and exercise of the intellect.

—**Noel Annan** (1916–2000)
Vice-chancellor, University of London

1968, "First glimpses of a new world," in Norman Cousins (ed.), *What I Have Learned,* p. 185.

I would say that the object of all education is to prepare students to participate in the Civilization of the Dialogue and that the particular object of the university is to exemplify the dialogue and carry it further. A university that does this is a success, no matter what else it fails to do; a university that fails in this is a failure, no matter what else it succeeds in doing.

—**Robert Maynard Hutchins**
(1899–1977), President,
University of Chicago

1970, "Were those the days?," *Daedalus,* Summer, p. 555.

The university is for learning—not for politics, not for growing up, not even for virtue, except as these things cut in and out of learning, and except also as they are necessary elements of all good human activity. The university is for learning as an airplane is for flying. This is its elemental and defining purpose. There is both affirmative and negative reason for this purpose: no other institution has this mission,

and no other mission justifies the university.

—**McGeorge Bundy** (1919–1996),
Dean, Faculty of Arts and Sciences,
Harvard University

1971, *The Degradation of the Academic Dogma,* p. 207.

[T]he university's most feasible function for the future is in essence what it has been in the past: that of serving as a setting for the scholarly and scientific imagination.

p. 208.

What, in a civilized society, could possibly be wrong with, or stagnant, archaic, or antiquarian about, the vision of an enclave in the social order whose principal purpose is working creatively and critically with ideas through scholarship and teaching? Is not man's highest evolutionary trait thus far precisely his capacity for dealing with ideas: learnedly, imaginatively, and critically? Is there any more promising hallmark for a civilized society than its willingness to support a class of persons whose principal business is to think, to arrive at knowledge, and to induct others in this principal business?

—**Robert A. Nisbet** (1913–), professor of sociology, University of California, Riverside

1982, *The State of the Nation and the Agenda for Higher Education,* p. 86.

The free mind is a foremost ideal of contemporary higher education. Great importance is attached to freedom of thought and communication, to the obligation to seek the truth through untrammeled inquiry, to tolerance of new and different ideas, to a disposition to explore and to experiment, and to a willingness to break away from conventions, traditions, superstitions, folklore, and myth.

> —**Howard R. Bowen** (1908–1989),
> economist; President, Grinnell College;
> President, University of Iowa;
> Chancellor, Claremont University Center

Purpose: Latent

1907, *The Education of Henry Adams,* chapter IV.

For generation after generation, Adamses and Brookses and Boylstons and Gorhams had gone to Harvard College, and although none of them, as far as known, had ever done any good there, or thought himself the better for it, custom, social ties, convenience, and, above all, economy, kept each generation in the track. Any other education would have required a serious effort, but no one took Harvard College seriously. All went there because their friends went there, and the College was their ideal of social self-respect.

> —**Henry B. Adams** (1838–1918),
> U.S. historian

1936, *American Wonderland,* p. 182.

They [American students] emerge like luggage after a well-planned trip tour covered with the labels but with very little acquirement within. The Universities are largely the gifts of the very rich, handed back to the middle class. There is more philanthropy than philosophy about American education.

—**Shane Leslie** (1885–1971), Irish writer

1938, "The education of the young," *Mr. Dooley at His Best,* p. 215.

"If ye had a boy wud ye sind him to colledge?" asked Mr. Hennessy.

"Well," said Mr. Dooley, "at th' age whin a boy is fit to be in colledge I wudden't have him around th' house."

> —**Peter Finley Dunne** (1867–1936),
> U.S. journalist and author

1939, "Education gets longer and longer," in *Too Much College,* p. 6.

Even in the clutter and failure of youth's career among the blocked avenues of our misfit world the college comes into its own as a sort of refuge. "My son," said another parent, "doesn't seem to have any particular ability, so we think we'll have to send him to college. He seems no good for anything else." The one anxiety of such parents is, "Can he get in?" Beyond that no need to look. It's like being dipped in the Jordan.

> —**Stephen Butler Leacock**
> (1869–1944), professor of political
> economy, McGill University

1948, "Report of the President's Commission on Higher Education," *Educational Record,* April, p. 117.

To the disinterested observer the American educational system looks like a gigantic playroom, designed to keep the young out of worse places until they can go to work.

> —**Robert Maynard Hutchins**
> (1899–1977), President,
> University of Chicago

1962, *The American College,* p. 76.

[T]he American college exists as a vast WPA project, which gives promising adolescents work to do while keeping them out of the job market, and also keeping several hundred thousand faculty members off the streets.

> —**Nevitt R. Sanford** (1909–1995),
> professor of psychology and education,
> Stanford University

1963, *Left-Handed Dictionary,* p. 235.

University—an institution for the postponement of experience.

—**Leonard L. Levinson** (1904–1974),
U.S. author

1965, interview in *Young Socialist,* 18
January, quoted in Anita King,
Quotations in Black, 1981, p. 201.

The colleges and universities in the American educational system are skillfully used to miseducate.

—**Malcolm X** (1925–1965),
social activist

1968, *The Academic Revolution,* p. 28.

The confrontation between teachers and students is . . . usually a confrontation between those who are in some sense mature and those who are less so. The central purpose of a college can thus be defined as socialization.

pp. 99–100.

[O]ne of the central functions of higher education—along with providing jobs for scholars—is to control access to the upper-middle social strata.

p. 137.

The driving force behind public support of higher education has always been middle-class parents eager to send their children to college at less than cost.

—**Christopher Jencks** (1936–),
professor of social policy,
Harvard University; **David Riesman**
(1909–2002) professor of sociology,
Harvard University

1970, *The American College and
American Culture,* pp. 11–12.

No sooner was Harvard established than embarrassed parents perceived its potential as an asylum for 14- or 15-year-old sons who were idle, disobedient, or too much interested in plantation sports.

—**Oscar Handlin** (1915–), professor of
history, Harvard University; **Mary F.
Handlin** (1913–1976), research editor,
Harvard University

1989, *Composing a Life,* quoted in
Rosalie Maggio, *The Beacon Book of
Quotations by Women,* 1992, p. 97.

Most higher education is devoted to affirming the traditions and origins of an existing elite and transmitting them to new members.

—**Mary Catherine Bateson** (1939–),
professor of anthropology and English,
George Mason University

Purpose: Societal

1880, inscriptions on Dexter Gate,
Harvard Yard.

Enter to grow in wisdom.
Depart to serve better thy country and thy kind.

—**Charles William Eliot** (1834–1926),
President, Harvard University

1896, *Mere Literature and Other Essays,*
pp. 73–74, quoted in *The Columbia
World of Quotations, 1996.*

It is the object of learning, not only to satisfy the curiosity and perfect the spirits of ordinary men, but also to advance civilization.

—**Woodrow Wilson** (1856–1924),
President, Princeton University;
President of the United States

1903, *The Souls of Black Folk,* chapter 5.

The function of the university is not simply to teach bread-winning, or to furnish teachers for the public schools, or to be a centre of polite society; it is, above all, to be the organ of that fine adjustment between real life and the growing knowledge of life, an adjustment which forms the secret of civilization.

—**W. E. B. Du Bois** (1868–1963), professor of sociology, Atlanta University

1903, "The talented tenth," in *The Negro Problem: A Series of Articles by Representative American Negroes of Today.*

If we make money the object of man-training, we shall develop money-makers but not necessarily men; if we make technical skill the object of education, we may possess artisans but not, in nature, men. Men we shall have only as we make manhood the object of the work of the schools—intelligence, broad sympathy, knowledge of the world that was and is, and of the relation of men to it—this is the curriculum of that Higher Education which must underlie true life. On this foundation we may build bread winning, skill of hand and quickness of brain, with never a fear lest the child and man mistake the means of living for the object of life. . . .

—**W. E. B. Du Bois** (1868–1963), professor of sociology, Atlanta University

1910, motto, quoted in Frederick Rudolph, *The American College and University: A History,* 1962, p. 481.

Let knowledge grow from more to more, and thus be human life enriched.

—**University of Chicago**

1914, *Treatise on Parents and Children.*

The function of a university is not to teach things that can now be taught as well or better by University Extension lectures or by private tutors or modern correspondence classes with gramophones. We go to them to become socialized; to acquire the hall mark of communal training; to become citizens of the world instead of inmates of the enlarged rabbit hutches we call homes; to learn manners and become unchallengeable ladies and gentlemen.

—**George Bernard Shaw** (1856–1950), Irish playwright

1944, *The Mission of the University,* chapter II, p. 40.

[I]t is imperative to set up once more, in the university, the teaching of the culture, the system of vital ideas, which the age has attained. This is the basic function of the university. This is what the university must be, above all else.

chapter VI, pp. 89–91.

The university must be open to the whole reality of its time. It must be in the midst of real life, and saturated with it. . . . [T]he university must intervene, *as* the university, in current affairs, treating the great themes of the day from its own point of view: cultural, professional, and scientific.

—**José Ortega Y Gassett** (1883–1955), professor of metaphysics, University of Madrid

no date, attributed in August Kerber, *Quotable Quotes on Education,* 1968, p. 227.

The university is the archive of the Western mind, it's the keeper of the Western culture—the guardian of our heritage, the teacher of our teachers—the dwelling place of the free mind.

—**Adlai E. Stevenson, Jr.** (1900–1965), U.S. statesman

no date, attributed in Harold W. Stoke, *The American College President,* 1959, p. 3.

Education may not save us, but it is the only hope we have.

—**Robert Maynard Hutchins**
(1899–1977), President,
University of Chicago

1966, "The university," *The New Republic,* May 28, p. 17.

[T]here has fallen to the universities a unique, indispensable and capital function in the intellectual and spiritual life of modern society. . . . [A] way will have to be found to perform these functions if the pursuit of the good life, to which this country is committed, is to continue and to be successful. . . . [T]he modern void, which results from the vast and intricate process of emancipation and rationalization, must be filled and . . . the universities must fill the void because they alone can fill it.

—**Walter Lippman** (1889–1974),
U.S. editor and author

1967, "The future of the nineteenth century idea of a university," *Minerva,* August, p. 3.

The university is a mechanism for the inheritance of the western style of civilisation.

—**Eric Ashby** (1904–1992), botanist;
Vice-chancellor, Cambridge University

1977, *Missions of the College Curriculum,* p. 32.

In American society, the communications media often act as diagnosticians. Educational institutions are expected, often unrealistically, to produce cures.

—**Carnegie Foundation for the
Advancement of Teaching**

1988, *A Free and Ordered Space,* p. 41.

American colleges and universities do not play the role in our society as centers for independent thought, or the open pursuit of truth, for the protection of minority or dissenting or critical views—they do not serve America—when they mimic governmental institutions or private businesses or allow themselves to be simply holding pens for competing dogmas.

—**A. Bartlett Giamatti** (1938–1989),
President, Yale University

1990, *Universities and the Future of America,* p. 105.

Armed with the security of tenure and the time to study the world with care, professors would appear to have a unique opportunity to act as society's scouts to signal impending problems long before they are visible to others. Yet rarely have members of the academy succeeded in discovering emerging issues and bringing them vividly to the attention of the public.

—**Derek Bok** (1930–), President,
Harvard University

Purpose: Transcendent

c. first century B.C.E., *Epistles, volume 2,* 2,45, quoted in David Watson, *The Works of Horace,* 1792, p. 342,4.

Polite Athens gave me some finishing strokes in this education; by enabling me to distinguish between a right and a curve line, and to pursue truth through all her windings in the groves of the academy [i.e., the Groves of Academe].

—**Horace [Quintus Horatius Flaccus]**
(65–8 B.C.E.), Roman poet and satirist

1624, Sermon No. 11, in Evelyn M. Simpson and George R. Potter, *The Sermons of John Donne, Volume VI, 1953,* p. 227.

The University is a Paradise, Rivers of Knowledge are there, Arts and Sciences flow from thence . . . ; bottomless depths of unsearchable Counsels there.

—**John Donne** (1572–1631),
metaphysical poet; Anglican divine

1858, lecture, Christian Library Association, 22 June, quoted in Richard Hofstadter and Wilson Smith (eds.), *American Higher Education: A Documentary History, Volume II,* 1961, p. 517.

Of all mere human institutions there is none so important and mighty in their influence as Universities; because, when rightly constituted, they are made up of the most enlightened, and the choicest spirits of our race; they embrace the means of all human culture, and they act directly upon the fresh and upspringing manhood of a nation.

—**Henry P. Tappan** (1805–1881),
President, University of Michigan

1873, Speech to the House of Commons, 11 March, quoted in Burton Stevenson, *The Home Book of Quotations,* 1967, p. 2068.

A university should be a place of light, of liberty, and of learning.

—**Benjamin Disraeli,
Earl of Beaconsfield** (1804–1881),
English statesman

1903, *The Souls of Black Folk,* chapter 5.

The riddle of existence is the college curriculum that was laid before the Pharaohs, that was taught in the groves by Plato, that formed the trivium and quadrivium, and is to-day laid before the freedmen's sons by Atlanta University. And this course of study will not change; its methods will grow more deft and effectual, its content richer by toil of scholar and sight of seer; but the true college will ever have one goal,—not to earn meat, but to know the end and aim of that life which meat nourishes.

—**W. E. B. Du Bois** (1868–1963),
professor of sociology, Atlanta University

1912, quoted in Abraham Flexner, *Universities: American English German,* 1930, p. 186.

[I]t is in universities that . . . the soul of a people mirrors itself.

—**Richard Burdon (Viscount) Haldane**
(1856–1928), British statesman;
Chancellor, University of Bristol

1934, Inaugural Address, *School and Society,* 20 October, p. 506.

The liberal college has existed . . . to interpret the possibilities of large and noble living.

—**Dixon Ryan Fox** (1887–1945),
President, Union College

1936, *Notes on the Harvard Tercentenary,* p. 70

He who enters a university walks on hallowed ground.

—**James Bryant Conant** (1893–1978),
President, Harvard University

1936, *The Higher Learning in America,* p. 71.

[T]he aim of education is to connect man with man, to connect the present with the past, and to advance the thinking of the race.

—**Robert Maynard Hutchins**
(1899–1977), President,
University of Chicago

1938, "The aim of philosophy," in *Modes of Thought,* p. 233.

The task of a University is the creation of the future, so far as rational thought, and civilized modes of appreciation, can effect the issue.

—Alfred North Whitehead
(1861–1947), English philosopher and mathematician; professor of philosophy, Harvard University

1943, *Education for Freedom,* pp. 23–24.

Now wisdom and goodness are the aims of higher education. How can it be otherwise? Wisdom and goodness are the end of human life.

—Robert Maynard Hutchins
(1899–1977), President,
University of Chicago

1946, "The University," 25 June, *Johns Hopkins Magazine,* February 1953, pp. 21–30.

There are few earthly things more splendid than a university. In these days of broken frontiers and collapsing values, when the dams are down and the floods are making misery, when every future looks somewhat grim and every ancient foothold has become something of a quagmire, wherever a university stands, it stands and shines; wherever it exists, the free minds of men, urged on to full and fair inquiry, may still bring wisdom into human affairs.

—John Masefield (1878–1967),
English poet

1959, *The Idea of the University,* pp. 70, 75.

The idea becomes concrete in the institution. The extent to which it does this determines the quality of the university. Stripped of its idea the university loses all value. Yet 'institution' necessarily implies compromises. The idea is never perfectly realized. . . . The idea is not something that can be touched, seen, or heard. It glimmers in the ashes of the institution, flaring up from time to time in individuals or groups. One need not always belong to a university to live by its ideal. But the idea is attracted to the institution, without which it feels incomplete, sterile, and isolated.

—Karl Jaspers (1883–1969),
German philosopher

no date, attributed in August Kerber, *Quotable Quotes on Education,* 1968, p. 217.

The ideal campus is a monument to the unknown.

—John Ciardi (1916–1986),
U.S. poet and editor

1968, "Parting shots: A century of commencement speeches," *Saturday Review,* 12 May 1979, p. 38.

A university is not a service station. Neither is it a political society, nor a meeting place for political societies. With all its limitations and failures, and they are invariably many, it is the best and most benign side of our society insofar as that society aims to cherish the human mind.

—Richard Hofstadter (1916–1970),
professor of American history,
Columbia University

1976, *The Purposes of Education,* p. 76.

The ultimate business of education is human freedom.

—Stephen K. Bailey (1916–1982),
professor of education;
Harvard University, Vice President,
American Council on Education

1977, *Investment in Learning,* p. 296.

If higher education performed no other function than to maintain fruitful continuity with the past, it might well be worth every dollar currently spent on it.

—**Howard R. Bowen** (1908–1989),
economist; President, Grinnell College;
President, University of Iowa;
Chancellor, Claremont University Center

no date, attributed at <http://www.top-quotations.com/quocards/>.

The university should teach you to become one with the universe. That is the meaning of the word 'university'.

—**Osho Rajneesh** (1931–1990),
Hindu mystic

1988, *A Free and Ordered Space,* pp. 24–25.

The university . . . is still a constant conversation between young and old, between students, among faculty; between faculty and students; a conversation between past and present, a conversation the culture has with itself, on behalf of the country. . . . Perhaps it is the sound of all those voices, over centuries overlapping, giving and taking, that is finally the music of civilization, the sound of human beings shaping and sharing, mooring ideals to reality, making the world, for all its pain, work.

p. 49.

The University is the guardian of the imagination that both defines and asserts our humanity.

—**A. Bartlett Giamatti** (1938–1989),
President, Yale University

2001, *Chronicle of Higher Education,* 28 September, p. A16.

A university is a historic wager that people of different beliefs can sustain passionate conversations.

—**Michael Brooks** (?–),
Executive Director, Hillel,
University of Michigan

Chapter 2

Social Issues

Affirmative Action

1965, commencement address at Howard University, June, quoted in Steven M. Cahn, *The Affirmative Action Debate,* 2nd edition, 2002, p. xii.

You do not take a person who, for years, has been hobbled by chains and liberate him, bring him up to the starting point of a race, and then say, "You're free to compete with all the others," and still justly believe that you have been completely fair. Thus it is not enough just to open the gates of opportunity. All our citizens must have the ability to walk through those gates. . . . We seek not . . . just equality as a right and a theory but equality as a fact and equality as a result.

—Lyndon Baines Johnson
(1908–1973),
President of the United States

1973, *The Purposes and the Performance of Higher Education in the United States,* p. 38.

Admissions standards should be relaxed for members of disadvantaged groups, provided that the chances are good that such students can meet graduation requirements in full.

**—Carnegie Commission
on Higher Education**

1975, *Affirmative Action Reconsidered: Was It Necessary in Academia?,* p. 39.

What is most lacking in the arguments for affirmative action programs is a detailed specification of who is expected to benefit, in what manner, with what likelihood, and at what risk of negative effects on net balance.

—Thomas Sowell (1930–),
U.S. economist

1978, judgment of the court, *University of California Regents v. Bakke,* 438 U.S. 265.

This [attainment of a diverse student body] clearly is a constitutionally permissible goal for an institution of higher education.

—Lewis F. Powell, Jr. (1907–1998),
Associate Justice, U.S. Supreme Court

1978, separate opinion, *University of California Regents v. Bakke,* 438 U.S. 265.

I suspect that it would be impossible to arrange an affirmative action program in a racially neutral way and have it successful. To ask that this be so is to demand the impossible. In order to get beyond racism, we must first take account of race.

—**Harry A. Blackmun** (1908–1999)
Associate Justice, U.S. Supreme Court

1989, "Why the racial slogans?"
Washington Post, 20 September, quoted in Dinesh D'Souza, *Illiberal Education,* 1991, p. 238.

[Y]ou cannot claim both full equality and special dispensation.

—**William Raspberry** (1935–),
U.S. journalist

1991, *Illiberal Education,* p. 31.

It is mathematically impossible to achieve ethnic proportionality without decreasing "overrepresented" groups. In the zero-sum game of admissions to highly competitive colleges like Berkeley, affirmative action gains by some minorities seem to require affirmative action losses for others.

p. 249.

No community can be built on the basis of preferential treatment and double standards, and their existence belies university rhetoric about equality. Conflicting standards of excellence and justice are the root of bitter and divisive controversies over admissions, curricular content, and race relations on campus.

—**Dinesh D'Souza** (1961–),
writer and policy analyst

1995, "Affirmative action policies have helped minorities, women progress," in *Higher Education and National Affairs,* ACE, 25 September, p. 18.

I am not wedded to affirmative action. All I ask of critics is, show me another way to overcome the inequities of an American society that is filled with racism and sexism.

—**Reginald Wilson** (1927–), President, Wayne Community College; Senior Scholar, American Council on Education

1995, speech, July

We should reaffirm the principle of affirmative action and fix the practice. We should have a simple slogan: Mend it, but don't end it.

—**William Jefferson Clinton** (1946–),
President of the United States

1996, *Hopwood v. Texas,* 78 F. 3d 932,946 (5th Cir.).

The use of race, in and of itself, to choose students simply achieves a student body that looks different. Such a criterion is no more rational on its own terms than would be choices based upon the physical size or blood type of applicants. . . . [R]ace is often said to be justified in the diversity context, not on it own terms, but as a proxy for other characteristics that institutions of higher education value. . . . Unfortunately, this approach simply replicates the very harm that the Fourteenth Amendment was designed to eliminate.

—**Jerry E. Smith** (1946–),
federal judge

1999, quoted in Bob Pool, "Protest over UCLA Law School 'resegregation' education," *The Los Angeles Times,* 17 April, p. B1.

The real world has people of color in it. You can't teach in a segregated atmosphere—it just can't be done.

—**Gary L. Blasi** (1945–), professor of law, University of California, Los Angeles

2003, quoted in David Koenig, "University of Texas Minorities Drop," *The Associated Press,* 16 January.

There's a prevailing view that you can have diversity and not consider race. None of the alternatives work very well. All the alternatives produce fewer minorities and much more distortion of academic standards.

—**Douglas Laycock** (1948–), professor of law, University of Texas

2003, oral arguments, *Gratz and Hamacher v. Bollinger,* U.S. Supreme Court, 2 April.

If this value of having everybody in a mix of people with other people is so significant to you [the University of Michigan], just lower your qualification standards. You don't have to be the great college you are. You could be a lesser college, if this value is important enough to you.

—**Antonin Scalia** (1936–), Associate Justice, U.S. Supreme Court

2003, majority opinion, *Grutter v. Bollinger.*

In order to cultivate a set of leaders with legitimacy in the eyes of the citizenry, it is necessary that the path to leadership be visibly open to talented and qualified individuals of every race and ethnicity. All members of our heterogeneous society must have confidence in the openness and integrity of the educational institutions that provide this training.

—**Sandra Day O'Connor** (1930–), Associate Justice, U.S. Supreme Court

Commoditization

1897, *The American College in American Life,* p. 36.

The fear is often expressed that the materialism and commercialism of the time are causing the college, standing for things of the mind, to lose influence.

—**Charles F. Thwing** (1853–1937), President, Adelbert College; President, Western Reserve University

1904, *Papers and Addresses of the Association of Colleges and Preparatory Schools of the Southern States,* quoted in Edgar W. Knight, *What College Presidents Say,* 1940, p. 61.

There is hardly any conceivable limit to the ingenuity and genius of the advertising spirit in many of our colleges of today. Some institutions are engaged in the work of "university extension" for the publicity it gives them, professing to do "at long range" what they have never learned to do thoroughly within their own walls.

—**George H. Denny** (1870–1955), President, Washington and Lee University; President, Hamden-Sydney College; President, University of Alabama

1918, *The Higher Learning in America,* Chapter 8.

The underlying business-like presumption . . . appears to be that learning is a merchantable commodity, to be produced on a piece-rate plan, rated, bought and sold by standard units, measured, counted and reduced to staple equivalence of impersonal, mechanical tests. In all its bearings the work is hereby reduced to a mechanistic, statistical consistency, with numerical standards and units. . . .

—**Thorstein Veblen** (1857–1929),
U.S. sociologist

1930, *Universities: American English German,* p. 5.

[A] university should not be a weather vane, responsive to every variation of popular whim. Universities must at times give society, not what society wants, but what it needs. Inertia and resistance have their uses, provided they be based on reasonable analysis, on a sense of values, not on mere habit.

—**Abraham Flexner** (1866–1959),
U.S. educator

1965, speech at Dearborn, Michigan, 1 February, quoted in Jacques Barzun, *The American University,* 1968, p. 63.

America's educational system is in danger of becoming a vast factory committed to the production of specialists, technicians, and fact collectors . . . making it increasingly difficult for the college student to achieve a mature understanding of himself and his proper relation to society—to achieve, in short, a liberal education.

—**David B. Truman** (1913–),
President, Mt. Holyoke College

1975, *The Case Against College,* p. 8.

The Madison Avenue campaigns sell colleges like soap, promoting those features that market analysts think the customers really want: innovative programs, an environment conducive to meaningful personal relationships, and a curriculum so free that it doesn't sound like college at all—"We shape our curriculum to your individual needs."

—**Caroline Bird** (1915–), U.S. author

1977, "The liberal learning," *The Center Magazine,* March/April, p. 22.

At best, most college presidents are running something that is somewhere between a faltering corporation and a hotel.

—**Leon Botstein** (1946–),
President, Bard College

1980, *On Higher Education,* p. 117.

Even the most shoddy, cut-rate, and cutthroat degrees are not necessarily frauds on the student consumer. They may, in fact, be examples of collusion between academic vendor and student buyer to secure a credential at some monetary cost but almost no cost in time and effort.

—**David Riesman** (1909–2002),
professor of sociology,
Harvard University

1985, *Integrity in the College Curriculum,* p. 2.

There is so much confusion as to the mission of the American college and university that it is no longer possible to be sure why a student should take a particular program of courses. . . . The curriculum has given way to a marketplace philosophy: it is a supermarket where students are shoppers and professors are merchants of learning. Fads and fashions, the demands of popularity and success, enter where wisdom and experience should prevail.

—**Association of American Colleges**

1987, *College,* p. 22.

As the competitive pressure for students grows, abuses are likely to increase while the quality of the information may decline. A small advertisement in the classified section of *The New York Times* reflects the temper of the times. "Wanted: an exp'd person for ADMISSIONS OFFICE. Must have good speaking voice, telephone skills, and ability to close."

—**Ernest L. Boyer** (1928–1995), Chancellor, State University of New York

1990, *The University: An Owner's Manual,* pp. 233–34.

A university cannot be run by cost accountants or as a commercial enterprise responding only to changing markets. That is bad for us and worse for the societies we seek to serve.

—**Henry Rosovsky** (1927–), Dean, Faculty of Arts and Sciences, Harvard University

1992, *On Q: Causing Quality in Higher Education,* p. 128.

[H]igher education has the same operating characteristics as a bank, an airline, or a restaurant. The fact is that we do have customers. We provide them with a service and an exchange takes place. . . .

—**Daniel Seymour** (1947–), education and management consultant

1994, "Total Quality Management in the culture of higher education," *Review of Higher Education, 17,* p. 459.

When bringing TQM [Total Quality Management] to campus, one brings a language developed in the realm of commodity production into the community of specialized academic discourse. . . . [I]t is not useful to compare the acquisition of knowledge in a college classroom with purchasing chicken nuggets in a fast-food establishment, or even purchasing a car, unless one is attempting to illustrate absurdity.

—**DeVillo Sloan** (1956–), associate director of public relations, Wells College

1994, *In Defense of Elitism,* p. 158.

[O]ne need look no further than the curricular wars to understand that most students are not looking to broaden their spiritual or intellectual horizons. They see themselves as consumers buying a product, and insist on applying egalitarian rules of the marketplace to what used to be an unchallenged elitism of the intellect.

—**William A. Henry III** (1950–), writer and social critic

1995, *Once Upon a Campus,* p. x.

[S]takeholders expect the same thing in a college education that they expect in a toaster oven or a new home—utility. Skip the rhetoric. Forget about the cute accessories or the quaint features. People want to be assured that what they purchase today will be useful tomorrow.

—**Daniel Seymour** (1947–), education and management consultant

2001, "Research is valuable. Let's give it away," *Chronicle of Higher Education,* 14 September, p. B14.

Scholarship is a communal activity, so experimental results are not deemed valuable until they are given to others, and scholars are honored according to how many results they give. The recent tendency to treat research results like commodities, goods to be exchanged for cash, threatens the contributions that university-based scholarship makes to society. . . . Important and unexpected experimental results once led university scientists to rush down the hall and share their excitement with their colleagues. When the rush is instead to consult a patent attorney and a venture capitalist, I worry about the long-term future of scientific discovery.

—**John R. Menninger** (1935–), professor of biological sciences, University of Iowa

2001, "Higher education as a mature industry," in Philip Altbach et al., *In Defense of American Higher Education,* p. 45.

Students today increasingly bring to higher education exactly the same consumer expectations they have for every other commercial enterprise with which they deal. Their focus is on convenience, service, quality, and low cost.

—**Arthur Levine** (1948–), President, Bradford College; President, Teachers College, Columbia University

Diversity: People

c. 1900, attributed in Shirley M. Tilghman, 2003 Commencement Address, Princeton University.

One of the things that makes us unserviceable citizens is that there are certain classes of men with whom we have never been able to associate, and whom we have, therefore, been unable to understand. I believe that the process of a university should be a process of unchosen contacts.

—**Woodrow Wilson** (1856–1924), President, Princeton University; President of the United States

1903, "The talented tenth," in *The Negro Problem: A Series of Articles by Representative American Negroes of Today.*

All men cannot go to college, but some men must; every isolated group or nation must have its yeast, must have for the talented a few centers of training where men are not so mystified and befuddled by the hard and necessary toil of earning a living, as to have no aims higher than their bellies, and no God greater than Gold.

—**W. E. B. Du Bois** (1868–1963), professor of sociology, Atlanta University

1925, *Report for 1924–25,* quoted in Edward C. Elliott (ed.), *The Rise of a University, Vol. II,* 1937, p. 210.

It takes all sorts and kinds of people to make a world, and not all of the best of them will be college graduates by any means.

—**Nicholas Murray Butler** (1862–1947), President, Columbia University

1927, *Annual Report,* quoted in Barbara Miller Solomon, *In the Company of Educated Women,* 1985, p. 141.

No one would wish a college to be homogeneous in the wealth or race or social status of the families of its students, but a certain homogeneity in aims, aspirations, and intellectual ability in the student group has value in the education which the College offers.

—**Ada L. Comstock** (1876–1973), President, Radcliffe College

1966, *The Reforming of General Education,* p. 20.

The different strains in the membership, particularly the boys of various foreign stocks, the influx of freshmen from out of town, and the students from other colleges, all unite in producing a social diversity which is a factor often unappreciated in college life.

—**Daniel Bell** (1919–), professor of sociology, Columbia University; Harvard University

1975, *The Case Against College,* p. 23.

Equalizing opportunity through universal higher education subjects the whole population to the intellectual mode natural only to a few. It violates the fundamental egalitarian principle of respect for the differences between people.

—**Caroline Bird** (1915–), U.S. author

1987, *Ever the Teacher,* p. 151.

[A]n appreciation for "otherness" is central to the very idea of the liberal arts.

—**William G. Bowen** (1933–),
President, Princeton University

1991, *Illiberal Education,* p. 14.

Universities are a microcosm of society. But they are more than a reflection or mirror; they are a leading indicator. In universities, an environment where students live, eat, and study together, racial and cultural differences come together in the closest possible way. Of all American institutions, perhaps only the military brings people of such different backgrounds into more intimate contact.

p. 17.

Diversity, tolerance, multiculturalism, pluralism—these phrases are perennially on the lips of university administrators. They are the principles and slogans of the victim's revolution.

p. 214.

The monolithic ideological focus of the so-called "studies" programs seems to have produced a relentless, even fanatical, conformity of thought in which "diversity" loses its procedural meaning and assumes substantive content. In other words, "diversity" does not refer to a range of views on a disputed question, but rather entails enlisting in a regiment of ideological causes which are identified as being "for diversity."

p. 230.

The question is not whether universities should seek diversity, but what kind of diversity. It seems that the primary form of diversity which universities should try to foster is diversity of mind.

—**Dinesh D'Souza** (1961–),
writer and policy analyst

1996, *The Opening of the American Mind,* p. xvii.

The university is no longer the site of homogeneity in class, gender, ethnicity, and race.

p. 146.

The serious historical examination of the culture and the activities of those long considered to be insignificant appears to many in and outside the academe [sic] to be trivial pursuits.

—**Lawrence W. Levine** (1933–),
professor of history,
University of California, Berkeley

1997, "Diversity: Walk the walk and drop the talk," *Change,* July/August, p. 36.

Somehow, in an awfully short time, we have pounded and bleached the word diversity into nothingness.

—**Clifford Adelman** (1942–), research scholar, U.S. Department of Education

1997, "Why diversity is a smoke screen for affirmative action," *Change,* July/August, pp. 26–27.

In the best of cases, "diversity" becomes something of an affirmative-action smoke screen for institutions committed to opening up opportunities for historically disadvantaged minorities, but leery of running afoul of recent court cases. But in far more cases today, diversity is a smoke screen for the elimination of all real efforts to assist African Americans and other underrepresented minorities.

—**Samuel L. Myers, Jr.** (1949–),
professor of human relations and social justice, University of Minnesota

1999, *Annual Report: Diversity.*

We live in an age in which the dirty words on college campuses are no longer four letters; they are at least six letters—racist, sexist, and homophobic. No one wants to be called these things or to be subjected to harsh attacks, which so often seem to accompany disagreements over diversity. So it has frequently seemed the wiser course to ignore or at least attempt to duck the issue of diversity and hope that it will go away.

—**Arthur Levine** (1948–), President, Bradford College; President, Teachers College, Columbia University

Ivory Tower

1836, "On the conduct of life," *Literary Remains, Vol. 2,* p. 89.

There is one almost certain drawback on a course of scholastic study, that it unfits men for active life.

—**William Hazlitt** (1778–1830), English essayist

1912, *Teaching in School and College,* pp. 6–7, quoted in Lawrence R. Veysey, *The Emergence of the American University,* 1965, p. 216.

Academic life is delightful to men and women of scholarly tastes; one is removed from the sordid and material side of the struggle, and one's associations and friendships are based on a community of intellectual interest. One does not dwell in a daily atmosphere of cloth and pork.

—**William Lyon Phelps** (1865–1943), professor of English literature, Yale University

1936, *Journal of the Association of University Women,* January, quoted in Stephen Donadio et al. (eds.), *The New York Public Library Book of Twentieth-Century Quotes,* 1992, p. 164.

A university studies politics, but it will not advocate fascism or communism. A uni-

versity studies military tactics, but it will not promote war. A university studies peace, but it will not organize crusades of pacifism. It will study every question that affects human welfare, but it will not carry a banner in a crusade for anything except freedom of learning.

—**Lotus D. Coffman** (1875–1938), President, University of Minnesota

1936, "Harvard: The future," *Atlantic Monthly,* 158, p. 267.

[U]napplied knowledge is knowledge shorn of its meaning. The careful shielding of a university from the activities of the world around is the best way to chill interest and to defeat progress. Celibacy does not suit a university. It must mate itself with action.

—**Alfred North Whitehead** (1861–1947), English philosopher and mathematician; professor of philosophy, Harvard University

1937, *The Nature of a Liberal College,* p. 19.

If it [the college] were wholly alien to its environment, it could not perform its function. . . . On the other hand, if it yields completely to its environment, it equally fails in its objectives. It must maintain a realistic contact without compromising its essential function.

—**Henry M. Wriston** (1889–1978), President, Lawrence College; President, Brown University

1950, *Reflections on Life,* quoted in Stephen Donadio et al. (eds.), *The New York Public Library Book of Twentieth-Century Quotes,* 1992, p. 164.

The atmosphere of libraries, lecture rooms and laboratories is dangerous to those who shut themselves up in them too long. It separates us from reality like a fog.

> —**Alexis Carrell** (1873–1944),
> Nobel Laureate in medicine

no date, attributed in August Kerber, *Quotable Quotes on Education,* 1968, p. 217.

The great universities of the world have been more often fields of battle than ivory towers of contemplation.

> —**James Bryant Conant** (1893–1978),
> President, Harvard University

1955, "The administrator: Leader or officeholder?," *Freedom, Education, and the Fund,* 1956, p. 194.

The object of universities, hospitals, and foundations is not the preservation of the status quo. It is the improvement of the conditions of human life and the clarification of its aims. . . . Yet universities, hospitals, and foundations that do these things must inevitably engage in criticism of existing practices, and if they do they must expect to be criticized in turn.

> —**Robert Maynard Hutchins** (1899–1977), President, University of Chicago

1963, "A reply to Robert Hutchins: The aimlessness of American education," in *Rumbles Left and Right,* p. 134.

[I] should sooner live in a society governed by the first two thousand names in the Boston telephone directory than in a society governed by the two thousand faculty members of Harvard University . . . because I greatly fear intellectual arrogance, and that is a distinguishing characteristic of the university which refuses to accept any common premise.

> —**William F. Buckley, Jr.** (1925–),
> U.S. journalist and author

1967, quoted by Theodore H. White, "In the halls of power," *Life,* 9 June, p. 57.

A politician or businessman must pay a price for being wrong: the academic never does.

> —**Edward C. Banfield** (1916–1999),
> professor of government,
> Harvard University

1972, *The Future Executive,* p. 45.

Members of every academic community are learning that they cannot have it both ways. If they presume to raise questions about international and national and local decisions, which as citizens they do and should, the international and national and local decision-makers will naturally raise questions about how professors work and students live. Those who want the protection of a monastery have to live like monks. On a relevant campus there's no hiding place down here.

> —**Harlan Cleveland** (1918–), political scientist; President, University of Hawaii

1973, *The Concept of a University,* p. 76.

[T]o treat universities simply as institutions which provide educational services for society is like treating a Ming vase as a cut glass flower bowl: plausible, but crass. There is an important and neglected sense in which the belief that universities are ivory towers—an image seldom invoked these days without sneer or repudiation—is precisely true.

p. 86.

[O]ne of the primary distinctions between the academic and the practical worlds rests upon the simplest and most luminous of facts: that in a university, no one has to come to a conclusion upon which a decision must be based.

p. 100.

The remoteness of academic from practical concerns must be regarded not as a surviving tradition from less enlightened days, but as an essential condition of the maintenance of the academic world. The practical world is one we cannot help living in, but the academic world requires special cultivation, and did not come into existence in any significant form until recent times. And the condition of its survival is that it should be isolated from the essentially practical task of making decisions.

—**Kenneth P. Minogue** (1930–),
senior lecturer in political science,
London School of Economics and
Political Science

no date, attributed in Keith Allan Noble, *The International Education Quotations Encyclopaedia,* 1995.

The university must be a tributary to a larger society, not a sanctuary from it.

—**A. Bartlett Giamatti** (1938–1989),
President, Yale University

no date, attributed in Keith Allan Noble, *The International Education Quotations Encyclopaedia,* 1995.

Our troubled planet can no longer afford the luxury of pursuits confined to an ivory tower. Scholarship has to prove its worth, not on its own terms, but by service to the nation and the world.

—**Oscar Handlin** (1915–),
professor of history, Harvard University

1987, speech, University of South Carolina, 16 September, quoted in Bill Swainson, *Encarta Book of Quotations,* 2000, p. 437.

In American society, the university is traditionally considered to be a psychosocial moratorium, an ivory tower where you can withdraw from the problems of society and the world around you to work on important things like your career and your marriage.

—**Abbie Hoffman** (1936–1989),
U.S. political activist

1988, *Nice Work,* p. 170.

Universities are the cathedrals of the modern age. They shouldn't have to justify their existence by utilitarian criteria. The trouble is, ordinary people don't understand what they're about, and the universities don't really bother to explain themselves to the community.

—**David Lodge** (1935–),
British novelist and critic

1999, "Castles in a bog," *National Crosstalk,* Summer.

Colleges and universities tend to take credit for much of the good that occurs in a society, but remain shockingly oblivious to the greatest human follies and catastrophes.

—**Gordon Davies** (1938–),
President, Kentucky Council on
Postsecondary Education

Outcomes: Society

1850, "Boston," *American Notes.*

There is no doubt that much of the intellectual refinement and superiority of Boston is referable to the quiet influence of the University of Cambridge, which is within three or four miles of the city. The resident professors at that university are gentlemen of learning and varied attainments; and are, without one exception that I can call to mind, men who would shed a grace upon, and do honour to, any society in the civilised world. Many of the resident gentry in Boston and its neighbourhood, and I think I am not mistaken in adding, a large majority of those who are attached to the liberal professions there, have been educated at this same school. Whatever the defects of American universities may be, they disseminate no prejudices; rear no bigots; dig up the buried ashes of no old superstitions; never interpose between the people and their improvement; exclude no man because of his religious opinions; above all, in their whole course of study and instruction, recognise a world, and a broad one too, lying beyond the college walls.

—**Charles Dickens** (1812–1870), English novelist

1858, *The Idea of a University,* Discourse VII.

[A] university training is the great ordinary means to a great but ordinary end; it aims at raising the intellectual tone of society, at cultivating the public mind, at purifying the national taste, at supplying true principles to popular enthusiasm and fixed aims to popular aspiration, at giving enlargement and sobriety to the ideas of the age, at facilitating the exercise of political power, and refining the intercourse of private life.

—**John Henry (Cardinal) Newman** (1801–1890), Rector, Catholic University of Ireland

1869, Inaugural Address, 19 October, in *A Turning Point in Higher Education,* 1969, p. 32.

With good methods, we may confidently hope to give young men of twenty to twenty-five an accurate general knowledge of all the main subjects of human interest, besides a minute and thorough knowledge of the one subject which each may select as his principal occupation in life. To think this impossible is to despair of mankind; for unless a general acquaintance with many branches of knowledge, good so far as it goes, be attainable by great numbers

of men, there can be no such thing as an intelligent public opinion; and in the modern world the intelligence of public opinion is the one indispensable condition of social progress.

p. 63.

The university must accommodate itself promptly to significant changes in the character of the people for whom it exists. The institutions of higher education in any nation are always a faithful mirror in which are sharply reflected the national history and character. In this mobile nation the action and reaction between the university and society at large are more sensitive and rapid than in stiffer communities.

p. 63.

And what will the University do for the community? First, it will make a rich return of learning, poetry, and piety. Secondly, it will foster the sense of public duty—that great virtue which makes republics possible.

—**Charles William Eliot** (1834–1926), President, Harvard University

1895, *The Universities of Europe in the Middle Ages,* chapter 1.

The institutions which the Middle Age has bequeathed to us are of greater and more imperishable value even than its cathedrals. . . . The universities and the immediate products of their activity may be said to constitute the great achievement of the Middle Ages in the intellectual sphere. Their organization and their traditions, their studies and their exercises affected the progress and intellectual development of Europe more powerfully, or (perhaps it should be said) more exclusively than any schools in all likelihood will ever do again.

—**Hastings Rashdall** (1858–1924), Dean of Carlisle, University of Oxford

1897, *The American College in American Life,* p. 45.

There cannot be an over supply of educated men. There can be no absolute over supply of any good thing. We cannot educate too many men; neither can we educate men too much. Can humanity become too good, or too able, or too learned, or too reasonable?

—**Charles F. Thwing** (1853–1937),
President, Adelbert College;
President, Western Reserve University

1901, "Colleges and degrees," *Mr. Dooley's Opinions,* p. 204.

"D'ye think th' colledges has much to do with th' progress iv th' wurruld?" asked Mr. Hennessy. "D'ye think," said Mr. Dooley, " 'tis th' mill that makes th' wather run?"

—**Peter Finley Dunne** (1867–1936),
U.S. journalist and author

1913, *University Control,* p. 13.

[T]he development of the American university, especially the state university, is one of the greatest achievements of our people, promising moral, social and intellectual leadership and supremacy in the course of the present century.

—**J. McKeen Cattell** (1860–1944),
professor of psychology,
Columbia University

1925, *Arrowsmith,* chapter 2.

The University of Winnemac . . . is not a snobbish rich-man's college, devoted to leisurely nonsense. It is the property of the people of the state, and what they want— or what they are told they want—is a mill to turn out men and women who will lead moral lives, play bridge, drive good cars, be enterprising in business, and occasionally mention books, although they are not expected to have time to read them. It is a Ford Motor Factory, and if its products rattle a little, they are beautifully standardized, with perfectly interchangeable parts. . . . [B]y 1950, one may expect it to have created an entirely new world-civilization, a civilization larger and brisker and purer.

—**Sinclair Lewis** (1885–1951),
U.S. writer

1927, *Life and the Student,* pp. 175–76.

An American university is something new under the sun; not merely, perhaps not chiefly, an institution of learning, but a vast social and economic enterprise, a struggling organ of confused democracy, striving to grow, to make good, to find a popular function and pecuniary support.

—**Charles Horton Cooley** (1864–1929),
professor of sociology,
University of Michigan

1966, "The gross national mind," in *The Most of Malcolm Muggeridge,* p. 93.

Higher education is booming in the United States; the Gross National Mind is mounting along with the Gross National Product.

—**Malcolm Muggeridge** (1903–1990),
English journalist

1973, *The Purposes and the Performance of Higher Education in the United States,* pp. 76–77.

[H]igher education should not promise too much. It can contribute substantially to equality of opportunity but only in a minor degree to equality of economic results. It can contribute significantly to a higher GNP, but it cannot by itself cause the GNP to rise. It can provide a favorable climate for student development, but it cannot take responsibility for such development; it cannot save souls. It can assist pure scholarship, but it cannot guarantee that the products of such scholarship will add to human happiness. It can provide opportunities for commentary on the conduct of society, but it cannot assure the validity of such commentary; it cannot save the world. It should not promise more than it can reasonably expect to deliver.

—**Carnegie Commission
on Higher Education**

1977, *Investment in Learning,* p. 12.

Learning, the chief product of higher education, consists primarily of changes in people—changes in their knowledge, their characteristics, and their behavior. Production in higher education, then, is not the transformation of resources into tangible products; rather, it is the transformation of resources into desired intangible qualities of human beings.

p. 447.

The monetary returns alone . . . are probably sufficient to offset all the costs. But over and above the monetary returns are the personal development and life enrichment of millions of people, the preservation of the cultural heritage, the advancement of knowledge and the arts, a major contribution to national prestige and power, and the direct satisfactions derived from college attendance and from living in a society where knowledge and the arts flourish. These nonmonetary benefits surely are far greater than the monetary benefits—so much greater, in fact, that individual and social decisions about the future of higher education should be made primarily on the basis of nonmonetary considerations and only secondarily on the basis of monetary factors.

—**Howard R. Bowen** (1908–1989), economist; President, Grinnell College; President, University of Iowa; Chancellor, Claremont University Center

1977, editorial, 21 December, quoted in Carnegie Council on Policy Studies in Higher Education, *Three Thousand Futures,* 1980, p. 97.

Taken together, the universities are probably the strongest of all institutional influences on the American future.

—*Washington Post*

Radicals

c. 1960, student slogan, quoted in Joseph R. Conlin, *The Morrow Book of Quotations in American History,* 1984, p. 336.

I am a student. Please do not fold, spindle or mutilate.

—**Author Unknown**

no date, attributed in Leonard L. Levinson, *Bartlett's Unfamiliar Quotations,* 1971, p. 47.

I can remember when the academic life was a meadow of mediation in an island of tranquility. Now the president and faculty get combat pay.

—**Hubert H. Humphrey** (1911–1978), U.S. politician, Vice President of the United States

1968, "Reply to Uncle Grayson [Kirk, president, Columbia University], *Up Against the Wall,* Columbia SDS (Students for a Democratic Society) newspaper, 22 April, quoted in Immanuel Wallerstein and Paul Starr, *The University Crisis Reader, Volume Two,* 1971, p. 428.

You call for order and respect for authority; we call for justice, freedom, and socialism. There is only one thing left to say. It may sound nihilistic to you, since it is the opening shot in a war of liberation. I'll use the words of LeRoi Jones, whom I'm sure you don't like a whole lot: "Up against the wall, motherfucker, this is a stick-up."

—**Mark Rudd** (1947–), student radical leader, Columbia University

1968, speech at Columbia University, April, quoted in Joseph R. Conlin, *The Morrow Book of Quotations in American History,* 1984, p. 257.

If we win, we will take control of your world, your corporations, your university, and attempt to mold a world in which we and other people can live as human beings.

—**Mark Rudd** (1947–), student radical leader, Columbia University

1968, Charlottesville, Virginia, 12 April, quoted in <http://beatl.barnard.columbia.edu/columbia68/documents/doc3.htm>.

Our young people, in disturbing numbers, appear to reject all forms of authority, from whatever source derived, and they have taken refuge in a turbulent and inchoate nihilism whose sole objectives are destruction. I know of no time in our history when the gap between the generations has been wider or more potentially dangerous.

—**Grayson Kirk** (1903–1997), President, Columbia University

1968, "Parting shots: A century of commencement speeches," *Saturday Review,* 12 May 1979, p. 38.

To imagine that the best way to change a social order is to start by assaulting its most accessible centers of thought and study and criticism is not only to show a complete disregard for the intrinsic character of the university, but also to develop a curiously self-destructive strategy for social change.

—**Richard Hofstadter** (1916–1970), professor of American history, Columbia University

1968, SDS pamphlet distributed in Chicago, August, quoted in Immanuel Wallerstein and Paul Starr, *The University Crisis Reader, Volume Two,* 1971, p. 209.

We indict the universities because they function primarily to train young people for technical and managerial jobs in the big corporations. The way we see it, these corporations are the source of poverty and stupid long-hour jobs because of their calculated mis-management of the productive resources of America. These same corporations are the source of America's holy war against movements of national liberation because they want their foreign investment empire well protected. Forget it! We don't wanna work on Maggie's farm no more. Shut it down!

—**Les Coleman** (?–?), Students for a Democratic Society (SDS) officer

1968, *Berkeley Barb,* 2–8 February, quoted in Immanuel Wallerstein and Paul Starr, *The University Crisis Reader, Volume Two,* 1971, p. 350.

[T]he thing to do is to get a traveling yippee guerrilla theater band roaming through college campuses burning books, burning degrees and exams, burning school records, busting up classrooms, and freeing our brothers from the prison of the university. . . . The universities cannot be reformed. They must be abandoned or closed down. They should be used as bases for actions against society, but never taken seriously. The professors have nothing to teach; we learn in action confronting America. We can learn more from any jail than we can from any university.

—**Jerry Rubin** (1938–1994), antiwar activist and entrepreneur

1969, title of a statement prepared for the SDS National Convention, 18 June, quoted in Immanuel Wallerstein and Paul Starr, *The University Crisis Reader, Volume Two,* 1971, p. 260.

You don't need to be a weatherman to know which way the wind blows.

—Students for a Democratic Society (SDS)

1969, poster, April, quoted in Immanuel Wallerstein and Paul Starr, *The University Crisis Reader, Volume Two,* 1971, p. 10.

> STRIKE FOR THE EIGHT DEMANDS STRIKE BE CAUSE YOU HATE COPS STRIKE BECAUSE YOUR ROOMMATE WAS CLUBBED STRIKE TO STOP EXPANSION STRIKE TO SEIZE CONTROL OF YOUR LIFE STRIKE TO BECOME MORE HUMAN STR IKE TO RETURN PAINE HALL SCHOLARSHIPS STRIKE BE CAUSE THERE'S NO POETRY IN YOUR LECTURES STRIKE BECAUSE CLASSES ARE A BORE STRIKE FOR POWER STRIKE TO SMASH THE CORPORATION STRIKE TO MAKE YOURSELF FREE STRIKE TO ABOLISH ROTC STRIKE BECAUSE THEY ARE TRYING TO SQUEEZE THE LIFE OUT OF YOU STRIKE

—Students, Harvard School of Design

1969, "Columbia," *Movement,* March, quoted in Immanuel Wallerstein and Paul Starr, *The University Crisis Reader, Volume Two,* 1971, p. 194.

Our strength was greatest at the time of our greatest militancy. . . . At that time, nothing could defeat us, not the police, not the jocks, not the liberal faculty, so treacherous and yet so important, only our own (we found out later) weakness and bad political judgment. The liberal world was para-

lyzed; radicals had a vision of what victory seems like. . . . Above all, we learned almost accidentally the great truth stated by Chairman Mao Tse-tung, "Dare to struggle, dare to win."

—Mark Rudd (1947–), student radical leader, Columbia University

1969, "Harvard: The voice of a non-striker," *Wall Street Journal,* 6 May, quoted in Immanuel Wallerstein and Paul Starr, *The University Crisis Reader, Volume Two,* 1971, p. 324.

The problem at Harvard is not SDS. The problem is not the use of the police, nor is it the student strike. The problem is the Harvard faculty: Its leniency, its blindness and its cowardice.

—J. C. Helms (?–?), graduate student, Harvard University

1969, letter to disciplined students, 4 June, quoted in Immanuel Wallerstein and Paul Starr, *The University Crisis Reader, Volume Two,* 1971, p. 14.

Violence is simply not compatible with the serious and sustained intellectual work which is the essence of a University. The very intellectual processes on which study, teaching and research depend cannot proceed in the atmosphere of destructive emotions which invariably accompany violence and which are too often unleashed by it.

—Faculty Committee of Fifteen, Harvard University

1969, speech at General Beadle State College, 3 June, quoted in James B. Simpson, *Simpson's Contemporary Quotations,* 1988.

The student who invades an administration building, roughs up a dean, rifles the files and issues "nonnegotiable demands" may have some of his demands met by a permissive university administration. But the greater his "victory" the more he will have undermined the security of his own rights.

—**Richard M. Nixon** (1913–1994),
President of the United States

1972, *Where Has All the Ivy Gone?,*
p. 273.

I have never understood why they tried to start the revolution by taking over the universities. It should have been self-evident that the net result of success would be to close the universities but leave the nation unaffected—at least, for quite a long time. Nor do I find it easy to believe that the rebels, as intelligent as most of them were, seriously expected that they could keep the universities alive as corporate bodies, once they had control of them, if they made the fundamental alterations in organization and role that they proposed to.

—**Muriel Beadle** (1915–1994),
U.S. author and community organizer

1977, *We Must March, My Darlings,*
p. 80.

Touch a university with hostile hands and the blood you draw is prompt, copious and real.

—**Diana Trilling** (1905–1996)
U.S. author and critic

Reform

1519, letter to Martin Luther, May, quoted in Henry S. Pritchett, "Preface," in Howard J. Savage, *American College Athletics,* 1929, p. v.

Instead of holding the universities in contempt, we ought rather to recall them to more sober studies.

—**Desiderius Erasmus** (1466–1536),
Dutch humanist; professor of divinity
and Greek, Cambridge University

1776, *Wealth of Nations,* Book Five, Chapter I.

The improvements which, in modern times, have been made in several different branches of philosophy have not, the greater part of them, been made in universities. . . . [S]everal of those learned societies have chosen to remain, for a long time, the sanctuaries in which exploded systems and obsolete prejudices found shelter and protection after they had been hunted out of every other corner of the world.

—**Adam Smith** (1723–1790),
Scottish philosopher and economist

1828, *Report of the Faculty, Part I,* quoted in Arthur Levine, *Handbook of Undergraduate Curriculum,* 1978, p. 545.

[P]erhaps the time has come, when we ought to pause, and inquire, whether it will be sufficient to make gradual changes, as heretofore; and whether the whole system is not rather to be broken up, and a better one substituted in its stead. From different quarters, we have heard the suggestion, that our colleges must be new-modelled; that they are not adapted to the spirit and wants of the age; that they will soon be deserted, unless they are better accommodated to the business character of the nation.

—**Faculty of Yale College**

c. nineteenth century, attributed in Henry M. Wriston, *Academic Procession,* 1959, p. 70.

No man ought to meddle with universities who does not know them well and love them well.

—**Thomas Arnold** (1795–1842),
Headmaster, Rugby School

1831, "On the state of the English universities, with more especial reference to Oxford," *Edinburgh Review,* June, p. 427, quoted in J. B. Lon Hefferlin, *Dynamics of Educational Reform,* 1969, p. 136.

All experience proves that Universities, like other corporations, can only be reformed from without.

—**William Hamilton** (1788–1856), Scottish philosopher; professor of logic and metaphysics, Edinburgh University

1869, Inaugural Address, 19 October, in *A Turning Point in Higher Education,* 1969, p. 32.

A university is not built in the air, but on social and literary foundations which preceding generations have bequeathed. If the whole structure needs rebuilding, it must be rebuilt from the foundation. Hence, sudden reconstruction is impossible in our high places of education.

—**Charles William Eliot** (1834–1926), President, Harvard University

c. 1885, letter to the Reverend Rufus Anderson, quoted in J. B. Lon Hefferlin, *Dynamics of Educational Reform,* 1969, p. 105.

I consider that a great step is made in a reformation when it has been granted that the present system is open to examination, and not stereotyped for all ages. Wherever that is done, light will break in. . . . It begins to be admitted that college systems may be examined. When this is done there is hope of amendment.

—**Francis Wayland** (1796–1865), President, Brown University

1909, *Report for 1908–9,* quoted in Edward C. Elliott (ed.), *The Rise of a University, Vol. II,* 1937, p. 330.

There are those now busily instructing the public who seem to believe . . . that if only they can have access to Treasurer's Reports and Registrar's statistics and rearrange them in some new and occult fashion, like men on a chessboard, higher education will at once be reformed and rise to new planes of achievement. These are the delusions of the mechanically minded. . . . There is really only one fundamental problem in higher education, and that is to find the teacher.

—**Nicholas Murray Butler** (1862–1947), President, Columbia University

1929, *The Aims of Education and Other Essays,* Chapter One.

In the history of education, the most striking phenomenon is that schools of learning, which at one epoch are alive with a ferment of genius, in a succeeding generation exhibit merely pedantry and routine. The reason is that they are overladen with inert ideas. Education with inert ideas is not only useless: it is above all things harmful—*Corruptio optimi, pessima.*

—**Alfred North Whitehead** (1861–1947), English philosopher and mathematician; professor of philosophy, Harvard University

1929, "Alfred North Whitehead," in Alfred North Whitehead, *The Aims of Education and Other Essays.*

The need for breaking down sterilizing departmentalization has been widely felt. Unfortunately, however, a too frequent way of doing it has been, wittily but not too unfairly, described as the cross-sterilization of the social sciences. That is a tendency by which a difficult problem, say of the law, is solved by relying on the formulation of a dubious truth in some other field.

—**Felix Frankfurter** (1882–1965), Associate Justice, U.S. Supreme Court

1944, *The Mission of the University,* chapter II, p. 27.

The reform of higher education cannot be limited, nor can even its main features be limited, to the correction of abuses. Abuses are always of minor importance. . . . Any reform movement which is limited to correcting slovenly or slipshod abuses in our university will lead inevitably to a reform which is equally slovenly.

—**José Ortega Y Gassett** (1883–1955), professor of metaphysics, University of Madrid

1946, "The administrator," *Journal of Higher Education,* November, p. 402.

The fact that the purpose of universities is rapidly lost has led to the suggestion that they should be burned down every twenty-five years, or that the original faculty should consist of men forty years old, that no additions should be made, and that they should all retire at the age of sixty-five. These proposals seem drastic, but they are little more so than the facts demand. It is imperative to force the periodic reconsideration of the purpose of an institution.

—**Robert Maynard Hutchins** (1899–1977), President, University of Chicago

1959, *Academic Procession,* p. 39.

[R]eform easily exhausts the energies of its proponents and . . . the stubborn, silent, but destructive effect of passive resistance is continuous, pervasive, and insidious. A change voted is merely a challenge to resistance; the vote is preliminary to the real battle.

—**Henry M. Wriston** (1889–1978), President, Lawrence College; President, Brown University

1963, *The Uses of the University,* pp. 94–95.

Few institutions are so conservative as the universities about their own affairs while their members are so liberal about the affairs of others; and sometimes the most liberal faculty member in one context is the most conservative in another.

—**Clark Kerr** (1911–2003), Chancellor, University of California, Berkeley; President, University of California

1967, speech at the Twenty-Second National Conference on Higher Education, 7 March, quoted in J. B. Lon Hefferlin, *Dynamics of Educational Reform,* 1969.

When a college is on the verge of oblivion there is no problem in achieving instant curricular revision. . . . Dynamic, creative, dictatorial leadership is therefore welcomed by all. . . . The history of American higher education contains many evidences of the pressures of imminent failure providing the condition for immediate radical curricular change. Panic always produces action that is unobtainable during normal times.

—**Miller Upton** (1916–), President, Beloit College

1971, *Deschooling Society,* p. 38.

Any attempt to reform the university without attending to the system of which it is an integral part is like trying to do urban renewal in New York City from the twelfth story up.

—**Ivan Illich** (1926–), U.S. educator

1978, *The Perpetual Dream,* p. 8.

American higher education needs more inventiveness, more imagination, more willingness to experiment and hence to fail, than is generally present.

—**Gerald P. Grant** (1938–), professor of education and sociology, Syracuse University; **David Riesman** (1909–2002), professor of sociology, Harvard University

1980, *On Higher Education,* p. 294.

If one is thinking of what is consciously labeled "reform," the number of institutions that have attempted anything of a systematic sort might be as many as 250 out of 3,000 institutions. And even in this small number, the students affected in any appreciable degree by the changes are likely to be a minority.

—**David Riesman** (1909–2002), professor of sociology, Harvard University

1986, *Higher Learning,* p. 40.

[A]nyone who studies the history of curricular reform since 1900 will emerge stripped of the notion that this subject holds the key to many insights about the course of American civilization. Over this period, all of the fundamental issues have remained the same. Almost every important proposal has already been tried. No permanent victories are ever won, nor are serious arguments ever conclusively defeated.

p. 58.

The professors who vote for new majors or curricular reforms know very little about whether these initiatives will actually help students progress toward the educational goals of the institution. And rarely, if ever, do they make a serious effort to find out.

p. 192.

Presidents can explain the faculty's actions to the outside world; they can raise money, build new buildings, and defend the insti-

tution from hostile attacks; but they lack the authority to bring about serious educational reform.

—**Derek Bok** (1930–), President, Harvard University

1988, *ProfScam,* p. 151.

Reform may be the most popular leisure activity of the American university. The history of higher education is littered with grandiose blueprints for change—the debris of dozens of well-intentioned but ultimately failed efforts. But the rhetoric of reform is one of the proudest traditions of the academy.

—**Charles J. Sykes** (1954–), U.S. journalist

1991, *BAD, or the Dumbing of America,* p. 65.

[A]mericans devised a reformed system of higher education, one more in keeping with American desires, especially the urge to succeed in public, defined largely as making a pile and living a life untroubled by thought.

—**Paul Fussell** (1924–), professor of English, University of Pennsylvania

Service

1802, address, quoted in Frederick Rudolph, *The American College and University: A History,* 1962, p. 58.

It ought always to be remembered, that literary institutions are founded and endowed for the common good, and not for the private advantage of those who may resort to them for education. It is not that they may be able to pass through life in an easy or reputable manner, but that their mental powers may be cultivated and improved for the benefit of society. If it be true no man should live for himself alone, we may safely assert that every man who has been aided by a public institution to acquire an education and to qualify himself for usefulness, is under peculiar obligations to exert his talents for the public good.

—**Joseph McKeen** (1757–1807),
President, Bowdoin College

1896, "Princeton for the nation's service," Inaugural Address, December, quoted in Edgar W. Knight, *What College Presidents Say,* 1940, p. 24.

[I]n days quiet and troubled alike Princeton has stood for the nation's service, to produce men and patriots.

—**Woodrow Wilson** (1856–1924),
President, Princeton University;
President of the United States

1897, *The American College in American Life,* p. 62.

No youth has been more eager than the college youth to doff the student's gown and to don the soldier's uniform. It has been said that, except for Harvard College, the Revolution would have been put off half a century.

—**Charles F. Thwing** (1853–1937),
President, Adelbert College;
President, Western Reserve University

1902, "The university and democracy," in *The Trend in Higher Education,* 1905, p. 28.

Some [universities] are deaf to the cry of suffering humanity; some are exclusive and shut up in themselves; but the true university, the university of the future, is one the motto of which will be: Service for mankind wherever mankind is, and whether within scholastic walls or without those walls and in the world at large.

—**William Rainey Harper** (1856–1906),
President, University of Chicago

1908, *Report for 1907–8,* quoted in Edward C. Elliott (ed.), *The Rise of a University, Vol. II,* 1937, p. 3.

The modern university must be conceived of as a public service institution. Its men, its books, its influence, its information, must always be at the service of the public when a good and unselfish end is to be served. The university rests on the public will and on public appreciation. To shut itself up, cloister-like, in its own sufficiency, or to turn all its energies and resources inward, are alike to be false to its own ideal and to waste its most valuable opportunities.

—**Nicholas Murray Butler**
(1862–1947), President,
Columbia University

1910, Address at the University Club of Chicago, 12 May, quoted in Arthur S. Link (ed.), *The Public Papers of Woodrow Wilson,* vol. 20, p. 438.

Princeton is no longer a thing for Princeton men to please themselves with. Princeton is a thing with which Princeton men must satisfy the country.

—**Woodrow Wilson** (1856–1924),
President, Princeton University;
President of the United States

1912, quoted in John S. Brubacher and Willis Rudy, *Higher Education in Transition,* 1958, p. 157.

[I] have endeavored to induce every citizen to regard himself as a stockholder in the Institution, who had a real interest in helping make it of the greatest service to his children and those of his neighbors.

—**James Burrill Angell** (1829–1916),
President, University of Vermont;
President, University of Michigan

1960, "Education—to what end?", *Morehouse College Bulletin,* March, p. 6, quoted in Samuel DuBois Cook, "The socio-ethical role and responsibility of the black college graduate," pp. 59–60, in Charles V. Willie and Ronald R. Edmonds (eds.), *Black Colleges in America,* 1978.

[I]f one has a better mind than his fellows, more wealth than his fellows, is more favorably circumstanced than his fellows, has a better opportunity to develop than his fellows, he is obligated to use skills in the interest of the common good. To use education for the common good is mandatory because trained minds are rare. . . . And to whom much is given, much is required. . . . [M]an can fulfill his true destiny in this life only in proportion as his skills are used in the service of mankind.

> —**Benjamin E. Mays** (1895–1984), President, Morehouse College

1962, *The American College and University: A History,* p. 59.

[C]olleges of early nineteenth-century America were committed to social needs rather than to individual preference and self-indulgence. When college presidents thought of their students they were reminded not of society's obligation to young men but of the obligation of young men to society.

> —**Frederick Rudolph** (1920–), professor of history, Williams College

1983, "A crisis of purpose: Reexamining the role of the university," *Change,* October, p. 53.

[I]t is the increasing responsibility of the university not merely to be a principal source of new knowledge, but also to be instrumental in analyzing and applying this knowledge and in making it rapidly useful to all societal sectors.

> —**Ernest A. Lynton** (1926–1998), senior vice president for academic affairs, University of Massachusetts

1994, *The Chronicle of Higher Education,* 9 March.

I'm concerned that in recent years higher education's historic commitment to service seems to have diminished. I'm troubled that many now view the campus as a place where professors get tenured and students get credentialed; the overall efforts of the academy are not considered to be at the vital center of the nation's work. And what I find most disturbing is the growing feeling in this country that higher education is a *private* benefit, not a *public* good.

> —**Ernest L. Boyer** (1928–1995), Chancellor, State University of New York

1996, "The scholarship of engagement," *Journal of Public Service and Outreach,* 1 (1), p. 11.

The academy must become a more vigorous partner in the search for answers to our most pressing social, civic, economic, and moral problems and must reaffirm its historic commitment to what I call the scholarship of engagement.

> —**Ernest L. Boyer** (1928–1995), Chancellor, State University of New York

1997, "Higher education and rebuilding civic life," *Change,* January/February, p. 13.

[W]e need to get over the traditional research culture that has sapped the vitality of most of our colleges and universities by drawing faculty away from commitment to their institutions and communities. The denigration of applied research and problem solving has further eroded higher education's connection to the world.

—**Zelda F. Gamson** (1936–),
professor of education,
University of Massachusetts, Boston

Sex and Gender

1776, letter to John Adams, 14 August, quoted in Barbara Miller Solomon, *In The Company of Educated Women,* 1985, p. 1.

I most sincerely wish that some more liberal plan might be laid and executed for the Benefit of the rising Generation, and that our new constitution may be distinguished for Learning and Virtue. If we mean to have Heroes, Statesmen and Philosophers, we should have learned women ... If much depends as is allowed upon the early Education of youth and the first principals [sic] which are instilld take the deepest root, great benefits must arise from literary accomplishments in women.

—**Abigail Adams** (1744–1818),
First Lady

1793, salutatorian commencement address, Philadelphia Academy, quoted in Barbara Miller Solomon, *In The Company of Educated Women,* 1985, p. 28.

They have denied women a liberal education and now if we should prove capable of speaking, where could we speak? The Church, the Bar, the Senate are closed against us. Who shut them? Man, Despotic Man.

—**Priscilla Mason** (c. 1770–?),
student, Philadelphia Academy

1868, Letter to her mother, September, quoted at <http://anthropology.vassar.edu/bianco/hidden/ellen.html>

I am really astonished at the amount of work we do. The only trouble here, they wont [sic] let us study enough. I think few men in college do as much as we do here [at Vassar].

—**Ellen Henrietta Swallow Richards** (1842–1911), U.S. chemist and ecologist

1872, Thomas Woody, *A History of Women's Education in the United States,* 1929, quoted in Frederick Rudolph, *The American College and University: A History,* 1962, p. 318.

It is too late, amid the noontime splendours of the nineteenth century, to ignore the claims of woman to higher education.... Whatever shall make her wiser and better, that she may learn; whatever knowledge she may be able to use, either in adding to her own happiness or in promoting the happiness of others—that knowledge she may rightfully acquire.

—**Board of Visitors,**
University of Wisconsin

c. 1874, review of Edward Clarke's *Sex in Education,* quoted in Barbara Miller Solomon, *In The Company of Educated Women,* 1985, p. 62.

To resist the demand that women are making for education is a hopeless task.

—**Henry B. Adams** (1838–1918),
U.S. historian

1876, inauguration speech, quoted in Edwin E. Slosson, *Great American Universities,* 1910, p. 121.

Of this I am certain, they are not among the wise who deprecate the intellectual capacity of women, and they are not among the prudent who would deny to women the best opportunity for education and culture.

—**Daniel Coit Gilman** (1831–1908),
President, Johns Hopkins University

no date, quoted in Edith Finch, *Carey Thomas of Bryn Mawr,* 1947, p. 31–2.

[O]ne thing I am determined on is that by the time I die *my* brain shall weigh as much as a man's if study and learning can make it so and then I'll leave it in the hands of some physiologist to be weighed so after that no miserable man can stand up on a platform and tell a miserable audience that my brain weighed "a few ounces less than any other man's." Just wait til equal education takes place and see if that remark can be made!

—**M. Carey Thomas** (1857–1935), President, Bryn Mawr College

1881, *Report for 1880–81,* quoted in William F. Russell (ed.), *The Rise of a University, Vol. I,* 1937, p. 271–72.

No one is any longer weak enough to argue that women should be denied the educational advantages which universities offer, on the ground of any natural incapacity in the sex to profit by them. Nor is it any longer contended that the physical organization of women is too delicate to permit them with safety to grapple with those difficult subjects which are commonly supposed to require for their mastery a severe course of study long protracted. . . . Nor does it appear that their intellectual triumphs have been purchased at any expense to their physical vigor.

—**Frederick A. P. Barnard** (1809–1889), President, Columbia University

1881, "Experiments," *Common Sense About Women,* 1882, p. 199, quoted in Patricia A. Palmieri, "From republican motherhood to race suicide: Arguments

on the higher education of women in the United States, 1820–1920," in Lester F. Goodchild and Harold S. Wechsler (eds.), *ASHE Reader on the History of Higher Education, 2nd Edition,* 1997, p. 173.

Why is it, that, whenever anything is done for women in the way of education it is called "an experiment"—something that is to be long considered, stoutly opposed, grudgingly yielded, and dubiously watched,—while if the same thing is done for men, its desirableness is assumed as a matter of course, and the thing is done?

—**Thomas Wentworth Higginson** (1823–1911), social critic and reformer

c. 1890, in Charles W. Dabney, *Universal Education in the South,* 1936, quoted in Edgar W. Knight, *What College Presidents Say,* 1940, pp. 302–3.

Educate a man and you have educated only one person; educate a mother and you educate a whole family. . . . The proper training of women is the strategic point in the education of the race. . . . Money invested in the education of women yields better dividends than that invested in men. Woman is the priestess in humanity's temple and she presides at the fountain head of civilization.

—**Charles D. McIver** (1860–1906), President, Normal and Industrial Institute [now University of North Carolina-Greensboro]

1895, *An Ideal Husband,* Act II.

Lady Chiltern: Robert is a great champion of the Higher Education of Women, and so, I am afraid, am I.
Mrs. Cheverley: The higher education of men is what I should like to see. Men really need it so sadly.

Lady Markby: They do, dear. But I am afraid such a scheme would be quite impractical. I don't think man has much capacity for development. He has got as far as he can, and that is not far, is it?

—**Oscar Wilde** (1854–1900),
Irish playwright, author, and wit

1905, Ida Husted Harper, *Life and Work of Susan B. Anthony,* vol. 3, 1908, quoted in Mary Briggs, *Women's Words: The Columbia Book of Quotations by Women,* 1995, p. 107.

I can't say that the college-bred woman is the most contented woman. The broader her mind the more she understands the unequal conditions between men and women, the more she chafes under a government that tolerates it.

—**Susan B. Anthony** (1820–1906), U.S. social reformer and suffragist

1905, *Story of My Life, Part I.*

When I was a little girl, I visited Wellesley and surprised my friends by the announcement, "Some day I shall go to college—but I shall go to Harvard!" When asked why I would not go to Wellesley, I replied that there were only girls there.

—**Helen Keller** (1880–1968), U.S. writer

1958, *The Academic Marketplace,* p. 226.

Women scholars are not taken seriously and cannot look forward to a normal professional career. This bias is part of the much larger pattern which determines the utilization of women in our economy. It is not peculiar to the academic world, but it does blight the prospects of senior scholars.

—**Theodore Caplow** (1920–), professor of sociology, University of Virginia;
Reese J. McGee (1929–), professor of sociology, Purdue University

1961, *The Ground I Walked On,* p. 3.

[Y]ou ought not to educate a woman as if she were a man, or to educate her as if she were not.

—**George N. Shuster** (1894–1977), President, Hunter College

1975, *New York Times,* 9 October, p. 43.

Equality is not when a female Einstein gets promoted to assistant professor. Equality is when a female schlemiel moves ahead as fast as a male schlemiel.

—**Ewald B. Nyquist** (1914–1987), commissioner of education, State of New York

1979, "Toward a woman-centered university," in *On Lies, Secrets, and Silence,* p. 127.

What we have at present is a man-centered university, a breeding ground not of humanism, but of masculine privilege.

p. 155.

Consciously woman-centered universities—in which women shape the philosophy and the decision-making though men may choose to study and teach there—may evolve from existing institutions. Whatever the forms it may take, the process of women's repossession of ourselves is irreversible. Within and without academe, the rise in women's expectations has gone far beyond the middle class and has released an incalculable new energy—not merely for changing institutions but for human redefinition; not merely for equal rights but for a new kind of being.

—**Adrienne Rich** (1929–), U.S. poet

1982, *The Classroom Climate: A Chilly One for Women?,* p. 3.

A chilling classroom climate puts women students at a significant educational disadvantage. Overtly disparaging remarks about women, as well as more subtle differential behaviors, can have a critical and lasting effect. When they occur frequently ... such behaviors can have a profoundly negative impact on women's academic and career development. ...

—**Roberta A. Hall** (1946–), assistant to the president, University of St. Thomas; **Bernice R. Sandler** (1928–), senior scholar, Women's Research and Education Institute

1988, *MisEducation,* p. 2.

Anyone who has contact with a university learns that men are more important than women, and that men's ideas are the ones that matter.

—**Anne Innis Dagg** (1933–), academic advisor, Independent Studies, University of Waterloo (Canada); **Patricia J. Thompson** (1967–), graduate student

1999, *Writing the Social: Critique, Theory, and Investigations,* p. 203.

To women who know enough of feminist discourse to know how to name and see what is going on around them in the university, the taken-for-granted everyday practices of a male-dominated society display an ordinary, and pervasive, sexism. This is the reason the phrase "a chilly climate for women" resonates.

—**Dorothy E. Smith** (1926–), professor of sociology, Ontario Institute for Studies in Education

Social Mobility

1825, Inaugural Address, quoted in Richard Hofstadter and Wilson Smith (eds.), *American Higher Education: A Documentary History, Volume I,* 1961, p. 329.

[R]aise colleges among yourselves, and you reduce the charges of a liberal edu-

cation so considerably that hundreds and thousands can immediately avail themselves of their aid. ... Such is the peculiar genius and excellence of our republican institutions, that, moral and mental worth is the surest passport to distinction. The humblest individual, by the diligent cultivation of his faculties, may, without the aid of family or fortune, attain the most exalted stations within the reach or gift of freemen.

—**Philip Lindsley** (1786–1855), President, University of Nashville

1857, *Colleges: Their Place Among American Institutions* (pamphlet), quoted in Edgar W. Knight, *What College Presidents Say,* 1940, p. 264.

Scarcely anything in America is more distinctly American than the relations between the colleges and the common people. The people have made the colleges what they are, and the colleges have made the people what they are. All classes have contributed to the establishment and the support of the colleges and all classes have reaped the benefits.

—**William S. Tyler** (1810–1897), professor of Greek, Amherst College

1864, quoted in Edgar W. Knight, *What College Presidents Say,* 1940, p. 82.

It is one of the glories of our American colleges, that their doors are open to all classes in society, and that the only nobility known within their walls has its basis in intellectual power, high attainment and moral worth. ... Within the walls of an American college all factitious distinctions vanish. ...

—**Theron Baldwin** (1801–1870), U.S. clergyman and educator

1898, *Educational Reform,* p. 235.

I am not acquainted with any portion of American society, high or low, rich or poor, in which there are so few distinctions and separations based on social inequalities as in the American colleges.

—**Charles William Eliot** (1834–1926),
President, Harvard University

1899, *Going to College,* pp. 41–42.

[T]he most perfect democracy in the world is the college. Here as nowhere else brains, character, and application are the only qualities that count. . . . Nobody cares who his grandfather was, nor how much his father is worth, but the questions are, What does he know? and, What can he do?

—**Waitman Barbe** (1864–1925),
assistant to the president,
West Virginia University

1962, *The American College,* p. 14.

The social benefits of college seem to be regarded as highly as the economic ones, and to be inseparably inter-related with them. For the great middle class, college has become a social necessity, while for members of the lower classes it is a prime means for social advancement. Everyone has a chance to advance socially—or to maintain his existing high status—by attending one of the colleges of higher prestige.

—**Nevitt R. Sanford** (1909–1995),
professor of psychology and education,
Stanford University

1974, *The Great School Wars,* quoted in Rosalie Maggio, *The Beacon Book of Quotations by Women,* 1992, p. 98.

The ladder was there, "from the gutter to the university," and for those stalwart enough to ascend it, the schools were a boon and a path out of poverty.

—**Diane Ravitch** (1938–), professor of
history and education,
New York University

2001, "From mass higher education to universal access," in Philip Altbach et al., *In Defense of American Higher Education,* p. 124.

Through its role in fostering social mobility and the belief in a society open to talent, American higher education legitimates the social and political system and thus is a central element in this society as it is nowhere else.

—**Martin A. Trow** (1926–),
professor of sociology,
University of California, Berkeley

Town and Gown

1869, Inaugural Address, 19 October, in *A Turning Point in Higher Education,* 1969, p. 63.

What can the community do for the University? It can love, honor, and cherish it. Love it and honor it. The University is upheld by this public affection and respect. In the loyalty of her children she finds strength and courage.

—**Charles William Eliot** (1834–1926),
President, Harvard University

1936, *Alma Mater,* p. 4.

The campus and the college buildings dominated its architecture like the temple and citadel of a Greek city-state, a difficult relationship since there was always some doubt in the minds of the town folk whether the college was an asset or a parasite. The town with its college was like a woman's club committee with a celebrity in tow, a credit to them but also an embarrassment and sometimes a nuisance. . . .

p. 20.

This college town was the egg in which nested the college yolk.

—**Henry Seidel Canby** (1878–1961),
U.S. editor and critic

1959, *The American College President,* p. 5.

Town and gown are more indistinguishable than they once were and this is itself a testimony to the rising level of education. If college professors are more like townspeople, townspeople are also more like college professors.

—**Harold W. Stoke** (1903–1982), President, University of New Hampshire; President, Louisiana State University; President, Queens College

1982, *Beyond the Ivory Tower,* p. 217.

In city or town, the culture of the university—with its bohemian life-styles and youthful exuberance—is often an irritant, as well as a source of pride, to the surrounding community.

—**Derek Bok** (1930–), President, Harvard University

Section Two

Academic Affairs

Chapter 3

Educational Policy

Academic Culture

1856, "Universities," *English Traits,* p. 882.

Universities are, of course, hostile to geniuses, which, seeing and using ways of their own, discredit the routine: as churches and monasteries persecute youthful saints.

—**Ralph Waldo Emerson** (1803–1882),
U.S. poet, philosopher, and essayist

1858, lecture, Christian Library Association, 22 June, quoted in Richard Hofstadter and Wilson Smith (eds.), *American Higher Education: A Documentary History, Volume II,* 1961, p. 519.

Governments cannot make universities by enactments of laws: Nor corporations by the erection of edifices: The church cannot create them under the authority of heaven: The flattering eulogies of orators cannot adorn them with learning: Newspapers cannot puff them into being. Learned men—scholars—these are the only workmen who can build up universities. Provide charters and endowments—the necessary protection and capital: provide books and apparatus—the necessary tools: Then seek out the sufficient scholars, and leave them to the work, as the intellectual engineers who are alone competent to do it.

—**Henry P. Tappan** (1805–1881),
President, University of Michigan

1865, *Sketches from Cambridge, By a Don,* pp. 5–6.

[I]f you wish at once to do nothing and be respectable now-a-days, the best pretext is to be at work on some profound study.

—**Leslie Stephen** (1832–1904),
English author and critic

1869, Inaugural Address, 19 October, in *A Turning Point in Higher Education,* 1969, pp. 35–36.

The worthy fruit of academic culture is an open mind, trained to careful thinking, instructed in the methods of philosophic investigation, acquainted in a general way with the accumulated thought of past generations, and penetrated with humility.

—**Charles William Eliot** (1834–1926),
President, Harvard University

1892, "Notes on first faculty meeting," quoted in Richard J. Storr, *Harper's University: The Beginnings,* p. 99.

The question before us is how to become one in spirit, though not necessarily in opinions.

—**William Rainey Harper** (1856–1906),
President, University of Chicago

1922, *My Discovery of England.*

Oxford trains scholars of the real type better than any other place in the world. Its methods are antiquated. It despises science. Its lectures are rotten. It has professors who never teach and students who never learn. It has no order, no arrangement, no system. Its curriculum is unintelligible. It has no president. It has no state legislature to tell it how to teach, and yet,—it gets there. Whether we like it or not, Oxford gives something to its students, a life and a mode of thought, which in America as yet we can emulate but not equal.

—**Stephen Butler Leacock**
(1869–1944), professor of political
economy, McGill University

1923, *College Days,* p. v.

[I] have lived and breathed so long in a college atmosphere that I am convinced that all colleges are in a measure alike, and that what is said of one is true of all.

—**Stephen Butler Leacock**
(1869–1944), professor of political
economy, McGill University

1926, *The Mauve Decade,* p. 207.

[U]niversities where individualism is dreaded as nothing else. . . .

—**Thomas Beer** (1889–1940),
U.S. author

1970, "Governance and functions," *Daedalus,* Winter, p. 116.

It [the university] is a church with a religion. It believes in the unfettered search for truth, in free expression of opinion without fear, in preservation of the past, including books however offensive they may be currently, and in access on merit and the granting of grace on merit. Its principles are more important than service, or rules, or votes, or consumer preference. It is the keeper of the good, the true, and the beautiful; of culture. It perpetuates a spirit of inquiry and integrity. Its religion is not subject to compromise.

—**Clark Kerr** (1911–2003), Chancellor,
University of California, Berkeley;
President, University of California

1971, *An Uncertain Glory,* p. 23.

Everything in academic life is vastly more charged with emotion than with intellect.

—**Frederic W. Ness** (1914–1998),
President, Fresno State College

1977, *Investment in Learning,* p. 269.

The ideals of the academy are mostly radical ideals. Insofar as they are practiced, they are disturbing to superstition, prejudice, provincialism, ignorance, and discrimination, the enemies of change. They are not the ideals of an educational system that is intended to buttress the status quo merely by socializing its students.

—**Howard R. Bowen** (1908–1989),
economist; President, Grinnell College;
President, University of Iowa;
Chancellor, Claremont University Center

1983, "Contradictions in a community of scholars: The cohesion-accuracy tradeoff," *Review of Higher Education,* Summer, p. 253.

The phrase "community of scholars" contains a contradiction. Actions that strengthen the community weaken the scholarship. And actions that strengthen the scholarship weaken the community.

—**Karl E. Weick** (1936–), professor of organizational behavior and psychology, University of Michigan

1987, "Foreword," Burton R. Clark, *The Academic Life,* 1987, p. xvii.

[U]niversities and colleges give the highest rewards to those faculty members who may not be committed to giving their best effort to the students who pay their tuitions with an expectation that they will be well taught. Although many faculty members sincerely assert their fondness for students and are excited by the satisfaction they derive from teaching well, the academic culture too often holds such enthusiasms in low regard.

—**Ernest L. Boyer** (1928–1995), Chancellor, State University of New York

1990, "Through thick and thin: Two ways of talking about the academy and moral responsibility," in William B. May (ed.), *Ethics and Higher Education,* p. 59.

[W]e are the heirs of a tradition that found in higher education a high moral calling. And we can remind ourselves that part of what we are called to do is stewardship of our institutions as a dwelling place for the human spirit—a habitation where faculty members, administrators, and students alike can become habituated to a vision of the good society by inhabiting a good community of scholars.

—**James Laney** (1927–), President, Emory University

Academic Freedom

1820, letter to Mr. Roscoe, quoted in John S. Brubacher and Willis Rudy, *Higher Education in Transition,* 1958, p. 300.

[H]ere [the University of Virginia] we are not afraid to follow truth wherever it may lead, nor to tolerate error so long as reason is left free to combat it.

—**Thomas Jefferson** (1743–1826), father of the University of Virginia; President of the United States

1837, "The American Scholar," delivered before the Phi Beta Kappa Society, at Cambridge, August 31, *Nature; Addresses and Lectures,* 1849.

Free should the scholar be,—free and brave. Free even to the definition of freedom, "without any hindrance that does not arise out of his own constitution."

—**Ralph Waldo Emerson** (1803–1882), U.S. poet, philosopher, and essayist

1869, Inaugural Address, 19 October, in *A Turning Point in Higher Education,* 1969, pp. 57–58.

A university must be indigenous; it must be rich; but, above all, it must be free. The winnowing breeze of freedom must blow through all its chambers. . . . The Corporation demands of all its teachers that they be grave, reverent, and high minded; but it leaves them, like their pupils, free.

—**Charles William Eliot** (1834–1926), President, Harvard University

1894, quoted in Walter P. Metzger, *Academic Freedom in the Age of the University,* 1955, p. 153.

In all lines of academic investigation it is of the utmost importance that the investigator should be absolutely free to follow the indications of truth wherever they may lead. Whatever may be the limitations which trammel inquiry elsewhere, we believe the great State University of Wisconsin should ever encourage that continual and fearless sifting and winnowing by which alone the truth can be found.

—**Board of Regents,**
University of Wisconsin

1915, "Declaration of principles on academic freedom and academic tenure," AAUP *Policy Documents and Reports, Ninth Edition,* 2001, p. 297.

[The university] should be an intellectual experiment station, where new ideas may germinate and where their fruit, though still distasteful to the community as a whole, may be allowed to ripen until finally, perchance, it may become part of the accepted intellectual food of the nation or the world.

p. 298.

The liberty of the scholar within the university to set forth his conclusions, be they what they may, is conditioned by their being conclusions gained by a scholar's method and held in a scholar's spirit; that is to say, they must be the fruits of competent and patient and sincere inquiry, and they should be set forth with dignity, courtesy, and temperateness of language.

—**American Association**
of University Professors

c. 1915, "The Professor's Union" (editorial), quoted in Walter P. Metzger, *Academic Freedom in the Age of the University,* 1955, p. 208.

Academic freedom, that is the unalienable right of every college instructor to make a fool of himself and his college by . . . intemperate, sensational prattle about every subject under the sun, to his classes and the public, and still keep on the payroll or be reft therefrom only by elaborate pro-

cess, is cried to all the winds by the organized dons.

—*New York Times*

1915, *Report for 1914–15,* quoted in Edward C. Elliott (ed.), *The Rise of a University, Vol. II,* 1937, p. 409.

[P]rofessors of established reputation, sound judgment and good sense rarely if ever find themselves under serious criticism from any source. Such men and women may hold whatever opinions they please, since they are in the habit of expressing them with discretion, moderation, good taste and good sense. . . . It is a misnomer to apply the high and splendid term "academic freedom" to exhibitions of bad taste and bad manners.

—**Nicholas Murray Butler**
(1862–1947), President,
Columbia University

1917, "Annual report for 1916–17," *Educational Review,* December 1920, quoted in Robert P. Ludlum, "Academic freedom and tenure: A history," *The Antioch Review,* March 1950, pp. 23–24.

If a university or college censors what its professors may say, if it restrains them from uttering something that it does not approve, it thereby assumes responsibility for that which it permits them to say.

—**Abbot Lawrence Lowell** (1856–1943),
President, Harvard University

1918, *The Higher Learning in America,* Chapter 3.

A free hand is the first and abiding requisite of scholarly and scientific work.

—**Thorstein Veblen** (1857–1929),
U.S. sociologist

1925, Session Laws, pp. 50–51, quoted in Edgar W. Knight, *Fifty Years of American Education,* 1952, p. 273.

Be it enacted by the general assembly of the state of Tennessee. That it shall be unlawful for any teacher in any of the universities, normals, and all other public schools of the state, which are supported in whole or in part by the public school funds of the state, to teach any theory that denies the story of the divine creation of man, as taught in the Bible, and to teach instead that man has descended from a lower order of animals.

—State of Tennessee

1927, *Report for 1926–27,* quoted in Edward C. Elliott (ed.), *The Rise of a University, Vol. II,* 1937, p. 42.

The scholar who in sincerity and knowledge criticizes or dissents from some well-established institution, idea or practice or some new exhibition of folly or stupidity is as much entitled to that dissent as his fellow who defends what this scholar condemns. This is one of the hardest lessons for public opinion in a democracy to learn.

—Nicholas Murray Butler
(1862–1947), President,
Columbia University

1934, *Transactions and Proceedings of the National Association of State Universities,* quoted in Edgar W. Knight, *What College Presidents Say,* 1940, p. 223.

I think that the original need for academic freedom has almost passed out and the tradition stands on, and it has come to be academic license rather than freedom.

—Lee Paul Sieg (1879–1963), President, University of Washington

1936, "Statement on academic freedom," *Bulletin of the American Association of University Professors,* October, p. 366.

[A]cademic freedom is not academic license. It does not guarantee to any individual the right to teach whatever he pleases nor to impose on the immature, the uncritical, the unwary, his own untested intellectual idiosyncrasies. . . .

**—National Catholic
Educational Association**

1936, *The Higher Learning in America,* p. 21.

Academic freedom is simply a way of saying that we get the best results in education and research if we leave their management to people who know something about them.

—Robert Maynard Hutchins
(1899–1977), President,
University of Chicago

1940, "Statement of principles on academic freedom and tenure," AAUP *Policy Documents and Reports, Ninth Edition,* 2001, p. 3.

Institutions of higher education are conducted for the common good and not to further the interest of either the individual teacher or the institution as a whole. The common good depends upon the free search for truth and its free exposition.

**—American Association
of University Professors**

1952, "On academic freedom," *Time,* 8 December, quoted in James B. Simpson, *Simpson's Contemporary Quotations,* 1988.

Education is a kind of continuing dialogue, and a dialogue assumes different points of view.

—**Robert Maynard Hutchins**
(1899–1977), President,
University of Chicago

1954, quoted in Duane DeMello, *The McCarthy Era: 1950–54,* 1968, p. 54.

The thing that the American people can do is to be vigilant day and night to make sure they don't have Communists teaching the sons and daughters of America. Now, I realize that the minute anyone tries to get a Communist out of a college, out of a university, there'll be raised the phony cry that you're interfering with academic freedom. I would like to emphasize that there is no academic freedom where a Communist is concerned. He is not a free agent. . . . [I] don't care how much of a screwball or crackpot any professor or teacher may be as long as he or she is a free agent.

—**Joseph McCarthy** (1909–1957),
U.S. Senator

1957, *Sweezy v. New Hampshire,* 354 U.S. 234.

It is the business of a university to provide that atmosphere which is most conducive to speculation, experiment and creation. It is an atmosphere in which there prevail "the four essential freedoms" of a university—to determine for itself on academic grounds who may teach, what may be taught, how it shall be taught, and who may be admitted to study.

—**Felix Frankfurter** (1882–1965),
Associate Justice, U.S. Supreme Court

1957, *Sweezy v. New Hampshire,* 354 U.S. 234.

The essentiality of freedom in the community of American universities is almost self-evident. . . . To impose any strait jacket upon the intellectual leaders in our colleges and universities would imperil the future of our Nation. . . . Teachers and students must always remain free to inquire, to study and to evaluate, to gain new maturity and understanding; otherwise our civilization will stagnate and die.

—**Earl Warren** (1891–1974),
Chief Justice, U.S. Supreme Court

1958, *The Academic Marketplace,* p. 222.

The ideal of academic freedom includes the assumption that men working on the fringes of established knowledge will often dissent from the truths of the majority, will appear unreasonable, eccentric, or disloyal, or will be unable to explain to others their motives for pursuing a particular line of effort.

—**Theodore Caplow** (1920–), professor of sociology, University of Virginia; **Reese J. McGee** (1929–), professor of sociology, Purdue University

1964, Inaugural address, 11 April, quoted in James B. Simpson, *Simpson's Contemporary Quotations,* 1988.

Universities should be safe havens where ruthless examination of realities will not be distorted by the aim to please or inhibited by the risk of displeasure.

—**Kingman Brewster** (1919–1988),
President, Yale University;
Master, University College, London

1967, *Keyishian v. Board of Regents,* 385 U.S. 589 at 603 (1967).

Our Nation is deeply committed to safeguarding academic freedom, which is of transcendent value to all of us and not merely to the teachers concerned. . . . The classroom is peculiarly the "marketplace of ideas." The Nation's future depends upon leaders trained through wide exposure to that robust exchange of ideas which discovers truth "out of a multitude of tongues, [rather] than through any kind of authoritative selection."

—**William J. Brennan, Jr.** (1906–1997), Associate Justice, U.S. Supreme Court

1968, "Parting shots: A century of commencement speeches," *Saturday Review,* 12 May 1979, p. 38.

[A university's] essential character as a center of free inquiry and criticism—a thing not to be sacrificed for anything else.

—**Richard Hofstadter** (1916–1970), professor of American history, Columbia University

1971, *An Uncertain Glory,* p. 29.

Academic freedom is something the top administrator is not supposed to understand but is expected to defend with his life. Probably the quickest way to distinguish between an academician and a "nonacad" is that the former, on this subject, will always begin, "I believe in academic freedom, *and . . .*"; while the latter, assuming he has a modicum of sophistication, will begin, "I believe in academic freedom, *but. . . .*"

—**Frederic W. Ness** (1914–1998), President, Fresno State College

1971, *The Degradation of the Academic Dogma,* p. 67.

Academic freedom meant to those scholars who founded the wider guild of professors in the United States freedom for *academic* man: not freedom for political man, economic man, or for those who be-

lieved the university to be primarily a privileged sanctuary for each and every dereliction, delinquency, and desolation of intellect known since Adam.

—**Robert A. Nisbet** (1913–), professor of sociology, University of California, Riverside

no date, attributed in Peter Hebblethwaite, *John Paul II and the Church,* 1995, p. 165.

If church or state or any other power outside the university can dictate who can teach and who can learn, the university is not free and, in fact, is not a true university where the truth is sought and taught. It is rather a place of political or religious indoctrination.

—**Theodore M. Hesburgh, C.S.C.** (1917–), President, University of Notre Dame

no date, attributed in Nat Hentoff, *Free Speech for Me—but Not for Thee,* 1992, p. 152.

The university has a fundamental mission which is to search for the truth. And a university is a place where people have to have the right to speak the unspeakable and think the unthinkable and challenge the unchallengeable.

—**Benno Schmidt** (1942–), President, Yale University

Access

1869, Inaugural Address, 19 October, in *A Turning Point in Higher Education,* 1969, p. 32.

The American college is obliged to supplement the American school. Whatever elementary instructions the schools fail to give, the college must supply.

p. 48.

The poorest and the richest students are equally welcome here, provided that with their poverty or their wealth they bring capacity, ambition, and purity.

—**Charles William Eliot** (1834–1926),
President, Harvard University

1895, "What the Germans lack," in
Twilight of the Idols.

'Higher education' and *multitude*—the two contradict each other from the outset. Any higher education belongs only to the exception: you must be privileged in order to have a right to such an exalted privilege. All great things, all beautiful things can never be common property. . . .

—**Friedrich Wilhelm Nietzsche**
(1844–1900), German philosopher;
professor of classical philology, Basel.

1904, *Inaugural Address of Charles Richard Van Hise,* pp. 13–14, quoted in R. Freeman Butts, *The College Charts Its Course,* 1939, p. 227.

A state university can only permanently succeed where its doors are open to all of both sexes who possess sufficient intellectual endowment, where the financial terms are so easy that the industrious poor may find the way, and where the student sentiment is such that each stands upon an equal footing with all. This is the state university ideal, and this is a new thing in the world.

—**Charles R. Van Hise** (1857–1918),
President, University of Wisconsin

1907, "The American type of university,"
Science, XXVI, p. 40.

The universities that would thrive must put away all exclusiveness and dedicate themselves to universal public service. They must not try to keep people out; they must help all who are worthy to get in.

—**Andrew S. Draper** (1848–1913),
President, University of Illinois

1910, *Great American Universities,*
p. 193.

The theory of the State University is that the State here offers at great expense, but free to all its young people, the opportunity for an education. It is like a fountain in a public square, giving its water freely to every passerby without regard to whether he has food and clothing, or whether he spills the water in carrying it to his lips. The assumption is that nobody will come to the university unless he is earnestly desirous of an education.

—**Edwin E. Slosson** (1865–1929),
chemist; U.S. writer

1917, *Why Go to College,* p. 1.

Any boy in America who has a good mind and good health can have a college education if he wants it. . . . The same thing may be said about girls.

—**William H. P. Faunce** (1859–1930),
President, Brown University

1931, Address, Haverford College, 17 April, quoted in Burton Stevenson, *The Home Book of Quotations,* 1967, p. 538.

The idea that going to college is one of the inherent rights of man seems to have obtained a baseless foothold in the minds of many of our people.

—**Abbot Lawrence Lowell** (1856–1943),
President, Harvard University

1938, *Saturday Evening Post,* 22 January,
p. 16.

Anyone should go to college who has demonstrated both an aptitude and a desire for more education than he has been able to get in elementary and high school. And I may add that to deprive any such person of a college education because his parents cannot afford to give him one is to commit an offense not only against the individual but also against society at large.

—**Robert Maynard Hutchins**
(1899–1977), President,
University of Chicago

1947, *Higher Education for American Democracy, Vol. 1,* p. 36.

The American people should set as their ultimate goal an educational system in which at no level—high school, college, graduate school, or professional school—will a qualified individual in any part of the country encounter an insuperable economic barrier to the attainment of the kind of education suited to his aptitudes and interests. . . . The time has come to make education through the fourteenth grade available in the same way that high school education is now available.

—**President's Commission
on Higher Education**

1960, *Encounter,* July, p. 9.

The delusion that there are thousands of young people about who are capable of benefitting from university training, but have somehow failed to find their way there, is . . . a necessary component of the expansionist case. . . . University graduates, however, are like poems or bottles of hack, and unlike cars and tins of salmon, in that you cannot *decide* to have more good ones. All you can decide to have is more, and MORE will mean WORSE.

—**Kingsley Amis** (1922–1995),
English novelist and poet

1964, quoted in Earl J. McGrath (ed.) *Universal Opportunity for Education Beyond the High School,* 1966, pp. 20–21.

The goal of universal education beyond the high school is no more Utopian than the goal of full citizenship for all Americans, for the first is becoming prerequisite to the second. If a person is adjudged incapable of growth toward a free mind today, he has been adjudged incapable of the dignity of full citizenship in a free society. This is a judgment which no American conscious of his ideal and traditions can make.

—**Educational Policies Commission**

1965, *The Sheepskin Psychosis,* p. 5.

I cannot believe that a college education would be a good thing for everybody. I am convinced that too many, not too few, high school graduates go to college.

—**John Keats** (1920–2000), U.S. author

1967, *The Vale of Laughter,* p. 57.

I am not impressed by the Ivy League establishments. Of course they graduate the best—it's all they'll take, leaving to others the problem of educating the country. They will give you an education the way the banks will give you money—provided you can prove to their satisfaction that you don't need it.

—**Peter DeVries** (1910–1993),
U.S. author

1975, *The Case Against College,* p. 10.

[J]ust as society has systematically damaged women by insisting that their proper place was in the home, so we may now be systematically damaging eighteen-year-olds by insisting that their proper place is in college.

—**Caroline Bird** (1915–), U.S. author

no date, attributed in August Kerber, *Quotable Quotes on Education,* 1968, p. 219.

Colleges aren't strictly for geniuses. We can't afford to slam the door of opportunity in the faces of C-level high school seniors, who will help make our country's future. We must fight for our average students.

—**Arthur S. Flemming** (1905–1996),
President, Macalester College;
President, University of Oregon;
President, Ohio Wesleyan University

1982, recalled at his death, 16 June, quoted in James B. Simpson, *Simpson's Contemporary Quotations,* 1988.

Over the years, we have come to identify quality in a college not by whom it serves but by how many students it excludes. Let us not be a sacred priesthood protecting the temple, but rather the fulfillers of dreams.

—**Robert J. Kibbee** (1920–1982),
Chancellor, City University of New York

Change

1827, *Two Reports of the Faculty to the Board of Trustees of Amherst College,* quoted in Edgar W. Knight, *What College Presidents Say,* 1940, p. 57.

The complaint is, and if our ears do not deceive us, it daily waxes louder and louder, that while everything else is on the advance, our colleges are stationary; or, if not quite stationary, that they are in danger of being left far behind, in the rapid march of improvement.

—**Faculty of Amherst College**

1910, *Great American Universities,* p. 75.

At every one of the fourteen universities I visited I was met by the remark: "You have

come to us at a critical moment. This university is just now in a transition stage." No doubt the remark was to certain extent true of all. It should have been more true than it was, for in some cases the transit was so slow that I was not able to detect it.

—**Edwin E. Slosson** (1865–1929),
chemist; U.S. writer

1911, *Administration of the college curriculum,* quoted in Frederick Rudolph, *Curriculum,* 1978, p. 17.

The progress of this institution . . . will be directly proportional to the death rate of the faculty.

—**William T. Foster** (1879–1950),
President, Reed College

1921, address at Yale University, *At War with Academic Traditions,* 1934, pp. 151–52.

Universities have outlived every form of government, every change of tradition, of law, and scientific thought, because they minister to one of man's undying needs. Of his creations none has more endured through the devouring march of time; and those who administer them, or teach therein, are but living links in an ever lengthening chain that stretches forward measureless to the unknown.

—**Abbot Lawrence Lowell** (1856–1943),
President, Harvard University

1926, *The College President,* p. 234.

In a long administration, if it be good, or even if it be bad, the ease of thinking and of doing in and through a well-recognized method may become an easily worn habit which makes for stagnation. . . . Tradition is a heavy, and often a cold and deadening, hand.

—**Charles F. Thwing** (1853–1937),
President, Adelbert College;
President, Western Reserve University

1926, *Which Way Parnassus?,* p. 43.

There is nothing in this world more conservative than the academic mind, nothing so violently frightened by a new idea, nothing that so instinctively shrinks from any suggestion of change.

—**Percy Marks** (1891–1956),
U.S. writer and instructor of English

1930, inaugural address, October, quoted in George A. Pettitt, *Twenty-eight Years in the Life of a University President,* 1966, p. 56.

That university man is rare indeed who would claim that the present system of higher education is adequate, yet we stick to it because it is easier than to make a radical change. The lockstep is hard to break. . . . Why should we not look on education as a problem for experimentation just as we so look on a problem in physics or astronomy?

—**Robert G. Sproul** (1891–1975),
President, University of California

1930, *Universities: American English German,* p. 27.

Universities that are held to their appropriate tasks will be unfit to do other things.

—**Abraham Flexner** (1866–1959),
U.S. educator

1939, "Editor's introduction," in R. Freeman Butts, *The College Charts Its Course,* p. xv.

America's most ancient legend is found in its old tradition of being young and new. This notion is particularly ludicrous in the field of higher education, since the American college is in fact one of the oldest educational institutions in the modern world. It has in full measure, moreover, the appurtenances of advanced age; the myopic, reverent following of time-worn routines, the pious mumbling of old spells and incantations, the supremely naive faith in its own magic worth.

—**Harold Benjamin** (1893–1969),
Dean, College of Education,
University of Maryland

1956, *Constraint and Variety in American Higher Education,* pp. 34–35.

[I]n education it is perhaps not so easy as it is in manufacturing to say who is the leader, who is at the top, or which way is up: there is no World Series or All-American team. . . . It may be illuminating to see the avant-garde, both educational and more generally cultural, as the head of a snake-like procession—the head of which is often turning back upon itself, as at present, while the middle part seeks to catch up with where the head once was. When the middle part becomes aware, as doesn't always happen, that the position of the head has shifted, it may try to turn in two directions at once.

—**David Riesman** (1909–2002),
professor of sociology,
Harvard University

1963, *The Uses of the University,* pp. 37–38.

"Innovation" may be the historical "measure of success," the great characterizing feature of the "giants of the past;" but innovations sometimes succeed best when they have no obvious author.

—**Clark Kerr** (1911–2003), Chancellor, University of California, Berkeley; President, University of California

1968, "A different way to restructure the university," *New York Times Magazine,* 18 December, p. 50.

[T]o ask the American professoriat to restructure itself is as sensible as if one had asked Marie Antoinette to establish a republican government in France. Whether or not it coincided with her long-term interests was immaterial; the poor woman couldn't even conceive of the possibility.

—**Irving Kristol** (1920–), U.S. editor

1972, "Tactics for change," in *Two Papers on Academic Change,* 1972, p. 5.

If all else fails [in your efforts to provoke change], resign: You may be the problem.

—**Robert L. Halfman** (1923–), professor of aeronautics and astronautics, Massachusetts Institute of Technology

1977, *Curriculum,* p. 3.

Assemble a cluster of professors in a country town, surround them with scenic grandeur, cut them off from the world beyond, and they will not have much trouble congratulating themselves into curricular torpor. Let someone knock on the door with a vision of change, he will discover that access is blocked by those within the gate. Let him argue on behalf of some perceived need or desire of the students, and he will soon discover his mistake: The institution is really not for the students, after all, but for the professors.

p. 3.

Values change, and so does the curriculum, as the more than 300 years since the founding of Harvard College clearly say. Since that time, long ago, when a peculiarly self-demanding band of alienated Englishmen got themselves a college almost before they had built themselves a privy, change in the course of study has been constant, conscious and unconscious, gradual and sudden, accidental and intentional, uneven and diverse, imaginative and pedestrian.

—**Frederick Rudolph** (1920–), professor of history, Williams College

1982, " 'The Uses of the University' two decades later: Postscript 1982," *Change,* October, p. 24.

About eighty-five institutions in the Western world established by 1500 still exist in recognizable forms, with similar functions and unbroken histories, including the Catholic church, the Parliaments of the Isle of Man, of Iceland, and of Great Britain, several Swiss cantons, and seventy universities. Kings that rule, feudal lords with vassals, and guilds with monopolies are all gone. These seventy universities, however, are still in the same locations with some of the same buildings, with professors and students doing much the same things, and with governance carried on in much the same ways. There have been many intervening variations on the ancient themes, it is true, but the eternal themes of teaching, scholarship, and service, in one combination or another, continue. Looked at from within, universities have changed enormously in the emphases on their several functions and in their guiding spirits, but looked at from without and comparatively, they are among the least changed of institutions.

—**Clark Kerr** (1911–2003), Chancellor, University of California, Berkeley; President, University of California

1990, *The University: An Owner's Manual,* p. 284.

From an intellectual point of view, American universities have changed more—and more creatively—than schools in other parts of the world. That fact is not unrecognized: abroad, proposals for reform of higher education usually begin with a consideration of the American model.

—**Henry Rosovsky** (1927–), Dean of the Faculty of Arts and Sciences, Harvard University

1996, *Taking Charge of Change.*

Institutions ignore a changing environment at their peril. Like dinosaurs, they risk becoming exhibits in a kind of cultural Jurassic Park: places of great interest and curiosity, increasingly irrelevant in a world that has passed them by.

—**Kellogg Commission of the Future of State and Land-Grant Colleges, National Association of State Universities and Land-Grant Colleges**

1998, *Creating Entrepreneurial Universities,* p. 143.

A long-standing popular misconception places a Great Person with a Large Idea at the front end of change. . . . But the reality of change in complex organizations, especially in universities, is different. . . . New organizational ideas are but symbolic experiments in the art of the possible.

—**Burton R. Clark** (1921–),
professor of sociology,
University of California, Los Angeles

Coeducation

1856, letter to the "Gentlemen of the Medical Faculty of Harvard College," 12 November, quoted in Mary Briggs, *Women's Words: The Columbia Book of Quotations by Women,* 1995, p. 104.

In opening your doors to woman, it is mind that will enter the lecture room, it is intelligence that will ask for food; sex will never be felt where science leads for the atmosphere of thought will be around every lecture.

—**Harriot K. Hunt** (1805–1875),
U.S. physician and feminist

1868, *American Journal of Education,* January, quoted in Edgar W. Knight, *What College Presidents Say,* 1940, p. 300.

Have young ladies the ability in mental vigor and bodily health to maintain a fair standing in the class with young men? . . . I answer, where there has been the same preparatory training, we find no difference in ability to maintain themselves in the recitation room. . . . A breaking down of health does not appear to be more frequent than with young men.

—**James H. Fairchild** (1917–1902),
President, Oberlin College

1869, Inaugural Address, 19 October, in *A Turning Point in Higher Education,* 1969, p. 50.

The Corporation will not receive women as students into the College proper, nor into any school whose discipline requires residence near the school. The difficulties involved in the common residence of hundreds of young men and women of immature character and marriageable age are very grave. The necessary police regulations are exceedingly burdensome. The Corporation are not influenced to this decision, however, by any crude notions about the innate capacities of women. The world knows next to nothing about the mental capacities of the female sex. Only after generations of civil freedom and social equality will it be possible to obtain the data necessary for an adequate discussion of woman's natural tendencies, tastes, and capabilities.

—**Charles William Eliot** (1834–1926),
President, Harvard University

1871, *Woman Suffrage and Woman's Profession,* quoted in Mary Briggs, *Women's Words: The Columbia Book of Quotations by Women,* 1995, p. 65.

I regard the effort to introduce women into colleges for young men as very undesirable, and for many reasons. That the two sexes should be united, both as teachers and pupils, in the same institution seems very desirable, but rarely in early life by a method that removes them from parental watch and care, and from the protecting influences of home.

—**Catherine E. Beecher** (1800–1878),
U.S. educator and author

1879, *Report for 1878–79,* quoted in William F. Russell (ed.), *The Rise of a University, Vol. I,* 1937, p. 256.

The presence of young women in colleges is distinctly conducive to good order. Nothing is more certain than that the complete isolation of young men in masses from all society except their own tends to the formation of habits of rudeness, and to disregard of the ordinary proprieties of life. . . .

—**Frederick A. P. Barnard**
(1809–1889), President,
Columbia University

1894, letter to a friend, quoted in Henry W. Bragdon, *Woodrow Wilson: The Academic Years,* 1967, p. 215.

I have had just enough experience of co-education to know that, even under the most favorable circumstances, it is most demoralizing. It seems to me that in the South it would be fatal to the standards of delicacy between men and women that we most value. . . . I do not mean that it leads to vice, although occasionally it does; but it *vulgarizes* the whole relationship of men and women.

—**Woodrow Wilson** (1856–1924),
President, Princeton University;
President of the United States

1894, in Paul N. Garber, *John Carlisle Kilgo,* 1937, quoted in Edgar W. Knight, *What College Presidents Say,* 1940, p. 303.

Brothers and sisters grow up in the same home, boys and girls play together in the yards, attend the village school together, go to picnics together, attend the same Sunday schools, and are expected to be social companions after college days, and become man and wife for a lifetime association; then why should college training, the supreme part of education, be separate? There is no answer, except that the thing began in other ways and should continue.

—**John C. Kilgo** (1861–1922), President,
Trinity College (North Carolina)

c. 1900, quoted in Edgar W. Knight, *Fifty Years of American Education,* p. 128.

To behold the campus dotted with couples, billing and cooing their way to an A. B., is a thing it is said to rejoice Venus or Pan rather than Minerva, and were it the frequent or necessary outcome of coeducation, the future of the system would certainly be in jeopardy.

—**James R. Angell** (1829–1916),
president, University of Chicago

1900, personal diary, 10 September, quoted in Mary Briggs, *Women's Words: The Columbia Book of Quotations by Women,* 1995, p. 107.

They [the University of Rochester] let the girls in.

—**Susan B. Anthony** (1820–1906),
U.S. social reformer and suffragist

1904, *Proceedings of the National Education Association,* quoted in Edgar W. Knight, *What College Presidents Say,* 1940, p. 306.

It is now well established that higher education in this country reduces the rate of both marriage and offspring. . . . I think it is established that mental strain in early womanhood is a cause of imperfect mammary function which is the first stage of the slow evolution of sterility. . . . The girls' colleges think it wisest to train for self-support, and hold that if marriage comes it can best take care of itself. I urge the precise reverse.

—**G. Stanley Hall** (1844–1924), President, Clark University

1904, *Proceedings of the National Education Association,* quoted in Edgar W. Knight, *What College Presidents Say,* 1940, pp. 305–6.

[B]est of all for each sex is the coeducational university, in which men and women, side by side where association is wise, and apart where separation is wise, acquire together and partly from each other that training of mind, morals, body and social habits which fits best for larger usefulness.

—**Richard Henry Jesse** (1853–1921), President, University of Missouri

1910, speech at the Semi-Centennial of Louisiana State University, quoted in Edgar W. Knight, *What College Presidents Say,* 1940, p. 308.

The very presence of the opposite sex has a restraining influence, preventing the expression of coarse and unrefined thoughts. . . . To object to co-education on the score of morals sounds like an echo from the far-off past.

—**Thomas D. Boyd** (1854–1932), President, Louisiana State University

1910, *Great American Universities,* pp. 64–65.

In the [Yale] Graduate School about one tenth are women—34 this year. They are well treated by the professors and respectfully ignored by the students, which is all

they have a right to demand. They are admitted to work for the Ph. D., but not for M. A., lest in the latter case some of the undergraduate classes be contaminated by their presence. The university is anxious to provide dormitories, dining halls, etc., for all its men students, but the women students are left to look after themselves. This is a good plan, for it tends to promote independence and self-reliance, in which the sex is apt to be deficient.

—**Edwin E. Slosson** (1865–1929), chemist; U.S. writer

Crisis

1922, "College education: An inquest, I," *The Freeman,* New York, 22 February, p. 562.

[T]he academic ship rolls and careens with every wind, its top-gallant is torn to shreds, its rudder is churned to pulp, its compass whirls about under a thousand stray magnetic currents, and its decks are awash, but it still sails on. The brave captain in the crow's nest sings out to the ever loyal and faithful alumni that all is well. Perhaps it is. But there can be no doubt that we have been blown very far from the old course and we are adrift.

—**Somnia Vana** (pseudonym)

1928, *The Effective College,* p. vii.

The American college is fearfully and wonderfully made. For many years the doctors have been watching it, thumping it and probing into it in the hope of understanding its anatomy and physiology. More recently its psychology and hygiene also have been subject to careful observation. Its unaccountable behavior has attracted the attention of the general public, who have been convinced it has a high fever, or a weak heart, or a diseased brain or arteriosclerosis, or all put together. Nearly everybody agrees it must be incurably sick and yet siren-like it draws increasingly thousands of our best youth into its atmosphere and life.

—**Robert Lincoln Kelly** (1865–1954), President, William Penn College; President, Earlham College

1939, *The College Charts Its Course,* p. vi.

Each age has assumed that *it* was uniquely a period of transition when the college for the first time was "on trial for its life." A study of the history of higher education shows plainly that the issues so hotly contested today are part of long continuing controversies the problems of which were defined in the large more than a hundred years ago.

—**R. Freeman Butts** (1910–), professor of education, Teachers College, Columbia University

1962, *Educating the Expert Society,* quoted in Keith Allan Noble, *The International Education Quotations Encyclopaedia,* 1995.

Many schools and colleges are unable to make a major change until confronted by crisis—near bankruptcy or an exodus of staff or an explosive split among key personnel. Crisis is the common condition under which old enterprises are reborn, allowed once more to begin anew with a sense of starting down an uncharted road.

—**Burton R. Clark** (1921–), professor of sociology, University of California, Los Angeles

1966, *The Reforming of General Education,* p. x.

The liberal arts college, whose imminent demise has been announced repeatedly for nearly a century, has frequently confounded the forecasters.

—**Daniel Bell** (1919–), professor of sociology, Columbia University; Harvard University

1969, "The financing of higher education," in John Caffrey, *The Future Academic Community,* p. 206.

I doubt if there was ever a time in the history of higher education when educators could predict past cost trends into the future and count confidently on finding the necessary funds. 'Crisis' in this sense is a normal situation for higher education; we are always faced with the necessity of securing a progressively increasing share of the national income.

—**Howard R. Bowen** (1908–1989), economist; President, Grinnell College; President, University of Iowa; Chancellor, Claremont University Center

1970, "The crisis of American authority" *Daedalus,* Summer, p. 573.

[T]he annals of colleges and universities offer less a glimpse of Eden than of Armageddon.

—**Walter P. Metzger** (1922–), professor of history, Columbia University

1978, *A Free and Ordered Space,* p. 27.

Most of the voices one hears tend to be those announcing the Apocalypse. Few are the assertions for the public at large of the ideals to which higher education must aspire, few are the assertions of the shape an institution of higher education must attain and why, and few are the consistent visions of the purpose of an undergraduate education. In the last generation, the field has been, with few exceptions, left to the promoters of a political system or of lament.

—**A. Bartlett Giamatti** (1938–1989), President, Yale University

1987, *Educational Access and Achievement in America,* p. 7.

In higher education, as in other areas of public policy, the American political system seems unable to engage in a serious debate about policy change—let alone to undertake action—unless some form of doom is widely felt to be impending.

—**Alice Rivlin** (1931–), U.S. economist

1992, *An Aristocracy of Everyone,* p. 9.

[C]risis by definition cannot be chronic. On tenth hearing, the alarm bells inspire despair rather than action. Tired out by our repeated crises, we roll over in bed.

—**Benjamin R. Barber** (1939–), professor of political science, Rutgers University

Degrees: Earned

1642–50, Laws of Harvard College, quoted in John S. Brubacher and Willis Rudy, *Higher Education in Transition,* 1958, p. 21.

Every scholar that on proofe is found able to read the originall of the old and New testament into the Latin toungue, and to Resolve them Logically withall being of honest life and conversation and at any publicke act hath the approbation of the overseers, and master of the College may bee invested with his first degree.

—**Harvard College**

1755, quoted in Richard Hofstadter and Wilson Smith (eds.), *American Higher Education: A Documentary History, Volume I,* 1961, p. 118.

Such as have diligently pursued their studies for three years after being admitted to the Bachelor's degree; and have been guilty of no gross immorality shall be admitted to the degree of Master of Arts.

—**Laws and Orders of Kings College**

1851, *University Education,* p. 68.

[U]niversities . . . where the mind may be cultivated according to its wants, and where, in the lofty enthusiasm of growing knowledge and ripening scholarship, the bauble of an academic diploma is forgotten.

—**Henry P. Tappan** (1805–1881), President, University of Michigan

1872, *Annual report 1871–72,* quoted in Henry James, *Charles W. Eliot,* 1930, volume I, p. 264.

College degrees have fallen into just disrepute in this country through the ignorant carelessness with which Legislatures have granted the right to confer degrees to hundreds of institutions which had no just claim to the possession of such a power.

—**Charles William Eliot** (1834–1926), President, Harvard University

1901, "Colleges and degrees," in *Mr. Dooley's Opinions,* p. 203.

Ivry public man is entitled ex-officio to all th' degrees there are. An' no public or private man escapes. Ye haven't got wan, ye say? Ye will though. Some day ye'll see a polisman fr'm the University iv Chicago at th' dure an' ye'll hide undher th' bed. But he'll get ye an' haul out. Ye'll say: "I haven't done annything," an' he'll say: "Ye'd betther come along quite [sic]. I'm sarvin' a degree on ye from Prisidint Harper." Some iv th' thriftier univarsities is makin' a degree th' alternytive iv a fine. Five dollars or docthor iv laws.

p. 203.

But annyhow degrees is good things because they livils all ranks.

—**Peter Finley Dunne** (1867–1936), U.S. journalist and author

1903, "University tendencies," *Popular Science Monthly,* June, p. 142.

The college degree is an incident in scholarship, a childish toy, so far as the real function of building up men is concerned. Prizes, honors, badges, and degrees,—all of these have no necessary place in the machinery of higher education.

> **—David Starr Jordan** (1851–1931),
> President, Stanford University

1911, *A Thousand and One Epigrams.*

A college degree, like a certificate of character, is a good thing for those who need it.

1911, *A Thousand and One Epigrams.*

A college degree is a social certificate, not a proof of competence.

> **—Elbert Hubbard** (1856–1915),
> U.S. writer and publisher

no date, attributed in August Kerber, *Quotable Quotes on Education,* 1968, p. 227.

Some men are graduated from college *cum laude,* some are graduated *secuima cum laude,* and some are graduated *mirabile dictu* [wonderful to relate].

> **—William Howard Taft** (1857–1930),
> President of the United States

1923, *The Rise of the Universities,* p. 1.

A great teacher like Socrates gave no diplomas; if a modern student sat at his feet for three months, he would demand a certificate, something tangible and external to show for it—an excellent theme, by the way, for a Socratic dialogue.

> **—Charles Homer Haskins**
> (1870–1937), professor of history,
> Harvard University

1926, *History of England, bk. 2,* chapter 4, quoted in *The Columbia World of Quotations,* 1996.

Socrates gave no diplomas or degrees, and would have subjected any disciple who demanded one to a disconcerting catechism on the nature of true knowledge.

> **—G. M. Trevelyan** (1876–1962),
> professor of history,
> Cambridge University

1930, *Universities: American English German,* p. 53.

The sort of easy rubbish which may be counted towards an A. B. degree or the so-called combined degrees passes the limit of credibility.

> **—Abraham Flexner** (1866–1959),
> U.S. educator

1931, "The boon of culture," in *A Mencken Chrestomathy,* 1949, pp. 313–14.

The virtue of a college degree is that it shuts off the asking of certain kinds of questions, some of them embarrassing. It is a certificate of safety, both to the holder and to the nation in general. A graduate is one who has been trained to act according to a pattern that is publicly considered to be normal and trustworthy. When he gets his diploma he makes a change, not in mere station, but in status. It lifts him over a definite fence, and maketh him to lie down in greener pastures.

> **—H. L. Mencken** (1880–1956),
> U.S. editor and writer

1936, *The Higher Learning in America,* p. 2.

The degree it [the college of liberal arts] offers seems to certify that the student has passed an eventful period without violating any local, state, or federal law, and that he has a fair, if temporary, recollection of what his teachers have said to him. . . . [L]ittle pretense is made that many of the things said to him are of much importance.

—**Robert Maynard Hutchins**
(1899–1977), President,
University of Chicago

1943, *Education for Freedom,* pp. 75–76.

The national passion for the bachelor's degree has been deplored for many years. The late Professor Barrett Wendell of Harvard saw no way to remedy the sad consequences of this passion except to confer the degree on every American at birth. This proposal would be better than leaving it where it is.

—**Robert Maynard Hutchins**
(1899–1977), President,
University of Chicago

1958, *Higher Education in Transition,* p. 188.

As late as 1825 the master of arts was awarded "in course" to any holder of a Harvard bachelor's degree after the lapse of three years and the payment of a fee. . . . In this period, it was frequently remarked by the townspeople of Cambridge that "all a Harvard man has to do for his Masters degree is to pay five dollars and stay out of jail."

—**John S. Brubacher** (1898–1988),
professor of higher education, University
of Michigan; **Willis Rudy** (1920–),
professor of history,
Fairleigh Dickinson University

1961, *Prospect for America,* p. 385.

Education is never finished. One must be continually exposed to it if one does not wish to stagnate. A degree is not an education and the confusion on this point is perhaps the greatest weakness in American thinking about education.

—**Rockefeller Brothers Fund**

no date, attributed in *Your Ultimate Success Quotation Library* (software program) at <http://www.cybernation. com/>.

The college graduate is presented with a sheepskin to cover his intellectual nakedness.

—**Robert Maynard Hutchins**
(1899–1977), President,
University of Chicago

1965, "Nationwide standards and accreditation," in Logan Wilson, *Emerging Patterns in American Higher Education,* 1965, p. 214.

A similar principle [to Gresham's Law] can be applied to education: *as a society places greater value on the attainment of academic degrees, the degrees from colleges and universities whose academic programs are superficial and shoddy will undermine the value of similar degrees from institutions whose educational offerings are excellent.*

—**William K. Selden** (1911–),
President, Illinois College

1968, *The Academic Revolution,* p. 61.

The crucial *raison d'etre* of the American college, the *sine qua non* of its survival and current importance, may not be education but certification.

—**Christopher Jencks** (1936–),
professor of social policy, Harvard
University; **David Riesman** (1909–2002)
professor of sociology,
Harvard University

1974, *Zen and the Art of Motorcycle Maintenance,* p.195.

The idea that the majority of students attend a university for an education independent of the degree and grades is a little hypocrisy everyone is happier not to expose.

> —**Robert M. Pirsig** (1928–),
> U.S. author

1976, *New York Times,* 17 October, p. 26.

Most of our students . . . are here to get the credentials they believe are central to admission to the Dream. Everyone here does the rhetoric bit—Fascist pig this and that—but push them and they ask you to write recommendations for jobs with banks and insurance companies.

> —**John Gargan** (?–?), professor of
> political science, Kent State University

1988, *ProfScam,* p. 82.

[T]he bachelor's degree has been so completely stripped of meaning that employers cannot even be sure if its holder has minimum skills that were once taken for granted among college graduates.

> —**Charles J. Sykes** (1954–),
> U.S. journalist

no date, attributed in
<www.quotationspage.com>.

Everyone has a right to a university degree in America, even if it's in Hamburger Technology.

> —**Clive James** (1939–),
> Australian author

1990, *The University: An Owner's Manual,* p. 105.

A bachelor's degree may signify little more than the satisfactory completion of a fixed number of undergraduate courses. It is a matter of simple observation that not all college graduates are educated persons, nor are all educated persons necessarily college graduates.

> —**Henry Rosovsky** (1927–), Dean of
> the Faculty of Arts and Sciences,
> Harvard University

1992, *Times* (London), 11 October, quoted in *The Columbia World of Quotations,* 1996.

University degrees are a bit like adultery: you may not want to get involved in that sort of thing, but you don't want to be thought incapable.

> —**Peter Imbert** (1933–),
> British police commissioner

1996, <http://groups.google.com/groups?selm=4dugii%241td%40panix.com&output=>.

No one wants a good education. Everyone wants a good degree.

> —**Lee Rudolph** (1948–), professor of
> mathematics, Clark University

Degrees: Honorary

1771–1778, *Autobiography.*

The business of the postoffice occasion'd my taking a journey this year to New England, where the College of Cambridge, of their own motion, presented me with the degree of Master of Arts. Yale College, in Connecticut, had before made me a similar compliment. Thus, without studying in any college, I came to partake of their honours.

> —**Benjamin Franklin** (1706–1790),
> U.S. statesman

1848, commencement address, quoted in Richard Hofstadter and Wilson Smith (eds.), *American Higher Education: A Documentary History, Volume I,* 1961, p. 377.

Colleges confer degrees on unworthy candidates.—I admit the fact. I wish it were otherwise. Of honorary doctorates, perhaps the least said the better.

> —**Philip Lindsley** (1786–1855),
> President, University of Nashville

1855, comment on declining an honorary degree from Oxford University, attributed in <www.bemorecreative.com>.

I had not the advantage of a classical education, and no man should, in my judgment, accept a degree he cannot read.

—**Millard Fillmore** (1800–1874),
President of the United States

1907, quoted in R. Kent Rasmussen (ed.) *The Quotable Mark Twain,* 1997, p. 76, citing Charles Neider (ed.), *The Autobiography of Mark Twain,* 1959, pp. 348–49.

It pleased me beyond measure when Yale made me a Master of Arts, because I didn't know anything about art; I had another convulsion of pleasure when Yale made me a Doctor of Literature, because I was not competent to doctor anybody's literature but my own, and couldn't even keep my own in a healthy condition without my wife's help. I rejoiced again when Missouri University made me a Doctor of Laws, because it was all clear profit, I not knowing anything about laws except how to evade them and not get caught. And now at Oxford I am to be made a Doctor of Letters—all clear profit, because what I don't know about letters would make me a multi-millionaire if I could turn it into cash.

—**Mark Twain [Samuel Langhorne Clemens]** (1835–1910), U.S. author

1911, *The Devil's Dictionary.*

LL.D. Letters indicating the degree *Legumptionorum Doctor,* one learned in laws, gifted with legal gumption. Some suspicion is cast upon this derivation by the fact that the title was formerly *LL.d.,* and conferred only upon gentlemen distinguished for their wealth. At the date of this writing Columbia University is considering the expediency of making another degree for clergymen, in place of the old D.D.— *Damnator Diaboli.* The new honor will be known as *Sanctorum Custus,* and written *$$c.*

—**Ambrose G. Bierce** (1842?–1914?),
U.S. journalist

no date, attributed by Alistair Cooke in a speech before the National Press Club, 8 October, 1986, in <http://www.lhup.edu/~dsimanek/mencken.htm>.

The honorary degree is a way of honoring a pompous ass. No honest person would accept a degree he hadn't worked for. Honorary degrees are suitable only for realtors, chiropractors and presidents of the United States.

—**H. L. Mencken** (1880–1956),
U.S. editor and writer

1984, Edward B. Fiske, "Honorary degrees for 5,000," *New York Times,* 27 May, p. 1,38.

The Greeks had their laurel wreaths. The English have their honors list. The French are always wearing ribbons in their lapels. In this country honorary degrees from universities serve that function. It's one way of honoring accomplishments.

—**Jack W. Peltason** (1923–),
Chancellor, University of Illinois, Urban-Champaign; Chancellor, University of California, Irvine; President, University of California; President, American Council on Education

1984, *New York Times,* 4 June, p. B5.

People with honorary degrees are looked upon with disfavor. Would you let an honorary mechanic fix your brand-new Mercedes? You must realize that honorary degrees are given generally to people whose SAT scores were too low to get them into schools the regular way.

—**Neil Simon** (1927–), U.S. playwright

Ethics, Morality, Values

1787, letter to Peter Carr, 10 August, quoted in Eugene Ehrlich and Marshall DeBruhl, *The International Thesaurus of Quotations,* 1996, p. 184.

State a moral case to a ploughman and a professor. The former will decide it as well, and often better than the latter, because he has not been led astray by artificial rules.

—**Thomas Jefferson** (1743–1826),
father of the University of Virginia;
President of the United States

1871, "Inaugural Address," in G. S. Merriam (ed.), *Noah Porter,* 1893, quoted in Lawrence R. Veysey, *The Emergence of the American University,* 1965, p. 45.

The most efficient of all moral influences in a college are those which proceed from *the personal characteristics of the instructors.* . . . A noble character becomes light and inspiration, when dignified by eminent intellectual power and attainments.

—**Noah Porter** (1811–1892), President,
Yale University

1878, *American Colleges: Their Students and Their Work,* p. 52.

The upright character of the professor is the first condition for demanding the upright character in the student.

—**Charles F. Thwing** (1853–1937),
President, Adelbert College; President,
Western Reserve University

1898, "The college woman and the family claim," in Ellen Condliffe Lageman (ed.), *Jane Addams On Education,* 1985.

The colleges have long been full of the best ethical teaching. . . . But while the college teaching has included an ever-broadening range of obligation, and while it has insisted upon the recognition of the claims of human brotherhood, the training has been singularly individualistic, it has fostered ambitions for personal distinction and has trained the faculties almost exclusively in the direction of intellectual accumulation.

—**Jane Addams** (1860–1935),
social reformer

1915, "Declaration of principles on academic freedom and tenure," AAUP *Policy Documents and Reports, Ninth Edition,* pp. 294–95.

To the degree that professional scholars, in the formation or promulgation of their opinions, are, or by the character of their tenure appear to be, subject to any motive other than their own scientific conscience and a desire for the respect of their fellow experts, to that degree the university teaching profession is corrupted; its proper influence upon public opinion is diminished and vitiated; and society at large fails to get from its scholars, in an unadulterated form, the peculiar and necessary service which it is the office of the professional scholar to furnish.

—**American Association
of University Professors**

1943, *Liberal Education,* p. 61.

Those communities are most vociferous about morality in which the least intellectual life goes on. So a college which advertises that it teaches character is sure to be one which knows how to do little else.

—**Mark Van Doren** (1894–1972),
professor of English,
Columbia University

1948, "Morals, religion, and higher education," *Freedom, Education, and the Fund,* 1956, pp. 95–96.

If a college or university is to think and think about important things, then it must think about morals, for we have admitted throughout that morals are most important. It may not be necessary that all the faculty should be good; it would be desirable that most of them, at least, take goodness seriously.

—**Robert Maynard Hutchins**
(1899–1977), President,
University of Chicago

1952, "The function of religious life," in *The Conquest of Life,* p. 78.

For the earnest young man who is seeking seriously in spite of human frailty to up-build character, this college is a tender and forgiving mother; for the sunken and sodden libertine who does not desire to rise out of his sensual life, she is an avenging goddess, angry-eyed and armed with all the lightnings of heaven.

—**John W. Cavanaugh, C.S.C.**
(1870–1935), President,
University of Notre Dame

1958, "The examined life," 8 June, quoted in Stephen James Nelson, *Leaders in the Crucible,* 2000, p. 82.

We hear more praise of talent today, than of values. Talent, however, is useless, even dangerous, without values. A man of great talent and no values is like a powerful sports car without a steering wheel—there is no direction for the power and no meaning to its journey.

—**Theodore M. Hesburgh, C.S.C.**
(1917–), President,
University of Notre Dame

1968, *The American University,* p. 72.

The same disclaimer must be made against the demand sometimes heard from earnest students that the university should teach them "values." The wish is not so laudable as it sounds, being only the wish to have one's perplexities removed by someone else. . . . Values (so-called) are not taught; they are breathed in or imitated.

—**Jacques Barzun** (1907–),
Dean of Faculties and Provost,
Columbia University

1970, "The role of the university: Ivory tower, service station, or frontier post?" *Daedalus,* Winter, p. 78.

Passive acceptance of the goals and values of society deprives the university of the claim to intellectual leadership and encourages its involvement in ventures of dubious ethical and intellectual value.

—**Salvador E. Luria** (1912–1991),
professor of biology, Massachusetts
Institute of Technology; **Zella Luria**
(1924–), professor of psychology,
Tufts University

1977, *Curriculum,* p. 289.

Colleges and universities, of course, can be counted on to continue to teach and support values haphazardly. Can there be any question about the values a college or university teaches when it says: "We don't care what courses you take; you can have a B. A. and not know how to write, how to understand nuclear fission, look at a painting, or listen to music"?

—**Frederick Rudolph** (1920–),
professor of history, Williams College

1979, *The Hesburgh Papers,* p. xi.

I realize full well that education is essentially a work of the intellect, the formation of intelligence, the unending search for knowledge. Why then be concerned with values? Because wisdom is more than knowledge, man is more than his mind, and without values, man may be intelligent but less than fully human.

—**Theodore M. Hesburgh, C.S.C.**
(1917–), President,
University of Notre Dame

1979, "The college presidency: Life between a rock and a hard place," *Change,* May-June, p. 44.

Every decision is not, of course, a great moral crisis. But I have found few decisions that did not have a moral dimension that could only be ignored with considerable risk, not just for oneself, but particularly for justice, whose final spokesmen all presidents are. When the president abdicates this fundamental responsibility, people are deeply hurt.

—**Theodore M. Hesburgh, C.S.C.**
(1917–), President,
University of Notre Dame

1982, *Beyond the Ivory Tower,* p. 10.

If we would teach our students to care about important social problems and think about them rigorously, then clearly our institutions of learning must set a high example in the conduct of their own affairs.

p. 126.

A university that refuses to take ethical dilemmas seriously violates its basic obligations to society. And a university that fails to engage its members in debate on these issues and to communicate with care the reasons for its policies gives an impression of moral indifference that is profoundly dispiriting to large numbers of students and professors who share a concern for social issues and a desire to have their institution behave responsibly.

p. 127.

An instructor does not indoctrinate his students merely by disclosing his own ethical values. The critical line is crossed only

when a teacher attempts to force his values on his students by refusing to entertain contrary arguments or by using his power as a grader and discussion leader to coerce students into accepting his views.

—**Derek Bok** (1930–), President,
Harvard University

1986, *The Effective Administrator,* p. 23.

At the heart of the moral vision of the university is the centrality of the individual. The belief that operates as a conscious and unconscious dynamic is that the individual celebrating his or her own intelligence through industry informed by moral vision will make the best contribution to the university and to the world. People are regarded as more important than procedures. It's not a bad formula.

—**Donald E. Walker** (1921–),
President, Idaho State University;
President, Southeastern Massachusetts University; Chancellor, Grossmont-Cuyamaca Community College District

1987, *Reconstructing American Education,* p. 180.

Universities are less able than ever to define the ways in which they are distinct from other social institutions, how the principles on which they operate differ from those in business and government, and why they should enjoy special privileges. Therefore, the next great crisis of the university may not be demographic, fiscal, or organizational. Instead, it may be moral.

—**Michael B. Katz** (1939–), professor of history, University of Pennsylvania

1988, *A Free and Ordered Space,* p. 47.

A civilized order is the precondition of freedom, and freedom—of belief, speech, and choice—the goal of responsible order. A university cannot expound those goals and expect a larger society to find them compelling, it cannot become a repository of national hope and a source of national leadership, unless it strives to practice what it teaches. If its goals are noble, so must be its acts.

—**A. Bartlett Giamatti** (1938–1989),
President, Yale University

1990, *The University: An Owner's Manual,* p. 107.

It may well be that the most significant quality in educated persons is the informed judgment that enables them to make discriminating moral choices.

—**Henry Rosovsky** (1927–),
Dean of the Faculty of Arts and
Sciences, Harvard University

1991, *Keeping Faith With the Student Athlete,* March.

If the university is not itself a model of ethical behavior, why should we expect such behavior from students or from the larger society?

—**Knight Foundation Commission
on Intercollegiate Athletics**

1999, "Liberal education, moral education: Can—and should—a university teach its students to be better citizens and better people," *Princeton Alumni Weekly,* 27 January, pp. 20–21.

One aspect of a student's moral education lies not in the curriculum but in the behavior of the faculty, staff, and administration and in the policies of the institution. . . . Students will be smart enough to discern if the University remains a symbol of enlightenment or an institution whose defining ambition is to sustain the status quo and its own special privileges.

—**Harold T. Shapiro** (1935–),
President, University of Michigan;
President, Princeton University

2000, "The moral purposes of the university: An exchange," *Hedgehog Review,* Fall, p. 108.

If I were writing a history of the American university, I would tell an upbeat story about the gradual replacement of the churches by the universities as the conscience of the nation. . . . Today the American universities not only form the best system of higher education in the world, but they are morally impressive institutions.

—**Richard Rorty** (1931–), professor of
philosophy, University of Virginia

Quality and Standards

1841, report to the Brown Corporation, quoted in Frederick Rudolph, 1977, *Curriculum,* p. 99.

Students frequently enter college almost wholly unacquainted with English grammar and unable to write a tolerably legible hand.

—**Francis Wayland** (1796–1865),
President, Brown University

c. 1864, quoted in Donald G. Tewksbury, *The Founding of American Colleges and Universities Before the Civil War,* 1932, p. 24.

Colleges rise up like mushrooms in our luxurious soil. They are duly lauded and puffed for a day, and then they sink to be heard no more. Already Western colleges thus established have become the objects of ridicule and contempt in every enlightened corner of the land.

—**Philip Lindsley** (1786–1855),
President, University of Nashville

1910, *Report for 1909–1910,* quoted in Edward C. Elliott (ed.), *The Rise of a University, Vol. II,* 1937, p. 405.

One main difficulty with which the higher institutions of learning throughout the world have to struggle today is militant mediocrity. . . . The searching question is being asked, where are to be found fit successors to the scholars of the generation that is now passing off the stage? Many are sought, but few are found.

—**Nicholas Murray Butler**
(1862–1947), President,
Columbia University

1939, *Too Much College,* p. 138.

Much of our study [in schools of liberal arts] is turning to mere wool-gathering, to pretentious nonsense. The rigour of it is melting like butter. A lot of it is so easy, so vague and silly that anything nicely above an anthropoid ape can get a degree in it.

—**Stephen Butler Leacock**
(1869–1944), professor of political economy, McGill University

1943, *Liberal Education,* p. 153.

Education is honored when it is hard, and it is more honored when it is hard and good.

—**Mark Van Doren** (1894–1972),
professor of English,
Columbia University

1955, *Yale: The University College,*
p. vii.

In the coming half century, if no disaster intervenes, we may become as famous for our universities as were the Romans for their roads and their laws.

—**George Wilson Pierson** (1904–1993),
professor of history, Yale University

1959, *The House of Intellect,* p. 127.

To judge by words, the academic world is very much alive to the desirability of maintaining standards. Not a minute passes without some reference to this sacred duty.

Carrying it out is another thing. . . . The very customs of the academic grove militate against standards. The system of credits turns attention away from substance.

—**Jacques Barzun** (1907–),
Dean of Faculties and Provost,
Columbia University

1961, *Excellence, Can We Be Equal and Excellent Too?,* p. 86.

An excellent plumber is infinitely more admirable than an incompetent philosopher. The society which scorns excellence in plumbing because plumbing is a humble activity and tolerates shoddiness in philosophy because it is an exalted activity will have neither good plumbing nor good philosophy. Neither its pipes nor its theories will hold water.

—**John W. Gardner** (1912–2002),
educational statesman; professor of
public service, Stanford University

1962, *The American College,* p. 2.

One does not need any fixed conceptions of educational goals to be convinced that American colleges are failing rather badly. They fail to achieve their own stated purposes; and they fail by other reasonable standards of accomplishment.

—**Nevitt R. Sanford** (1909–1995),
professor of psychology and education,
Stanford University

c. 1965, in Stuart W. Leslie, "Playing the educational game to win," *Historical Studies in the Physical and Biological Sciences, Vol. 18,* 1987.

The game of improving an educational operation is great fun to play, because it is so easy to win. Most of the competition just doesn't realize that education is a competitive business, like football, only with no conference rules.

—**Frederick E. Terman** (1900–1982),
Provost, Stanford University

1966, *An Assessment of Quality in Graduate Education,* p. 4.

[Q]uality is someone's subjective assessment, for there is no way of objectively measuring what is in essence an attribute of value.

> —**Allan M. Cartter** (1922–1976),
> Vice President, American Council
> on Education; Chancellor,
> New York University

1968, *The Academic Revolution,* p. 403.

The general rule of the academic world is that the rich grow richer even faster than the poor do. If one looks, for example, at scholarly ratings of universities over the years, one discovers few new faces.

> —**Christopher Jencks** (1936–),
> professor of social policy,
> Harvard University; **David Riesman**
> (1909–2002) professor of sociology,
> Harvard University

1971, quoted in Myron Farber, "New City U. head seeks rise in level of teaching," *New York Times,* 28 July, p. 39.

The quality of a university is measured more by the kind of student it turns out than by the kind it takes in.

> —**Robert J. Kibbee** (1920–1982),
> Chancellor, City University of New York

c. 1973, attributed in Thomas L. Martin, Jr., *Malice in Blunderland,* 1973, p. 22.

The quality of a department is inversely proportional to the number of courses it lists in its catalog.

> —**Joel Hildebrand** (1881–1983),
> professor of chemistry,
> University of California, Berkeley

1980, *Three Thousand Futures,* p. 135.

The United States has the most adequate all-around system of higher education in the world. It offers access to more of the population and finds talent more adequately in all parts of society than in any other nation. Its research contributions since about 1930 have been preeminent.

> —**Carnegie Council on Policy Studies
> in Higher Education**

1983, *A Nation at Risk,* p. 5.

[W]hile we can take justifiable pride in what our schools and colleges have historically accomplished and contributed to the United States and to the well being of its people, the educational foundations of our society are presently being eroded by a rising tide of mediocrity that threatens our very future as a Nation and a people. . . . If an unfriendly foreign power had attempted to impose on America the mediocre educational performance that exists today, we might well have viewed it as an act of war.

> —**National Commission on
> Excellence in Education**

1985, *Achieving Educational Excellence,* pp. 60–61.

[T]rue excellence lies in the institution's ability to affect its students and faculty favorably, to enhance their intellectual and scholarly development, and to make a positive difference in their lives. The most excellent institutions are, in this view, those that have the greatest impact—"add the most value" as the economists would say—on the student's knowledge and personal development, and on the faculty member's scholarly and pedagogical ability and productivity.

> —**Alexander Astin** (1932–), professor
> of higher education, University of
> California, Los Angeles

1986, *Higher Learning,* pp. 30–31.

The students educated at marginal institutions in America would not go to college at all in most other nations. . . . A number of the colleges that would earn the scorn of European intellectuals do at least an adequate job of making up for the failings of our public schools and preparing students for occupations of their choice. This may not seem intellectually elevated, but it is valuable just the same.

—**Derek Bok** (1930–), President,
Harvard University

1988, *ProfScam,* p. 8.

For students, it [control by the professors] has meant watered-down courses; unqualified instructors; a bachelor's degree of dubious value; and an outrageous bill for spending four or five years in a ghetto of appalling intellectual squalor and mediocrity.

—**Charles J. Sykes** (1954–),
U.S. journalist

1990, *The University: An Owner's Manual,* p. 29.

[F]ully two thirds to three quarters of the best universities in the world are located in the United States. (That we are also home to a large share of the world's worst colleges and universities is not now my concern). What sector of society can make a similar statement? One can think of baseball, football, and basketball teams, but that pretty much exhausts the list.

—**Henry Rosovsky** (1927–), Dean of
the Faculty of Arts and Sciences,
Harvard University

1992, *Telling the Truth,* p. 1.

The idea that there is no truth to pursue has a corollary: There are no standards to meet.

—**Lynne Cheney** (1941–), U.S. writer

1993, *An American Imperative,* p. 1.

A disturbing and dangerous mismatch exists between what American society needs of higher education and what it is receiving. Nowhere is the mismatch more dangerous than in the quality of undergraduate preparation provided on many campuses. The American imperative for the 21st century is that society must hold higher education to much higher expectations or risk national decline.

—**Wingspread Group on
Higher Education**

1994, *A Different Shade of Crimson,* p. 45.

There may be a two-billion dollar endowment and ten-million books in the library, but anyone who has attended Harvard can tell you that it has only one truly priceless treasure: its students.

—**Ruben Navarrette, Jr.** (?–),
U.S. journalist and writer

Chapter 4

Learning

Grades and Examinations

1910, *Great American Universities,* p. 497.

The instructor in a technical school always has in the back of his mind the thought that if he passes this doubtful student in mathematics, he is likely to be called upon sometime to certify to his ability to build a bridge and will not be able to refuse, whatever his private misgivings. Consequently he gives himself the benefit of the doubt and flunks him. The humanist has no such fear of the future. He fears rather the loss of a student in the present. Consequently he gives him the benefit of the doubt and passes him. If the professor of English literature had to certify that all his graduates could unerringly tell a bad book from a good one and point out its fault, as the professor of toxicology has to certify that his graduates can detect the minutest trace of poison in a food, he would be more stringent in his grading.

—**Edwin E. Slosson** (1865–1929), chemist; U.S. writer

1923, "Some thoughts on examinations," *Laughter from a Cloud,* p. 120.

In Examinations those who do not wish to know ask questions of those who cannot tell.

—**Walter Raleigh** (1861–1922), professor of English literature, Oxford University

1928, *The Campus,* pp. 2–3.

[T]here has been for several years a certain element among the male students at least which considers it bad form to receive high marks, unless they are undeserved; in the latter case, the individual has "put one over" on his professor and is to be congratulated.

—**Robert Cooley Angell** (1899–1984), professor of sociology, University of Michigan

1944, *Teacher in America,* p. 217.

Marks are conventions, a language agreed upon and therefore to be respected. . . . It is absurd to say that marks are unimportant and that real students should disregard them. Cruel nonsense!

—**Jacques Barzun** (1907–), Dean of Faculties and Provost, Columbia University no date, attributed in August Kerber, *Quotable Quotes on Education,* 1968, p. 214.

In the honor system the professors have the honor and the students have the system.

—**Havilah Babcock** (1898–1964), professor of English, University of South Carolina

1959, *An Atmosphere to Breathe,* p. 19.

The game of outwitting the teacher is an ancient one, but the commitments of the modern scholar have tilted the scales in favor of the mark-hound. Objective concern for the subject is just what the mark-hound thrives on—tell him what you want, and he will give it to you. He will even imitate thought if that is what you ask for.

—**McGeorge Bundy** (1919–1996), Dean, Faculty of Arts and Sciences, Harvard University

1977, in the film *Annie Hall.*

Alvy Singer: I was thrown out of NYU my freshman year . . . for cheating on my metaphysics final. You know, I looked within the soul of the boy sitting next to me.

—**Woody Allen** (1935–), U.S. screenwriter and author

1983, "Grades: One more tilt at the windmill," in Arthur W. Chickering (ed.), *Bulletin,* Memphis State University Center for the Study of Higher Education, quoted in Roger Peters, "Some Snarks are Boojums," *Change,* November/December, 1994, p. 18.

[A course grade is] an inadequate report of an inaccurate judgment by a biased and variable judge of the extent to which a student has attained an undefined level of mastery of an unknown portion of an indefinite material.

—**Paul Dressel** (1910–1989), professor of university research, Michigan State University

no date, attributed in Louis E. Boone, *Quotable Business,* 1992, p. 232.

I think the world is run by C students.

—**Al McGuire** (1928–2001), basketball coach, Marquette University

1988, Josef Martin (pseudonym), *To Rise Above Principle,* p. 159.

[S]tudents who receive grades of D or F suffer proportionately more misfortunes, including deaths of relatives, than do students who receive grades of A, B, or C. . . .

—**Henry H. Bauer** (1931–), Dean of Arts and Sciences, Virginia Polytechnic Institute and State University

1992, *Imposters in the Temple,* 1992, p. 59.

As grades lose their meaning and relevance, it becomes difficult to distinguish good students from bad students, an invidious thing to do perhaps, but the kind of judging that will happen to them once they receive their degree and walk into the outside world. Today a college degree has become more a certificate of attendance than a badge of achievement, its worth devalued in the market.

—**Martin Anderson** (1936–), senior fellow, Hoover Institution, Stanford University

1993, *The Chronicle of Higher Education,* 1 December.

Some students also complain that their professors are cheating *them*—spending more time consulting and publishing than teaching or preparing for classes. Those students see little reason why they should not cheat as well.

—**Leslie Fishbein** (1947–), associate professor of American studies and Jewish studies, Rutgers University

Learning

no date, attributed in *Your Ultimate Success Quotation Library* (software program) at <http://www.cybernation.com/>.

For a man to attain to an eminent degree in learning costs him time, watching, hunger, nakedness, dizziness in the head, weakness in the stomach, and other inconveniences.

—**Miguel De Cervantes** (1547–1616), Spanish novelist and poet

1828, *Report of the Faculty,* quoted in Frederick Rudolph, 1977, *Curriculum,* p. 70.

The object is not to *finish* his education: but to lay the foundation. . . . If he acquires here a thorough knowledge of the principles of science, he may then, in a great measure, educate himself. He has, at least, been taught *how* to learn.

—**Faculty of Yale College**

1836, *Journals,* quoted in Rhoda Thomas Tripp, *The International Thesaurus of Quotations,* 1970, p. 173.

Meek young men grow up in colleges and believe it is their duty to accept the views which books have given, and grow up slaves.

—**Ralph Waldo Emerson** (1803–1882), U.S. poet, philosopher, and essayist

1867, commencement address, College of California, quoted in Frederick Rudolph, 1977, *Curriculum,* p. 105.

If we cannot excuse the self-conceit of the so-called practical man who conceals his ignorance beneath his empiricism, neither can we pardon the college which has turned out its graduate in arts so artless that his learning fails him when brought face to face with nature and experience.

—**Benjamin Silliman, Jr.** (1816–1885), professor of chemistry, Yale University

no date, attributed in Henry Morton Robinson, "Ivy superiority," *Holiday Magazine,* 1955, November, p. 136.

I propose to raise up a generation of students who will disagree with me, and I propose further to give them very poor grades if they don't.

—**Andrew D. White** (1832–1918), President, Cornell University

1901, *Up from Slavery,* Chapter III.

The older I grow, the more I am convinced that there is no education which one can get from books and costly apparatus that is equal to that which can be gotten from contact with great men and women. Instead of studying books so constantly, how I wish that our schools and colleges might learn to study men and things!

—**Booker T. Washington** (1856–1915), President, Tuskegee Normal and Industrial Institute

1901, "Mr. Carnegie's gift," *Mr. Dooley's Opinions,* p. 149.

Ye can lade a man up to th' university, but ye can't make him think.

—**Peter Finley Dunne** (1867–1936), U.S. journalist and author

1905, *Story of My Life, Part I.*

One goes to college to learn, it seems, not to think. When one enters the portals of learning, one leaves the dearest pleasures—solitude, books and imagination—outside with the whispering pines. I suppose I ought to find some comfort in the thought that I am laying up treasures for future enjoyment, but I am improvident enough to prefer present joy to hoarding riches against a rainy day.

—**Helen Keller** (1880–1968), U.S. writer

1909, "The spirit of learning," Phi Beta Kappa Address, Cambridge, 1 July, in Ray Stannard Baker and William E. Dodd (eds.), *College and State, Volume II,* 1925, p. 110.

What we should seek to support in our college, therefore, is not so much learning itself as the spirit of learning. . . . It is citizenship in the world of knowledge, but not ownership of it.

—**Woodrow Wilson** (1856–1924), President, Princeton University; President of the United States

1911, *A Thousand and One Epigrams.*

Academic education is the act of memorizing things read in books, and things told by college professors who got their education mostly by memorizing things read in books and told by college professors.

—**Elbert Hubbard** (1856–1915), U.S. writer and publisher

1918, *The Higher Learning in America,* Chapter 1.

The student who comes up to the university for the pursuit of knowledge is expected to know what he wants and to want it, without compulsion. If he falls short in these respects, if he has not the requisite interest and initiative, it is his own misfortune, not the fault of his teacher.

—**Thorstein Veblen** (1857–1929), U.S. sociologist

no date, attributed in David J. Loftus, *The Unofficial Book of Harvard Trivia,* 1985, p. 36.

You can always tell a Harvard man—but you can't tell him much.

—**James Barnes** (1866–1936), Harvard alumnus

1923, *How to Make the Best of Life,* p. 70.

University education cannot be handed out complete like a cake on a tray. It has to be fought for, intrigued for, conspired for, lied for, and sometime simply stolen. If it had not it would scarcely be education.

—**Arnold Bennett** (1867–1931), British novelist and playwright

no date, attributed in <www.quotationspage.com>.

Instead of giving money to found colleges to promote learning, why don't they pass a constitutional amendment prohibiting anybody from learning anything? If it works as good as the Prohibition one did, why, in five years we would have the smartest race of people on earth.

—**Will Rogers** (1879–1935), U.S. humorist

1929, *The Aims of Education and Other Essays,* Chapter One.

Culture is activity of thought, and receptiveness to beauty and humane feeling. Scraps of information have nothing to do with it. A merely well-informed man is the most useless bore on God's earth. What we should aim at producing is men who possess both culture and expert knowledge in some special direction.

Chapter Two.

Your learning is useless to you till you have lost your text-books, burnt your lecture notes, and forgotten the minutiae which you had learnt by heart for the examination.

—**Alfred North Whitehead**
(1861–1947), English philosopher and mathematician; professor of philosophy, Harvard University

1931, *Autobiography,* volume I, chapter 17, p. 124.

It is possible to get an education at a university. It has been done; not often. But the fact that a proportion, however small, of college students do get a start in interested, methodological study proves my thesis. . . .

—**Lincoln Steffens** (1866–1936),
U.S. journalist and social reformer

1943, *Liberal Education,* p. 100.

College is the place where youth first realizes how imperfect and yet how distinguishing the acts of reason are: the acts not alone of logic, but of abstraction too, of seeing what does not change among all the things that do, and of manipulating objects in the light of ideas that have first been understood. College is not the final school. But it is the school which makes possible any end.

—**Mark Van Doren** (1894–1972),
professor of English,
Columbia University

1943, *Education for Freedom,* p. 9.

I am sure that in what is called "the curriculum" of the conventional school, college, or university the only people who are getting an education are the teachers. They

work in more or less coherent, if somewhat narrow, fields, and they work in more or less intelligible ways. The student, on the other hand, works through a multifarious collection of disconnected courses in such a way that the realms of knowledge are likely to become less and less intelligible as he proceeds. In such an institution the only way to learn anything is to teach it.

—**Robert Maynard Hutchins**
(1899–1977), President,
University of Chicago

no date, attributed in Mark Van Doren, *Liberal Education,* 1943, p. 15.

No one can become really educated without having pursued some study in which he took no interest—for it is a part of education to learn to interest ourselves in subjects for which we have no aptitude.

—**T. S. Eliot** (1888–1965),
U.S.-born British poet

no date, attributed in *Your Ultimate Success Quotation Library* (software program) at <http://www.cybernation. com/>.

It's fairly obvious that American education is a cultural flop. Americans are not a well-educated people culturally, and their vocational education often has to be learned all over again after they leave school and college. On the other hand, they have open quick minds and if their education has little positive sharp value, it has not the stultifying effects of a more rigid training.

—**Raymond Chandler** (1888–1959),
U.S. author

1952, *Dance to the Piper,* quoted in Rosalie Maggio, *The Beacon Book of Quotations by Women,* 1992, p. 98.

I learned three important things in college—to use a library, to memorize quickly and visually, to drop asleep at any time given a horizontal surface and fifteen minutes. What I could not learn was to think creatively on schedule.

—**Agnes de Mille** (1905–1993),
U.S. dancer, choreographer

1958, *Quote,* 3 August, quoted in James B. Simpson, *Simpson's Contemporary Quotations,* 1988.

It is not so important to be serious as it is to be serious about the important things. The monkey wears an expression of seriousness which would do credit to any college student, but the monkey is serious because he itches.

—**Robert Maynard Hutchins**
(1899–1977), President,
University of Chicago

1961, "The private world of a man with a book," *Saturday Review,* 7 January, pp. 17–18.

[M]ost of the most important experiences that truly educate cannot be arranged ahead of time with any precision. . . . True learning is not a matter of the formal organization of knowledge of books. It is a series of personal experiences.

—**Harold Taylor** (1914–1993),
President, Sarah Lawrence College

1962, "The crisis of the state universities," in Nevitt Sanford, *The American College,* 1962, p. 448.

Our students do not expect to learn in the profound and the only meaningful sense of the word learning. They do not expect that their understandings of the world will change, that their beliefs will be altered, that old interests will be replaced by new ones, and that on the day of their graduation they will be—as human beings—quite different from the freshmen who entered

the university four years ago. They attend the university not as the truly religious person attends to worship, for the sake of an experience which will transform him; but rather as does the average Sunday churchgoer, for the sake of social conformity and from habit.

—**Frank Pinner** (1914–1999),
professor of political science,
Michigan State University

1963, *Left-Handed Dictionary,* p. 235.

University—an institution of higher yawning.

—**Leonard L. Levinson** (1904–1974),
U.S. author

1976, *Waco Tribune-Herald,* 18 March, quoted in Keith Allan Noble, *The International Education Quotations Encyclopaedia,* 1995.

A number of people who are essentially ignorant now have degrees and diplomas to certify they are educated. These people either know how ignorant they are, and thus realize education is a fraud, or they go around saying they are just as good as everybody else. Ignorance is curable. Stupidity is not.

—**John Ciardi** (1916–1986),
U.S. poet and editor

no date, attributed in *Your Ultimate Success Quotation Library* (software program) at <http://www.cybernation.com/>.

Studying literature at Harvard is like learning about women at the Mayo clinic.

—**Roy Blount, Jr.** (1941–),
U.S. author and humorist

no date, attributed in <www. famous-quotations.com>.

Learning is what most adults will do for a living in the 21st century.

—**Bob Perelman** (1947–), U.S. poet;
professor of English,
University of Pennsylvania

Life Experience

no date, attributed in Keith Allan Noble, *The International Education Quotations Encyclopaedia,* 1995.

Common sense has availed many a man more than the seven arts, however liberal they might be.

—**Baltasar Gracián** (1601–1658),
Spanish philosopher and writer

1709, *Tattler,* 2 August, quoted in *The Columbia World of Quotations,* 1996.

To behold her [Lady Elizabeth Hastings] is an immediate check to loose behavior; to love her is a liberal education.

—**Sir Richard Steele** (1672–1729),
British essayist, dramatist, and editor

1732, "First dialogue," in *Alciphron; or The Minute Philosopher.*

He that wants the proper materials of thought may think and meditate forever to no purpose: those cobwebs spun by scholars out of their own brains being alike unserviceable, either for use or for ornament. Proper ideas or materials are only to be got by frequenting good company. I know several gentlemen who, since their appearance in the world, have spent as much time in rubbing off the rust and pedantry of a college education as they have done before in acquiring it.

—**George Berkeley** (1685–1753),
Irish bishop; philosopher

1821, "Ignorance of the learned," in *Table Talk,* p. 75.

You will hear more good things on the outside of a stage-coach from London to Oxford, than if you were to pass a twelve-month with the under-graduates, or heads of colleges, of that famous university. . . .

—**William Hazlitt** (1778–1830),
English essayist

1851, *Moby Dick,* chapter 24.

[A] whaleship was my Yale College and my Harvard.

—**Herman Melville** (1819–1891),
U.S. novelist and poet

no date, attributed in <www.houseof quotes.com>.

Life is my college. May I graduate well, and earn some honors.

—**Louisa May Alcott** (1832–1888),
U.S. writer

1889, U.S. Commissioner of Education, *Report, 1889–90,* II, 1143, quoted in Lawrence R. Veysey, *The Emergence of the American University,* 1965, p. 13–14.

While the college student has been learning a little about the barbarous and petty squabbles of a far-distant past, or trying to master languages which are dead, such knowledge seems adapted for life upon another planet than this as far as business affairs are concerned, the future captain of industry is hotly engaged in the school of experience, obtaining the very knowledge required for his future triumphs. . . . College education as it exists is fatal to success in that domain.

—**Andrew Carnegie** (1835–1919),
U.S. industrialist

no date, attributed at <http://www.quote world.org>.

Some people get an education without going to college; the rest get it after they get out.

—**Mark Twain [Samuel Langhorne Clemens]** (1835–1910), U.S. author

no date, attributed in <www.allthings william.com>.

The higher education so much needed today is not given in the school, is not to be bought in the marketplace, but has to be wrought out in each one of us for himself; it is the silent influence of character on character.

—**Sir William Osler** (1849–1919),
physician and writer

no date, attributed in <www.quotations page.com>.

A thorough knowledge of the Bible is worth more than a college education.

—**Theodore Roosevelt** (1858–1919),
President of the United States

no date, quoted in Waitman Barbe,
Going to College, 1899, p. 8.

It has been my fortune . . . to become intimately acquainted with hundreds of men who, without any equipment of education, have accumulated millions of dollars. I have never met with any one of them whose regret was not profound and deep that he had not an education . . . who did not feel in the presence of cultured people a certain sense of mortification which no money paid for. . . . I never met one of them who was not prepared to sacrifice his whole fortune that his boy should not feel that mortification.

—**Chauncey M. Depew** (1834–1928),
U.S. Senator

no date, attributed in August Kerber,
Quotable Quotes on Education, 1968,
p. 218.

Life, itself, without the assistance of colleges and universities, is becoming an advanced institution of learning.

—**Thomas Alva Edison** (1847–1931),
U.S. inventor

1920, speech at the Oxford Union, 2 December, quoted in Keith Allan Noble, *The International Education Quotations Encyclopaedia,* 1995.

I have not had your advantages. What poor education I have received has been gained in the University of Life.

—**Horatio Bottomley** (1860–1933),
British newspaper publisher and financier

1930, *Fifteen Minutes a Day: The Reading Guide,* p. 7.

[I]n my opinion, a five-foot—at first a three-foot—shelf would hold books enough to afford a good substitute for a liberal education for anyone who would read them with devotion, even if he could spare but fifteen minutes a day for reading.

—**Charles William Eliot** (1834–1926),
President, Harvard University

no date, attributed in August Kerber,
Quotable Quotes on Education, 1968,
p. 216.

To be two years a widow exceedeth a college education.

—**Gelett Burgess** (1866–1951),
U.S. writer

1935, "The sheep look up," address, the Modern Forum, 25 November, quoted in Henry A. Ashmore, *Unseasonable Truth,* 1989, p. 149.

Education is not a substitute for experience. It is preparation for it. There is no substitute for experience.

> —**Robert Maynard Hutchins**
> (1899–1977), President,
> University of Chicago

1951, "August 31," *Once Around the Sun,* p. 252.

It takes most men five years to recover from a college education, and to learn that poetry is as vital to thinking as knowledge.

> —**Brooks Atkinson** (1894–1984),
> U.S. journalist and drama critic

no date, attributed in Louis E. Boone, *Quotable Business,* 1992, p. 232.

I learned more about economics from one South Dakota dust storm than I did in all my years at college.

> —**Hubert H. Humphrey** (1911–1978),
> U.S. politician, Vice President of the
> United States

1969, "Bridges to other people," in *Redbook,* quoted in Rosalie Maggio, *The Beacon Book of Quotations by Women,* 1992, p. 96.

Education is a private matter between the person and the world of knowledge and experience, and has little to do with school or college.

> —**Lillian Smith** (1897–1969),
> U.S. author

1974, *Barefoot in Arcadia,* p. 158.

Common sense—one of the rarest of commodities—is an asset that man ought to desire, and more common sense can be induced by observing the diversity of human beings in a small town than can be learned in academia.

> —**Louis B. Wright** (1899–1984),
> director, Folger Shakespeare Library

1975, *Vital Speeches,* 15 April, quoted in James B. Simpson, *Simpson's Contemporary Quotations,* 1988.

Much that passes for education . . . is not education at all but ritual. The fact is that we are being educated when we know it least.

> —**David P. Gardner** (1933–),
> President, University of Utah;
> President, University of California

no date, attributed in <www.quote garden.com>.

I think everyone should go to college and get a degree and then spend six months as a bartender and six months as a cabdriver. Then they would really be educated.

> —**Al McGuire** (1928–2001),
> U.S. basketball coach

no date, attributed in <www.bemore creative.com>.

Being considerate of others will take you and your children further in life than any college or professional degree.

> —**Marian Wright Edelman** (1939–),
> U.S. social reformer; author

Outcomes: Individual

c. 1603, *Valerius Terminus of the Interpretation of Nature.*

[U]niversities incline wits to sophistry and affectation.

> —**Francis Bacon** (1561–1626), English
> philosopher, essayist, and statesman

1673, *The Imaginary Invalid,* quoted in Keith Allan Noble, *The International Education Quotations Encyclopaedia,* 1995.

Once you have the cap and gown all you need do is, open your mouth. Whatever nonsense you talk becomes wisdom and all the rubbish, good sense.

—**Molière [Jean-Baptiste Poquelin]** (1622–1673), French playwright

1722, Boston *Courant,* 14 May, (under the pen name "Silence Dogood"), quoted in David J. Loftus, *The Unofficial Book of Harvard Trivia,* 1985, p. 34.

[Harvard students] learn little more than how to carry themselves handsomely, and enter a room genteely (which might as well be acquired at a Dancing School), and . . . they return, after abundance of trouble and Changes, as great Blockheads as ever, only more proud and self-conceited.

—**Benjamin Franklin** (1706–1790), U.S. statesman

1784, in Benjamin Franklin, *Two Tracts, Information to Those Who Would Remove to America, And Remarks Concerning the Savages of North America,* quoted in Paul Boyer, *Native American Colleges,* 1997, p. 9.

Several of our young people were formally brought up at the College of the Northern Provinces; they were instructed in all your Sciences; but, when they came back to us, they were bad Runners, ignorant of every means of living in the Woods, unable to bear either Cold or Hunger, knew neither how to build a Cabin, take a Deer, or kill an Enemy, spoke our Language imperfectly, were therefore neither fit for Hunters, Warriors, nor Counselors, they were totally good for nothing. We are however not the less oblig'd by your kind Offer, tho' we decline accepting it; and, to show our grateful Sense of it, [if] the Gentlemen of Virginia will send us a Dozen of their Sons, we will take great Care of their Education, instruct them in all we know, and make *Men* of them.

—**Unnamed Indian Leader**, declining offer by the College of William and Mary to educate Indian youth

1844, "New England Reformers," *Essays, Second Series.*

We are students of words: we are shut up in schools, and colleges, and recitation-rooms, for ten or fifteen years, and come out at last with a bag of wind, a memory of words, and do not know a thing.

—**Ralph Waldo Emerson** (1803–1882), U.S. poet and essayist

1848, commencement address, quoted in Richard Hofstadter and Wilson Smith (eds.), *American Higher Education: A Documentary History, Volume I,* 1961 p. 377.

No college professors can work miracles, or convert a blockhead into a Solomon. "Though the ass may make pilgrimage to Mecca, yet an ass he will come back."

—**Philip Lindsley** (1786–1855), President, University of Nashville

1858, *The Idea of a University,* Discourse VII.

A man of well improved faculties has the command of another's knowledge. A man without them, has not the command of his own.

Discourse VII.

[E]ducated men can do what illiterate cannot; and the man who has learned to think and to reason and to compare and to discriminate and to analyze, who has refined his taste, and formed his judgment, and sharpened his mental vision, will not indeed at once be a lawyer, or a pleader, or an orator, or a statesman, or a physician, or a good landlord, or a man of business, or a soldier, or an engineer, or a chemist, or a geologist, or an antiquarian, but he will be placed in that state of intellect in which he can take up any one of the sciences or callings I have referred to, or any other for which he has a taste or special talent, with an ease, a grace, a versatility, and a success, to which another is a stranger.

—**John Henry (Cardinal) Newman** (1801–1890), Rector, Catholic University of Ireland

no date, attributed in August Kerber, *Quotable Quotes on Education,* 1968, p. 218.

One of the benefits of a college education is to show the boy its little avail.

—**Ralph Waldo Emerson** (1803–1882), U.S. poet and essayist

1869, Inaugural Address, 19 October, in *A Turning Point in Higher Education,* 1969, p. 40.

[T]he young man of nineteen or twenty ought to know what he likes best and is most fit for. . . . When the revelation of his own peculiar taste and capacity comes to a young man, let him reverently give it welcome, thank God, and take courage. Thereafter he knows his way to happy, enthusiastic work, and, God willing, to usefulness and success.

—**Charles William Eliot** (1834–1926), President, Harvard University

1870, quoted in Frederick Rudolph, *The American College and University,* 1962, p. 89.

The effects [of colleges] are so powerful and salutary that it may well be questioned whether the education which they impart does not of itself more than repay the time

and money which it costs, even to those idlers at college who derive from their residence little or nothing more than those accidental or incidental advantages. . . . Such idlers sometimes awake to manliness and to duty when they leave college. . . . To many who persistently neglect the college studies, the college life is anything rather than a total loss. Even those who sink downward with no recovery find their descent retarded.

—**Noah Porter** (1811–1892), President, Yale University

no date, attributed in *Your Ultimate Success Quotation Library* (software program) at <http://www.cybernation.com/>.

The exquisite art of idleness, one of the most important things that any university can teach.

—**Oscar Wilde** (1854–1900), Irish playwright, author, and wit

1894, "Abraham Lincoln," in *The Works of Robert C. Ingersoll,* vol. 3, 1929, p. 166.

[C]olleges are places where pebbles are polished and diamonds are dimmed. If Shakespeare had graduated at Oxford, he might have been a quibbling attorney, or a hypocritical parson.

—**Robert G. Ingersoll** (1833–1899), U.S. orator and lawyer

1894, *Pudd'nhead Wilson,* chapter 5, p. 44.

Training is everything. The peach was once a bitter almond; cauliflower is nothing but cabbage with a college education.

—**Mark Twain [Samuel Langhorne Clemens]** (1835–1910), U.S. author

1896, S. S. Koteliansky and Leonard Woolf (translators), *Note-Book of Anton Chekhov,* 1921, p. 53.

The university brings out all abilities including incapability.

—**Anton Chekhov** (1860–1904),
Russian writer, dramatist

1899, *Going to College,* p. 7.

We may regret almost any other step in life, but I believe it is safe to say that there is not a college graduate in the world today, who went to college with serious and honest purpose, who will not say it was time, money and labor well spent.

—**Waitman Barbe** (1864–1925),
assistant to the president,
West Virginia University

no date, attributed in <http://www.quote garden.com/college.html>.

A man who has never gone to school may steal from a freight car, but if he has a university education he may steal the whole railroad.

—**Theodore Roosevelt** (1858–1919),
President of the United States

1907, *The Education of Henry Adams,* chapter IV.

The chief wonder of education is that it does not ruin everybody concerned in it, teachers and taught. . . . Harvard College was probably less hurtful than any other university then in existence. It taught little, and that little ill, but it left the mind open, free from bias, ignorant of facts, but docile. The graduate had few strong prejudices. . . . If the student got little from his mates, he got little more from his masters. The four years passed at the college were, for his purposes, wasted. . . .

—**Henry B. Adams** (1838–1918),
U.S. historian

1910, *Great American Universities,* p. 60.

A distinguished alumnus of Harvard, when asked why he sent his son to Yale, replied: "I used to think that Harvard gave the better training, but at my time of life I find that all the Harvard men are working for Yale men."

p. 119.

Does a boy get a chance for personal development in a crowd of two thousand or five thousand—it will soon be ten thousand in some places—other boys? There can be but one president of a class, but one editor in chief of the daily, but one champion orator, but one speediest sprinter, and but one star pitcher, however numerous the students. Consequently, the crowd on the bleachers gets bigger year by year.

—**Edwin E. Slosson** (1865–1929),
chemist; U.S. writer

1911, *A Thousand and One Epigrams.*

No one knows the vanity of riches save he who has been rich; therefore, I would have every man rich, and I would give every youth a college education that he might know the insignificance of it.

—**Elbert Hubbard** (1856–1915),
U.S. writer and publisher

1913, *An Autobiography,* Chapter I.

I thoroughly enjoyed Harvard, and I am sure it did me good, but only in the general effect, for there was very little in my actual studies which helped me in after life.

—**Theodore Roosevelt** (1858–1919),
President of the United States

no date, attributed at <http://www.quote world.org>.

College don't make fools. They only develop them.

—**George Horace Lorimer**
(1867–1937), U.S. editor and writer

1939, *Too Much College,* p. 19.

For the vastly great part of it [education] the student's one aim is to get it done with. There comes a glad time to his life when he has "finished" mathematics, a happy day when he has done philosophy, an exhilarating hour when he realizes that he is finished with "compulsory English." Then at last his four years are out, his sentence expired, and he steps out of college a free man, without a stain on his character—and not much on his mind. . . . Later on, he looks back wistfully and realizes how different it might have been.

—**Stephen Butler Leacock** (1869–1944), professor of political economy, McGill University

no date, attributed in <www. famous-quotations.com>.

Harvard takes perfectly good plums as students, and turns them into prunes.

—**Frank Lloyd Wright** (1868–1959), U.S. architect

1943, *Liberal Education,* pp. 2–3.

It is impossible to find a man who believes that the right things were done to his mind. He was forced to learn too many things, or too few. It was all too general, or too special. The present was ignored; or the past. Something was left out entirely, or at best skimmed over; mathematics, poetry, the method of science, the secret of religion, the history of this or that. The result is, he will say, that he does not feel at home in the realms of nature and intellect; he is not securely centered between thoughts and things; he is not a philosopher. And whereas once he did not care, now—if he is middle-aged—he does. He knows that he has missed something, and he suspects that all the king's horses could not find it for him again.

—**Mark Van Doren** (1894–1972), professor of English, Columbia University

1958, "Science vs. the humanities: A truce to the nonsense on both sides," *Saturday Evening Post,* 3 May, p. 26.

The test and the use of man's education is that he finds pleasure in the exercise of his mind.

—**Jacques Barzun** (1907–), Dean of Faculties and Provost, Columbia University

1959, *Academic Procession,* p. 2.

I went to college for no purpose except the experience itself; it seemed to me then—and has ever since—an adequate objective.

—**Henry M. Wriston** (1889–1978), President, Lawrence College; President, Brown University

1961, Baccalaureate Address, *Time,* 23 June, p. 30.

If you feel that you have both feet planted on level ground, then the university has failed you.

—**Robert Goheen** (1919–), President, Princeton University

1972, *The Guardian,* quoted in Jonathon Green, *Morrow's International Dictionary of Contemporary Quotations,* 1982, p. 359.

If a man is a fool, you don't train him out of being a fool by sending him to a university. You merely turn him into a trained fool, ten times more dangerous.

—**Desmond Bagley** (1923–1983), British writer

1974, "So brief a time," *Yale Alumni Magazine,* June, p. 9.

[T]he tragedy of not using the college years . . . is that never again does one receive impressions with quite the same emotional intensity with which one receives them between the ages of 17 and

21. It is so brief a time, so very brief, yet one can build a lifetime on the exploitation of it.

—**Louis Auchincloss** (1917–),
U.S. lawyer; writer

1975, *The Case Against College,* p. 70.

[T]here is no real evidence that the higher income of college graduates is due to college at all. . . . [C]ollege may simply attract people who are slated to earn more money anyway; those with higher IQs, better family backgrounds, a more enterprising temperament.

p. 122.

College doesn't make people intelligent, ambitious, happy, liberal, or quick to learn new things. It's the other way around. Intelligent, ambitious, happy, liberal, quick-learning people are attracted to college in the first place. Going to college in hopes of being like them, if you are not, is like playing tennis to look like the tennis-playing rich. It doesn't work.

—**Caroline Bird** (1915–), U.S. author

1977, *Song of Solomon,* p. 189.

Bryn Mawr had done what a four-year dose of liberal education was designed to do; unfit her for eighty per cent of the useful work of the world.

—**Toni Morrison** (1931–), U.S. writer

no date, attributed in <www.quote garden.com>.

A lot of fellows nowadays have a B.A., M.A., or Ph.D. Unfortunately, they don't have a J.O.B.

—**"Fats" Domino** (1928–),
U.S. entertainer and composer

1993, *Conversations: Straight Talk with America's Sister President,* p. 170.

[A]n education that produces people who know a lot but do so very little is hardly a true education.

—**Johnetta B. Cole** (1936–),
President, Spelman College

Chapter 5

Research and Scholarship

Conferences

1959, *The House of Intellect,* p. 189.

For the participants, the conference has become a principal form of intellectual togetherness. . . . A conference could be, indeed, a temporary materialization of the House of Intellect. What is regrettable is that, despite our ample means and best wits, the conference has become rather a tribal rite and the possible House of Intellect a nomad's tent. The ritual is even growing more complex: the biggest and best conferences, it is now believed, require a preconference conference.

—**Jacques Barzun** (1907–),
Dean of Faculties and Provost,
Columbia University

1984, Prologue, *Small World.*

The modern conference resembles the pilgrimage of Medieval Christendom in that it allows the participants to indulge themselves in all the pleasures and diversions of travel while appearing to be austerely bent on self-improvement. To be sure, there are certain penitential exercises to be performed—the presentation of a paper, perhaps, and certainly listening to the papers of others. . . .

—**David Lodge** (1935–),
English novelist

1988, *ProfScam,* p. 13.

One of the inevitable signs of academic prosperity is an invitation to deliver papers to conventions of one's peers, a ritual in which professors bore other professors by reading aloud obscure products of their research.

—**Charles J. Sykes** (1954–),
U.S. journalist

1990, *Killing the Spirit,* p. 143.

Professors . . . seem to love conferences. I must say that to me they seem a dreadful penance, where the proportion of intellectual gold to dross is usually infinitesimal. But if professors are to bore their students, they might, I suppose, just as well bore each other.

—**Page Smith** (1917–1995),
historian; Provost, University of
California at Santa Cruz

Knowledge

1858, *The Idea of a University,*
Discourse V.

The principle of real dignity in Knowledge, its worth, its desirableness, considered irrespectively of its results, is this germ within it of a scientific or a philosophical process. That is how it comes to be an end in itself; this is why it admits of being called Liberal. Not to know the relative disposition of things is the state of slaves or children; to have mapped out the Universe is the boast, or at least the ambition, of Philosophy.

Discourse V.

[T]hat alone is liberal knowledge, which stand on its own pretensions, which is independent of sequel, expects no complement, refuses to be *informed* (as it is called) by any end, or absorbed into any art, in order to duly present itself to our contemplation. The most ordinary pursuits have this specific character, if they are self-sufficient and complete; the highest lose it, when they minister to something beyond them.

Discourse V.

I am asked what is the end of University Education, and of the Liberal or Philosophical Knowledge which I conceive it to impart: I answer . . . that it has a very tangible, real, and sufficient end, though the end cannot be divided from that knowledge itself. Knowledge is capable of being its own end. Such is the constitution of the human mind, that any kind of knowledge, if it really be such, is its own reward.

Discourse IX.

Truth has two attributes—beauty and power; and while Useful Knowledge is the possession of truth as powerful, Liberal

Knowledge is the apprehension of it as beautiful.

> **—John Henry (Cardinal) Newman**
> (1801–1890), Rector,
> Catholic University of Ireland

c. 1870s, *The Mask of Balliol,* quoted in *Oxford Dictionary of Quotations* (electronic edition), 1995.

> First come I; my name is Jowett.
> There's no knowledge but I know it.
> I am the Master of this college:
> What I don't know isn't knowledge.

> **—H. C. Beeching** (1859–1919),
> English divine

1908, Albert Bigelow Paine (ed.), *Mark Twain's Notebook,* 1935, quoted in R. Kent Rasmussen (ed.) *The Quotable Mark Twain,* 1997, p. 87.

All schools, all colleges, have 2 great functions: to confer, and to conceal, valuable knowledge.

> **—Mark Twain [Samuel Langhorne Clemens]** (1835–1910), U.S. author

no date, attributed by August Kerber, *Quotable Quotes on Education,* 1988, p. 223.

Universities are full of knowledge; the freshmen bring a little in and the seniors take none away, and knowledge accumulates.

> **—Abbott Lawrence Lowell**
> (1856–1943), President,
> Harvard University

1929, *The Aims of Education and Other Essays,* Chapter Seven.

Knowledge doesn't keep any better than fish. . . . [I]t must come to the students, as it were, just drawn out of the sea and with the freshness of its immediate importance.

—**Alfred North Whitehead** (1861–1947), English philosopher and mathematician; professor of philosophy, Harvard University

1943, "Introduction," in *Education for Freedom,* 1943, p. xii.

It is probable that the most "practical" education will prove to be a theoretical one. Habituation to routine will be valueless, or even a handicap.

—**Robert Maynard Hutchins** (1899–1977), President, University of Chicago

no date, attributed in <www.quote garden.com>.

No man should escape our universities without knowing how little he knows.

—**J. Robert Oppenheimer** (1904–1967), U.S. physicist; professor of physics, University of California, Berkeley

1966, "The university," *The New Republic,* May 28, p. 18.

[T]he community of professors is, in the modern world, the best available source of guidance and authority in the field of knowledge. There is no other court to which men can turn and find what they once found in tradition and in custom, in ecclesiastical and civil authority. Because modern man in his search for truth has turned away from kings, priests, commissars and bureaucrats, he is left, for better or worse, with the professors.

—**Walter Lippman** (1889–1974), U.S. editor and author

1971, *The Degradation of the Academic Dogma,* pp. 23–24.

What is the dogma that the university is built on? *Knowledge is important.* Just

that. Not "relevant" knowledge; not "practical" knowledge; not the kind of knowledge that enables one to wield power, achieve success or influence others. *Knowledge!*

—**Robert A. Nisbet** (1913–), professor of sociology, University of California, Riverside

1973, *The Concept of a University,* p. 67.

We need not doubt that dogmatism is the prime academic sin in order to recognize that a whiff of it may be valuable in ballasting academic identities. However important rationality may be, it ought not to be allowed an instant and unchallenged dominion of the mind. Intellectual life would be hopelessly unstable if theories were abandoned at the first successful challenge. On the other hand, hard gemlike flames soon burn out, the mastery of a well-developed vocabulary is substituted for thought, and perceptions turn into formulae: these are the processes of the human mind, almost as inexorable as the rotation of the seasons.

—**Kenneth P. Minogue** (1930–), senior lecturer in political science, London School of Economics and Political Science

1978, motto, in the film *Animal House.*

Knowledge is good.

—**Faber College**

no date, attributed in <http:// www.geocities.com/~spanoudi/ topic-u1.html#university>.

The university is not engaged in making ideas safe for students. It is engaged in making students safe for ideas.

—**Clark Kerr** (1911–2003), Chancellor, University of California, Berkeley; President, University of California

1983, *In Search of Our Mother's Gardens,* quoted in Rosalie Maggio, *The Beacon Book of Quotations by Women,* 1992, p. 97.

Ignorance, arrogance, and racism have bloomed as Superior Knowledge in all too many universities.

—**Alice Walker** (1944–), U.S. author

1992, convocation address, September, quoted in Stephen James Nelson, *Leaders in the Crucible,* 2000, p. 46.

A man white, black or yellow; Christian, Jew, Mahommedan [sic] or heathen may enter and enjoy all the advantages of the institution . . . and go out believing in one God, in many Gods, or in no God. But it will be impossible for anyone to continue with us long without knowing what we believe to be the truth and our reasons for that belief.

—**Peter Pouncy** (1937–), President, Amherst College

1998, "The art of the presidency," *The President,* Spring, p. 12.

Knowledge is the new economic currency. In the past, a nation's natural assets—its geography, its climate, its landscape, its natural resources—shaped its destiny. All these will remain important, but more important still will be knowledge. Unlike other natural resources, it is undepleted by use; it is endlessly renewable, autocatalytic in its influence, undiminished by its application.

—**Frank H. T. Rhodes** (1926–), President, Cornell University

Ph.D.

1903, "The Ph.D. octopus," *The Harvard Monthly,* March, pp. 4–5.

Will anyone pretend for a moment that the doctor's degree is a guarantee that its pos-

sessor will be successful as a teacher? Notoriously his moral, social and personal characteristics may utterly disqualify him for success in the class-room; and of these characteristics his doctor's examination is unable to take any account whatever. . . . The truth is that the Doctor-Monopoly in teaching, which is becoming so rooted an American custom, can show no serious grounds whatsoever for itself in reason. As it actually prevails and grows in vogue among us, it is due to childish motives exclusively. In reality it is but a sham, a bauble, a dodge whereby to decorate the catalogues of schools and colleges.

—**William James** (1842–1910), professor of philosophy, Harvard University

1911, *Report for 1911–12,* quoted in Edward C. Elliott (ed.), *The Rise of a University, Vol. II,* 1937, pp. 240–41.

During the last twenty-five years there has developed among the colleges and schools of the United States a deplorable form of educational snobbery, which insists that a candidate for appointment for a teaching position shall have gained the privilege of writing the letters Ph.D. after his name. . . . As a matter of fact, few persons are less well equipped to make good secondary school and college teachers than the most recent possessors of the degree of Doctor of Philosophy.

—**Nicholas Murray Butler** (1862–1947), President, Columbia University

1926, *Which Way Parnassus?,* p. 71.

Some Ph.D.'s are scholars; many of them are blind earthworms burrowing a long, thin hole that leads nowhere.

—**Percy Marks** (1891–1956), U.S. writer and instructor of English

1930, *Universities: American English German,* p. 124.

Fifty years ago, the degree of Ph.D. had a meaning in the United States; today, it has practically no significance. The same is true of research.

—**Abraham Flexner** (1866–1959), U.S. educator

1945, *A Texan in England,* p. 26.

The average Ph.D. thesis is nothing but a transference of bones from one graveyard to another.

—**J. Frank Dobie** (1888–1964), professor of English, University of Texas

1964, *New York Times,* 20 May, quoted in Keith Allan Noble, *The International Education Quotations Encyclopaedia,* 1995.

Where there are two Ph.D.s in a developing country, one is head of State and the other is in exile.

—**Edwin Herbert Samuel** (1898–1978), English writer and governmental official

1964, *The Observer,* quoted in Jonathon Green, *Morrow's International Dictionary of Contemporary Quotations,* 1982, p. 360.

Life at university, with its intellectual and inconclusive discussions at a postgraduate level is on the whole a bad training for the real world. Only men of very strong character surmount this handicap.

—**Paul Chambers** (1904–1981), British industrialist

1968, *The American University,* p. 261.

The next nut to crack is the Ph.D., and for this I urge a radical device. The best would

be: give every native-born American a Ph.D. at birth and start from there.

—**Jacques Barzun** (1907–), Dean of Faculties and Provost, Columbia University

1969, *The Ideal of the University,* p. 26.

No one will ever total up the marriages ruined, the children neglected, the anguish suffered, and the years of fruitful work blighted by the curse of the unfinished dissertation.

—**Robert Paul Wolff** (1933–), professor of Afro-American studies and philosophy, University of Massachusetts, Amherst

no date, attributed in David J. Loftus, *The Unofficial Book of Harvard Trivia,* 1985, p. 76.

I never took a Ph.D. It's what saved me, I think. If I had taken a doctoral degree, it would have stifled my writing capacity.

—**Barbara Tuchman** (1912–1989), U.S. historian

1978, attributed in Paul Dickson, *The Official Rules,* p. 41.

To every Ph.D. there is an equal and opposite Ph.D.

—**Duggans' Law**

1990, "The Ph.D. squid," *The American Scholar,* Spring, p. 182.

The Ph.D. has not just multiplied, it has spread. . . . The Ph.D. Octopus is well and thriving. Indeed, for the contemporary situation the generally small, timid octopus, which tends to confine itself mainly to coastal waters, provides an image less compelling than another cephalopod: the large, aggressive, and highly mobile squid with two prehensile arms in addition to its eight grasping tentacles.

p. 193.

At the very least, the dissertation as an exercise should prepare the new Ph.D. to organize his or her first college course and to appreciate what it takes to write a good book.

—**Theodore Ziolkowski** (1932–),
graduate Dean, Princeton University

1990, *The University: An Owner's Manual,* pp. 137–38.

Graduate students are the faculty's young disciples who ensure the continuity of learning. They are also the children and heirs of the faculty. In Germany, the professor who guides the Ph.D. dissertation is called a *Doctorvater* (doctor-father) and that aptly describes the ideal.

—**Henry Rosovsky** (1927–),
Dean of the Faculty of Arts and
Sciences, Harvard University

Publication

1942, *The Academic Man,* p. 197.

There is the necessity of bringing results to light in the form of publication, for in the academic scheme of things results unpublished are little better than those never achieved.

—**Logan Wilson** (1907–1990),
President, University of Texas at Austin;
President, American Council
on Education

1983, *Scholarship and Its Survival,* p. 61.

[T]he scholarly record is ultimately a written one: this is the foundation for the principle, often maligned and sometimes abused, of "publish or perish."

—**Jaroslav Pelikan** (1923–),
historian, Dean of the Graduate School,
Yale University

1986, "Guarding the guardians: A conference on editorial peer review," *JAMA,* 256, p. 2391–92.

[D]espite this system [of peer review], anyone who reads journals widely and critically is forced to realize that there are scarcely any bars to eventual publication. There seems to be no study too fragmented, no hypothesis too trivial, no literature citation too biased or too egotistical, no design too warped, no methodology too bungled, no presentation of results too inaccurate, too obscure, and too contradictory, no analysis too self-serving, no argument too circular, no conclusions too trifling or too unjustified, and no grammar and syntax too offensive for a paper to end up in print.

—**I. Drummond Rennie** (1936–),
deputy editor, *Journal of the American
Medical Association*

1990, *Killing the Spirit,* p. 180.

Under the publish-or-perish standard, the university is perishing. Research *and* publication are not necessarily related.

—**Page Smith** (1917–1995),
historian; Provost, University of
California at Santa Cruz

1992, *Education without Impact,* p. 91.

[T]he old edict "publish or perish" has something rather comical about it. For the most part, professors don't publish a great deal, but they usually don't perish either.

—**George H. Douglas** (1934–),
professor of English, University of
Illinois, Urbana-Champaign

1992, *Imposters in the Temple,* 1992, p. 81.

[E]very article authored in a prestigious journal in a scholar's field of study is like a notch in the six-gun of an Old West gunfighter, a proof of talent and visible building block of the academic intellectual's reputation pyramid.

—**Martin Anderson** (1936–),
senior fellow, Hoover Institution,
Stanford University

Research

no date, attributed in Keith Allan Noble, *The International Education Quotations Encyclopaedia,* 1995.

Research! A mere excuse for idleness; it has never achieved, and will never achieve any results of the slightest value.

—**Benjamin Jowett** (1817–1893),
Master, Balliol College; Vice-chancellor,
Oxford University

1902, "University building," in *Popular Science Monthly,* August, p. 332.

The crowning function of a university is that of original research. On this rests the advance of civilization.

—**David Starr Jordan** (1851–1931),
President, Stanford University

1918, *The Higher Learning in America,* Chapter 1.

Men instinctively seek knowledge, and value it. The fact of this proclivity is well summed up in saying that men are by native gift actuated with an idle curiosity,— "idle" in the sense that a knowledge of things is sought, apart from any ulterior use of the knowledge so gained.

—**Thorstein Veblen** (1857–1929),
U.S. sociologist

1925, *Report for 1924–25,* quoted in Edward C. Elliott (ed.), *The Rise of a University, Vol. II,* 1937, p. 69.

It was Garrick, a great admirer of George Whitefield's preaching, who said that

Whitefield's eloquence was such that he could reduce his hearers to tears merely by uttering the word Mesopotamia. The word research has come to be something like the blessed word Mesopotamia. It is used to reduce everything to silence, acquiescence, and approbation. The fact of the matter is that something between 75 per cent and 90 per cent of what is called research in the various universities and institutions of the land is not properly research at all. . . . Not many persons in any one generation are capable of real research.

—**Nicholas Murray Butler**
(1862–1947), President,
Columbia University

1934, "Education and research I," *No Friendly Voice,* 1936, p. 175.

A university may be a university without doing any teaching. It cannot be one without doing any research.

—**Robert Maynard Hutchins**
(1899–1977), President,
University of Chicago

1937, *The Nature of a Liberal College,* p. 60.

The greatest single source of academic refreshment is research.

—**Henry M. Wriston** (1889–1978),
President, Lawrence College;
President, Brown University

no date, attributed in *Your Ultimate Success Quotation Library* (software program) at <http://www.cybernation. com/>.

If we knew what we were doing it wouldn't be research.

—**Albert Einstein** (1879–1955),
U.S. physicist

1941, "Teaching and research,"
Association of American Colleges Bulletin, March, p. 76.

If research had no other value, its service in keeping professors alive and interested in their fields of knowledge would amply justify it.

—**Louis B. Wright** (1899–1984),
director, Folger Shakespeare Library

1971, *The Degradation of the Academic Dogma,* pp. 71–72.

The first man who, having enclosed a piece of the university, bethought himself of saying, "This is my institute," and found members of the faculty simple enough to believe him, was the real founder of the university's higher capitalism. . . . The first million dollars given to a university for project research was far too much. Today ten billion dollars is not enough. So we have fallen.

—**Robert A. Nisbet** (1913–),
professor of sociology,
University of California, Riverside

no date, attributed in *Your Ultimate Success Quotation Library* (software program) at <http://www.cybernation.com/>.

It is a good morning exercise for a research scientist to discard a pet hypothesis every day before breakfast. It keeps him young.

—**Konrad Lorenz** (1903–1989),
Austrian zoologist, ethnologist

no date, attributed at <http://www.quote world.org>.

University President: "Why is it that you physicists always require so much expensive equipment? Now the Department of Mathematics requires nothing but money for paper, pencils, and erasers . . . and the Department of Philosophy is better still. It doesn't even require erasers."

—**Isaac Asimov** (1920–1992),
U.S. scientist; writer

1986, *Higher Learning,* pp. 76–77.

[R]esearch represents the ultimate expression of a scholar's powers, intellectual labor brought to its highest, most exalted state. . . . As a result, published research emerges as the common currency of academic achievement, a currency that can be weighed and evaluated across institutional and even national boundaries. It is, therefore, the chief determinant of status within the guild.

—**Derek Bok** (1930–), President,
Harvard University

1990, *Killing the Spirit,* p. 7.

"Research" is a word without soul or substance, as broad as the ocean and as shallow as a pond. [T]he vast majority of the so-called research turned out in the modern university is essentially worthless. . . . It is busywork on a vast, almost incomprehensible scale.

—**Page Smith** (1917–1995),
historian; Provost,
University of California at Santa Cruz

1990, *The University: An Owner's Manual,* p. 89.

Research is an expression of faith in the possibility of progress. . . . Research, especially academic research, is a form of optimism about the human condition.

—**Henry Rosovsky** (1927–), Dean of the Faculty of Arts and Sciences,
Harvard University

Research vs. Teaching

1852, "On university education," in *Introductory Lectures on the Opening of Owens College, Second Edition,* p. 22, quoted in George Leslie Brook, *The Modern University,* 1965, p. 22.

He who learns from one occupied in learning, drinks from a running stream. He who learns from one who has learned all he is to teach, drinks "the green mantle of the stagnant pool."

—A. J. Scot (?–?)

1858, *The Idea of a University,* Preface.

To discover and to teach are distinct functions; they are also distinct gifts, and are not commonly found united in the same person. He, too, who spends his day in dispensing his existing knowledge to all comers is unlikely to have either leisure or energy to acquire new. The common sense of mankind has associated the search after truth with seclusion and quiet. The greatest thinkers have been too intent on their subject to admit of interruption; they have been men of absent minds and idiosyncratic habits, and have, more or less, shunned the lecture room and the public school.

—John Henry (Cardinal) Newman
(1801–1890), Rector,
Catholic University of Ireland

1891, "Ideals of the new American university," *The Forum,* September, p. 14, quoted in W. H. Cowley and Don Williams, *International and Historical Roots of American Higher Education,* 1991, p. 141.

Investigation is the basis of all good instruction. No second-hand man was ever a great teacher, and I very much doubt if any really great investigator was ever a poor teacher.

—David Starr Jordan (1851–1931),
president, Stanford University

1902, *Report for 1901–2,* quoted in Edward C. Elliott (ed.), *The Rise of a University, Vol. II,* 1937, p. 342.

The best teacher is a constant student, and the constant student sooner or later tends to become an investigator. . . . We shall not reach an ideal condition until every department in the University, without exception, regards itself as charged with the duty of investigating as well as that of teaching.

—Nicholas Murray Butler
(1862–1947), President,
Columbia University

1906, "The reaction of graduate work on the other work of the university," *Journal of Proceedings and Addresses of the Association of American Universities,* 1906, p. 60, quoted in Christopher J. Lucas, *American Higher Education,* 1994, p. 180.

It must, I think, be admitted that most university teachers . . . have chosen their profession not so much from the love of teaching as from the desire to continue the study of their speciality. While the number of those who have a positive distaste for teaching is small, there are many whose interest in teaching is secondary to their interest in investigation.

—Jacob Gould Schurman (1854–1942),
president, Cornell University

1919, *Report for 1918–19,* quoted in Edward C. Elliott (ed.), *The Rise of a University, Vol. II,* 1937, p. 343.

Very few persons are able to make important contributions to knowledge, and such persons are only in the rarest instances good teachers. It is very often true that the most distinguished scholars and men of science in a university are among its poorest teachers. The reason is simple. Their intellectual interests lie elsewhere and they have neither the mental energy nor the fund of human sympathy to give to struggling and often ill-prepared youth who may come to them for instruction and advice.

—**Nicholas Murray Butler** (1862–1947), President, Columbia University

1929, *The Aims of Education and Other Essays,* Chapter Seven.

Do you want your teachers to be imaginative? Then encourage them to do research. Do you want your researchers to be imaginative? Then bring them into intellectual sympathy with the young. . . .

—**Alfred North Whitehead** (1861–1947), English philosopher and mathematician; professor of philosophy, Harvard University

1936, quoted in Edgar W. Knight, *Fifty Years of American Education,* 1952, p. 263.

The true teacher is a man of inquiring mind, not satisfied with a parasitical intellectual life but eager to discover truth as yet unknown. The college teacher who views knowledge as something in a dish to pass around among his students without spilling any of it is promptly exposed by undergraduates quick to detect the bluffer.

—**Harold W. Dodds** (1889–1980), President, Princeton University

1940, "Competition between teaching and research in American universities," in Milton R. Konvitz (ed.), *Education for Freedom and Responsibility,* 1952, p. 100, quoted in Richard M. Huber, *How Professors Play the Cat Guarding the Cream,* 1992, p. 126–27.

The idea is that teaching and research go hand in hand; that the successful teacher will inevitably be engaged in fruitful research; and that the successful scholar or sci-

entist just as surely will be an effective teacher. This proposition in this general form is wishful thinking of the baldest sort. The eminent scholar or scientist who is also an inspiring teacher is, of course, for the university administrator an answer to prayer; we know all too well that answers to this particular prayer appear in the flesh *very infrequently.*

—**Edmund E. Day** (1883–1951), President, Cornell University

1941, "Teaching and research," *Association of American Colleges Bulletin,* March, p. 77.

[T]he best teachers are those who are actively engaged in the pursuit of truth, not those who simply report what has already been found. . . . When a professor quits trying to learn the truth for himself and becomes merely the purveyor of second-hand knowledge, his own education ceases, and his usefulness as a teacher at that point begins to decline.

p. 79.

The purely inspirational teacher, the man who never goes to the springs of knowledge, presently runs dry. He may whip up his zeal by reading secondary books, but soon the most callow students can see through his devices. When he has exhausted his original capital he has nothing to fall back upon.

—**Louis B. Wright** (1899–1984), director, Folger Shakespeare Library

1944, *Teacher in America,* p. 202.

If teaching is unimportant, and scholarship all-important, then it is logical to make the Ph.D. the prerequisite that it is. But in that case, parents and students must be reconciled to indifferent teaching as a rule, and men choosing the academic career must either give up hope of advancement or be master-jugglers of their early years, at the cost of other goods of life—health, friendship, and contemplation.

—**Jacques Barzun** (1907–),
Dean of Faculties and Provost,
Columbia University

1958, *The Academic Marketplace,* p. 84.

For most members of the profession, the real strain in the academic role arises from the fact that they are, in essence, paid to do one job [teaching], whereas the worth of services is evaluated on the basis of how well they do another [research].

—**Theodore Caplow** (1920–), professor of sociology, University of Virginia; **Reese J. McGee** (1929–), professor of sociology, Purdue University

1959, *Academic Procession,* p. 34.

When the students discover that the professor publishes, and gets good reviews, their receptiveness to his instruction is heightened. Learning is a voluntary act; the attitude of the students is decisive, and particularly so at the higher levels. The reputation of a professor profoundly affects their readiness to respond to his instruction.

—**Henry M. Wriston** (1889–1978),
President, Lawrence College;
President, Brown University

1965, "What makes a college good?," in *The Age of the Scholar,* p. 148.

[I]t is therefore necessary that he [the professor] be a scholar, that his scholarship shall have brought him a secure knowledge of his subject, that his knowledge be his own—alive and growing, and not a textbook's information—and that he have some ability, some method or artistry, to communicate both his learning and his enthusiasm for the field of his inquiry, and his

sense of its importance, to younger minds finding their way into that world illuminated by intellect where his own chief pleasure is found.

—**Nathan Pusey** (1907–2001),
President, Harvard University

1968, *The Academic Revolution,* p. 13.

College instructors have become less and less preoccupied with educating young people, more and more preoccupied with educating one another by doing scholarly research which advances their discipline.

—**Christopher Jencks** (1936–),
professor of social policy, Harvard University; **David Riesman** (1909–2002), professor of sociology, Harvard University

1982, speech at Engineering Dean's Institute, Salt Lake City, Utah, 29 March, attributed in Frank H. T. Rhodes, "The university and its critics," in William G. Bowen and Harold T. Shapiro (eds.), *Universities and Their Leadership,* 1998, p. 11.

Research is to teaching as sin is to confession. If you do not participate in the one, then you have nothing to say in the other.

—**John B. Slaughter** (1934–),
Chancellor, University of Maryland, College Park; President, Occidental College

1985, *Integrity in the College Curriculum,* p. 10.

Research, not teaching, pays off in enhanced reputation, respect of peers beyond one's own campus, and access to funds. The language of the academy is revealing: professors speak of teaching *loads* and research *opportunities,* never the reverse.

—**Association of American Colleges**

1990, *The University: An Owner's Manual,* p. 90.

A research-oriented faculty is less likely to be the home of intellectual deadwood. Active, lively, thoroughly current minds that enjoy debate and controversy make better teachers.

—**Henry Rosovsky** (1927–), Dean of the Faculty of Arts and Sciences, Harvard University

1992, *How Professors Play the Cat Guarding the Cream,* p. 11.

Faculty who teach undergraduates advance in rank, not on the basis of their competence in teaching, but on the basis of their contributions to knowledge through published research. And that is why *university teaching is the only profession in which you can become a success without satisfying the client.*

—**Richard M. Huber** (1922–), Dean of General Studies, Hunter College

1998, *The Pleasures of Academe,* p. 61.

Professors must have something to profess. They can pass on someone else's discoveries and hard-won knowledge at second or third hand—which all teachers must do to some extent—or they can present their own data, syntheses, and ways of viewing the world, gained by wrestling with the primary sources of the subject. To profess is to maintain a continuous search for new knowledge and to teach others not only what one has learned but how to do the research itself.

—**James Axtell** (1941–), professor of humanities, College of William and Mary

Scholar

c. 600, attributed in <http://www.understanding-islam.com/related/text.asp?type=question&qid=283>.

The ink of the scholar is more important than the blood of a martyr.

—**Muhammad** (c. 570–c. 632), Meccan spiritual leader

1601, "Of studies," in *The Essays or Counsels Civil and Moral.*

Studies serve for delight, for ornament, and for ability. Their chief use for delight, is in privateness and retiring; for ornament, is in discourse; and for ability, is in the judgment, and disposition of business. . . . To spend too much time in studies is sloth; to use them too much for ornament, is affectation; to make judgment wholly by their rules, is the humor of a scholar.

—**Francis Bacon** (1561–1626), English philosopher and statesman

no date, attributed in *Your Ultimate Success Quotation Library* (software program) at <http://www.cybernation.com/>.

The scholar without good breeding is a nitpicker; the philosopher a cynic; the soldier a brute and everyone else disagreeable.

—**Lord Chesterfield** (1694–1773), British statesman; author

no date, attributed in *Your Ultimate Success Quotation Library* (software program) at <http://www.cybernation.com/>.

People often become scholars for the same reason they become soldiers: simply because they are unfit for any other station. Their right hand has to earn them a livelihood; one might say they lie down like bears in winter and seek sustenance from their paws.

—**Georg C. Lichtenberg** (1742–1799), German physicist

1836, "On the conduct of life," *Literary Remains, Vol. 2,* p. 91.

It is the vice of scholars to suppose that there is no knowledge in the world but that of books.

—**William Hazlitt** (1778–1830), English essayist

1837, "The American scholar," delivered before the Phi Beta Kappa Society, at Cambridge, August 31, *Nature; Addresses and Lectures,* 1849.

The office of the scholar is to cheer, to raise, and to guide men by showing them facts amidst appearances.

—**Ralph Waldo Emerson** (1803–1882), U.S. poet, philosopher, and essayist

1839, *Hyperion,* book 1, chapter 8.

The mind of the scholar, if you would have it large and liberal, should come in contact with other minds. It is better that his armor should be somewhat bruised by rude encounters, even, than hang forever rusting on the wall.

—**Henry Wadsworth Longfellow** (1807–1882), professor of literature, Harvard University

1854, "Solitude," *Walden.*

A man thinking or working is always alone, let him be where he will. Solitude is not measured by the miles of space that intervene between a man and his fellows. The really diligent student in one of the crowded hives of Cambridge College is as solitary as a dervish in the desert.

—**Henry David Thoreau** (1817–1862), U.S. author

1855, *Journals,* quoted in Eugene Ehrlich and Marshall DeBruhl, *The International Thesaurus of Quotations,* 1996, p. 599.

A scholar is a man with this inconvenience, that, when you ask him his opinion on any matter, he must go home and look up his manuscripts to know.

—**Ralph Waldo Emerson** (1803–1882), U.S. poet, philosopher, and essayist

1858, *The Autocrat of the Breakfast Table,* chapter 6, p. 151.

The world's great men have not commonly been great scholars, nor its great scholars great men.

—**Oliver Wendell Holmes, Sr.** (1809–1894), author; professor of medicine, Harvard University

1898, *Educational Reform,* p. 231.

A university is a society of learned men, each a master in his field; each acquainted with what has been achieved in all past time in his special subject; each prepared to push forward a little the present limits of knowledge; each expecting and hoping to clear up some tangle or bog on the frontier, or to pierce, with his own little searchlight, if only by a hand's-breadth, the mysterious gloom which surrounds on every side the area of ascertained truth.

p. 233.

[T]he university develops a very peculiar and interesting kind of human being—the scientific specialist. The motives, hopes, and aims of the investigator . . . are different from those of ordinary humanity. . . . He is an intense and diligent worker; but the masses of mankind would think he was wasting his time. He eagerly desires what he calls results of investigation; but these results would seem to the populace to have no possible human interest.

—**Charles William Eliot** (1834–1926), President, Harvard University

1904, "Emerson," in *Critical Miscellanies,* Vol. I, p. 311.

This is ever the test of the scholar: whether he allows intellectual fastidiousness to stand between him and the great issues of his time.

—**John Morely** (1871–1908), British author

no date, attributed in "Wit of wisdom," *Wisdom,* 1956, October, p. 65.

An expert is one who knows more and more about less and less.

—**Nicholas Murray Butler** (1862–1947), President, Columbia University

1951, "Religion and the mind of the university," in Amos N. Wilder (ed.) *Liberal Learning and Religion,* pp. 154–5.

[T]he university professor is a fearful creature who knows that his sense of security and well-being hang on slender threads. The god of the university professor is specialized competence. His whole intellectual life is defined in terms of it and all the rest of his life is dependent upon it.

—**Bernard M. Loomer** (1912–1985), Dean, Divinity School, University of Chicago

no date, attributed in *Your Ultimate Success Quotation Library* (software program) at <http://www.cybernation. com/>.

By the worldly standards of public life, all scholars in their work are of course oddly virtuous. They do not make wild claims, they do not cheat, they do not try to persuade at any cost, they appeal neither to prejudice nor to authority, they are often frank about their ignorance, their disputes are fairly decorous, they do not confuse what is being argued with race, politics, sex or age, they listen patiently to the young and to the old who both know everything. These are the general virtues of scholarship, and they are peculiarly the virtues of science.

—**Jacob Bronowski** (1908–1974), British scientist; author

1963, quoted in Beverly Smith, Jr., "A Yank returns to Oxford," *Saturday Evening Post,* 23 March, p. 72.

[Senator William J.] Fulbright is responsible for the greatest movement of scholars across the face of the earth since the fall of Constantinople in 1453.

—**Ronald B. McCallum** (1898–1973), Master, Pembroke College, University of Oxford

1980, "The cleric of treason," in *George Steiner: A Reader,* 1984, pp. 197–98.

The absolute scholar is in fact a rather uncanny being. . . . A man will invest his sum of living in the study of Sumerian potsherds, in the vertiginous attempt to classify the dung beetles of one corner of New Guinea, in a study of the mating patterns of wood lice, in the biography of a single writer or statesman, in the synthesis of one chemical substance, in the grammar of a dead language. . . . To the utmost scholar, sleep is a puzzle of wasted time, and flesh a piece of torn luggage that the spirit must drag after it. . . . It is indeed a daunting and haunted business.

—**George Steiner** (1929–), professor of comparative literature, University of Oxford

no date, attributed in *Your Ultimate Success Quotation Library* (software program) at <http://www.cybernation. com/>.

I am an old scholar, better looking now than when I was young. That's what sitting on your ass does for your face.

> —**Leonard Cohen** (1934–), Canadian songwriter, musician, and writer

Scholarship

no date, attributed in *Your Ultimate Success Quotation Library* (software program) at <http://www.cybernation. com/>.

True scholarship consists in knowing not what things exist, but what they mean; it is not memory but judgment.

> —**James Russell Lowell** (1819–1891), professor of literature, Harvard University

1894, "The study of literature; Fragments from the lectures of Professor Lowell," *Harvard Crimson,* quoted in Lawrence R. Veysey, *The Emergence of the American University,* 1965, p. 201.

Mere scholarship is as useless as the collecting of old postage stamps.

> —**James Russell Lowell** (1819–1891), professor of literature, Harvard University

1903, "Maxims for revolutionists," *Man and Superman.*

A learned man is an idler who kills time with study. Beware of his false knowledge: it is more dangerous than ignorance.

1903, "Maxims for revolutionists," *Man and Superman.*

At the University every great treatise is postponed until its author attains impartial judgment and perfect knowledge. If a horse could wait as long for its shoes and would pay for them in advance, our blacksmiths would all be college dons.

> —**George Bernard Shaw** (1856–1950), Irish playwright

1907, "The present dilemma in philosophy," *Pragmatism.*

Whatever universe a professor believes in must at any rate be a universe that lends itself to lengthy discourse. A universe definable in two sentences is something for which the professorial intellect has no use. No faith in anything of that cheap kind!

> —**William James** (1842–1910), professor of philosophy, Harvard University

1923, *Report for 1922–23,* quoted in Edward C. Elliott (ed.), *The Rise of a University, Vol. II,* 1937, p. 249.

In a commercial sense it is true that the higher and finer scholarship does not pay. When measured by the standard of intellectual and spiritual values, on the other hand, few things bring richer reward than scholarship. Its possession is a constant source of joy and satisfaction, and the power which invisibly flows from it is of untold benefit to all men.

> —**Nicholas Murray Butler** (1862–1947), President, Columbia University

1933, "Polymaths: Technicians, specialists, and genius," *Sigma Xi Quarterly,* September, pp. 97–98.

[T]here is such a thing as specialization, and also such a thing as narrow specialization. We not only have 'scientists,' we have 'chemists.' We not only have 'chemists,' we have 'colloid chemists.' We not only have 'colloid chemists,' we have 'inorganic colloid chemists.' We not only have 'inorganic colloid chemists,' we have 'aerosol inorganic colloid chemists,' we have 'high temperature aerosol inorganic colloid chemists,' and so on indefinitely until the scientist is fractionated to a single paragraph of his doctor's thesis.

—**Charles S. Slichter** (1864–1946), graduate Dean, University of Wisconsin

1950, "A modest proposal for some stress on scholarship in graduate training," Address before the Graduate Convocation, Brown University, 3 June, Brown University Papers XXIV.

Once the taste for it [scholarship] has been aroused, it gives a sense of largeness even to one's small quests, and a sense of fullness even to the small answers to problems large or small which it yields, a sense which can never in any other way be attained, for which no other source of human gratification can, to the addict, be a satisfying substitute, which gains instead of loses in quality and quantity in pleasure-yielding capacity by being shared with others—and which, unlike golf, improves with age.

—**Jacob Viner** (1892–1970), professor of economics, Princeton University

no date, attributed in *Your Ultimate Success Quotation Library* (software program) at <http://www.cybernation. com/>.

The ceaseless, senseless demand for original scholarship in a number of fields, where only erudition is now possible, has led either to sheer irrelevancy, the famous knowing of more and more about less and less, or to the development of pseudo-scholarship which actually destroys its object.

—**Hannah Arendt** (1906–1975), U.S. political philosopher

1961, *New York Herald Tribune,* 1 January, quoted in James B. Simpson, *Simpson's Contemporary Quotations,* 1988.

Scholarship is polite argument.

—**Philip Rieff** (1922–), professor of sociology, University of Pennsylvania

1966, "The university," *The New Republic,* May 28, p. 19.

The search for truth proceeds best if it is inspired by wonder and curiosity, if, that is to say, it is disinterested—if the scholar disregards all secondary considerations of how his knowledge may be applied, how it can be sold, whether it is useful, whether it is good or bad, respectable, fashionable, moral, popular and patriotic; whether it will work or whether it will make men happier or unhappier, whether it is agreeable or disagreeable, whether it is likely to win him a promotion or a prize or decoration, whether it will get him a good vote in the Gallup poll. Genius is most likely to expand the limits of our knowledge, on which the applied sciences depend, when it works in a condition of total unconcern with the consequences of its own findings.

—**Walter Lippman** (1889–1974), U.S. editor and author

1987, *College,* p. 131.

Scholarship is not an esoteric appendage; it is at the heart of what the profession is all about. All faculty, throughout their careers, should, themselves, remain students.

—**Ernest L. Boyer** (1928–1995), Chancellor, State University of New York

1990, *Scholarship Reconsidered,* p. 16.

[T]he work of the professoriate might be thought of as having four separate, yet overlapping, functions. These are: the scholarship of *discovery;* the scholarship of *in-*

tegration; the scholarship of *application;* and the scholarship of *teaching.*

—**Ernest L. Boyer** (1928–1995), Chancellor, State University of New York

1992, "Sexual personae: The canceled preface," *Sex, Art, and American Culture,* p. 120.

American universities are organized on the principle of the nuclear rather than the ex-tended family. Graduate students are grimly trained to be technicians rather than connoisseurs. The old German style of universal scholarship has gone.

—**Camille Paglia** (1947–), professor of humanities, University of the Arts

Chapter 6

Teaching

Canon

1820, *Western Review* (Cincinnati), quoted in R. Freeman Butts, *The College Charts Its Course,* p. 117.

Should the time ever come when Latin and Greek should be banished from our Universities, and the study of Cicero and Demosthenes, of Homer and Virgil should be considered as unnecessary for the formation of a scholar, we should regard mankind as fast sinking into absolute barbarism, and the gloom of mental darkness as likely to increase until it should become universal.

—**Author Unknown**

1885, *Educational Reform: Essays and Addresses,* p. 142.

[F]ree choice implies that there are no studies which are recognized as of supreme merit, so that every young man unquestionably ought to pursue them. Can this be? Is it possible that the accumulated wisdom of the race cannot prescribe with certainty the studies which will best develop the human mind in general between the ages of eighteen and twenty-two? At first it certainly seems strange that we have to answer no; but when we reflect how very brief the acquaintance of the race has been with the great majority of the subjects which are now taught in a university the negative answer seems less surprising.

—**Charles William Eliot** (1834–1926), President, Harvard University

1916, *Report for 1915–16,* quoted in Edward. C. Elliott (ed.) *The Rise of a University, Vol. II,* 1937, p. 221.

No educational substitute for Greek and Latin has ever been found, and none will be found so long as our present civilization endures, for the simple reason that to study Greek and Latin under wise and inspiring guidance is to study the embryology of the civilization which we call European and American.

—**Nicholas Murray Butler** (1862–1947), president, Columbia University

1930, "The American fear of literature," Nobel Prize address, 12 December, quoted in Tony Augarde, *The Oxford Dictionary of Modern Quotations,* 1991, p. 137.

Our American professors like their literature clear and cold and pure and very dead.

—**Sinclair Lewis** (1885–1951), U.S. author

1936, *The Higher Learning in America,* p. 59.

Unless students and professors (and particularly professors) have a common intellectual training, a university must remain a series of disparate schools and departments, united by nothing except the fact that they have the same president and board of trustees. Professors cannot talk to one another, not at least about anything important. They cannot hope to understand one another.

p. 78.

A book is a classic that is contemporary in every age. That is why it is a classic. . . . Such books are then a part, and a large part, of the permanent studies. They are so in the first place because they are the best books we know. How can we call a man educated who has not read any of the great books of the western world?

> **—Robert Maynard Hutchins**
> (1899–1977), President,
> University of Chicago

1940, *Memory Hold-the-Door,* p. 34.

This preoccupation with the classics was the happiest thing that could have befallen me. It gave me a standard of values. To live for a time close to great minds is the best kind of education.

> **—John Buchan** (1875–1940),
> British statesman, Chancellor,
> Edinburgh University

1944, *Teacher in America,* p. 316.

[L]et us be clear about the role of the classics: they are worth studying as examples of *how* to think, not of *what* to think.

> **—Jacques Barzun** (1907–),
> Dean of Faculties and Provost,
> Columbia University

1947, *Higher Education for American Democracy, Vol. 1,* pp. 48–9.

The failure to provide any core of unity in the essential diversity of higher education is a cause for grave concern. A society whose numbers lack a body of common experience and common knowledge is a society without a fundamental culture; it tends to disintegrate into a mere aggregation of individuals. Some community of values, ideas, and attitudes is essential as a cohesive force in this age of minute division of labor and intense conflict of special interests.

> **—President's Commission
> on Higher Education**

1948, "Morals, religion, and higher education," *Freedom, Education, and the Fund,* 1956, p. 99.

In order to communicate with one another, the members of the community must understand one another, and this means that they must have a common language and a common stock of ideas. Any system of education that is based on the training of individual differences is fraudulent in this sense. The primary object of education should be to bring out our common humanity. For though men are different, they are also the same, and their common humanity, rather than their individual differences, requires development today as at no earlier era in history.

pp. 99–100.

The Great Conversation began with the Greeks, the Hebrews, the Hindus, and the Chinese and has continued to the present day. . . . There may be many ways in which a college or university can continue the Great Conversation, but it would seem offhand that one of the best ways is through the reading and discussion by all the students of the books in which the Great Conversation has been carried on by the greatest men who have taken part in it. . . .

To continue and enrich the Great Conversation is the object of higher education.

—**Robert Maynard Hutchins**
(1899–1977), President,
University of Chicago

1952, *The Great Conversation,* p. 1.

The tradition of the West is embodied in the Great Conversation that began in the dawn of history and that continues to the present day. . . . No other civilization can claim that its defining characteristic is a dialogue of this sort . . . No dialogue in any other civilization can compare with that of the West in the number of great works of the mind that have contributed to this dialogue. The goal toward which Western society moves is the Civilization of the Dialogue.

—**Robert Maynard Hutchins**
(1899–1977), President,
University of Chicago

1966, *The Reforming of General Education,* p. 145.

There is not, I believe, in education—and perhaps not in life—a quota of eternal verities, a set of invariant truths, a single quadrivium and trivium that must be taught to a young man lest he be charged with the failure to be civilized or humane.

—**Daniel Bell** (1919–), professor of sociology, Columbia University; Harvard University

1992, *Loose Canons,* p. 35.

The return of "the" canon, the high canon of Western masterpieces, represents the return of an order in which my people were the subjugated, the voiceless, the invisible, the underrepresented and the unrepresent-able. Who would return us to that medieval never-never land?

p. 113.

Since the trivium and quadrivium of the Latin Middle Ages, "the humanities" has *not* meant the best that has been taught by all human beings; rather "the humanities" has meant the best that has been taught by white males in the Greco-Roman, Judeo-Christian traditions. A tyrannical pun obtains between the word *humanity,* on the one hand, and *humanities,* on the other.

—**Henry Louis Gates** (1950–),
professor of humanities,
Harvard University

1996, *The Opening of the American Mind,* p. 78.

[T]he classical canon in American colleges was a much-amended reproduction of a medieval curriculum which itself had already been seriously revised first during the Renaissance and then during its English adaption at Oxford and Cambridge. . . . The only truly permanent element in the classical American canon was the belief in its inspired timelessness.

p. 98.

The debate over the canon has been dominated by the fear that the canon is finite; add something and something else must be deleted. . . . [I]f there ever was a time when universities could teach the entire canon, or even the entire canon in any single subject area, that time has long since passed. . . .

—**Lawrence W. Levine** (1933–),
professor of history,
University of California, Berkeley

Culture Wars

1987, press release from Stanford University News Service, 16 January, quoted in Donald Kennedy, *Academic Duty,* 1997, p. 9.

Hey, hey, ho, ho, Western culture's got to go.

—**Stanford University students**

1988, *ProfScam,* p. 188.

Much of the push for dismantling the foundations of liberal education is based on political arguments: The traditional authors are too white, too male, too old, and too hard.

—**Charles J. Sykes** (1954–), U.S. journalist

1989, "Peace plan for the culture war," *The Nation,* March, p. 310, in James L. Nolan, Jr., *The American Culture Wars,* p. 8.

[C]urriculum is a microcosm of the culture; its inclusions and exclusions are an index of what the culture deems important. A conflict over 'the canon,' over what books to teach and how to teach them, is conflict over society's vision of itself.

—**Gerald Graff** (1937–), professor of English, Northwestern University; **William E. Cain** (1952–), professor of English, Wellesley College

1989, speech to the entering class, quoted in Nat Hentoff, *Free Speech for Me—but Not for Thee,* 1992, p. 132.

On some other campuses in this country, values of civility and community have been offered by some as paramount values of the university, even to the point of superseding freedom of expression. Such a

view is wrong in principle, and if extended, disastrous to freedom of thought.

—**Benno Schmidt** (1942–), President, Yale University

1990, "On differences," presidential address, Modern Language Association, *PMLA,* May, 1991, p. 404.

[M]ulticulturalism promises to bring dignity to the dispossessed and self-empowerment to the disempowered, to recuperate the texts and traditions of ignored groups, to broaden cultural history.

—**Catharine R. Stimpson** (1936–), Dean of the Graduate School, Rutgers University

1991, "Multiculturalism: An exchange," *American Scholar,* Spring, p. 268.

No longer can the structures of knowledge which supported white hegemony be defended: whites must take their place, not above or below, but alongside the rest of humanity.

—**Molefi Kete Asante** (1942–), professor of African American studies, Temple University

1991, *Illiberal Education,* p. 92.

Not only does the new multiculturalism deprive students of an opportunity for learning about themselves and others, but it distorts other cultures and peoples and makes future global understanding more difficult.

p. 229.

[I]nstead of a liberal education, what American students are getting is its diametrical opposite, an education in close-mindedness and intolerance, which is to say, illiberal education.

—**Dinesh D'Souza** (1961–), writer and policy analyst

1992, *How Professors Play the Cat Guarding the Cream,* p. 41.

Historical perspective helps our understanding of the curricular wars. Professor-bashing for inculcating subversive doctrines into innocent minds is as old as Socrates, as yesterday as McCarthyism, and as today as beliefs termed "politically correct."

—**Richard M. Huber** (1922–), Dean of General Studies, Hunter College

1992, *Loose Canons,* p. 108.

The rhetoric of liberal education remains suffused with the imagery of possession, patrimony, legacy, lineage, inheritance— call it cultural geneticism. . . .

p. 127.

[O]ur subject [African-American Studies] is open to all—whether to study or to teach. After all, the fundamental premise of the academy is that all things ultimately are knowable; all therefore are teachable. What would we say to a person who said that we couldn't teach Milton because we are not Anglo-Saxon, or male, or heterosexual—or blind!

—**Henry Louis Gates** (1950–), professor of humanities, Harvard University

1992, *Give War a Chance,* p. xxi.

Liberals have invented whole college majors—psychology, sociology, women's studies—to prove that nothing is anybody's fault.

—**P. J. O'Rourke** (1947–), U.S. writer

1996, "For English departments, a major change," *Washington Post,* 30 December, p. D2.

The final piece of evidence that the lunatics are running the academic asylum is now firmly in place. . . . [V]ulgarity is everywhere in the English departments, which no longer require students to study works of literature chosen by scholars for their quality, importance and universality. Instead they let students pick and choose in an academic supermarket where "popular culture" and the Holy Trinity of "race, gender and class" are the dominant elements.

—**Jonathan Yardley** (1939–), journalist

1996, *The Opening of the American Mind,* p. 17.

Convinced by everything I know and have seen that the American academic world is doing a more thorough and cosmopolitan job of educating a greater diversity of students in a broader and sounder array of courses covering the past and present of the worlds they inhabit than ever before in its history, I walk through the Looking Glass and find myself surrounded by those who see our enterprise as unhealthy and unreliable, built not on the solid foundations of serious inquiry and innovative approaches but on the sands of fashion and politics and coercion.

—**Lawrence W. Levine** (1933–), professor of history, University of California, Berkeley

Curriculum

no date, attributed in *Your Ultimate Success Quotation Library* (software program) at <http://www.cybernation. com/>.

Most subjects at universities are taught for no other purpose than that they may be retaught when the students become teachers.

—**Georg C. Lichtenberg** (1742–1799), German physicist

1828, *Report of the Faculty, Part I,* quoted in Arthur Levine, *Handbook of Undergraduate Curriculum,* 1978, p. 545.

The two great points to be gained in intellectual culture, are the *discipline* and the *furniture* of the mind; expanding its powers, and storing it with knowledge. . . . All this is not to be effected by a light and hasty course of study; by reading a few books, hearing a few lectures, and spending some months at a literary institution. The habits of thinking are to be formed, by long continued and close application.

—**Faculty of Yale College**

1841, *On Heroes, Hero-Worship, and the Heroic.*

If we think of it, all that a University, or final highest School can do for us, is still but what the first School began doing,—teach us to *read.* We learn to *read,* in various languages, in various sciences; we learn the alphabet and letters of all manner of Books. But the place where we are to get knowledge, is the Books themselves! It depends on what we read, after all manner of Professors have done their best for us. The true University of these days is a Collection of Books.

—**Thomas Carlyle** (1795–1881),
Scottish historian and
political philosopher

1869, Inaugural Address, 19 October, in *A Turning Point in Higher Education,* 1969, p. 29.

The endless controversies whether language, philosophy, mathematics, or science supplies the best mental training, whether general education should be chiefly literary or chiefly scientific, have no practical lesson for us today. This University recognizes no real antagonism between literature and science, and consents to no such narrow alternatives as mathematics or classics,

science or metaphysics. We would have them all, and at their best.

—**Charles William Eliot** (1834–1926),
President, Harvard College

1896, "Quarterly statement," cited in Richard J. Storr, *Harper's University,* 1966, p. 180.

[T]he athletic field, like the gymnasium, is one of the University's laboratories and by no means the least important one.

—**William Rainey Harper** (1856–1906),
President, University of Chicago

1907, letter to C. F. Adams, 21 October, quoted in Lawrence R. Veysey, *The Emergence of the American University,* 1965, p. 90.

I have often said that if I were compelled to have one required subject in Harvard college, I would make it dancing if I could.

—**Charles William Eliot** (1834–1926),
president, Harvard University

no date, attributed in <http://www.quotationspage.com//search.php3>.

Changing a college curriculum is like moving a graveyard—you never know how many friends the dead have until you try to move them!

—**Woodrow Wilson** (1856–1924),
President, Princeton University;
President of the United States

1922, *The Days of a Man,* quoted in R. Freeman Butts, *The College Charts Its Course,* 1939, p. 199.

Higher education should thus foster divergence instead of conformity, its function being not to bring youths to a predetermined standard, but to help each make the most of his inborn talents. A prearranged course of study is like ready-made clothing, fitting nobody in particular; it is the acme of educational laziness.

—**David Starr Jordan** (1851–1931),
President, Stanford University

1927, *Life and the Student,* p. 179.

I should advise a boy who is ambitious for culture to go to college, if he can, for the sake of leisure, books and possibly inspiring persons. The curriculum is not to be taken too seriously; let him follow a plan of his own, preferring courses in which he is encouraged to work his own way.

—**Charles Horton Cooley** (1864–1929),
professor of sociology,
University of Michigan

1927, "What college did to me," in *The Early Worm.*

In my day . . . a student could elect to take any courses in the catalogue, provided no two of his courses came at the same hour. The only thing we were not supposed to mix was scotch and gin. This was known as the elective system.

—**Robert Benchley** (1889–1945),
U.S. author and humorist

no date, attributed in August Kerber, *Quotable Quotes on Education,* 1968, p. 224.

The catalogue of a progressive institution of higher learning resembles nothing so much as a similar catalogue annually issued by Sears, Roebuck and Company.

—**Everett Dean Martin** (1880–1941),
social psychologist;
adult educator, Cooper Union

1929, *The Aims of Education and Other Essays,* Chapter One.

There is only one subject-matter for education, and that is Life in all its manifestations.

Chapter Two.

A well-planned University course is a study of the wide sweep of generality. . . .

—**Alfred North Whitehead**
(1861–1947), English philosopher and mathematician; professor of philosophy, Harvard University

1935, *McGill News,* quoted in Edgar W. Knight, *Fifty Years of American Education,* 1952, p. 128.

The colleges have gotten away from their original mission. They began as places of piety and learning. They did not teach people how to make money. . . . The college did not teach men a career. . . . But the colleges were supposed to fit men to die; there are no courses in this subject now. . . . Back to the Latin grammar with them. Make them learn the passive subjunctive of a deponent verb. Then they will be ready to die, and thus, since all life moves at back rounds, worthy to live.

—**Stephen Butler Leacock**
(1869–1944), professor of political economy, McGill University

1936, *The Higher Learning in America,* p. 29.

[F]ine associations, fine buildings, green grass, good food, and exercise are excellent things for anybody. You will note that they are exactly what is advertised by every resort hotel. The only reason why they are also advertised by every college and university is that we have no coherent educational program to announce.

p. 95.

The modern university may be compared with an encyclopedia. The encyclopedia contains many truths. It may consist of nothing else. But its unity can be found only in its alphabetical arrangement. The university is in much the same case. It has departments running from art to zoology;

but neither the students nor the professors know what is the relationship of one departmental truth to another, or what the relationship of departmental truths to those in the domain of another department may be.

—**Robert Maynard Hutchins**
(1899–1977), President,
University of Chicago

1939, *Too Much College,* pp. 137–38.

These [new] courses are carried along as a dead weight, like the barnacles that gather at the bottom of a sailing ship. The only purpose that they serve is to enable young people to come to college who could never have done so in the sterner days of the old-time curriculum—young men who can study tap dancing and social behavior but not Latin and physics; young women who can't learn algebra but can manage archery; and young people of both sexes whose minds are nicely fitted to a course on *Theory and Practice of Badminton,* or a course on *Marriage,* open only to seniors and pursued intensively in the spring quarter.

—**Stephen Butler Leacock**
(1869–1944), professor of political economy, McGill University

1943, *Liberal Education,* p. 108.

The college is meaningless without a curriculum, but it is more so when it has one that is meaningless.

p. 114.

A curriculum creates a world. It is important then that it have a center and an order or parts. Some studies are surely secondary to others, as some rest on others as a base. This should be made manifest, and no student should be permitted to ignore the primary, the basic matter.

—**Mark Van Doren** (1894–1972),
professor of English,
Columbia University

1943, *Education for Freedom,* p. 26.

The crucial error is that of holding that nothing is any more important than anything else, that there can be no order of goods and no order in the intellectual realm. There is nothing central and nothing peripheral, nothing primary and nothing secondary, nothing basic and nothing superficial. The course of study goes to pieces because there is nothing to hold it together. Triviality, mediocrity, and vocationalism take it over because we have no standard by which to judge them. We have little to offer as a substitute for a sound curriculum except talk of personality, "character," and great teachers, the slogans of educational futilitarianism.

—**Robert Maynard Hutchins**
(1899–1977), President,
University of Chicago

1951, "The democratic dilemma,"
Freedom, Education, and the Fund,
1956, p. 133.

A university student in America may be able to elect almost any courses he chooses. . . . This means that the student will elect those courses which are the easiest, or which are offered at the most convenient times and places. I once knew a student who boasted that he had graduated from college without taking any course that was offered above the first floor.

—**Robert Maynard Hutchins**
(1899–1977), President,
University of Chicago

1955, "Undergraduates on apron strings,"
Atlantic Monthly, October, p. 45.

I want to argue an unpopular cause: the cause of the old, free elective system in the academic world, or the untrammeled right of the undergraduate to make his own mistakes.

—Howard Mumford Jones
(1892–1980), professor of humanities,
Harvard University

1961, "Preface," *The Higher Learning in America,* p. xiii.

One of the easiest things in the world is to assemble a list of hilarious courses offered in the colleges and universities of the United States. Such courses reflect the total lack of coherent, rational purpose in these institutions.

—Robert Maynard Hutchins
(1899–1977), President,
University of Chicago

1962, *The American College,* p. 425.

[A]ll curricula either favor or hamper personality development, regardless of whether they were designed with such development in mind. . . .

—Nevitt R. Sanford (1909–1995),
professor of psychology and education,
Stanford University

1968, *The American University,* p. 71.

The belief that a curriculum can be devised and kept relevant to the present is an illusion. . . . What concerns (or "excites") one four-year generation will bore the next, as anyone can verify by reference to popular music. And so it is with literature, politics, and the current view of creeds and crises.

p. 216.

As for college courses, their range of subject matter is infinite from "Cosmetology" and "Advanced Ice-cream Making" to "The Pleasure Horse: Appreciation and Use," followed logically by "Blacksmith-

ing." After these, "Police Science" and "Fire Science" seem almost philosophical.

—Jacques Barzun (1907–), Dean of
Faculties and Provost,
Columbia University

no date, attributed in Keith Allan Noble, *The International Education Quotations Encyclopaedia,* 1995, p. 325.

They teach you anything in American universities today. You can major in mud pies.

—Orson Welles (1915–1985),
U.S. filmmaker

c. 1973, attributed in Thomas L. Martin, Jr., *Malice in Blunderland,* 1973, p. 23.

The number of courses in the catalogue is equal to twice the number of faculty. Corollary—At least one course listed by a faculty member will be his doctoral dissertation.

—Clark Kerr (1911–2003), Chancellor,
University of California, Berkeley;
President, University of California

1974, *Leadership and Ambiguity,* p. 104.

Academic "policy" is the accretion of hundreds of largely autonomous actions taken for different reasons, at different times, under different conditions, by different people in the college. This collection of actions is periodically codified into what is presented as an educational program by the college catalog or a student or faculty handbook.

—Michael D. Cohen (1945–), professor
of complex systems, information, and
public policy, University of Michigan;
James G. March (1928–), professor
of international management,
political science, and sociology,
Stanford University

1977, *Curriculum,* pp. 1–2.

Thinking about the curriculum historically presents many problems and requires a willingness to accept surprise, ambiguity, and a certain unavoidable messiness. If the world does not always make sense, why should the curriculum?

> —**Frederick Rudolph** (1920–),
> professor of history, Williams College

1977, *Missions of the College Curriculum,* p. 8.

[C]urricula are like huge beanbags that keep on being added to, bean by bean, as each new faculty member brings new courses with him or her, and these beanbags keep on reflecting, as they grow, the many impacts that come their way.

p. 18.

The curriculum is the major statement any institution makes about itself, about what it can contribute to the intellectual development of students, about what it thinks is important in its teaching service to society.

p. 30.

To a remarkable degree, the curricula of American colleges reflect the concerns of the general society and of the institutions that shape public opinion.

p. 164.

No curricular concept is as central to the endeavors of the American college as general education, and none is so exasperatingly beyond the reach of general consensus and understanding.

p. 185.

General education is that part of the undergraduate curriculum that permits a college or university, as an institution, to make a unique contribution to the education of its students. . . . No other effort to define the quality and character of the edu-cation to be offered is nearly as important as this one.

> —**Carnegie Foundation for the Advancement of Teaching**

1978, *Newsweek,* 29 May, p. 100.

A society that thinks the choice between ways of living is just a choice between equally eligible "lifestyles" turns universities into academic cafeterias offering junk food for the mind.

> —**George F. Will** (1941–),
> journalist and political commentator

1978, *Handbook on Undergraduate Curriculum,* p. xv.

Each week at the Brandeis Educational Policy Committee someone would insist that the future of the university rested on our dropping a given requirement or adding a proposed program. And each week we traded anecdotes and guesses about the effects of the proposals. The most compelling arguments were based on the experience of a relative or a friend or a friend of a relative at another school where the proposal or something like it had been adopted. Through the magic of parliamentary procedure, we were able to resolve the same issue at several consecutive meetings with any number of different conclusions. Everybody had an equal chance to win, and everyone did one week or another. But when a proposal went to the faculty for final approval, we all stood behind it. The faculty then repeated the same discussions that we had had and voted in their own way, basing their votes on their own feelings and their own anecdotes. And the resolutions that came out of the faculty meetings became educational policy.

> —**Arthur Levine** (1948–), President,
> Bradford College; President, Teachers
> College, Columbia University

1981, "The liberal arts revisited," in *Values, Leadership and Quality: The Administration of Higher Education,* 1990, p. 92.

It is the responsibility of universities to keep alive subjects and ideas that may not be fashionable, that may not be popular. . . . [I]f they are not to be preserved in universities, then that is a loss to civilization and a loss to the capacity and potential of generations to come, to education and scholarship in the future.

> —**Hanna Holborn Gray** (1930–),
> historian; President,
> University of Chicago

1985, *Integrity in the College Curriculum,* pp. 1–2.

Evidence of decline and devaluation is everywhere. . . . As for what passes as a college curriculum, almost anything goes. We have reached a point at which we are more confident about the length of a college education than its content and purpose.

> —**Association of American Colleges**

no date, attributed in <bemorecreative. com>.

As Oscar Wilde should have said, when bad ideas have nowhere else to go, they emigrate to America and become university courses.

> —**Frederick Raphael** (1931–),
> English novelist and screenwriter

no date, attributed in *Your Ultimate Success Quotation Library* (software program) at <http://www.cybernation. com/>.

I was planning to go into architecture. But when I arrived, architecture was filled up. Acting was right next to it, so I signed up for acting instead.

> —**Tom Selleck** (1945–), U.S. actor

1996, *The Opening of the American Mind,* p. 43.

Academic history in the United States . . . has not been a long happy voyage in a stable vessel characterized by blissful consensus about which subjects should form the indisputable curriculum; it has been marked by prolonged and often acrimonious struggle and debate, not very different from that which characterizes the academe [sic] in our own day.

> —**Lawrence W. Levine** (1933–),
> professor of history, University of
> California, Berkeley

Lecture

1781, in James Boswell, *Life of Samuel Johnson, 1791.*

Lectures were once useful; but now, when all can read, and books are so numerous, lectures are unnecessary. If your attention fails, and you miss a part of a lecture, it is lost; you cannot go back as you do upon a book.

> —**Samuel Johnson** (1709–1784),
> English author

1869, Inaugural Address, 19 October, in *A Turning Point in Higher Education,* 1969, p. 42.

There has been much discussion about the comparative merits of lectures and recitations. . . . Recitations alone readily degenerate into dusty repetitions, and lectures alone are too often a useless expenditure of force. The lecturer pumps laboriously into sieves. The water may be wholesome, but it runs through.

> —**Charles William Eliot** (1834–1926),
> President, Harvard University

1910, *Great American Universities,* p. 520.

As it is, the professors give too many lectures and the students listen to too many.

Or pretend to; really they do not listen, however attentive and orderly they may be. The bell rings and a troop of tired-looking boys, followed perhaps by a larger number of meek-eyed girls, file into the classroom, sit down, remove the expressions from their faces, open their notebooks on the broad chair arms, and receive. It is about as inspiring as a room full of phonographs holding up their brass trumpets.

—**Edwin E. Slosson** (1865–1929), chemist; U.S. writer

1912, *Report for 1911–12,* quoted in Edward C. Elliott (ed.), *The Rise of a University, Vol. II,* 1937, p. 169.

The habit of conveying information to college students by means of lectures is wholly deplorable. It is not only a waste of time, since the printed page would be far better than the spoken word, but it leads to unfortunate and undesirable intellectual habits on the part of the student.

—**Nicholas Murray Butler** (1862–1947), President, Columbia University

1914, *Arcadian Adventures with the Idle Rich.*

[He] was about to open his lecture, when one of his students rose in his seat and asked a question. It is a practice . . . which, I need hardly say, we do not encourage; the young man, I believe, was a newcomer in the philosophy class.

—**Stephen Butler Leacock** (1869–1944), professor of political economy, McGill University

1927, "Ideals for the development of Rollins College," *School and Society,* 6 August, p. 155.

The lecture system is probably the worst scheme ever devised for imparting knowledge. It assumes that what one man has taken perhaps a life-time to acquire by the most painstaking observation, hard thinking and long-continued reflection, can be relayed or spoon-fed to another man who has not gone through a like process.

—**Hamilton Holt** (1872–1951), President, Rollins College

1928, *Proper Studies,* pp. 169–70.

Lecturing as a method of instruction dates from classical and mediaeval times, before the invention of printing. When books were worth their weight in gold, professors had to lecture. Cheap printing has radically changed the situation which produced the lecturer of antiquity. And yet—preposterous anomaly!—the lecturer survives and even flourishes. In all the universities of Europe his voice still drones and brays just as it droned and brayed in the days of Duns Scotus and Thomas Aquinas. Lecturers are as much of an anachronism as bad drains or tallow candles; it is high time they were got rid of.

—**Aldous Huxley** (1894–1963), English writer

1944, *Teacher in America,* p. 31.

The man who yawned during his own lecture was correctly reproved by him who said: "The professor confirms our judgment but usurps our prerogative."

p. 37.

Lecturing comes so natural to mankind that it is hard to stop it by edict. It simply turns into bootleg form. Many teachers think that because they sit around a table with only a dozen students they are running a discussion group, but they are lecturing just the same if the stream of discourse flows in only one direction.

—**Jacques Barzun** (1907–), Dean of Faculties and Provost, Columbia University

no date, attributed in <www. famous-quotations.com>.

Some people talk in their sleep. Lecturers talk while other people sleep.

—**Albert Camus** (1913–1960),
French existentialist writer

no date, attributed in Keith Allan Noble, *The International Education Quotations Encyclopaedia,* 1995.

Professors simply can't discuss a thing. Habit compels them to deliver a lecture.

—**Harold V. (Hal) Boyle** (1911–1974),
U.S. journalist

Liberal Arts

no date, *Espitulae Ex Ponto,* bk. 2, quoted in *The Columbia World of Quotations,* 1996.

[A] faithful study of the liberal arts humanizes character and permits it not to be cruel.

—**Ovid [Publius Ovidius Naso]**
(43 B.C.E.–c. 17), Roman poet

1930, "The liberal arts," *Association of American Colleges Bulletin,* p. 337.

The liberal arts, we say, are the liberalizing arts, the studies that liberate the mind and send it questing on strange and alluring adventures.

—**Alfred H. Upham** (1877–1945),
President, University of Idaho; President,
Miami University (Ohio)

1943, *Liberal Education,* p. 75.

Life is monotonous. The arts, and especially the liberal arts, know what to make of the fact; how much to accept and dignify it with duties, how much to defy it or correct it with pleasure, pretense, play, and speculation. . . . When the liberal arts fail to do their work, civilization has become a disease. When they are dismissed as a luxury, practical affairs suffer the consequence. They are the most practical possessions men have. . . .

p. 79.

The subject matter of the liberal arts is life.

—**Mark Van Doren** (1894–1972),
professor of English,
Columbia University

1943, *Education for Freedom,* p. 14.

The liberal arts are the arts of freedom. To be free a man must understand the tradition in which he lives. A great book is one which yields up through the liberal arts a clear and important understanding of our tradition.

—**Robert Maynard Hutchins**
(1899–1977), President,
University of Chicago

1944, "The problem of the liberal arts college," *American Scholar,* p. 393.

The problem of securing to the liberal arts college its due function in democratic society is that of seeing to it that the technical subjects which are now socially necessary acquire a humane direction.

—**John Dewey** (1859–1952), professor
of philosophy, Columbia University

1952, *The Great Conversation,* pp. 4–5.

The method of liberal education is the liberal arts, and the result of a liberal education is discipline in those arts. . . . As we live in the tradition, whether we know it or not, so we are all liberal artists, whether we know it or not. We all practice the liberal arts, well or badly, all the time every day. . . . The liberal arts are not merely indispensable; they are unavoidable. Nobody can decide for himself whether he is going to be a human being. The only question open to him is whether he will be an ignorant, undeveloped one or one who has sought to reach the highest point he is capable of attaining. The question, in short, is whether he will be a poor liberal artist or a good one.

> **—Robert Maynard Hutchins**
> (1899–1977), President,
> University of Chicago

1977, *Curriculum,* p. 30.

The medieval universities organized and divided seven liberal arts into the *quadrivium* (arithmetic, geometry, astronomy, music), which was of a lower order than the *trivium* (logic, grammar, and rhetoric). . . . These basic studies provided the intellectual equipment that allowed the medieval university student to move into a study of the three philosophies of Aristotle: natural philosophy (physics), moral philosophy (ethics), and mental philosophy (metaphysics).

> **—Frederick Rudolph** (1920–),
> professor of history, Williams College

no date, attributed in <http://quote garden.com/college.html>.

A liberal-arts education is supposed to provide you with a value system, a standard, a set of ideas, not a job.

> **—Caroline Bird** (1915–), U.S. author

Liberal Education

1825, inaugural address, in LeRoy J. Halsey, *The Works of Philip Lindsley, D.D.,* 1866, quoted in Frederick Rudolph, *The American College and University: A History,* 1962, p. 214.

I affirm . . . that every individual, who wishes to rise above the level of a mere labourer at task-work, ought to endeavor to obtain a liberal education.

> **—Philip Lindsley** (1786–1855),
> President, University of Nashville

1858, *The Idea of a University,* Discourse V.

[L]iberal Education, viewed in itself, is simply the cultivation of the intellect, as such, and its object is nothing more or less than intellectual excellence. . . . The artist puts before him beauty of feature and form; the poet, beauty of mind; the preacher, the beauty of grace; then intellect too, I repeat, has its beauty, and it has those who aim at it.

Discourse VII.

The process of training, by which the intellect, instead of being formed or sacrificed to some particular or accidental purpose, some specific trade or profession, or study or science, is disciplined for its own sake, for the perception of its own proper object, and for its own higher culture, is called Liberal Education; . . . And to set forth the right standard, and to train according to it, and to help forward all students toward it according to their various capacities, this I conceive to be the business of a University.

Discourse VII.

If then the intellect is so excellent a portion of us, and its cultivation so excellent, it is not only beautiful, perfect, admirable, and noble in itself, but in a true and high sense it must be useful to the possessor and to all around him; not useful in any low, mechanical, mercantile sense, but as diffusing good, or as a blessing, or a gift, or power, or a treasure, first to the owner, then through him to the world. I say then, if a liberal education be good, it must necessarily be useful too.

> **—John Henry (Cardinal) Newman**
> (1801–1890), Rector,
> Catholic University of Ireland

1882, *Report for 1881–82,* quoted in William F. Russell (ed.), *The Rise of a University, Vol. I,* 1937, p. 352.

It is not . . . a reproach to collegiate education that it is not practical. It is only a mistake to suppose that it ought to be practical.

—**Frederick A. P. Barnard**
(1809–1889), President,
Columbia University

1907, quoted in Henrietta A. Huxley (ed.), *Aphorisms and Reflections,* #89, pp. 9–10.

That man, I think, has had a liberal education who has been so trained in youth that his body is the ready servant of his will, and does with ease and pleasure all the work that, as a mechanism, it is capable of; whose intellect is a clear, cold logic engine, with all its parts of equal strength and in smooth working order; ready, like a steam engine, to be turned to any kind of work, and spin the gossamers as well as forge the anchors of the mind. . . .

—**T. H. Huxley** (1825–1895),
British biologist and educator

1917, *Why Go to College,* p. 19.

[A] liberal education is one which liberates, releases the soul from the little, the provincial, the immediate, and makes us citizens of the world and so at home in any part of the world to which duty may call us.

—**William H. P. Faunce** (1859–1930),
President, Brown University

1925, *Report for 1924–25,* quoted in Edward C. Elliott (ed.), *The Rise of a University, Vol. II,* 1937, p. 324.

A liberal education is one that is fit for a free man who is worthy of his freedom. . . . The notion that intensive and very accurate knowledge of a narrow field, and nothing

more, can constitute a liberally educated man, is a grotesque absurdity.

—**Nicholas Murray Butler**
(1862–1947), President,
Columbia University

1930, *Fifteen Minutes a Day: The Reading Guide,* p. 8.

The best acquisition of a cultivated man is a liberal frame of mind or way of thinking; but there must be added to that possession acquaintance with the prodigious store of recorded discoveries, experiences, and reflections which humanity in its intermittent and irregular progress from barbarism to civilization has acquired and laid up. Liberal education accomplishes two objectives. It produces a liberal frame of mind, and it makes the studious and reflective recipient acquainted with the stream of the world's thought and feeling, and with the infinitely varied products of the human imagination.

—**Charles William Eliot** (1834–1926),
President, Harvard University

1943, *Liberal Education,* p. 65.

Liberal education is nothing if not practical. It studies an art, or a system of arts, designed both by nature and by man to secure that human beings shall be precisely and permanently human.

p. 67.

The aim of a liberal education is one's own excellence, the perfection of one's own intellectual character; not merely to know or to do, but also, indeed chiefly, to be.

—**Mark Van Doren** (1894–1972),
professor of English,
Columbia University

1952, *The Great Conversation,* p. 3.

The aim of liberal education is human excellence, both private and public (for man is a political animal). Its object is the excellence of man as man and man as citizen. It regards man as an end, not as a means; and it regards the ends of life, and not the means to it. For this reason it is the education of free men.

—**Robert Maynard Hutchins** (1899–1977), President, University of Chicago

1954, *Time,* quoted in Jonathon Green, *Morrow's International Dictionary of Contemporary Quotations,* 1982, p. 361.

The true business of a liberal education is greatness.

—**Nathan Pusey** (1907–2001), President, Harvard University

no date, attributed in Ned Sherrin, *The Oxford Dictionary of Humorous Quotations,* 1995, p. 105.

I read Shakespeare and the Bible and I can shoot dice. That's what I call a liberal education.

—**Tallulah Bankhead** (1903–1968), U.S. actress

no date, attributed in Keith Allan Noble, *The International Education Quotations Encyclopaedia,* 1995.

A liberal education . . . frees a man from the prison-house of his class, race, time, place, background, family, and even his nation.

—**Robert Maynard Hutchins** (1899–1977), President, University of Chicago

1964, Commencement Address, 31 May, quoted in James B. Simpson, *Simpson's Contemporary Quotations,* 1988.

Any education that matters is liberal. All the saving truths, all the healing graces that distinguish a good education from a bad one or a full education from a half empty one are contained in that word.

—**Alan Simpson** (1912–1998), President, Vassar College

1966, *The Reforming of General Education,* p. 8.

When a subject is presented as received doctrine or fact, it becomes an aspect of specialization and technique. When it is introduced with an awareness of its contingency and of the conceptual frame that guides its organization, the student can then proceed with the necessary self-consciousness that keeps his mind open to possibility and to reorientation. All knowledge, thus, is liberal (that is, it enlarges and liberates the mind) when it is committed to continuing inquiry.

p. 152.

The university cannot remake a world (although in upholding standards it plays some part in such attempts). It cannot even remake men. But it can liberate young people by making them aware of the forces that impel them from within and constrict them from without.

—**Daniel Bell** (1919–), professor of sociology, Columbia University; Harvard University

1969, "Women and Creativity, *Motive,* quoted in Rosalie Maggio, *The Beacon Book of Quotations by Women,* 1992, p. 96.

It is the function of a liberal university not to give the right answers, but to ask the right questions.

—**Cynthia Ozick** (1928–), U.S. author

no date, attributed in <www.creative quotations.com>.

The primary purpose of a liberal education is to make one's mind a pleasant place to spend one's leisure.

—**Sydney J. Harris** (1917–1986),
U.S. journalist and author

1974, "So brief a time," *Yale Alumni Magazine,* June, p. 9.

From the perspective of today, it seems to me that my courses at Yale were thoroughly practical. For they have stayed with me for a lifetime, and what could be more practical than that?

—**Louis Auchincloss** (1917–),
U.S. lawyer; writer

1975, *The Case Against College,* p. 109.

Intellectuals have trouble describing the benefits of a liberal education because the liberal arts are a religion, the established religion of the ruling class. . . . As with religion, no proof is required, only faith.

—**Caroline Bird** (1915–), U.S. author

1978, "A promise of lifelong discontent," *Swarthmore College Bulletin,* p. 2, quoted in Ernest L. Boyer, *College: The Undergraduate Experience in America,* 1987, p. 101.

If you have a liberal education . . . you will live at more than one level. You won't simply respond passively to events, and you won't be concerned about them *only* personally. At least sometimes you will see your fate, whatever it is, as an illustration of the human condition and the destiny of man.

—**Charles Frankel** (1917–1979),
professor of philosophy,
Columbia University

1991, *Illiberal Education,* p.250.

[L]iberal education is an opportunity for all citizens in a democratic society. Contrary to what some activists allege, liberal education is consistent with democracy; indeed it enables democratic rule to reach its pinnacle.

—**Dinesh D'Souza** (1961–),
writer and policy analyst

Teachers and Teaching

c. first century, *Epistulae Morales, no. 7, section 8,* quoted in Elizabeth Knowles, *The Oxford Dictionary of Phrase, Saying, and Quotation,* 1997.

Even while they teach, men learn.

—**Seneca [the Younger]** (4 B.C.E.?–65),
Roman philosopher and poet

1776, *Wealth of Nations,* Book Five, Chapter I.

The discipline of colleges and universities is in general contrived, not for the benefit of the students, but for the interest, or more properly speaking, for the ease of the masters. Its object is, in all cases, to maintain the authority of the master, and whether he neglects or performs his duty, to oblige the students in all cases to behave to him, as if he performed it with the greatest diligence. . . . Where the masters, however, really perform their duty, there are no examples, I believe, that the greater part of the students ever neglect theirs. No discipline is ever requisite to force attendance upon lectures which are really worth the attending. . . .

—**Adam Smith** (1723–1790),
Scottish philosopher and economist

c. 1795, quoted in Charles F. Thwing, *The American College in American Life,* 1897.

It is the priceless privilege of a University teacher to help the manly youth around him in their souls' living, to make them more generous, more truthful, more fit for life in this earnest and struggling world, more worthy of love and respect.

—**Timothy Dwight** (1752–1817),
President, Yale University

1831, William H. Gilman and Albert R. Ferguson (eds.) *The Journals and Miscellaneous Notebooks of Ralph Waldo Emerson, Vol. III,* 1963, p. 274.

The things taught in schools and colleges are not an education, but the means of an education.

—**Ralph Waldo Emerson** (1803–1882),
U.S. poet and essayist

1836, presidential address, quoted in Frederick Rudolph, 1977, *Curriculum,* p. 93.

It is easy to see what it is that constitutes the first excellence of an instructor. It is not his amount of knowledge, nor yet his facility of communication, important as these may be; but it is his power to give an impulse to the minds of his pupils, and to induce them to labor. For this purpose, nothing is so necessary as a disinterested devotion to the work, and a certain enthusiasm which may act by sympathy on the minds of the young.

—**Mark Hopkins** (1802–1887),
President, Williams College

no date, attributed in David J. Loftus, *The Unofficial Book of Harvard Trivia,* 1985, p. 33.

I am not aware that any one single thing is well taught to the undergraduates of Harvard College. Certainly I left it without knowing anything.

—**Charles Sumner** (1811–1874),
U.S. Senator

1869, Inaugural Address, 19 October, in *A Turning Point in Higher Education,* 1969, p. 35.

Philosophical subjects should never be taught with authority. . . . It is not the function of the teacher to settle philosophical and political controversies for the pupil, or even to recommend to him any one set of opinions as better than another. Exposition, not imposition, of opinions is the professor's part. The student should be made acquainted with all sides of these controversies. . . .

pp. 35–36.

The very word "education" is a standing protest against dogmatic teaching. The notion that education consists in the authoritative inculcation of what the teacher deems true may be logical and appropriate in a convent, or a seminary of priests, but it is intolerable in universities and public schools, from primary to professional.

pp. 52–53.

Two kinds of men make good teachers—young men and men who never grow old.

—**Charles William Eliot** (1834–1926),
President, Harvard University

1871, speech at Williams College Alumni Dinner, New York, 28 December, quoted in Frederick Rudolph, *Mark Hopkins and the Log,* 1956, p. 227.

The ideal college is Mark Hopkins at one end of a log and a student on the other. [See *SHE* p. xvi.]

—**James Garfield** (1831–1881),
President of the United States

1886, speech at Harvard commencement dinner, quoted in Samuel Eliot Morison, *Three Centuries of Harvard, 1636–1936,* 1936, p. 347.

Formerly, the only business of a teacher was to hear recitations, and make marks for merit. Now he has the opportunity of teaching. This is one of the greatest discoveries of modern time—that the business of a teacher is to teach.

—**James Freeman Clarke** (1810–1888), professor of religion, Harvard University

1902, "University building," *Popular Science Monthly,* August, p. 331.

[T]he best teacher is more important than the best study.

—**David Starr Jordan** (1851–1931), President, Stanford University

1903, "Maxims for revolutionists," *Man and Superman.*

He who can, does. He who cannot, teaches.

—**George Bernard Shaw** (1856–1950), Irish playwright

1907, quoted in Harold T. Shapiro, "University presidents—then and now," in William G. Bowen and Harold T. Shapiro (eds.), *Universities and Their Leadership,* 1998, pp. 77–78.

No system of teaching which depends upon methods and not upon persons, or which imagines the possibility of any substitution of the written word for the living person, can work any but mechanical effects. The teacher's own spirit must, with intimate and understanding touch, mold and fashion the spirit of the pupil; there is no other way to hand the immortal stuff of learning on.

—**Woodrow Wilson** (1856–1924), President, Princeton University; President of the United States

1909, "The spirit of learning," presentation to the Harvard Chapter of

Phi Beta Kappa, 1 July, quoted in McGeorge Bundy, *An Atmosphere to Breathe,* 1959, p. 13.

Contact, companionship, familiar intercourse is the law of life for the mind. The comradeship of undergraduates will never breed the spirit of learning. The circle must be widened. It must include the older men, the teachers, the men for whom life has grown more serious and to whom it has revealed more of its meanings.

—**Woodrow Wilson** (1856–1924), President, Princeton University; President of the United States

1910, *Great American Universities,* p. 50.

The teaching of Professor Phelps [of Yale University] differs from what is commonly found in English classrooms in that many of his students like poetry even after they have studied it.

p. 90.

One cannot tell anything about the character of the training given by a certain course from its name or department. Their names come mostly from the chance of historical development or connection with a particular profession. Whether a study trains the eye, cultivates the memory, stimulates the imagination, improves the taste or inspires the soul depends not so much upon the subject-matter as upon the way it is taught.

—**Edwin E. Slosson** (1865–1929), chemist: U.S. writer

1912, *Report for 1911–12,* quoted in Edward C. Elliott (ed.), *The Rise of a University, Vol. II,* 1937, p. 170.

One important obstacle to the improvement of college teaching is the tradition which has grown up . . . that the classroom work of college teachers should not be supervised. It is now usual to leave a poor teacher alone with his poverty.

—**Nicholas Murray Butler**
(1862–1947), President,
Columbia University

1915, "Declaration of principles on academic freedom and tenure," *AAUP Policy Documents and Reports, Ninth Edition,* p. 296.

It is not only the character of the instruction but also the character of the instructor that counts; and if the student has reason to believe that the instructor is not true to himself, the virtue of the instruction as an educative force is incalculably diminished. There must be in the mind of the teacher no mental reservation. He must give the student the best of what he has and what he is.

—**American Association of University Professors**

1918, *The Higher Learning in America,* Chapter 1.

[T]he instruction that falls legitimately under the hand of the university man is necessarily subsidiary and incidental to the work of inquiry, and it can effectually be carried on only by such a teacher as is himself occupied with the scrutiny of what knowledge is already in hand and with pushing the inquiry to further gains. And it can be carried on by such a teacher only by drawing his own students into his own work of inquiry. The student's relation to his teacher necessarily becomes that of an apprentice to his master, rather than that of a pupil to his schoolmaster.

—**Thorstein Veblen** (1857–1929),
U.S. sociologist

1927, *Life and the Student,* p. 169.

Whatever else students do or do not get they will always get your attitudes—as open-minded or dogmatic, adventurous or conventional, confident or suspicious, self-absorbed or appreciative of their personalities. For the last they will always be grateful.

p. 171.

If you must choose it is better that students should not understand than that fine things should be made coarse in the telling. Let them become vaguely aware of something to divine and aspire toward.

p. 174.

Nothing more pitiable than one trying to interest a roomful of students in something he doesn't care for himself.

—**Charles Horton Cooley** (1864–1929),
professor of sociology,
University of Michigan

1929, *The Aims of Education and Other Essays,* Chapter Three.

It should be the chief aim of a university professor to exhibit himself in his own true character—that is, as an ignorant man thinking, actively utilising this small share of knowledge.

Chapter Seven.

Imagination is a contagious disease. It cannot be measured by the yard, or weighed by the pound, and then delivered to the students by members of the faculty. It can only be communicated by a faculty whose members themselves wear their learning with imagination.

—**Alfred North Whitehead**
(1861–1947), English philosopher and mathematician; professor of philosophy,
Harvard University

1936, *The Higher Learning in America,* p. 27.

Under [the great-man theory of education], you pay no attention to what you teach. . . . You get great men for your faculty. Their mere presence on the campus inspires, stimulates, and exalts. . . . This is a variant of the nauseating anecdote about Mark Hopkins on one end of the log and the student on the other. Under any conditions that are likely to exist in this country the log is too long and there are too many people sitting on both ends of it to make the anecdote apposite.

—**Robert Maynard Hutchins**
(1899–1977), President,
University of Chicago

1942, *The Academic Man,* p. 184.

Nearly everybody can listen to a teacher and give some judgment of his ability, but apparently nobody can tell precisely what the characteristics of the successful teacher are, much less how to attain them.

—**Logan Wilson** (1907–1990),
President, University of Texas at Austin;
President, American Council
on Education

1943, *Liberal Education,* p. 171.

The teacher learns by teaching, which is the highest form of study. . . . There is no substitute for the natural teacher, and no formula whereby he may be made.

—**Mark Van Doren** (1894–1972),
professor of English,
Columbia University

1944, *Teacher in America,* p. 12.

Teaching is not a lost art, but the regard for it is a lost tradition.

p. 27.

An hour of teaching is certainly the equivalent of a whole morning of office work. The pace, the concentration, the output of energy in office work are child's play compared with handling a class, and the smaller the class, the harder the work. Tutoring a single person—as someone has said—makes you understand what a dynamo feels like when it is discharging into a nonconductor.

p. 29.

Teaching in America is a twenty-four-hour job, twelve months in the year: sabbatical leaves are provided so you can have your coronary thrombosis off the campus.

p. 44.

Ideally a teacher should speak with the tongue of an angel and look like one. In saying this, I deny a common half-truth which seems to me to rest on false democratic feeling. I refer to the elder-brother notion that the teacher is simply a student who has been at it somewhat longer than his charges. I have heard a teacher tell a class that all he could do, really, was by a timely word here and there to help his juniors avoid this or that pitfall. And I seemed to hear the echo answer, "Piffle!"

—**Jacques Barzun** (1907–),
Dean of Faculties and Provost,
Columbia University

1958, *The Academic Marketplace,*
p. 159.

Where men are hired to teach only on the basis of their research productivity, what happens to teaching? With the exception of some humanities departments and a few atypical natural science and social science departments, the answer to this query takes two general forms: (1) Teaching doesn't matter—it isn't important; and (2) There's nothing to worry about—any Ph.D. can teach.

—**Theodore Caplow** (1920–), professor of sociology, University of Virginia;
Reese J. McGee (1929–), professor of sociology, Purdue University

1959, *The House of Intellect,* p. 127.

Small classes *are* in favor, but I suspect more for 'human' than for intellectual reasons. In small classes more reading is done, perhaps, and more 'participating,' but somehow not much more instruction. There often is about the small class something of the illusion of work one finds in the committee meeting. It can be an agreeable chat.

—**Jacques Barzun** (1907–),
Dean of Faculties and Provost,
Columbia University

1963, quoted in Beverly Smith, Jr., "A Yank returns to Oxford," *Saturday Evening Post,* 23 March, p. 72.

It is a rare thing for a student to be taught by only one tutor. If he should by rare chance have been indoctrinated by Mr. A, he will certainly be liberated by Mr. B.

—**C. A. Simpson** (1892–1969),
Dean, Christ Church College,
University of Oxford

1963, *The Uses of the University,* pp. 21–22.

The faculty may, in fact, appoint the faculty, but within this faculty group the students choose the real teachers.

—**Clark Kerr** (1911–2003), Chancellor, University of California, Berkeley; President, University of California

1963, *Redbook* magazine, July, quoted in Gorton Carruth and Eugene Ehrlich, *The Harper Book of American Quotations,* p. 209.

If one cannot state a matter clearly enough so that even a twelve-year-old can understand it, one should remain within the cloistered walls of the university and lab-

oratory until one gets a better grasp of one's subject matter.

—**Margaret Mead** (1901–1978),
U.S. anthropologist

1967, "The future of teaching" in Calvin B. T. Lee, *Improving College Teaching,* pp. 58–59.

At present the universities are as uncongenial to teaching as the Mojave Desert to a clutch of Druid priests. If you want to restore a Druid priesthood, you cannot do it by offering prizes for Druid-of-the-Year. If you want Druids, you must grow forests.

—**William Arrowsmith** (1924–1992),
professor of classics, University of Texas

1968, *The American University,* pp. 35–36.

The presumption holds that anyone who possesses certified knowledge and is not a deaf-mute can teach. No formal attempt is made to impart to the novice any notions of lecturing, examining, grading, or conducting a discussion group. College and university teaching is thus the only profession (except the proverbially oldest in the world) for which no training is given or required.

p. 90.

We believe in a teaching magic that does not require the student to be "willing to be taught"; with us, after failure, the burden of proof is on the teacher.

pp. 90–91.

[W]e have dimmed our wits with the . . . idea that there is no difference between teacher and taught; they are "both students, exploring together, each learning from the other." . . . That instructor and instructed are both still learning does not mean that they do so hand in hand and from the same starting point. A good teacher will tolerate a certain overconfidence in undergraduates—that is part of pedagogy—but to make believe that their knowledge and his are equal is an abdication and a lie.

—**Jacques Barzun** (1907–),
Dean of Faculties and Provost,
Columbia University

1973, *Malice in Blunderland,* p. 103.

Waffle's Law: A professor's enthusiasm for teaching the introductory course varies inversely with the likelihood of his having to do it.

—**Thomas L. Martin, Jr.** (1921–),
President, Illinois Institute of Technology

1974, *Zen and the Art of Motorcycle Maintenance,* p. 147.

At a teaching college you . . . teach and teach and teach until your mind grows dull and your creativity vanishes and you become an automaton saying the same dull things over and over to endless waves of innocent students who cannot understand why you are so dull, lose respect and fan this disrespect out into the community.

—**Robert M. Pirsig** (1928–),
U.S. writer

no date, quoted in David P. Gardner, "The charge of the byte brigade," *Educational Record,* Winter, 1986, p. 15.

Five centuries of the printed book have not diminished the need for the lecture, seminar, and tutorial. In most fields of knowledge—even in science and technology—the intuitive value judgment, the leap of imagination, the processing of data by analogy rather than by deduction, are characteristic of the best kind of education. We know no way to elicit these except through dialogue between the teacher and the pupil. The most precious qualities transmitted from teacher to pupil are not facts and

theories, but attitudes of mind and styles of thinking.

—**Eric Ashby** (1904–1992), botanist;
Vice-chancellor, Cambridge University

1978, "Introduction," in Joel Seligman, *The High Citadel,* 1978, p. xv.

[T]he Socratic method is a game at which only one (the professor) can play. . . .

—**Ralph Nader** (1934–),
U.S. social activist

1985, *Integrity in the College Curriculum,* p. 32.

Every course should be taught differently, as if it were the only course that defined the difference, for the student, between catching hold and falling off.

—**Association of American Colleges**

1986, *Higher Learning,* p. 43.

Only in colleges where teaching is the dominant concern of the faculty is one likely to find a large number of professors making a sustained effort to connect different fields of learning.

—**Derek Bok** (1930–), President,
Harvard University

1986, "Conceptual difficulties in science," in Marian R. Rice (ed.), *Undergraduate Education in Chemistry and Physics,* pp. 23–24.

What we do in our instruction is predicated on the following rule: You take an enormous breadth of subject matter—the bigger the better—and if you pass it by the student at sufficiently high velocity, the Lorentz contraction shortens it to the point where it drops into the hole that is the student's mind. I think that is a fair description of our teaching procedures. It doesn't work in physics, and it doesn't work in education either. . . .

—**Arnold B. Arons** (1916–2001),
professor of physics,
University of Washington

1987, "Foreword," Burton R. Clark, *The Academic Life,* 1987, p. xix.

[A]t every institution, teaching should be valued as the responsibility of every faculty member.

—**Ernest L. Boyer** (1928–1995),
Chancellor, State University of New York

1988, *A Free and Ordered Space,* p. 193.

A liberal education is at the heart of a civil society, and at the heart of a liberal education is the act of teaching.

—**A. Bartlett Giamatti** (1938–1989),
President, Yale University

no date, attributed at <http://www.quote world.org>.

We have inadvertently designed a system in which being good at what you do as a teacher is not formally rewarded, while being poor at what you do is seldom corrected nor penalized.

—**Elliot Eisner** (1933–), professor of education, Stanford University

1988, *ProfScam,* p. 4.

[T]he modern professors would rather have root-canal work done than spend time with any undergraduates. . . .

—**Charles J. Sykes** (1954–),
U.S. journalist

1989, Book Review, *Guardian,* 30 September, quoted in *The Columbia World of Quotations,* 1996.

In universities and intellectual circles, academics can guarantee themselves pop-ularity—or, which is just as satisfying, unpopularity—by being opinionated rather than by being learned.

—**A. N. Wilson** (1950–), British author

1990, *Killing the Spirit,* p. 7.

There is no decent, adequate, respectable education, in the proper sense of that much abused word, without personal involvement by a teacher with the needs and concerns, academic and personal, of his/her students. All the rest is "instruction" or "information transferral," "communication technique," or some other impersonal and antiseptic phrase, but *it is not teaching* and the student is not really learning.

p. 199.

It can be said unequivocally that good teaching is far more complex, difficult, and demanding than mediocre research, which may explain why professors try so hard to avoid it.

—**Page Smith** (1917–1995), historian;
Provost, University of California
at Santa Cruz

1991, "The professor's life," *Dartmouth Alumni Magazine,* February, p. 14.

At the close of long days of work, at the conclusion of long years of scholarly solitude, professors are entitled to feel that rapture, to recognize that their teaching will create a ripple of influence that will be felt in the lives of students years after graduation.

—**James O. Freedman** (1935–),
President, University of Iowa;
President, Dartmouth College

1992, "Reclaiming the public trust," *Change,* July/August, pp. 17–18.

[T]eaching remains one of the few human activities that does not get demonstrably better from one generation to the next.

—**Derek Bok** (1930–), President, Harvard University

Technology

1858, *The Idea of a University,* Discourse VI.

What the steam engine does with matter, the printing press is to do with mind; it is to act mechanically, and the population is to be passively, almost unconsciously, enlightened, by the mere multiplication and dissemination of volumes. . . . The best telescope does not dispense with eyes; the printing press or the lecture room will assist us greatly, but we must be true to ourselves, we must be parties in the work.

—**John Henry (Cardinal) Newman** (1801–1890), Rector, Catholic University of Ireland

1910, *Great American Universities,* p. 498.

It is to be hoped that more of our universities will adopt moving pictures, for it is doubtless a legitimate and useful mode of conveying information.

—**Edwin E. Slosson** (1865–1929), chemist; U.S. writer

1944, *Teacher in America,* pp. 42–43.

It is idle to talk about what *could* be done by gadgets—gramophone disks or sound films. We know just what they can do: they aid teaching by bringing to the classroom irreplaceable subject matter or illustrations of it. . . . But this will not replace the teacher—even though through false economy it might here and there *dis*place him.

—**Jacques Barzun** (1907–), Dean of Faculties and Provost, Columbia University

1977, *Curriculum,* p. 269.

Under the impact of new technology and numbers, closed-circuit television lifted the constraints that the size of lecture halls had placed on class size. Someone quipped: "The ideal college is Mark Hopkins on one end of a television tube and a student on the other."

—**Frederick Rudolph** (1920–), professor of history, Williams College

1981, *Human Options,* p. 187.

The book is still the finest portable university known to man.

—**Norman Cousins** (1912–1990), U.S. editor and author

1996, "Virtual universities could produce only virtual learning," *Chronicle of Higher Education,* 2 May, p. A29.

The kind of virtual university envisioned by the Western governors [Western Governor's University] seems likely to produce only virtual learning.

—**Kenneth H. Ashworth** (1932–), Commissioner, Texas College and University System Coordinating Board

1997, quoted in R. Lenzner and S. S. Johnson, "Seeing things as they really are," *Forbes,* 10 March, p. 127.

Thirty years from now the big university campuses will be relics. Universities won't survive. It's [technology] as big a change as when we first got the printed book. . . . Already we are beginning to deliver more lectures and classes off campus via satellite or two-way video at a fraction of the cost. The college won't survive as a residential institution. Today's buildings are hopelessly unsuited and totally unneeded.

> —**Peter Drucker** (1909–),
> U.S. management consultant and writer

1998, "The next information revolution," *Forbes ASAP,* 24 August, p. 54.

Long-distance learning . . . may well make obsolete within 25 years that uniquely American institution, the freestanding undergraduate college. It is becoming clearer every day that these technical changes will—indeed must—lead to redefining what is meant by *education.*

> —**Peter Drucker** (1909–),
> U.S. management consultant and writer

2001, "The technological revolution," in Philip Altbach et al., *In Defense of American Higher Education,* p. 210.

Each of these technologies (book, audio tapes, video tapes, and television) has had a time of hype followed by disillusionment (at least on the part of the proponents). They have all had their place, but they all failed to replace the professor—because they cannot do what a *good* professor does. A good professor interacts with the students, stimulates them to think, prods them into new insights, motivates them through personal interaction, and provides a role model for intellectual inquiry.

p. 210.

Some faculty members view change with quite a bit of trepidation. I have been asked more than once, "If you can put my course on a website, then why would you need me any more?" I always answer, "If you can be replaced by a website, then you should be replaced by a website."

> —**Jack M. Wilson** (1945–), Dean of Faculty, Rensselaer Polytechnic Institute

Section Three

Institutions and Processes

Chapter 7

The Campus

Alma Mater

1796, *Memoirs of My Life,* chapter 3.

To the University of Oxford I acknowledge no obligation, and she will as cheerfully renounce me as a son, for I am willing to disclaim her for a mother. I spent fourteen months at Magdalen College: they proved to be the most idle and unprofitable of my whole life. . . .

—**Edward Gibbon** (1737–1794),
English historian

1818, argument before the Supreme Court of the United States in *Trustees of Dartmouth College v. Woodward,* quoted in Richard Hofstadter and Wilson Smith (eds.), *American Higher Education: A Documentary History, Volume I,* 1961, p. 212.

Sir, you may destroy this little institution; it is weak; it is in your hands! I know it is one of the lesser lights in the literary horizon of our country. You may put it out. But, if you do so, you must carry through your work! You must extinguish, one after another, all those greater lights of science which, for more than a century, have thrown their radiance over our land. It is,

Sir, as I have said, a small College. And yet, there are those who love it.

—**Daniel Webster** (1782–1852),
U.S. Senator

1858, *The Idea of a University,* Discourse VI.

The University is, according to the usual designation, an Alma Mater, knowing her children one by one, not a foundry, or a mint, or a treadmill.

—**John Henry (Cardinal) Newman** (1801–1890), Rector,
Catholic University of Ireland

c. 1881, "Bright College Years," song, (Yale Alma Mater), quoted in <http://www.yale.edu/athletic/songs/son.html>.

Oh, let us strive that ever we
May let these words our watchcry be,
Where'er upon life's seas we sail:
"For God, for Country, and for Yale!"

—**H. S. Durand** (?–?),
Yale Class of 1881

1897, *The American College in American Life,* p. 177.

[H]arvard stands as the mother of movements [i.e., Unitarianism, Transcendentalism, Elective System], and Yale as the mother of men.

—**Charles F. Thwing** (1853–1937), President, Adelbert College; President, Western Reserve University

1899, speech to students, quoted in George A. Pettitt, *Twenty-eight Years in the Life of a University President,* 1966, p. 200.

This University shall be a family's glorious old mother, by whose hearth you shall love to sit down. Love her. It does a man good to love noble things, to attach his life to noble allegiances ... [I]t is good to be loyal to the University, which stands in life for the purest things and the cleanest, loftiest ideals. Cheer for her; it will do your lungs good. Love her; it will do your heart and life good.

—**Benjamin Ide Wheeler** (1854–1927), President, University of California

1902, *Report for 1901–2,* quoted in Edward C. Elliott (ed.), *The Rise of a University, Vol. II,* 1937, p. 230.

College life and college spirit are real things as well as most effective educational instrumentalities. It is living together, not attending classes or listening to lectures together, which develops that strong attachment to Alma Mater, its ideals and its interests, which counts for so much both in the life of the individual student and in that of the university.

—**Nicholas Murray Butler** (1862–1947), President, Columbia University

1904, *College Life,* pp. 60–61.

[T]he youth who loves his Alma Mater will always ask, not "What can she do for me?" but "What can I do for her?"

—**LeBaron Russell Briggs** (1855–1934), Dean, Harvard College

1910, *Great American Universities,* p. 304.

The man educated in a State university has a unity of loyalty that no other gets. His college spirit, his State pride, and his patriotism are inextricably commingled, for they have grown up together. When a Princeton man gives the Princeton yell he is not hurrahing for New Jersey. But when an Illinois student yells "Illinois" he means the campus, the State, and the country altogether. It is a football game and a Fourth of July rolled into one. His alma mater is his motherland. If he serves his country on the battlefield he marches under the same flag and bears on his cap the same initial as when he was a student.

—**Edwin E. Slosson** (1865–1929), chemist; U.S. writer

1929, *American College Athletics,* p. 191.

The tender and peculiar place which the university or the college should occupy in the affections of its alumni is not to be denied or impugned. It is compounded of gratitude which prompts to service, a love that springs from impressionable years passed as an undergraduate under the protection of the Fostering Mother, and the tendency common to many men and women to look into their past for the Golden Age. These considerations form the ideal basis for the relation of the alumnus to his college.

—**Howard J. Savage** (1886–1973), staff member, Carnegie Foundation for the Advancement of Teaching

1970, *The American College and American Culture,* p. 59.

The athletic contest was the occasion for a display of loyalty akin to patriotism. The massed crowds in the stadium, the show of distinctive colors, the songs, all were evidences of an attachment to the college which it was not ludicrous to juxtapose with that to God and country. It was significant that the youths, here away from home, thought of themselves as sons of an alma mater.

> —**Oscar Handlin** (1915–), professor of history, Harvard University; **Mary F. Handlin** (1913–1976), research editor, Harvard University

1993, *Alma Mater: A College Homecoming,* p. 2.

Sometimes I think of it as an island, with all the island qualities: a sense that everything is connected, nothing is ever over, and everything that happens ought to be taken personally. The kind of place that, on its good days, can feel like the heart of the universe, the perfect center of a well-spent life. On other days, it's simply nowhere, it's nowhere squared: not just a small college, but a small rural college, a small rural college in the Midwest, a lightly endowed, wrist-slicingly isolated college with English roots and eastern airs, national and international aspirations, some wishful, some warranted, a college poor but proud, less conservative than old-fashioned, less elitist than peculiar, not a pushy, voguish college, not this one, but a college that stands on the edge of the party and waits and waits politely, sometimes it seems like forever, to be recognized and remembered and appropriately introduced: Kenyon College, Gambier, Ohio. A place I sometimes love, with a history that rolls like the seasons, down through the years, and moods that change like the weather.

> —**P. F. Kluge** (1942–), U.S. author

Campus Architecture

1810, letter to Hugh L. White et al., quoted in Paul Venable Turner, *Campus: An American Planning Tradition,* 1984, p. 79.

I consider the common plan, followed in this country but not in others, of making one large and expensive building, as unfortunately erroneous. It is infinitely better to erect a small and separate lodge for each separate professorship . . . joining these lodges by barracks for a certain portion of the students. . . . The whole of these arranged around an open square of grass and trees, would make it, what it should be in fact, an academical village. . . .

> —**Thomas Jefferson** (1743–1826), father of the University of Virginia; President of the United States

1870, *Annual report 1869–1870,* quoted in Henry James, *Charles W. Eliot,* 1930, volume I, p. 242.

The college grounds ought to be kept in such condition that they shall be an ornament to the city and a source of pleasure to all its citizens, as well as to the students who most frequent them.

> —**Charles William Eliot** (1834–1926), President, Harvard University

1902, "Concerning the American university," in *Popular Science Monthly,* June, p. 179.

As the loving devotion and art of the community were once lavished on its cathedral, so they should now go toward making the university stately and beautiful.

> —**J. McKeen Cattell** (1860–1944), professor of psychology, Columbia University

1910, *Great American Universities,*
p. 206.

I have alluded to the similarity in spirit and principles between Harvard and Michigan. The resemblance extends to their architecture. The campus in both cases has been built up on the elective principle. The arrangement of the buildings is much the same as when a child dumps his Swiss village out of the box on the floor.

—**Edwin E. Slosson** (1865–1929),
chemist; U.S. writer

no date, attributed in *Your Ultimate Success Quotation Library* (software program) at <http://www.cybernation.com/>.

I wonder anybody does anything at Oxford but dream and remember, the place is so beautiful. One almost expects the people to sing instead of speaking. It is all like an opera.

—**William Butler Yeats** (1865–1939),
Irish poet, playwright

1937, *When The Cathedrals Were White,* 1964, p. 135, quoted in Paul Venable Turner, *Campus: An American Planning Tradition,* 1984, p. 160.

Everything in the interest of comfort, everything for the sake of calm and serenity, everything to make solid bodies. Each college or university is an urban unit in itself, a small or large city. But a green city. Lawns, parks, stadiums, cloisters, dining halls, a whole complex of comfortable quarters. . . . The American university is a world in itself, a temporary paradise, a gracious stage of life. . . .

—**Le Corbusier** (1887–1965),
Swiss architect and artist

no date, *Architectural Forum,* quoted in Thomas A. Gaines, *The Campus as a Work of Art,* 1991.

The average American university is an architectural mess.

—**Aymar Embury II** (1880–1966),
U.S. architect

1963, quoted in Walter McQuade, "College architecture: The economics and aesthetics," *Fortune,* May, p. 149.

Man wants to express something that he sees in his mind, or feels in his soul, but few men get the chance—especially college students. But every time a student walks past a really urgent, expressive piece of architecture that belongs to his college, it can help reassure him that he does have that mind, does have that soul.

—**Louis I. Kahn** (1901–1974),
U.S. architect

1991, *The Campus as a Work of Art,*
p. ix.

The first thing to know about the campus as a work of art is this: It rarely is.

p. 36.

On the whole, religious buildings have been more consistently well designed than any other type of building on campus (no doubt due to divine intervention).

—**Thomas A. Gaines** (1923–),
architectural writer

Campus Life

1837, "The American scholar," delivered before the Phi Beta Kappa Society, at Cambridge, August 31, *Nature; Addresses and Lectures,* 1849.

[C]olleges can only highly serve us, when they aim not to drill, but to create; when they gather from far every ray of various genius to their hospitable halls, and, by the concentrated fires, set the hearts of their youth on flame.

—**Ralph Waldo Emerson** (1803–1882), U.S. poet, philosopher, and essayist

1858, *The Idea of a University,* Discourse VI.

[I]f I had to choose between a so-called University, which dispensed with residence and tutorial superintendence, and gave its degrees to any person who passed an examination in a wide range of subjects, and a University which had no professors or examinations at all, but merely brought a number of young men together for three or four years and then sent them away . . . I have no hesitation in giving the preference to that University which did nothing, over that which exacted of its members an acquaintance with every science under the sun. . . . When a multitude of young men, keen, open-hearted, sympathetic, and observant, as young men are, come together and freely mix with each other, they are sure to learn from one another, even if there be no one to teach them; the conversations of all is a series of lectures to each, and they gain for themselves new ideas and views, fresh matters of thought, and distinct principles for judging and acting, day by day.

—**John Henry (Cardinal) Newman** (1801–1890), Rector, Catholic University of Ireland

1871, "What is a university," *Rise and Progress of Universities—Historical Sketches,* volume 3, chapter 2.

The general principles of any study you may learn by books at home; but the details, the color, the tone, the air, the life which makes it live in us, you must catch all these from those in whom it lives already.

—**John Henry (Cardinal) Newman** (1801–1890), Rector, Catholic University of Ireland

1879, "On the campus," in *The Princeton Book,* p. 375.

There is no spell more powerful to recall the memories of college life than the word Campus. . . . One might as well try to keep a flask full of sunshine, as to preserve in words the spirit and delight of college days.

—**Henry J. Van Dyke, Jr.** (1852–1933), professor of English literature, Princeton University

1894, *Aspects of Modern Oxford,* p. 133, quoted in Charles F. Thwing, *The American College in American Life,* 1897, p. 127.

It is a great thing to be able to loaf well; it softens the manners and does not allow them to be fierce; and there is no place for it like the streams and gardens of an ancient university.

—**Alfred Denis Godley** (1856–1925), don, Oxford University

no date, attributed in John W. Gardner, *Know or Listen to Those Who Know,* 1975, p. 83.

Organization and method mean much, but contagious human characters mean more in a university.

—**William James** (1842–1910), professor of philosophy, Harvard University

1903, "University tendencies," *Popular Science Monthly,* June, p. 148.

Higher education, properly speaking, begins when a young man goes away from home to school. The best part of higher education is the development of the instincts of the gentleman and the horizon of the scholar.

—**David Starr Jordan** (1851–1931), President, Stanford University

1909, "The spirit of learning," presentation to the Harvard Chapter of Phi Beta Kappa, 1 July, quoted in McGeorge Bundy, *An Atmosphere to Breathe,* 1959, p. 12.

The real intellectual life of a body of undergraduates, if there be any, manifests itself not in the classroom, but in what they do and talk of and set before themselves as their favorite objects between classes and lectures.

—**Woodrow Wilson** (1856–1924),
President, Princeton University;
President of the United States

1912, *Memories and Studies,* p. 362.

Methods of which we talk so much play but a minor part. . . . Above all things, offer the opportunity of higher personal contacts. . . . [W]e are only beginning in this country, with our extraordinary American reliance on organization, to see that the alpha and omega in a university is the tone of it, and that this tone is set by human personalities exclusively.

—**William James** (1842–1910),
professor of philosophy,
Harvard University

1922, *My Discovery of England.*

If I were founding a university . . . I would found first a smoking room; then when I had a little more money in hand I would found a dormitory; then after that, or more probably with it, a decent reading room and a library. After that, if I still had money over that I couldn't use, I would hire a professor and get some text books.

—**Stephen Butler Leacock**
(1869–1944), professor of political
economy, McGill University

1923, *How to Make the Best of Life,* p. 63.

The earnest undergraduate is important; he may be as important as a whole town, but compared to the university, he is somewhat like a town built by a river. The river was there centuries before the town, and it will be there centuries after the town has vanished. The town is a mere incident in the life of the river. The individual undergraduate is a mere incident in the life of a university.

—**Arnold Bennett** (1867–1931),
British novelist and playwright

1964, "Harvard in epigram," in *Harvard Alumni Bulletin,* 24 October, p. 130.

It really is the undergraduate who makes a university, gives it its lasting character, smell, feel, quality, tradition . . . whose presence creates it and whose memories preserve it.

—**Seán O'Faoláin** (1900–1991),
Irish writer

Campus Location

1839, *Hyperion,* book 1, chapter 8.

[W]here should the scholar live? In solitude, or in society, in the green stillness of the country, where he can hear the heart of Nature beat, or in the dark gray town, where he can hear and feel the throbbing heart of man? I will make answer for him, and say, in the dark, gray town.

—**Henry Wadsworth Longfellow**
(1807–1882), professor of literature,
Harvard University

1878, *American Colleges: Their Students and Their Work,* p. 48.

If Yale were located at Williamstown, Harvard at Hanover, Columbia at Ithaca, the moral character of their students would be elevated in as great a degree as the natural scenery of their localities would be increased in beauty.

—**Charles F. Thwing** (1853–1937),
President, Adelbert College; President,
Western Reserve University

1884, *The American University: When Shall It Be? Where Shall It Be? What Shall It Be?,* p. 8.

Where shall the American University be? Briefly, we answer, it must be at or near a centre of wealth and culture. The University anywhere is in great advantage when placed at or near such a centre, because of the aids and auxiliaries which it furnishes to University work,—its galleries and museums of art and science, its libraries, its hospitals, and its varied life.

—**John W. Burgess** (1844–1931), Dean, Columbia College

1902, *Report for 1901–2,* quoted in Edward C. Elliott (ed.), *The Rise of a University, Vol. II,* 1937, p. 84.

The whole form of modern university development has been conditioned by the growth of great cities. The life of the modern universities is becoming more and more of the urban type. Each of the world's great capitals which is or aims to be a center of influence in the largest sense of the word must and will be the home of a great university.

—**Nicholas Murray Butler** (1862–1947), President, Columbia University

1910, *Great American Universities,* p. 313.

I have heard the cultural value of the Cornell scenery estimated as equivalent to five full professors. Not knowing in what thermodynamic units professor power is measured, I was not able to verify this estimate.

—**Edwin E. Slosson** (1865–1929), chemist; U.S. writer

1923, "Report of the chancellor 1922–23," quoted at <http://ublib.buffalo.edu/libraries/units/archives/presidents/capen_quotes.html>.

A university is not a group of buildings. It is a group of persons. . . . If the group could meet and accomplish its purpose in an open lot, a university would be there. In northern climates, such arrangements would, of course, be impossible.

—**Samuel P. Capen** (1878–1956), director, American Council on Education; President, University of Buffalo

1930, *Report for 1929–30,* quoted in Edward C. Elliott (ed.), *The Rise of a University, Vol. II,* 1937, p. 86.

[T]he typical university of the twentieth century is no longer of the monastic or secluded type. It is not to be found in the village or the small town, in the secluded valley or on a remote hilltop. It is put where men congregate and work and think and act.

—**Nicholas Murray Butler** (1862–1947), President, Columbia University

1960, *The Urban University,* p. 67, quoted in Carnegie Commission on Higher Education, *The Campus and the City,* 1972, p.14.

The university is one of the few immovable islands in a sea of urban change. The American city is perhaps the most fluid, large social unit in the history of mankind. . . . As a permanent institution of strength the university serves as an anchor in the city's desperate effort to arrest its disintegration and achieve a new stability.

—**J. Martin Klotsche** (1907–1995), Chancellor, University of Wisconsin-Milwaukee

1963, *The Uses of the University,* p. 89.

An almost ideal location for a modern university is to be sandwiched between a middle-class district on its way to becoming a slum and an ultramodern industrial park—so that students may live in the one and faculty consult in the other.

—**Clark Kerr** (1911–2003), Chancellor, University of California, Berkeley; President, University of California

1974, *Zen and the Art of Motorcycle Maintenance,* p. 150.

The real University is a state of mind. It is that great heritage of rational thought that has been brought down to us through the centuries and which does not exist at any specific location.

—**Robert M. Pirsig** (1928–), U.S. writer

Chapter 8

Institutions

Black Colleges

1901, *Up from Slavery,* Chapter III.

I have spoken of my admiration for General [Samuel] Armstrong, and yet he was but a type of the Christ-like body of men and women who went into the Negro schools at the close of the war by the hundreds to assist in lifting up my race. The history of the world fails to show a higher, purer, and more unselfish class of men and women than those who found their way into those Negro schools.

> —**Booker T. Washington** (1856–1915), President, Tuskegee Normal and Industrial Institute

1901, letter to Wallace Butrick, January, quoted in James D. Anderson, "Training the apostles of liberal culture: Black higher education, 1900–1935," in Lester F. Goodchild and Harold S. Wechsler (eds.), *ASHE Reader on the History of Higher Education, 2nd Edition,* 1997, p. 441.

The one all-important function of these [black] institutions, the work to which they must give their strength for many years to come is that of raising up a competent leadership; men and women who can think; who are independent and self-reliant; who can persuade and lead their people; they should be men and women who are themselves models and examples of what their people can and ought to become, especially should they be persons capable of teaching and preaching. No modification of their spirit and purpose should be allowed to interfere in any manner with this as the supreme purpose of their existence,

> —**Thomas J. Morgan** (1839–1902), corresponding secretary, American Baptist Home Mission Society

1903, *The Souls of Black Folk,* chapter 6.

The function of the Negro college, then, is clear: it must maintain the standards of popular education, it must seek the social regeneration of the Negro, and it must help in the solution of problems of race contact and cooperation. And finally, beyond all this, it must develop men.

> —**W. E. B. Du Bois** (1868–1963), professor of sociology, Atlanta University

1916, *U.S. Bureau of Education Bulletin,* quoted in Dwight Oliver Wendell Holmes, *The Evolution of the Negro College,* p. 159.

No type of education is so eagerly sought by the colored people as college education. Yet no educational institutions for colored people are so poorly equipped and so ineffectively organized and administered as a majority of those claiming to give college education.

—**U.S. Bureau of Education**

1945, quoted in Charles V. Willie, "Racism, black education, and the sociology of knowledge," in Charles V. Willie and Ronald R. Edmonds (eds.), *Black Colleges in America,* 1978, p. 13.

It will not be sufficient for Morehouse College . . . to produce clever graduates, men fluent in speech and able to argue their way through; but rather honest men, men who can be trusted in public and private—men who are sensitive to the wrongs, the sufferings, the injustices of society and who are willing to accept responsibility for correcting their ills.

—**Benjamin E. Mays** (1895–1984),
President, Morehouse College

c. 1950, "Uniting method and purpose in higher education," in Charles V. Willie and Ronald R. Edmonds (eds.), *Black Colleges in America,* 1978, p. 267.

And now abideth Yale, Harvard, and Morehouse—these three. But the greatest of these must be Morehouse.

—**Charles V. Willie** (1927–), professor
of education and urban studies,
Harvard University

1969, "The black presence in American higher education," in Nathan Wright, Jr., *What Black Educators Are Saying,* 1970, p. 135.

[Black colleges and universities] have been the intellectual salvation of the black people in America. There would be no substantial group of college-educated men and women in the black community today, were their education left to the white or integrated institutions. . . . These have been islands of culture in the truest sense in a sea of hostile white racism, oppression, and indifference to the minds and spirits of black people.

—**Andrew Billingsley** (1926–),
President, Morgan State University

1971, *Born to Rebel: An Autobiography,* p. 188.

[M]orehouse has done "so much with so little and so few." . . .

—**Benjamin E. Mays** (1895–1984),
President, Morehouse College

1971, "Negro colleges face the future," in *Daedalus,* Summer, p. 649, quoted in Henry N. Drewry and Humphrey Doermann, *Stand and Prosper,* 2001, p. 2.

People generally discuss Negro colleges as if they were all alike, with a common future. This is nonsense. Negro colleges are located along a spectrum of quality ranging from excellent to poor, just as are other institutions.

—**William J. Trent, Jr.** (1910–1993),
executive director,
United Negro College Fund

1978, "The black college in higher education," in Charles V. Willie and Ronald R. Edmonds (eds.), *Black Colleges in America,* 1978, p. 22.

[T]he image of the black man and woman in education and their contribution to American life must be equated with the black colleges.

pp. 26–27.

This is no time for black colleges to apologize for their existence, to become weak-kneed, to stop striving for excellence, and to stop trying to raise money for their support. . . . [I]f America allows black colleges to die, it would be the worst kind of discrimination and denigration known in history. To decree that colleges born to serve Negroes are not worthy of surviving now that white colleges accept Negroes would be a damnable act.

—**Benjamin E. Mays** (1895–1984),
President, Morehouse College

1978, "Black colleges: Self-concept," p. 31, in Charles V. Willie and Ronald R. Edmonds (eds.), *Black Colleges in America,* 1978.

[P]erhaps the greatest and most distinctive contribution of black colleges to the American philosophy of higher education has been to emphasize and legitimate public and community service as a major objective of colleges and universities. The most superficial perusal of the catalogs and other publications of these colleges reveals how deeply ingrained this mission is in their consciousness. Enter to learn; go forth to serve is a common motto.

—**Gregory Kannerstein** (1941–),
director of athletics, Haverford College

1978, "The socio-ethical role and responsibility of the black-college graduate," in Charles V. Willie and Ronald R. Edmonds (eds.), *Black Colleges in America,* p. 55.

The class of phenomena called black colleges is marked by a distinctive philosophy, history, curriculum emphasis, and raison d'être. A central assumption is that students at black colleges, vis-à-vis white colleges, will acquire a set of values, a spirit of social service, social conscience, moral sensitivity, and sense of personal and social responsibility—principally with reference to social and racial justice—that will stay with them and motivate them after graduation.

—**Samuel DuBois Cook** (1928–),
President, Dillard University

1978, "Black colleges of the North," in Charles V. Willie and Ronald R. Edmonds (eds.), *Black Colleges in America,* p. 154.

If America is genuinely sincere about the elimination of racism, there will come a time when every institution in America will be just an institution, neither black nor white. The predominantly black college should move toward being an American institution irrespective of race.

—**Herman R. Branson** (1914–1995),
President, Lincoln University;
President, Central State University

1978, "Effective management of scarce resources," in Charles V. Willie and Ronald R. Edmonds (eds.), *Black Colleges in America,* p. 158.

[F]ar from being "disaster areas" as two Harvard scholars have charged, black colleges have been the most productive institutions in America, given their resources, their personnel, and the general attitude of the public toward them.

> —**Prezell R. Robinson** (1922–),
> President, Saint Augustine's College

1978, "Uniting method and purpose in higher education," in Charles V. Willie and Ronald R. Edmonds (eds.), *Black Colleges in America,* p. 268.

[B]lack and white schools complement each other; a system of higher education that has a Harvard without a Hampton is incomplete.

> —**Charles V. Willie** (1927–), professor
> of education and urban studies,
> Harvard University

1993, *Conversations: Straight talk with America's sister president,* p. 181.

In an atmosphere relatively free of racism and sexism, where teachers care and expect the very best, parents and kinfolks are involved, and the curriculum and those around students reflect in positive ways who the students are—there are no limits to what individuals can learn and who they can become.

> —**Johnetta B. Cole** (1936–), President,
> Spelman College

1997, "The case for all-black colleges," *The ERIC Review: The Path to College,* vol. 5, issue 3.

[Historically black colleges and universities] know how to take diamonds in the rough and make them more brilliant, as Harvard and Stanford do. But they also know how to do something other colleges cannot do. They know how to take a lump of coal and turn it into diamond by mentoring, expecting excellence, and hands-on teaching by faculty who have been there and care.

> —**William H. Gray III** (1941–),
> member, U.S. House of Representatives;
> president, United Negro College Fund

College

1858, *The Idea of a University,* Discourse VII.

[I]f a Liberal Education consists in the culture of the intellect, and if that culture be in itself a good . . . and if a College of Physicians is a useful institution, because it contemplates bodily health, why is not an Academical Body, though it were simply and solely engaged in imparting vigour and beauty and grasp to the intellectual portion of our nature?

> —**John Henry (Cardinal) Newman**
> (1801–1890), Rector,
> Catholic University of Ireland

no date, quoted in Edwin E. Slosson, *Great American Universities,* 1910, p. 108.

Our colleges should conceive of themselves as organizations into which young men are received as into a family of free persons bound together by common obligations and common privileges, living together, teacher and pupil, in an intercourse of common advantage; its main object study; its diversions diversions, not occupations; its sport sport, not competitive business; its society a free society of equals, not a congeries of rival social groups.

> —**Woodrow Wilson** (1856–1924),
> President, Princeton University;
> President of the United States

no date, attributed in Page Smith, *Killing the Spirit,* 1990, p. 217.

The ideal college . . . should be a community, a place of close, natural, intimate association, not only of the young men who are its pupils and novices in various lines of study, but also of young men with older men . . . of teachers with pupils, outside the classroom as well as inside.

—**Woodrow Wilson** (1856–1924),
President, Princeton University;
President of the United States

1917, *Why Go to College,* pp. 27–28.

The college may not teach us how to earn money, but it will teach us how to spend it—which is vastly more important. It can show us what are the real values of life, the things worth paying for and worth working for. . . . He who wants nothing more than a salary-raising education should not enter the American college, for the college aims at character-raising, mind-building, personality-developing.

—**William H. P. Faunce** (1859–1930),
President, Brown University

1917, *Report for 1916–17,* quoted in Edward C. Elliott (ed.), *The Rise of a University, Vol. II,* 1937, p. 336.

There is probably no college in the land where an ambitious young American cannot today secure a thorough college education of the best type, if he insists upon getting it; but, on the other hand, there are very few colleges in the land where it is quite certain that by spending four years he will get such an education.

—**Nicholas Murray Butler**
(1862–1947), President,
Columbia University

1926, *Which Way Parnassus?,* p. 70.

A college basically is composed of just two elements: the teachers and the students. All else is supplemental.

—**Percy Marks** (1891–1956),
U.S. writer and instructor of English

1927, *Report for 1926–27,* quoted in Edward C. Elliott (ed.), *The Rise of a University, Vol. II,* 1937, p. 234.

The business of the college . . . is to prepare for life and not for making a living.

—**Nicholas Murray Butler**
(1862–1947), President,
Columbia University

1955, "Conscience and the undergraduate," *Atlantic Monthly,* April, p. 31.

[T]he American liberal arts college (including the church colleges) can find a significant, even unique, mission in the duality of its historic purpose: to see men made whole in *both* competence and conscience.

—**John Sloan Dickey** (1907–1991),
President, Dartmouth College

1959, *An Atmosphere to Breathe,* p. 27.

[W]herever we turn the answer is the same: *a college is not only a body of studies but a mode of association; its courses are only its formal side, its contacts and contagions its realities.*

—**McGeorge Bundy** (1919–1996),
Dean, Faculty of Arts and Sciences,
Harvard University

1961, *Quote,* 9 July, quoted in Jonathon Green, *Morrow's International Dictionary of Contemporary Quotations,* 1982, p. 360.

Education doesn't change life much. It just lifts trouble to a higher plane of regard. . . . College is a refuge from hasty judgment.

—**Robert Frost** (1874–1963), U.S. poet

1962, *The American College,* p. 13.

It is a remarkable fact that a culture that places relatively little value upon learning or the intellectual life, and has little understanding of, or sympathy for, what professors are trying to do, nevertheless regards college—the experience of college for young people—as one of the greatest goods, virtually as one of the necessities of life.

—**Nevitt R. Sanford** (1909–1995), professor of psychology and education, Stanford University

1965, "A better partnership for the federal government and higher education," in Logan Wilson, *Emerging Patterns in American Higher Education,* 1965, p. 273.

The keen legislative interest in what medical research can do for the bodies of the elderly is obvious, even though there is apparently less interest in what liberal arts colleges can do for the minds of the young.

—**Logan Wilson** (1907–1990), President, University of Texas at Austin; President, American Council on Education

1966, *The Reforming of General Education,* p. 8.

[T]he distinctive feature of the college is to deal with the grounds of knowledge: not *what* one knows but *how* one knows.

—**Daniel Bell** (1919–), professor of sociology, Columbia University; Harvard University

Community College

1938, "The junior college," *Educational Record,* January, p. 5.

With notable exceptions, the junior college has so far done only a negative job. It has kept young people from going places and doing things that would have been worse for them. It has supplied an institution where they could pass the time in relatively harmless pursuits until they could go

to work. When boys and girls cannot get jobs and cannot afford to go away to college, the junior college is indispensable.

—**Robert Maynard Hutchins** (1899–1977), President, University of Chicago

1947, *Higher Education for American Democracy, Vol. 1,* p. 37.

[T]uition-free education should be available in public institutions to all youth for the traditional freshman and sophomore years or for the traditional 2-year junior college course. To achieve this, it will be necessary to develop much more extensively than at present such opportunities as are now provided in communities by the 2-year junior college, community institute, community college, or institute of arts and sciences. The name used does not matter, though community college seems to describe these schools best; the important thing is that the services they perform be recognized and vastly extended.

—**President's Commission on Higher Education**

1951, "The democratic dilemma," *Freedom, Education, and the Fund,* 1956, p. 135.

New institutions, continuing for two years beyond the secondary schools, will be established for the mass, who should not be allowed to clutter up existing institutions, because they are not bright enough. . . . These new two-year colleges therefore become a kind of gigantic play-room in which the young are detained, or retarded, until we are ready to have them enter upon active life.

—**Robert Maynard Hutchins** (1899–1977), President, University of Chicago

1958, "Many millions more,"
Educational Record, April, p. 102.

A prime virtue of the junior college, I think, is that most of its students succeed in what they set out to accomplish, and cross the finish line before they grow weary of the race.

—**Robert Gordon Sproul** (1891–1975),
President, University of California

1960, "The 'cooling-out' function in higher education," *American Journal of Sociobiology 65* (6), pp. 569, 576.

Certain components of American higher education perform what may be called the cooling-out function. . . . The junior college may be viewed as a place where all high-school graduates have the opportunity to explore possible careers and find the type of education appropriate to their individual ability; in short, as a place where everyone is admitted and everyone succeeds.

—**Burton R. Clark** (1921–), professor of sociology, University of California, Los Angeles

no date, *A New Social Invention: The Community College,* p. 1, quoted in Clyde E. Blocker et al., *The Two Year College, A Social Synthesis,* 1965, p. 33.

A good community college will be honestly, gladly, and clearly a community institution. It is in and of the community. The community is used as an extension of the classroom and laboratory.

—**Edmund J. Gleazer, Jr.** (1916–),
President, Graceland College

1970, "A time to change," *Community and Junior College Journal,* April.

We need new approaches to places of learning. We may even need a substitute word for college if it gets in the way—perhaps

community centers for educational development. And the walls between college and community are long overdue in their falling down.

—**Edmund J. Gleazer, Jr.** (1916–),
President, Graceland College

1972, *The Community Junior College, 3rd edition,* p. 42.

It is fair to say that most community college students are able to learn but are relatively unpracticed. Under good instruction they can succeed admirably, whereas pedestrian teaching is more likely to discourage and defeat them. . . . Either it [the community college] teaches excellently or it fails completely.

—**James W. Thornton, Jr.** (1908–1996),
professor of education,
San Jose State College

1975, *The Case Against College,* p. 12.

The neatest way to get rid of a superfluous eighteen-year-old is to amuse him all day long at a community college while his family feeds and houses him. This is not only cheaper than a residential college, but cheaper than supporting him on welfare, a make-work job, in prison, or in the armed forces.

—**Caroline Bird** (1915–), U.S. author

1976, *Second Best,* p. xvii.

[Community colleges] are commonly believed to be among the great equalizers in a society which professes to be democratic and egalitarian. The social effect of the community college, however, tends to be just the opposite. Instead of blunting the pyramid of the American social and economic structure, the community college plays an essential role in maintaining it. It has become just one more barrier put between the poor and the disenfranchised and the decent and respectable stake in the social system which they seek.

—**L. Steven Zwerling** (1938–),
U.S. educator

1978, "What is a college for?," *New Directions for Community Colleges 24,* pp. 9, 13.

Let's be candid about the major issue in the community college today: the low academic achievement of its students. . . . As it is now, the community college is a remedial center, a vocational center, an adult center, a career center, a community center, a senior citizen center, a center for non-English speaking people, a local recreation center, and last and least of all, a college.

—**Bette Slutsky** (?–?), professor of biology, Truman College

1980, "Coastline Community College 5th Anniversary Report," p. 5.

The community is in the campus. The citizens are the students.

—**Bernard J. Luskin** (1937–),
President, Coastline Community College;
President, Orange Coast College;
Chancellor, Jones International University

1980, *The Community College,* p. 4.

We are trapped in the traditional view of college.

p. 10.

The community college . . . is more a process than a place.

p. 38.

The community college is a vital part of an integrated system of community services. If it limits itself to the conventional academic area, no matter how great its numbers might become or how excellent its programs, it remains the lower level of

a pyramid of academic prestige with the graduate schools at the cap.

—**Edmund J. Gleazer, Jr.** (1916–),
President, Graceland College

1988, *Building Communities: A Vision for a New Century,* p. 7.

We propose . . . that the theme "Building Communities" become the new rallying point for the community college in America. We define the term "community" not only as a region to be served, but also as a climate to be created. . . . If the college itself is not a model community, it cannot advocate community to others.

—**Commission on the Future of Community Colleges, American Association of Community and Junior Colleges**

1990, *Killing the Spirit,* pp. 19–20.

These institutions [community colleges], with close ties to their parent communities, free for the most part of the snobbish pursuit of the latest academic fads that so warp their university counterparts, and also of the unremitting pressure to publish or perish are, I believe, the hope of higher education in America. Unheralded and scorned or patronized by "the big boys," they carry out their mission with spirit and élan. There are, I am sure, indifferent community colleges as well as good ones, but the ones I have visited have all charmed me. . . .

—**Page Smith** (1917–1995), historian;
Provost, University of California at Santa Cruz

1996, *The American Community College, 3rd edition,* p. 408.

The real benefit of the community college cannot be measured by the extent to which it contributes to the overthrow of the social-class system in America. Nor can it be measured by the extent to which the college changes the mores of its community. It is a system for individuals, and it does what the best educational forms have always done; it helps individuals learn what they need to know to be effective, responsible members of their society.

—**Arthur M. Cohen** (1927–), professor of higher education, University of California, Los Angeles; **Florence B. Brawer** (1922–), research director, University of California, Los Angeles

2001, "The community college and the American dream," self-published.

In America, the avenue through which most of us prepare to pursue the [American] dream is through our system of public education, including community college education. . . . Let us think for a moment of the community college as the port of entry—the Ellis Island—for many of our "new immigrants" to higher education. Think of what our nation would lose if these individuals were given no choices in life, if the community college did not exist.

—**George B. Vaughan** (1932–), President, Mountain Empire Community College; President, Piedmont Virginia Community College

2002, *The American Community College, 4th edition,* p. 181.

Does the learning college represent reality or is it yet another example of good intentions that fail to materialize? . . . If it but serves only to shift the working definition of instruction from an activity to a process leading to predictable goals, it will have made a major contribution. . . . So far, the term seems as tautological as "eating restaurant."

—**Arthur M. Cohen** (1927–), professor of higher education, University of California, Los Angeles; **Florence B. Brawer** (1922–), research director, University of California, Los Angeles

Diversity: Institutions

1910, *Great American Universities,* p. 56.

[I] think our American universities are coming to be altogether too much alike. They are really not so much alike as their catalogues; but there ought to be a greater diversity, originality, and specialization. Since there are nearly a thousand institutions in the United States calling themselves colleges and universities, one might expect to find among them examples of all kinds of educational processes. But as a matter of fact there are only three or four different types, and these are not very distinct or different.

p. 382.

There is something about the American atmosphere which compels to uniformity. However unique an institution may be in its origin or original in its aim, it gradually grows into the type now defined as "the standard American university." Whatever it may have started from, it develops the lacking parts like a crystal or a crab.

—**Edwin E. Slosson** (1865–1929), chemist; U.S. writer

1931, *Report for 1930–31,* quoted in Edward C. Elliott (ed.), *The Rise of a University, Vol. II,* 1937, p. 59.

In this country we have a virtual hodgepodge of higher education institutions. We have colleges which are not colleges; we have universities which are not universities; and we have universities which are neither colleges nor universities.

—**Nicholas Murray Butler** (1862–1947), President, Columbia University

1948, "Report of the President's Commission on Higher Education," *Educational Record,* April, p. 118.

The report [of The President's Commission on Higher Education, 1947] calls again and again for great diversification of education. . . . Since American institutions of higher education are already so diversified that neither the faculty nor the students can talk with one another except about the weather, politics, and last Saturday's game, the Commission's advice is a little like telling a drowning man that he can improve his position by drinking a great deal of water.

—**Robert Maynard Hutchins**
(1899–1977), President,
University of Chicago

1971, *Report on Higher Education,* p. ix.

The modern academic university has, like a magnet, drawn all institutions toward its organizational form, until today the same teaching method, the same organization by disciplines, and the same professional academic training for faculty are nearly universal. The shortcomings of the academic university as a model for all other institutions have been obscured by the dazzling success of the best known examples.

—**Task Force**

Prestige

1909, *Proceedings of the National Collegiate Athletic Association 4,* 28 December, quoted in Paul R. Lawrence, *Unsportsmanlike Conduct,* 1987, p. 7.

There are institutions that will not play or row with some other colleges whom they fear, because if beaten it would hurt their prestige and decrease the advertising value of their team or crew.

—**James R. Day** (1845–1923),
Chancellor, Syracuse University

1918, *The Higher Learning in America,* Chapter 4.

It is in the eyes of the unlettered, particularly the business community, that it is desirable for the university to present an imposing front; that being the feature of academic installation which they will readily appreciate. . . . [T]he university buildings should bulk large in the landscape, should be wastefully expensive, and should conform to the architectural mannerisms in present vogue. . . . [T]hey spread abroad the prestige of the university as an ornate and spendthrift establishment; which is believed to bring increased enrolment of students and, what is even more to the point, to conciliate the good-will of the opulent patrons of learning.

—**Thorstein Veblen** (1857–1929),
U.S. sociologist

1930, Inaugural address, October, quoted in George A. Pettitt, *Twenty-eight Years in the Life of a University President,* 1966, p. 38.

We cannot accept the dictum of certain self-styled "prestige" institutions, that a state university must be content to operate on a lower plane for the less gifted group of the population. . . .

—**Robert G. Sproul** (1891–1975),
President, University of California

no date, attributed in *Crown's Book of Political Quotations,* 1982, p. 61.

It might be said that I have the best of both worlds: a Harvard education and a Yale degree.

—**John F. Kennedy** (1917–1963),
President of the United States

1963, *The Uses of the University,* p. 90.

The mark of a university "on the make" is a mad scramble for football stars and professorial luminaries. The former do little studying and the latter little teaching, and so they form a neat combination of muscle and intellect.

> —**Clark Kerr** (1911–2003), Chancellor, University of California, Berkeley; President, University of California

1968, *The American University,* p. 252.

Ostentatious research comes from lust for prestige, not individual merely, but departmental and corporate, for prestige is thought to rub off indefinitely far. We saw how much faculties want presidents "prestigious." I suggest that instead of *prestige* we use the Hindi word *izzat* and see how absurd we are: "Has he *izzat?* Have we enough *izzat* in the house? Our friends across the street are getting ahead of us in *izzat.*" Newspapers could then rate institutions *izzat-wise.*

> —**Jacques Barzun** (1907–), Dean of Faculties and Provost, Columbia University

no date, attributed in David J. Loftus, *The Unofficial Book of Harvard Trivia,* 1985, p. 34.

Theoretically [as a semanticist], I should be immune to the impact of any label or symbol, but that Harvard label has always bothered me. Something happens to me when I'm in the presence of a Harvard man—I sort of lose my confidence, even though I know some of them are really stupid asses.

> —**S. I. Hayakawa** (1906–1992), U.S. Senator; President, San Francisco State College

no date, attributed in <quotationspage. com>.

Americans are the only people in the world known to me whose status anxiety prompts them to advertise their college and university affiliations in the rear window of their automobiles.

> —**Paul Fussell** (1924–), professor of English, University of Pennsylvania

1986, *American Professors,* p. 150.

As far as we know, no one has tallied the number of institutions claiming to be the Harvard of the South or the Princeton of the West or the Yale of the Midwest, but the total number of such claimants is probably large.

> —**Howard R. Bowen** (1908–1989), economist; President, Grinnell College; President, University of Iowa; Chancellor, Claremont University Center; **Jack H. Schuster** (1937–), professor of education and public polity, Claremont Graduate University

Professional Education

1858, *The Idea of a University,* Discourse V.

[H]ere are two methods of Education; the end of the one is to be philosophical, of the other to be mechanical; the one rises toward general ideas, the other is exhausted upon what is particular and external. Let me not be thought to deny the necessity, or to decry the benefit, of such attention to what is particular and practical, as belongs to the useful mechanical arts; life could not go on without them; we owe our daily welfare to them; their exercise is the duty of the many, and we owe the many a debt of gratitude for fulfilling that duty. I only say that Knowledge, in proportion as it tends more and more to be particular, ceases to be Knowledge. . . .

> —**John Henry (Cardinal) Newman** (1801–1890), Rector, Catholic University of Ireland

1867, "Inaugural address," in Francis W. Garforth, *John Stuart Mill on Education,* 1971, p. 155.

Universities are not intended to teach the knowledge to fit men for some special mode of gaining their livelihood. . . . What professional men should carry away with them from an university, is not professional knowledge, but that which should direct the use of their professional knowledge, and bring the light of general culture to illuminate the technicalities of a special pursuit.

—**John Stuart Mill** (1806–1873),
English philosopher, Rector,
St. Andrews University

1918, *The Higher Learning in America,* Chapter 1.

In aim and animus the technical and professional schools are "practical," in the most thoroughgoing manner; while the pursuit of knowledge that occupies the scientists and scholars is not "practical" in the slightest degree. . . . The animus of the one is worldly wisdom; of the other, idle curiosity. The two are incommensurably at variance so far as regards their purposes, and in great measure also as regards their methods of work, and necessarily so.

Chapter 7.

A college of commerce is designed to serve an emulative purpose only—individual gain regardless of, or at the cost of, the community at large—and it is, therefore, peculiarly incompatible with the collective cultural purpose of the university. It belongs in the corporation of learning no more than a department of athletics. . . .

Chapter 7.

[T]he law school belongs to the modern university no more than a school of fencing or dancing. . . . These schools devote themselves with great singleness to the training of practitioners, as distinct from jurists; and their teachers stand in a relation to their students analogous to that in which the "coaches" stand to the athletes.

—**Thorstein Veblen** (1857–1929),
U.S. sociologist

1928, "The Steel Box," in *Bang! Bang!,* p. 58.

"Whom are you?" he asked, for he had attended business college.

—**George Ade** (1866–1944),
U.S. humorist and playwright

1936, *The Higher Learning in America,* p. 47.

Turning professional schools into vocational schools degrades the universities and does not elevate the professions.

—**Robert Maynard Hutchins**
(1899–1977), President,
University of Chicago

no date, Colin R. Coote (ed.), *A Churchill Reader,* 1954, quoted in Edward F. Murphy, *The Crown Treasury of Relevant Quotations,* 1978, p. 235.

Young people at universities study to achieve knowledge and not to learn a trade. We must all learn how to support ourselves, but we must also learn how to live. We need a lot of engineers in the modern world, but we do not want a world of modern engineers.

—**Winston Churchill** (1874–1965),
British statesman

1951, "The democratic dilemma," *Freedom, Education, and the Fund,* 1956, p. 106.

The principal function of a professional school in a university is not to train men for the profession, but to criticize the profession.

—**Robert Maynard Hutchins**
(1899–1977), President,
University of Chicago

1977, *Curriculum,* p. 100.

As late as 1870 a college degree was not at all necessary for admission to Harvard Law School; in fact, there were no admissions requirements at all, and a degree was the automatic reward for the payment of three term bills (the equivalent of eighteen months of study).

—**Frederick Rudolph** (1920–),
professor of history, Williams College

1983, *The Academic Ethic,* p. 5.

Only training for those occupations which rest upon a foundation of fundamental knowledge, as distinct from consisting almost entirely of practical skills, is appropriate for universities.

—**Edward Shils** (1910–1995), professor
of sociology, University of Chicago

1990, *The University: An Owner's Manual,* p. 80.

Most of the graduate programs in a university do not affect the undergraduates in any way. Professional education is self-contained and inward-looking.

—**Henry Rosovsky** (1927–),
Dean of the Faculty of Arts and
Sciences, Harvard University

University

1755, *Alciphron; or the Minute Philosopher,* dialogue 5, section 21, p. 204.

[T]he most ingenious Men are now agreed, that [universities] are only Nurseries of Prejudice, Corruption, Barbarism, and Pedantry.

—**George Berkeley** (1685–1753),
Irish bishop and philosopher

1856, "Universities," in *English Traits,* p. 882.

The university must be retrospective. The gale that gives direction to the vanes on all its towers blows out of antiquity.

—**Ralph Waldo Emerson** (1803–1882),
U.S. poet, philosopher, and essayist

1867, "Inaugural address," in Francis W. Garforth, *John Stuart Mill on Education,* 1971, p. 216.

A university ought to be a place of free speculation.

—**John Stuart Mill** (1806–1873),
English philosopher; Rector,
St. Andrews University

no date, attributed in August Kerber, *Quotable Quotes on Education,* 1968, p. 214.

University, home of lost causes, and forsaken beliefs, and unpopular names, and impossible loyalties.

—**Matthew Arnold** (1822–1888),
English poet and critic

1887, President's Annual Report, Johns Hopkins University, p. 9, quoted in John S. Brubacher and Willis Rudy, *Higher Education in Transition,* 1958, p. 185.

It is one of the noblest duties of a university to advance knowledge, and to diffuse it not merely among those who attend the daily lectures . . . but far and wide.

—**Daniel Coit Gilman** (1831–1908),
President, Johns Hopkins University

1889, "The universities and colleges," in *The American Commonwealth,* Volume II.

While the German universities have been popular but not free, while the English universities have been free but not popular, the American universities have been both free and popular. . . . Accordingly, while a European observer is struck by their inequalities and by the crudeness of many among them, he is also struck by the life, the spirit, the sense of progress, which pervades them.

—**James Bryce** (1875–1938), professor of civil law, Oxford University

1892, Letter to E. Ray Lankester, 11 April, quoted in Bergen Evans, *Dictionary of Quotations,* 1968, p. 718.

The medieval university looked backwards; it professed to be a storehouse of old knowledge. . . . The modern university looks forward, and is a factory of new knowledge: its professors have to be at the top of the wave of progress.

—**T. H. Huxley** (1825–1895), British biologist and teacher

1898, *Educational Reform,* p. 229.

At the heart of every university there must be a great library.

—**Charles William Eliot** (1834–1926), President, Harvard University

1902, "University building," *Popular Science Monthly,* August, p. 332.

In the long run, the greatest university will be the one that devotes most care to its undergraduates.

—**David Starr Jordan** (1851–1931), President, Stanford University

1903, "Maxims for revolutionists," *Man and Superman.*

A fool's brain digests philosophy into folly, science into superstition, and art into pedantry. Hence university education.

—**George Bernard Shaw** (1856–1950), Irish playwright

1903, *The Souls of Black Folk,* chapter 5.

The roots of the tree, rather than the leaves, are the sources of its life; and from the dawn of history, from Academus to Cambridge, the culture of the University has been the broad foundation-stone on which is built the kindergarten's A B C.

—**W. E. B. Du Bois** (1868–1963), professor of sociology, Atlanta University

1910, letter to Herbert B. Brougham, quoted in Arthur S. Link (ed.), *The Public Papers of Woodrow Wilson, volume 20,* p. 70.

My own ideals for the University are those of genuine democracy and serious scholarship. These two, indeed, seem to me to go together.

—**Woodrow Wilson** (1856–1924), President, Princeton University; President of the United States

1912, *Memories and Studies,* p. 354.

The university most worthy of rational admiration is that one in which your lonely thinker can feel himself least lonely, most positively furthered, and most richly fed.

—**William James** (1842–1910), professor of philosophy, Harvard University

1913, *University Control,* p. 414.

It may be our part here in America to develop the true university: A place where each would gladly learn and gladly teach;

open summer and winter, night and day; a center in each community for the conservation of the best traditions and for the origination of the newest ideas; closely in touch with every forward movement of civic and national life; a home from which will go out, and to which will return, our leaders in every department of human activity.

—**J. McKeen Cattell** (1860–1944),
professor of psychology,
Columbia University

1927, *Life and the Student,* p. 177.

Every institution suffers from the sins of every other; and so our universities struggle as they can with deficiencies left by the family, the school, the economic system and the general trend of life, contributing, no doubt, a few errors of their own. It is all one problem.

—**Charles Horton Cooley** (1864–1929),
professor of sociology,
University of Michigan

1930, *Universities: American English German,* p. 3.

[A] university [is] . . . an expression of the age, as well as an influence operating upon both present and future.

p. 15.

The modern university must neither fear the world nor make itself responsible for its conduct.

p. 45.

The term "university" is very loosely used in America; I shall not pause to characterize the absurdities covered by the name.

—**Abraham Flexner** (1866–1959),
U.S. educator

1935, "What is a university," *No Friendly Voice,* 1936, p. 5.

A university is a community of scholars.

—**Robert Maynard Hutchins**
(1899–1977), President,
University of Chicago

1939, Lucien Price, *Dialogues of Alfred North Whitehead,* 1954, p. 127.

The universities are now having a great period, but universities may make themselves a great nuisance as did the monasteries, and for much the same reason.

—**Alfred North Whitehead**
(1861–1947), English philosopher and mathematician; professor of philosophy,
Harvard University

no date, attributed in August Kerber, *Quotable Quotes on Education,* 1968, p. 224.

Let us not burn the universities—yet. After all, the damage they do might be worse. . . .

—**H. L. Mencken** (1880–1956),
U.S. editor and writer

1941, Lucien Price, *Dialogues of Alfred North Whitehead,* 1954, p. 171.

The universities are like any other necessary implement—like a gun. We must have them, the work of civilization could scarcely be carried out without them; but while they are very valuable, they can also be very dangerous.

—**Alfred North Whitehead**
(1861–1947), English philosopher and mathematician; professor of philosophy,
Harvard University

1948, "Morals, religion, and higher education," *Freedom, Education, and the Fund,* 1956, pp. 82–83.

[I] believe that a university is a place where all professors and all students are engaged in independent study, and in this view a true university has not yet arisen in this country.

—**Robert Maynard Hutchins**
(1899–1977), President,
University of Chicago

1951, "The democratic dilemma,"
Freedom, Education, and the Fund,
1956, pp. 105–6.

The best definition of a university that I have been able to think of is that it is a center of independent thought. It may be a good many other things as well; but, if it is not this, it has failed.

—**Robert Maynard Hutchins**
(1899–1977), President,
University of Chicago

no date, attributed in August Kerber,
Quotable Quotes on Education, 1968,
p. 221.

A college teaches, a university both teaches and learns.

—**Robert Maynard Hutchins**
(1899–1977), President,
University of Chicago

1963, *The Uses of the University,* p. 1.

The university started as a single community—a community of masters and students. It may even be said to have had a soul in the sense of a central animating principle. Today the large American university is, rather, a whole series of communities and activities held together by a common name, a common governing board, and related purposes.

p. 17.

Universities have a unique capacity for riding off in all directions and still staying in the same place. . . .

p. 18.

A university anywhere can aim no higher than to be as British as possible for the sake of the undergraduates, as German as possible for the sake of the graduates and the research personnel, as American as possible for the sake of the public at large—and as confused as possible for the sake of the preservation of the whole uneasy balance.

—**Clark Kerr** (1911–2003), Chancellor,
University of California, Berkeley;
President, University of California

1966, "The university," *The New Republic,* May 28, p. 20.

The universities . . . are not only the depositories of wisdom. They are also laboratories where alchemists work, whose function it is to transmute knowledge into human wisdom.

—**Walter Lippman** (1889–1974),
U.S. editor and author

1968, "Parting shots: A century of commencement speeches," *Saturday Review,* 12 May 1979, p. 38.

The delicate thing about the university is that it has a mixed character, that it is suspended between its position in the eternal world, with all its corruption and evil and cruelties, and the splendid world of our imagination.

—**Richard Hofstadter** (1916–1970),
professor of American history,
Columbia University

no date, attributed in Keith Allan Noble,
The International Education Quotations Encyclopaedia, 1995.

A university is what a college becomes when the faculty loses interest in students.

—**John Ciardi** (1916–1986),
U.S. poet and editor

no date, attributed in <www.quote gallery.com>.

In social institutions, the whole is always less than the sum of its parts. There will never be a state as good as its people, or a church worthy of its congregation, or a university equal to its faculty and students.

—**Edward Abbey** (1927–1989), U.S. author

1977, attributed in Keith Allan Noble, *The International Education Quotations Encyclopaedia,* 1995.

There is only one justification for universities, as distinguished from trade schools. They must be centers of criticism.

—**Robert Maynard Hutchins** (1899–1977), President, University of Chicago

1978, *The Perpetual Dream,* p. 355.

Like the Church of Rome after Luther, the modern secular cathedrals we call universities remain strong and retain their hegemony on the academic landscape.

—**Gerald P. Grant** (1938–), professor of education and sociology, Syracuse University; **David Riesman** (1909–2002), professor of sociology, Harvard University

1982, *The Research Universities and their Patrons,* p. 1.

A research university is one whose mores and practices make it clear that enlarging and disseminating knowledge are equally important activities and that each is done better when both are done in the same place by the same people.

—**Robert M. Rosenzweig** (1931–), President, Association of American Universities

1991, *BAD, or the Dumbing of America,* p. 68.

Even if most American universities are hardly loci of thought at all but rather costly sports centers and health spas, the demands of pretension determine that the word *university* be attached to everything that might conceivably bear it, even as the real thing grows more and more rare.

—**Paul Fussell** (1924–), professor of English, University of Pennsylvania

Women's Colleges

1856, address to the Seventh National Women's Rights Convention, 25–26 November, quoted in Barbara Miller Solomon, *In the Company of Educated Women,* 1985, p. 43.

Our demand that Harvard and Yale Colleges should admit women, though not yielded, only waits for a little more time. And while they wait, numerous petty 'female colleges' have sprung into being, indicative of the justice of our claim that a college education should be granted to women. Not one of these female colleges . . . meets the demand of the age, and so will eventually perish.

—**Lucy Stone** (1818–1893), social activist

c. 1870, Last Will and Testament, quoted in Mary Briggs, *Women's Words: The Columbia Book of Quotations by Women,* 1995, p. 104.

It is not my design to render my sex any less Feminine, but to develop as fully as may be the powers of womenhood, and furnish women with the means of usefulness, happiness and honor, now withheld from them.

—**Sophia Smith** (1796–1870), U.S. philanthropist; founder of Smith College

1881, "Report for 1880–81," p. 74, quoted in Edgar W. Knight, *What College Presidents Say,* 1940, p. 302.

Without intending the slightest disparagement of the teaching in any of the certainly excellent colleges for women in the country at this time, it is certainly allowable to say of it that it cannot possibly compare with that which is given in those ancient seats of learning where, through a long series of years, have been gradually brought together all the appliances necessary to facilitate research or illustration in every department of knowledge, and where the teachers are men of celebrity universally recognized as authorities in the world of science or letters.

—**Frederick A. P. Barnard** (1809–1889), President, Columbia University

1887, personal diary, 20 October, quoted in Henry W. Bragdon, *Woodrow Wilson: The Academic Years,* 1967, p. 143.

Lecturing to young women of the present generation on the history and principles of politics is about as appropriate and profitable as would be lecturing to stone masons about the evolution of fashion in dress.

—**Woodrow Wilson** (1856–1924), President, Princeton University; President of the United States

1897, *The American College in American Life,* p. 26.

The purpose in the foundation of the colleges for women has not been to make women into better wives or worthier mothers, but it has been the same purpose which prevails in the higher education of men. . . . The college for women receives each woman, both as a woman and as a

human being; and it receives her in order to train her for the largest life.

—**Charles F. Thwing** (1853–1937), President, Adelbert College; President, Western Reserve University

1904, *Report for 1903–04,* quoted in Edward C. Elliott (ed.), *The Rise of a University, Vol. II,* 1937, p. 189.

The weakness in the program generally offered by women's colleges is that it follows closely or even slavishly that usual at colleges for men, and so fails to meet the peculiar needs that many college women feel. . . . The list of electives offered should contain carefully chosen courses in domestic science, domestic art, sanitary chemistry, the fine arts, and related subjects that are especially adapted to the training of college women.

—**Nicholas Murray Butler** (1862–1947), President, Columbia University

no date, attributed in Barbara Miller Solomon, *In the Company of Educated Women,* 1985, p. 84.

Our failures only marry.

—**M. Carey Thomas** (1857–1935), President, Bryn Mawr College

1954, *My Several Worlds,* p. 91.

We were soundly taught [at Randolph-Macon College, then a woman's institution] and the curriculum carried no hint that we were young women and not young men. We were not corrupted by home economics or dressmaking or cookery or any such soft substitute for hard thinking. We were compelled to take sciences whether we liked them or not, and mathematics and Latin were emphasized and excellently administered. Each year the student body petitioned for a course in home economics, for in that day no girl thought it possible that she might not marry, and each year the faculty sternly refused to yield to the request.

—**Pearl S. Buck** (1892–1973),
U.S. author

2001, *A Woman's Education,* p. 34.

Strong women's institutions should fight to become stronger, not give in to the fashion for coeducation.

—**Jill Ker Conway** (1934–),
President, Smith College

Chapter 9

Governance and Administration

Administration

1869, Inaugural Address, 19 October, in *A Turning Point in Higher Education,* 1969, p. 61.

An administrative officer who undertakes to do everything himself will do but little, and that little ill.

> —**Charles William Eliot** (1834–1926), President, Harvard University

1910, *Report for 1909–1910,* quoted in Edward C. Elliott (ed.), *The Rise of a University, Vol. II,* 1937, pp. 373–74.

[University] administration has been defined . . . as "doing extremely well what had better not be done at all."

> —**Nicholas Murray Butler** (1862–1947), President, Columbia University

1927, *Life and the Student,* p. 184.

It is usually possible to make a fair administrator out of a scholar, just as you can make over a touring car into a tolerable truck. The main thing is to suppress all irregular and exhausting excursions of the mind and use the energy thus saved for system and poise. You lower the gear and stiffen the frame.

> —**Charles Horton Cooley** (1864–1929), professor of sociology, University of Michigan

1932, "The unknowns in higher education," *The Management of Universities,* 1953, p. 91.

Administration may be a necessary evil, but it is at any rate necessary. . . .

> —**Samuel P. Capen** (1878–1956), director, American Council on Education; President, University of Buffalo

1936, *The Higher Learning in America,* Chapter 3, pp. 69–70.

It is a good principle of educational administration that a college or university should do nothing that another agency can do as well. This is a good principle because a college or university has a vast and complicated job even if it does only what it can do.

> —**Robert Maynard Hutchins** (1899–1977), President, University of Chicago

1938, *What a College President Has Learned,* p. 19.

[An administrator] should never feel hurried, or have the sense of working under pressure, for such things interfere gravely with the serenity of judgment that he should always retain.

—**Abbot Lawrence Lowell** (1856–1943),
President, Harvard University

1946, "The administrator," *Journal of Higher Education,* November, p. 395.

The longer an administrator administers, the more he is impressed by the peculiarities of his calling. These peculiarities are such that the administrator of any other enterprise can learn little from the study of university administration; and the administrator of a university, for whom these peculiarities have a sort of morbid fascination, has little to say about the administration of an enterprise which is without them.

p. 397.

Habits are formed by action. The way to become a good administrator is to administer. But this is also the way to become a bad administrator, for vice is a habit too.

p. 400.

The administrator should never do anything he does not have to do, because the things he has to do are so numerous that he cannot possibly have the time to do them. He should never do today what he can put off til tomorrow. He should never do anything he can get anybody else to do for him.

—**Robert Maynard Hutchins**
(1899–1977), President,
University of Chicago

1954, letter to Raymond T. McConnell, quoted at <http://ublib.buffalo.edu/libraries/units/archives/presidents/capen_quotes.html>.

The daily acts of an administrator are written in water. The wind passes over them and they are gone. But the results of his administrative policy if it is positive and constructive, remain. They constitute another stratum in the long process of sedimentation by which universities are slowly formed, and acquire stability and traditions and their individual characteristics. . . .

—**Samuel P. Capen** (1878–1956),
director, American Council on
Education; President,
University of Buffalo

1955, "The administrator: Leader or officeholder?," *Freedom, Education, and the Fund,* 1956, p. 172.

An administrator has all of these ways to lose and he has no way to win. Almost every decision an administrator makes is a decision against somebody.

—**Robert Maynard Hutchins**
(1899–1977), President,
University of Chicago

1958, *Time,* 17 November, p. 96.

I find that the three major administrative problems on campus are sex for the students, athletics for the alumni, and parking for the faculty.

—**Clark Kerr** (1911–2003), Chancellor,
University of California, Berkeley;
President, University of California

1959, letter to John J. Corson, 19 April, quoted in John J. Corson, *Governance of Colleges and Universities,* 1960, p. 18.

Administrative absurdity increases directly with the square of the distance between context and process.

—**Earl Latham** (1907–1977), professor of political science, Amherst College

1962, "The administrator: Bottleneck or pump?," *Daedalus,* Spring, p. 266.

Books on how to administer are as unconvincing as books on how to make love.

p. 269.

The secret of good administration . . . lies not in the administrator's vast and exact knowledge, but in his skill in navigating areas of ignorance.

p. 276.

Administration . . . is an uncodified art. Therefore, the only sure way to learn administration is to administer.

—**Eric Ashby** (1904–1992), botanist; Vice-chancellor, Cambridge University

1968, *The American University,* p. 96.

The simplest rebuttal [to faculty who object to the number of administrators] is to ask the objector "Do you want to bring your own chalk to the classroom?" Administration is seeing to it that the chalk is there.

p. 98.

Good administrators are frequently accused of wanting to keep everything tidy. The charge is correct, and so are the administrators. That is what they are there for—to contain natural chaos.

—**Jacques Barzun** (1907–), Dean of Faculties and Provost, Columbia University

1968, "A different way to restructure the university," *New York Times Magazine,* 18 December, p. 50.

University administration in the United States today combines relative powerlessness with near absolute mindlessness on the subject of education.

—**Irving Kristol** (1920–), U.S. editor

1971, *An Uncertain Glory,* pp. 4–5.

There is at least one popular fallacy I would dispose of immediately and unequivocally. I refer to the oft-repeated notion that the best administrators are the ones who least desire to administer. I have even known deans and one or two presidents to protest that they were shanghaied out of the classroom, to which they would return the instant they could persuade the trustees to unshackle the bonds. Nonsense! The successful presidents and deans I have known were in administration because they wanted to be in it and stayed because they had some sort of masochistic love for it.

—**Frederic W. Ness** (1914–1998), President, Fresno State College

1975, "Institutional paralysis," *Daedalus,* Winter, pp. 61–62.

No institution in the United States puts more constraints on its administration than a university. The administration cannot hire or fire a faculty member on its own initiative. It cannot initiate a new course offering, or modify or abandon an old one. It cannot determine the requirements for completion of a course of study, or decide whether or not a student has met those requirements. And in most cases, it can neither admit nor dismiss a student.

—**Adam Yarmolinski** (1923–2000), professor of public policy, University of Maryland, Baltimore County

1978, *The Art of Administration,* p. 26.

Though the mastery of simple skills does not comprise the whole of administration, carrying out simple tasks well is one distinguishing mark of a good administrator. No amount of fitful brilliance can offset day-to-day bumbling.

—**Kenneth E. Eble** (1923–1988), professor of English, University of Utah

1980, "How we talk and how we act: Administrative theory and administrative life," *Values, Leadership and Quality: The Administration of Higher Education,* 1990, p. 38.

[S]ome of our administrative precepts—the way we talk—may sometimes be less sensible than our administrative behavior—the way we act.

p. 49.

[M]any things that administrators do are essential to keeping the organization functioning; but if these vital things are only done when there is an unusually gifted individual at the top, the organization will not thrive. What makes an organization function well is the density of administrative competence, the kind of selection procedures that make all vice-presidents look alike from the point of view of their probable success. . . .

—**James G. March** (1928–), professor of sociology, political science, and management, Stanford University

1982, " 'The Uses of the University' two decades later: Postscript 1982," *Change,* October, p. 31.

I once said in the 1950s as Chancellor at Berkeley that the great administrative problems of the day were sex for the students, athletics for the alumni, and parking for the faculty; but it could be better said now that the problems are, instead, athletics for the students who have gone "straight," sex for the professors with some of whom the counter-culture still finds support, and parking for the alumni as they return for their refresher courses.

—**Clark Kerr** (1911–2003), Chancellor, University of California, Berkeley; President, University of California

1986, *The Effective Administrator,* p. 16.

[T]he best administrators I know are tutored by the recognition that they may be wrong and that if substantial numbers of their colleagues, faculty and staff members, and students disagree with them, probably they should carefully examine the position they have taken.

—**Donald E. Walker** (1921–), President, Idaho State University; President, Southeastern Massachusetts University; Chancellor, Grossmont-Cuyamaca Community College District

1988, Josef Martin (pseudonym), *To Rise above Principle,* p. 4.

Administration may be necessary, but it is certainly not important.

p. 151.

[M]uch that comes to a chair or dean is best handled by doing nothing at all, or by only pretending to do something, and innumerable other matters are best handled slowly rather than promptly. . . . [T]oo prompt an administrator can produce havoc.

—**Henry H. Bauer** (1931–), Dean of Arts and Sciences, Virginia Polytechnic Institute and State University

1992, *Book,* p. 9.

To his students he was autocratic and unfair, to his advisees distant and obtuse, to his colleagues earthbound and hollow. It was eventually apparent that these characteristics, displayed consistently and noted by all, ideally qualified Marshall for academic administration. . . .

> —**Robert Grudin** (1938–), professor of
> English, University of Oregon

2002, quoted in Lawrence Biemiller, "A storied approach to operations research," *Chronicle of Higher Education,* 14 June, p. A48.

I was a department head once. It was like running naked through a field of geese— it's not going to kill you, but there's enough pecking to keep you moving.

> —**Robert ED (Gene) Woolsey** (1936–),
> professor of operations research,
> Colorado School of Mines

2003, "First, kill all the administrators," *Chronicle of Higher Education,* 21 March.

James I of England once famously (and prophetically) said, "No bishops, no king." I say, no administrators, no life of the mind.

> —**Stanley E. Fish** (1938–), Dean,
> College of Liberal Arts and Sciences,
> University of Illinois at Chicago

Committees

1908, *Microcosmographia Academica,* reprinted in *Two Papers on Academic Change,* 1972, p. 10.

A Caucus is like a mouse-trap; when you are outside you want to get in; and when you are inside the mere sight of the other mice makes you want to get out.

> —**F. M. Cornford** (1874–1943),
> professor of ancient philosophy,
> Cambridge University

1918, *The Higher Learning in America,* Chapter 8.

It [the application of bureaucratic rules to specific cases] devolves, properly, on the clerical force, and especially on those chiefs of clerical bureaus called "deans," together with the many committees-for-the-sifting-of-sawdust into which the faculty of a well administered university is organized.

> —**Thorstein Veblen** (1857–1929),
> U.S. sociologist

1926, *Which Way Parnassus?,* p. 92.

The faculty politicians swarm into the committees, with the result that the least intelligent professors are very often the most powerful. Sometimes the president is fooled by a smooth professor, but more often he is balked by the good ones. He wants to put them on committees, and they don't want to serve; they insist that they give their time to study and teaching.

> —**Percy Marks** (1891–1956),
> U.S. writer and instructor of English

1944, *Teacher in America,* p. 179.

[T]here is no subject under the sun which has not, at one time or other been the *raison d'etre* of an academic committee. In general, the more "enlightened," "progressive," and "democratic" the college is, the more committees there are—and the less the life of a teacher is worth living.

> —**Jacques Barzun** (1907–),
> Dean of Faculties and Provost,
> Columbia University

1968, *The American University,* pp. 128–29.

[B]oth the committee and the large council are hampered by the very virtues of scholarly men. A scholar wants all the evidence before he reaches a conclusion; he is not to be hurried into a snap judgment. But running an institution calls again and again for intelligent guesses and a sense of timing. One reason why administrators keep long hours and deal in bad prose is that the report has to be done overnight for a meeting hastily called to fend off trouble or seize a real opportunity. The resulting state of mind is the antithesis of respectable scholarship and science; an able faculty group will want a semester to decide what has to be done next Thursday.

pp. 132–33.

There is no such thing as a self-propelled committee, any more than a report that writes itself. Coaxing and coaching are the two most delicate parts of administration. Too much input from the chair will retard the metabolism of the committee. Too little turns it into a party of lotus-eaters drifting downstream. A committee has been known to take nine years to come out with recommendations for a new program and a new building that all professed to want from the outset.

—**Jacques Barzun** (1907–), Dean of Faculties and Provost, Columbia University

1978, *A Free and Ordered Space,* p. 23.

[T]he Standing Committee on Special Interests . . . is the special-interest group that convenes to pursue a special interest if there is no preexistent special interest group empowered to pursue that special interest. It monitors public utterances to see who might be offended, and then it takes offense if no one else has the time or inclination; it watches power structures; it petitions for redress; it rallies, gathers, assembles, queries, blockades, and even assaults sincerely in good causes. It is an extraordinarily hardworking group, never at rest, always vigilant.

—**A. Bartlett Giamatti** (1938–1989), President, Yale University

1992, *Book,* p. 44.

Departmental committees report to department heads, who report to the deans,

who report to the provost, who reports to the president. The only trouble is, there's never been anything to report.

—**Robert Grudin** (1938–), professor of English, University of Oregon

1992, *A Semiempirical Life,* p. 94.

To me, any committee is a complete waste of time. Either the other members of a committee think the same way I do, in which case I might as well not be there, or they disagree, in which case I have to waste time arguing with a bunch of obstinate idiots.

—**Michael J. S. Dewar** (1918–1997), professor of chemistry and biochemistry, University of Texas, Austin

Conflict: Faculty–Administration

1912, "The administrative peril," in J. McKeen Cattell, *University Control,* 1913, p. 318.

The paramount danger, the most comprehensively unfavorable factor affecting ominously the prospects of higher education . . . is *the undue dominance of administration:* in policy, in measures, in personal relations, in all the distinctive interests of education, and the welfare of ideas and ideals.

1912, "The administrative peril in education," in J. McKeen Cattell, *University Control,* 1913, p. 336–37.

I wish it were possible always to speak of the presidency and the professorship and forget the president and the professor; yet personality persists despite the difficulty of recognizing in the glorified presidential butterfly the humble professorial worm.

—**Joseph Jastrow** (1863–1944), professor of psychology, University of Wisconsin

no date, attributed in Joseph Jastrow, "The administrative peril in education," in J. McKeen Cattell, *University Control,* 1913, p. 329.

We appear at present to be between the Scylla of presidential autocracy and the Charybdis of faculty and trustee incompetence. The more incompetent the faculties become, the greater is the need of executive autocracy, and the greater the autocracy of the president, the more incompetent do the faculties become.

1913, *University Control,* p. 31.

I once incited one of my children to call her doll Mr. President, on the esoteric ground that he would lie in any position in which he was placed.

—**J. McKeen Cattell** (1860–1944),
professor of psychology,
Columbia University

1941, "Teaching and research,"
Association of American Colleges Bulletin, March, p. 75.

For the past 500 years, to my certain knowledge, administrators have complained about the ineffectiveness of teachers, and teachers have retorted that their work was neither understood nor appreciated by the heads of their colleges.

—**Louis B. Wright** (1899–1984),
director, Folger Shakespeare Library

1941, "The professor as administrant,"
Bulletin of the AAUP, February, p. 19.

[W]hen a man becomes dean or president the reaction of many of his colleagues is from the start, and continues to be, adverse and suspicious. They seem to think that the man, by virtue of his acceptance of administrative responsibility, has suffered some sinister metamorphosis, has been transmogrified.

—**Ernest H. Wilkins** (1880–1966),
President, Oberlin College

1944, *Teacher in America,* p. 178.

In a large university, there are as many deans and executive heads as there are schools and departments. Their relations to one another are intricate and periodic; in fact "galaxy" is too loose a term: it is a planetarium of deans with the President of the University as a central sun. One can see eclipses, inner systems, and oppositions. But usually more sympathy obtains among fellow administrators than between them and the teaching personnel. If it came to a pitched battle, I feel sure that the more compact executive troops, animated by a single purpose, besides being better fed and disciplined, could rout the more numerous but disorderly rabble that teaches.

—**Jacques Barzun** (1907–),
Dean of Faculties and Provost,
Columbia University

1949, "Who should manage universities, and how?," *The Management of Universities,* 1953, p 13.

It should be obvious, it should always have been obvious, that a president cannot make a university and that a board cannot make a university. Either a president or a board can unmake one, however, in a very few months; and many presidents and boards, jointly or severally, have done just that. The only people who can make a university are the professors. But a faculty of cowed professors can only make a rabbit hutch.

—**Samuel P. Capen** (1878–1956),
director, American Council
on Education; President,
University of Buffalo

1955, "The administrator: Leader or officeholder?," *Freedom, Education, and the Fund,* 1956, p. 173.

An administrator who administers is bound to cause trouble. Administrative decisions affect the lives, the fortunes, and even the sacred honor, of members of the faculty. An administrator who wants the support of the faculty will make as few decisions as he can.

—**Robert Maynard Hutchins**
(1899–1977), President,
University of Chicago

1956, "On being retired," in T. C. Denise and M. H. Williams (eds.), *Retrospect and Prospect on the Retirement of T. V. Smith,* quoted in W. H. Cowley, *Presidents, Professors, and Trustees,* 1980, p. 1.

In almost every place which I visit, the academic administration is under continuous attack. . . . Fortunately, the worst malcontents do not often get into administration themselves: they only stand at the window and bark . . . I, for one, do not enjoy their raucous yapping.

—**T. V. Smith** (1890–1964), professor of philosophy, politics, and poetry, Syracuse University

1958, "A president's perspective," in Frank C. Abbot, *Faculty-Administrative Relationships,* pp. 1, 3.

A college or university is in theory an intellectual community in which conflict and tension are at a minimum. The actual state of affairs, however, is usually somewhat different. . . . It is of no particular value to list here the familiar symptoms or evidences of conflict. Perhaps we should expect what is referred to in the Army as "normal griping."

pp. 8, 9.

[I] think it is fairly said that whenever a serious conflict rends a college or university, the administration is necessarily more at fault than any person or group of persons on the faculty. My reason for this assertion is that one of the primary obligations of top administration is to prevent conflict, and, hence, any continuous and deep conflict is prima-facie evidence of administrative ineptness. . . .

—**Logan Wilson** (1907–1990), President, University of Texas at Austin; President, American Council on Education

1958, quoted in George A. Pettitt, *Twenty-eight Years in the Life of a University President,* 1966, p. 60.

Professors are hard to please, as they should be, because timid uncritical men cannot train youth for courage and adventure, and the president who retains his intellectual and moral stature under their cold scrutiny is indeed a good one.

—**Joel Hildebrand** (1881–1983), professor of chemistry, University of California, Berkeley

no date, attributed in Henry M. Wriston, *Academic Procession,* 1959, pp. 119–120.

The ideal faculty man, as I have rather romantically been thinking of him, ought properly to find administration distasteful. A man who positively enjoys sitting on committees, arguing about university affairs, or haggling about the wording of regulations, is unlikely to be passionately interested in teaching, scholarship or research.

—**Max Black** (1909–1988), professor of philosophy, Cornell University

1967, *Power, Presidents, and Professors,* p. 85.

Some presidents who were professors have found themselves regarded adversely and suspiciously by their erstwhile colleagues. To such faculty members, the very fact that a professor has turned president is evidence of his vanity, his thirst for power and public notice, or his impertinence as an educational administrator. At last he has revealed himself as a cormorant and a Machiavelli.

—**Nicholas J. Demerath** (1913–1996), professor of sociology, Washington University

1967, "The job of a college president," *Educational Record,* Winter, p. 68.

To college faculty members and students, "administration" is, though not a four-letter word, a dirty one. To his former colleagues, a professor who becomes dean or president is an emigre or a turncoat, a man who has renounced academic culture and scholarly values in favor of power and materialism.

—**Herbert A. Simon** (1916–), professor of computer sciences and psychology, Carnegie Institute of Technology

1979, "The university president," *The Hesburgh Papers,* p. 11.

Every day of every year, year in and year out, the president must prove himself to the faculty. Especially in a large institution, there is no such thing as a completely cordial and trusting relationship. The president is, in some sense, the symbolic adversary, since he is ultimately the bearer of whatever bad news comes to the faculty these days.

—**Theodore M. Hesburgh, C.S.C.** (1917–), President, University of Notre Dame

1980, "How we talk and how we act: Administrative theory and administrative life," *Values, Leadership and Quality: The Administration of Higher Education,* 1990, p. 37.

Administration is the art of disappointing people, and those who have been disap-

pointed do not always see administrative beauty in their tormentors. . . .

—**James G. March** (1928–), professor of sociology, political science, and management, Stanford University

1986, *The Many Lives of Academic Presidents,* p. 44.

Faculty members almost universally discount the performance of their current presidents at a rate that must be 25 to 75 percent below that of other observers. . . . A passing grade of "C" given by a faculty may be equivalent to a "B" or an "A" if given by more neutral observers.

—**Clark Kerr** (1911–2003), Chancellor, University of California, Berkeley; President, University of California; **Marian L. Gade** (1934–), research associate, University of California, Berkeley

1990, *The University: An Owner's Manual,* p. 243.

It is always bad form for a professor to admit the desire for administrative office. One of our clichés says: anyone who really wants these posts should be disqualified. Governance is a form of class treason, a leap from "we" to "they," and a betrayal of our primary mission—teaching and research. For this reason also, it is crucial—once a decanal or similar post is attained—to give evidence of continual suffering. Colleagues will offer condolences (congratulations would be a breach of manners) and the incumbent must always publicly yearn for a speedy return to laboratory or library or classroom, no matter what his or her real state of happiness.

—**Henry Rosovsky** (1927–), Dean of the Faculty of Arts and Sciences, Harvard University

1998, "University presidents—then and now," in William G. Bowen and Harold T. Shapiro (eds.) *Universities and Their Leadership,* p. 73.

The most common response of faculty to the news that a colleague has moved up to an administrative post is that they must, until that very moment, have overestimated the person's IQ!

> —**Harold T. Shapiro** (1935–), President, University of Michigan; President, Princeton University

2001, *Chronicle of Higher Education,* 14 December, p. A10.

I was a professor. I know the system. They're sons of bitches. These people are relentless. University administrators are unsparing. They will not say "uncle" until you have them up against the wall with your knee in their crotch.

> —**Jeffrey M. Duban** (1949–), U.S. attorney

2001, *A Woman's Education,* p. 65.

[A] president's relationship to a faculty involves more double binds than a bad marriage on the brink of collapse.

> —**Jill Ker Conway** (1934–), President, Smith College

Dean

no date, quoted in Harold W. Dodds, *The Academic President: Educator or Caretaker?,* 1977 p. 68.

A dean is too stupid to be a professor, but too bright to be a president.

> —**Author Unknown**

1943, *Cornell University: Founders and the Founding,* p. 200.

[T]he general opinion seemed to be that the appointment of professors to the office [of dean] was a useless waste of talent. "Why is it," asked Professor Nichols, "that as soon as a man has demonstrated that he has an unusual knowledge of books, some one immediately insists on making him a bookkeeper?"

> —**Carl Becker** (1873–1945), professor of history, Cornell University

1950, 5 April, quoted in Robert Ferrell, *The Eisenhower Diaries,* 1981, p. 173.

There is probably no more complicated business in the world than the picking of a new dean within a university. Faculties, including the retiring dean, feel an almost religious fervor in insisting on acceptance of their particular views. These are almost as varied as there are individuals involved, and every man's opinion is voiced in terms of urgency. The result is complete confusion, and I cannot see why universities have followed such a custom.

> —**Dwight D. Eisenhower** (1890–1969), President, Columbia University; President of the United States

1958, *The Academic Marketplace,* p. 200.

Popularity with the faculty is a doubtful merit in a dean. It is not uncommon for professors to rise to that position by leading local campaigns for faculty autonomy and then, once elevated, to grow into habits of despotism.

> —**Theodore Caplow** (1920–), professor of sociology, University of Virginia; **Reese J. McGee** (1929–), professor of sociology, Purdue University

1959, *Academic Procession,* p. 22.

[T]he duty of the dean is to make the college what the president has long asserted it already is.

> —**Henry M. Wriston** (1889–1978), President, Lawrence College; President, Brown University

1968, *The American University,* p. 116.

In this century an administrative job is less a post than a predicament, which is why few are the administrators who work a nine-to-five day or can notice a break between one week and the next. Rather it is a continuous scrimmage that nominally begins at 8:30 in the morning. A dean who has resigned, who is "out of the kitchen," *functus officio* [having discharged his duties], feels like a convict released for good behavior.

—**Jacques Barzun** (1907–),
Dean of Faculties and Provost,
Columbia University

1973, *Malice in Blunderland,* p. 90.

Those who can—do. Those who cannot—teach. Those who cannot teach become deans.

—**Thomas L. Martin, Jr.** (1921–),
President, Illinois Institute of Technology

1973, attributed in Thomas L. Martin, *Malice in Blunderland,*1973, p. 90.

Father Damian's Rules for Deans. Rule 1.—Hide!!! Rule 2.—If they find you, lie!!!

—**Father Damian C. Fandal, O. P.**
(1929–1994), Dean of Academic Affairs,
University of Dallas

1987, "Deaning," *Harvard Magazine,* January-February 1987, p. 34.

The dean is likely to know more members of the faculty than anyone else—usually by first name. . . . No ordinary professor can have as wide a circle of friends and associates: few will have the opportunity to make so many enemies.

—**Henry Rosovsky** (1927–),
Dean of the Faculty of Arts and
Sciences, Harvard University

1988, Josef Martin (pseudonym), *To Rise above Principle,* p. 82.

A dean qua dean has no friends, and a dean qua dean encounters no disinterested people.

p. 108.

[B]eing dean means being criticized, because no matter what goes wrong, there is always someone who knew it would; and if you ever find everyone going your way, then you may be sure that you're in the wrong lane.

—**Henry H. Bauer** (1931–), Dean of
Arts and Sciences, Virginia Polytechnic
Institute and State University

1990, *The University: An Owner's Manual,* p. 46.

A president views the university from an Olympian perspective, always prodding, seeking weakness, suggesting improvement. He stands on the shoulders of the deans peering into the distance, thinking of new challenges in spans of years, even five years, and on occasion decades. [As dean] I saw myself as a field commander, ducking bullets from unexpected directions. All too often goals were measured in hours, at best in weeks.

p. 53.

Deans prefer harmony and order.

pp. 213–14.

As a dean, my activities would consist of seeing many people, shuffling papers, writing letters, and chairing innumerable committees. Frequently these activities did not result in measurable progress or benefit, but I always returned home at night convinced that my time had been used productively. What is the basis of this constructive illusion? The difficulty of measuring executive output, and the natural tendency to give oneself the benefit of the doubt.

pp. 233–34.

Both professors and students have in their possession uninterrupted time. Time to write, read, think, dream—and to waste. A dean's schedule—any administrator's schedule—could not be more different: half-hour appointments lasting nearly all day and not infrequently beginning with breakfast. . . . Once I compared myself to a dentist: twelve to fourteen interviews a day, frequently accompanied by pain.

—**Henry Rosovsky** (1927–),
Dean of the Faculty of Arts and
Sciences, Harvard University

1997, *Straight Man,* p. 357.

A liberal arts dean in a good mood is a potentially dangerous thing. It suggests a world different from the one we know.

—**Richard Russo** (1949–), U.S. novelist

Governance

1776, *Wealth of Nations,* Book Five,
Chapter I.

If the authority to which he [the teacher] is subject resides in the body corporate, the college, or university, of which he himself is a member, and which the greater part of the other members are, like himself, persons who either are or ought to be teachers, they are likely to make a common cause, to be all very indulgent to one another, and every man to consent that his neighbour may neglect his duty, provided he himself is allowed to neglect his own. . . . If the authority to which he is subject resides, not so much in the body corporate of which he is a member, as in some other extraneous persons . . . it is not indeed in this case very likely that he will be suffered to neglect his duty altogether.

—**Adam Smith** (1723–1790),
Scottish philosopher and economist

1913, *University Control,* pp. 31–32.

The argument for giving a free hand to the president is that this is the way to get things done. It should, however, be remembered that it is quite as important—and this holds especially in the university—not to do the wrong thing as it is to do the right thing. The time of the president is largely occupied with trying to correct or to explain the mistakes he has made, and the time of the professor is too much taken up with trying to dissuade the president from doing unwise things or in making the best of them after they have been done.

—**J. McKeen Cattell** (1860–1944),
professor of psychology,
Columbia University

1918, *The Higher Learning in America,*
Chapter 8.

[A]s seen from the point of view of the higher learning, the academic executive and all his works are anathema, and should be discontinued by the simple expedient of wiping him off the slate; and that the governing board, in so far as it presumes to exercise any other than vacantly perfunctory duties, has the same value and should with advantage be lost in the same shuffle.

—**Thorstein Veblen** (1857–1929),
U.S. sociologist

1920, "The relation between faculties and governing boards," *At War With Academic Traditions in America,* 1934, pp. 290–91.

[T]he respective functions of the faculties and the governing boards—those things that each had better undertake, those it had better leave to the other, and those which require mutual concession—are best learned from experience and best embodied in tradition. Tradition has great advantages over regulations. It is a more delicate instrument; it accommodates itself to things that are not susceptible of sharp definition; it is more flexible in its application, making exceptions and allowances which it would be difficult to foresee or prescribe. It is also more stable. Regulations can be amended; tradition cannot, for it is not made, but grows, and can be altered only by a gradual change in general opinion, not by a majority vote. In short, it cannot be amended, but only outgrown.

—**Abbott Lawrence Lowell**
(1856–1943), President,
Harvard University

1955, "The administrator: Leader or officeholder?," *Freedom, Education, and the Fund,* 1956, p. 174.

A university administrator has at least five constituents: the faculty, the trustees, the students, the alumni, and the public. He could profitably spend all his time with any one of the five. What he actually does, of course, is to spend just enough with each of the five to irritate the other four.

—**Robert Maynard Hutchins**
(1899–1977), President,
University of Chicago

1959, *An Atmosphere to Breathe,* p. 9.

The truth is, as Lowell used to point out, that in a university no one has or should have final control over everything.

—**McGeorge Bundy** (1919–1996),
Dean, Faculty of Arts and Sciences,
Harvard University

1962, "Some myths about professors, presidents, and trustees," *Teachers College Record,* November, p. 165.

[C]ivil governments have created them [institutions of higher education] for the good of the general community. They have not been founded for the sole or even the primary benefit of professors, students, trustees, or all of them taken together but, instead, for the benefit of society at large.

Hence, in all countries civil government, the most inclusive agency of society, retains the right to set them in motion and, further, to require that their governing boards represent the public interest.

—**W. H. Cowley** (1899–1978),
President, Hamilton College

1963, *The Uses of the University,* p. 35.

There is a "kind of lawlessness" in any large university, with many separate sources of initiative and power; and the task is to keep this lawlessness within reasonable bounds.

p. 100.

The [faculty] group serves a purpose as a balance wheel—resisting some things that should be resisted, insisting on more thorough discussion of some things that should be more thoroughly discussed, delaying some developments where delay gives time to adjust more gracefully to the inevitable. All this yields a greater sense of order and stability.

—**Clark Kerr** (1911–2003), Chancellor,
University of California, Berkeley;
President, University of California

no date, attributed in Myron F. Wicke, *Handbook for Trustees,* 1963, p. 65.

[A]cademic governance is far too important to be left entirely in the hands of professors or entirely in the hands of boards of trustees. The enterprise requires the participation of both and, further, that of alumni and students. . . .

—**W. H. Cowley** (1899–1978),
President, Hamilton College

1965, "Myths and realities of independence," in Logan Wilson, *Emerging Patterns in American Higher Education,* 1965, p. 24.

Like the debutante's father who is fearful that young men will make passes at his daughter but is even more fearful that none will want to, every institution desires the interest and attention of its constituents, but does not want their interference.

—**Logan Wilson** (1907–1990),
President, University of Texas at Austin;
President, American Council
on Education

1966, "Statement on government of colleges and universities," *Policy Documents and Reports, Ninth Edition,* 2001, p. 220.

The governing board of an institution of higher education, while maintaining a general overview, entrusts the conduct of administration to the administrative officers—the president and the deans—and the conduct of teaching and research to the faculty. The board should undertake appropriate self-limitation.

p. 221.

The faculty has primary responsibility for such fundamental areas as curriculum, subject matter and methods of instruction, research, faculty status, and those aspects of student life which relate to the educational process. On these matters the power of review or final decision lodged in the governing board or delegated by it to the president should be exercised adversely only in exceptional circumstances, and for reasons communicated to the faculty.

—**American Association
of University Professors**

1973, *Governance of Higher Education: Six Priority Problems,* p. 3.

Governance is a means and not an end. It should be devised and adjusted not for its own sake but for the sake of the welfare of the academic enterprise.

p. 13.

Governance takes many forms and occurs in many environments. What can be said and be true about one place may not be true about another. What may be wise action in one situation may be unwise in another. The recognition of the great variety of patterns, conditions, and responses is the beginning of wisdom in approaching the problems of governance.

—**Carnegie Commission
on Higher Education**

1980, *At the Pleasure of the Board,* p. 56.

Despite one's legal authority, it is hard to operate a productive school against the will of those who are its teachers and students.

—**Joseph F. Kauffman** (1921–),
President, Rhode Island College

1982, " 'The Uses of the University' two decades later: Postscript 1982," *Change,* October, p. 29.

[W]ithin the range of alternatives considered in the United States, forms of governance make some difference but not as much as often supposed. . . . One specific arrangement in governance versus another has minor implications for what actually happens in a university.

—**Clark Kerr** (1911–2003), Chancellor,
University of California, Berkeley;
President, University of California

1982, *The Control of the Campus,* p. 88.

Governance guidelines in themselves have no animating power. In its most authentic sense, governance is simply the process by which people pursue common ends and, in the process, breathe life into otherwise lifeless forms. The best measure of the health of the governance structure at a college is not how it looks on paper, but the climate in which it functions.

> **—Carnegie Foundation for the Advancement of Teaching**

1989, "The cybernetics of university governance," in Jack H. Schuster et al., *Governing Tomorrow's Campus,* p. 40.

Governance is not in its essence a structure, but a shared idea about how to do higher education.

> **—Robert Birnbaum** (1936–), Chancellor, University of Wisconsin-Oshkosh

2001, "Leading higher education in an era of rapid change," 48th Annual Meeting of the State Higher Education Executive Officers, 30 July.

Universities have a style of governance that is more adept at protecting the past than preparing for the future.

> **—James J. Duderstadt** (1942–), President, University of Michigan

2003, "Academic values and the lure of profit," *Chronicle of Higher Education,* 4 April, p. B9.

Looking over the checkered history of commercial activity on campuses, one can more easily point to examples of costly unilateral decisions by impatient administrators, such as ill-advised Internet ventures or grandiose athletic projects, than to valuable opportunities lost through inordinate faculty delays.

> **—Derek Bok** (1930–), President, Harvard University

Leadership

1938, *The Educational Forum,* quoted in Edgar W. Knight, *What College Presidents Say,* 1940, p. 18.

Are there as many able college executives today as in past decades? Probably not. . . . The presidency is more complicated and less revered, than it was. In the State University field we have many able leaders today, but they are not, I fear, the equal of those of yesterday. . . .

> **—James L. McConaughy** (1887–1948), President, Wesleyan University

1955, "The administrator: Leader or officeholder?," *Freedom, Education, and the Fund,* 1956, p. 174.

Since the administrator's salary, prestige, and perquisites are high, he will be criticized under any conditions. But he will seldom be seriously disliked if he does nothing. People will say that he is a weak man and that he does not give the institution the leadership it should have. But everybody secretly yearns for the days of Coolidge, and academic communities, whatever their protestations to the contrary, really prefer anarchy to any form of government.

> **—Robert Maynard Hutchins** (1899–1977), President, University of Chicago

1956, "What does a president do?," unpublished lecture quoted in Robert F. Wert, "Leadership: The integrative factor," in Terry F. Lunsford (ed.), *The Study of Academic Administration,* 1963, p. 92.

Name a great American college or university, and I'll name a commanding leader or leaders who held its presidency. On the other hand, name an institution with a brilliant but now-withered past, and I can probably identify the weak . . . president or the faculty cabal, or the trustee clique that stopped its progress. . . . The fact seems to be that the great colleges and universities of this country became great under brilliant presidential leaders and that other institutions with comparable and sometimes better potential lagged or languished because of lack of a strong president.

—**W. H. Cowley** (1899–1978),
President, Hamilton College

1958, "A president's perspective," in Frank C. Abbot, *Faculty-Administrative Relationships,* p. 9.

Deans and presidents . . . are often lifted from virtually unrelated assignments into totally new and different responsibilities. No one is ever drafted against his will, to be sure, and most have presumably demonstrated some aptitude for educational leadership. But few people, including those who name administrators, realize that to move from a professorship to a presidency is to change occupation. . . .

—**Logan Wilson** (1907–1990),
President, University of Texas at Austin;
President, American Council
on Education

1968, *The American University,* pp. 135–36.

Where in the system leadership comes from is the one remaining question. Or rather, it is a question that is asked, impatiently, by those who think that the new university should show "capacity for change," "innovation," and "bold answers to the challenge of our times." This demand apparently discounts everything that has happened in universities during the past fifteen years, and takes for granted two manifest impossibilities: one, that a huge confederation staffed by highly independent individuals can move like an army at the command of a chief; two, that a modern

university can depart from practices common to its kind without loss in the competition for faculty and students.

—**Jacques Barzun** (1907–),
Dean of Faculties and Provost,
Columbia University

1968, *Leadership for Education: A Final Report,* p. 4, quoted in J. B. Lon Hefferlin, *Dynamics of Educational Reform,* 1969, p. 44.

The quickest way of changing an institution is to change its leadership.

—**James A. Perkins** (1911–1998),
President, Cornell University

1971, *An Uncertain Glory,* p. 49.

Regardless of what may appear in the charter and bylaws, the authority of the president, his real leadership, depends on the willingness of the campus to accept him as a leader. If it will not, well there are other ways for him to earn a living.

—**Frederic W. Ness** (1914–1998),
President, Fresno State College

1974, *Leadership and Ambiguity,* p. 203.

[T]he president is a bit like the driver of a skidding automobile. The marginal judgments he makes, his skill, and his luck may possibly make some difference in the survival prospects for his riders. As a result, his responsibilities are heavy. But whether he is convicted of manslaughter or receives a medal for heroism is largely outside his control.

—**Michael D. Cohen** (1945–), professor
of complex systems, information, and
public policy, University of Michigan;
James G. March (1928–), professor of
international management, political
science, and sociology,
Stanford University

1977, *Missions of the College Curriculum,* p. 16.

[A]dministrative leadership is very much in demand until it is exercised.

> **—Carnegie Foundation for the Advancement of Teaching**

1979, "The university president," *The Hesburgh Papers,* p. 156.

I have a strong belief, nurtured no doubt by my own prejudices, that the central person in exercising moral leadership for the life and prosperity of any academic institution must be its president. Presidential leadership demands that, for his speaking to be effective, he must somehow enlist the support of the various segments of the community. Otherwise, he is only speaking for himself and to himself, which is good posturing, but bad leadership.

> **—Theodore M. Hesburgh, C.S.C.** (1917–), President, University of Notre Dame

1980, *Being Lucky,* pp. 119–20.

The house of intellect is by nature averse to orders. Besides, one cannot command learning, cannot command an atmosphere; but one can, with the proper leadership, contribute to the nurture of all of these.

> **—Herman B Wells** (1902–2000), President, Indiana University

1980, "How we talk and how we act: Administrative theory and administrative life," *Values, Leadership and Quality: The Administration of Higher Education,* 1990, p. 53.

Where top leadership affects variation in outcomes, the system is probably not functioning well.

> **—James G. March** (1928–), professor of sociology, political science, and management, Stanford University

1982, " 'The Uses of the University' two decades later: Postscript 1982," *Change,* October, p. 30.

Presidents were used like Kleenex. The institutions survived, but their leader did not.

> **—Clark Kerr** (1911–2003), Chancellor, University of California, Berkeley; President, University of California

1983, *The youngest science: Notes of a medicine-watcher,* p. 172.

A good university doesn't need to be headed as much as to be given its head, and it is the administrator's task—not at all an easy one—to see that this happens. The temptations to intervene from the top, to reach in and try and change the way the place works, to arrive at one's desk each morning with one's mind filled with exhilarating ideas for revitalizing the whole institution, are temptations of the devil and need resisting with all the strength of the administrator's character.

> **—Lewis Thomas** (1913–1993), U.S. physician and author

1984, "Presidents will lead—if we let them," *AGB Reports,* July/August, p. 11.

I am convinced that it will be strong, assertive, and enlightened presidents that will lead us to a new and higher level of contribution. . . . Our future rests on the bold, decisive leadership of college and university presidents nationwide.

> **—James L. Fisher** (1931–), President, Towson State University

1984, "The ethical imperative of the college presidency," *Educational Record,* Spring, p. 25.

At its highest, most impressive levels, presidential leadership is an art form individualized by person, place, and circumstance. It is an art that invites imitation despite the evidence that exceptional leadership is by its nature inimitable.

—**Harold L. Enarson** (1919–),
President, Ohio State University

1988, *How Colleges Work,* p. 227.

Great credit is due to presidents and faculties when such a [campus] rebirth takes place. Less remembered are situations in which dramatic presidential acts generate negative consequences leading to a short and unhappy tenure. . . . Taking office in order to "turn the institution around" may be more often a prescription for joint misery than for success.

—**Robert Birnbaum** (1936–),
Chancellor, University of
Wisconsin-Oshkosh

1997, "Who will lead higher education's transformation?" *Planning for Higher Education,* Fall, pp. 50, 53.

Those who advocate change in higher education should stop all the fatuous talk and prose about consensus, joint decision making, leadership as followership, and collegial leadership—an oxymoron—as a way to move forward onto new ground. Structural changes require strong, responsible, daring, and action-oriented leadership. . . . [U]nless the college president is unshackled to become a strong transformational leader, higher education will not be able to make the changes that seem increasingly urgent.

—**James L. Fisher** (1931–), President,
Towson State University

Organization and Structure

1858, lecture, Christian Library Association, 22 June, quoted in Richard Hofstadter and Wilson Smith (eds.), *American Higher Education: A Documentary History, Volume II,* 1961, pp. 518–19.

How simple the idea of a university! An association of eminent scholars in every department of human knowledge; together with books embodying the results of human investigation and thinking, and all the means of advancing and illustrating knowledge. How simple the law which is to govern this association!—That each member as a thinker, investigator, and teacher shall be a law unto himself, in his own department.

—**Henry P. Tappan** (1805–1881),
President, University of Michigan

1923, *The Rise of the Universities,* pp. 24–25.

The essentials of university organization are clear and unmistakable, and they have been handed down in unbroken continuity. They have lasted more than seven hundred years—what form of government has lasted so long? Very likely all this is not final—nothing is in this world of flux—but it is singularly tough and persistent. . . .

—**Charles Homer Haskins**
(1870–1937), professor of history,
Harvard University

no date, quoted in Robert M. Hutchins, "The higher learning II," *No Friendly Voice,* 1936, p. 28.

[T]he increasing departmentalization of universities has trivialized the intellect of professors.

—**Alfred North Whitehead**
(1861–1947), English philosopher and
mathematician; professor of philosophy,
Harvard University

1939, "Hutchins of Chicago," in *Harper's Monthly Magazine,* March, p. 346.

One of the reasons why American universities are chaotic today is that they are so organized that the faculty can't run them and the president mustn't.

> —**Milton S. Mayer** (1908–1986), U.S. journalist

1959, *The American College President,* p. 60.

Colleges are gyroscopically controlled enterprises. Their directions and speed are set and sudden changes, while unlikely, are almost sure to be catastrophic. Colleges yield only to continuous pressures persistently applied. . . .

> —**Harold W. Stoke** (1903–1982), President, University of New Hampshire; President, Louisiana State University; President, Queens College

1960, *Governance of Colleges and Universities,* p. 43.

The administration of institutions of higher education presents a unique dualism in organizational structure.

> —**John J. Corson** (1905–1990), management consultant

no date, attributed in George Dennis O'Brien, *All the Essential Half-Truths about Higher Education,* 1998, p. 30.

The university is a collection of departments tied together by a common steam plant.

> —**Robert Maynard Hutchins** (1899–1977), President, University of Chicago

1963, "Faculty organization and authority," in Terry F. Lunsford (ed.), *The Study of Academic Administration,* p. 47.

The university and the large college are fractured by expertness, not unified by it. . . . The campus is a holding company for professional groups rather than a single association of professionals.

> —**Burton R. Clark** (1921–), professor of sociology, University of California, Los Angeles

1963, *The Uses of the University,* p. 20.

Hutchins once described the modern university as a series of separate schools and departments held together by a central heating system. In an area where heating is less important and the automobile more, I have sometimes thought of it as a series of individual faculty entrepreneurs held together by a common grievance over parking.

p. 41.

The "Idea of a University" was a village with its priests. The "Idea of a Modern University" was a town—a one-industry town—with its intellectual oligarchy. "The Idea of a Multiversity" is a city of infinite variety.

> —**Clark Kerr** (1911–2003), Chancellor, University of California, Berkeley; President, University of California

1972, *The Future Executive, p. 39.*

The analogy between an academic faculty and a political legislature is apt. Every faculty member is juridically free and equal—a politically acceptable (if practically unrealistic) organization chart for a university faculty could be drawn only by placing all the names in a horizontal line on a long roll of paper.

> —**Harlan Cleveland** (1918–), political scientist; President, University of Hawaii

1973, "The university and society's new demands upon it," in C. Kaysen (ed.), *Content and Context,* p. 397.

The faculty members have the rights of members of a community—control over their own activities and their time—without the normative constraints and demands that such a community provides. They have the rights of employees of a purposive corporation—the security of a salary and other perquisites of such employees—without the obligation to give up control over their time for use toward a corporate goal. The effect of this structural fault is to create a status with special privileges, a status with the autonomy of a community member, the security of a corporate employee, and the obligations of neither.

> —**James S. Coleman** (1926–1995),
> professor of sociology,
> University of Chicago

1973, *The University as an Organization,* p. 3.

Organizationally, the university is, in fact, one of the most complex structures in modern society; it is also increasingly archaic. It is complex because its formal structure does not describe either actual power or responsibilities; it is archaic because the functions it must perform are not and cannot be discharged through the formal structure provided in its charter.

> —**James A. Perkins** (1911–1998),
> President, Cornell University

1974, *Leadership and Ambiguity,* p. 3.

The American college or university is a prototypic organized anarchy. It does not know what it is doing. Its goals are either vague or in dispute. Its technology is familiar but not understood. Its major participants wander in and out of the or-

ganization. These factors do not make a university a bad organization or a disorganized one; but they do make it a problem to describe, understand, and lead.

> —**Michael D. Cohen** (1945–), professor of complex systems, information, and public policy, University of Michigan;
> **James G. March** (1928–), professor of international management, political science, and sociology, Stanford University

1978, "Anarchy and a built-in gyro," *AGB Reports,* May/June, p. 6.

[A]ny good undergraduate college resists rule, government, even law: it is at its most orderly a balance of anarchies. . . . [A]ny collegiate community, particularly in its faculty members and students, is essentially a self-correcting apparatus. It has its own gyros that will ultimately keep it stabilized and afloat. But it will generally react negatively to being aided, particularly from outside.

> —**Timothy S. Healy, S. J.** (1923–1992),
> President, Georgetown University

1986, *The Effective Administrator,* p. 86.

Universities have strong self-correcting tendencies. When bacteria invade the tissue of an organism, counteractions are immediately called forth, because the systems of that organism exist in a moving equilibrium. And therefore interference in one system calls forth compensating reactions in other systems. So with the university.

> —**Donald E. Walker** (1921–),
> President, Idaho State University;
> President, Southeastern Massachusetts University; Chancellor, Grossmont-Cuyamaca Community College District

Politics

1869, Inaugural Address, 19 October, in *A Turning Point in Higher Education,* 1969, p. 52.

The divisions within the faculty are never between the old and the young officers. There are always old radicals and young conservatives.

p. 63.

[H]owever important the functions of the President, it must not be forgotten that he is emphatically a constitutional executive. It is his character and his judgment which are of importance, not his opinions. He is the executive officer of deliberative bodies, in which decisions are reached after discussion by a majority vote. These decisions bind him. He cannot force his own opinions upon anybody. A university is the last place in the world for a dictator. Learning is always republican. It has idols, but not masters.

—**Charles William Eliot** (1834–1926), President, Harvard University

1908, *Microcosmographia Academica,* reprinted in *Two Papers on Academic Change,* 1972, p. 9.

You think (do you not?) that you have only to state a reasonable case, and people must listen to reason and act upon it at once. It is just this conviction that makes you so unpleasant. There is little hope of dissuading you; but has it occurred to you that nothing is ever done until everyone is convinced that it ought to be done, and has been convinced for so long that it is now time to do something else?

—**F. M. Cornford** (1874–1943), professor of ancient philosophy, Cambridge University

1911, quoted in Arthur Stanley Link, *Wilson,* vol. 1, 1947, p. 91.

I don't want you to suppose that when I was nominated for Governor of New Jersey I emerged from academic seclusion, where nothing was known of politics. I'll confide in you as I have already confided in others—that, as compared with the college politician, the real article seems like an amateur.

—**Woodrow Wilson** (1856–1924), President, Princeton University; President of the United States

no date, attributed in Keith Allan Noble, *The International Education Quotations Encyclopaedia,* 1995.

University politics are vicious precisely because the stakes are so small.

—**Henry A. Kissinger** (1923–), professor of government, Harvard University; U.S. Secretary of State

no date, attributed in Paul Dickson, *The Rules of the Game,* 1978, p. 164.

Academic politics . . . are the most vicious form of politics because the fighting is over issues decided five years earlier.

—**Wallace Sayre** (1905–1972), professor of political science, Columbia University

1963, in Robert M. Hutchins, et al., *On Science, Scientists and Politics,* quoted in Henry A. Ashmore, *Unseasonable Truth,* 1989, p. 423.

Though I do not know much about professional politics, I know a lot about academic politics—and that is the worst kind.

—**Robert Maynard Hutchins** (1899–1977), President, University of Chicago

1986, *The Effective Administrator,* p. 30.

[P]residential survival operates relatively independently of presidential competence, and is nothing more than an accurate reflection of the political nature of the office and sometimes the institution.

p. 194.

An administrator works with the consent of the governed. The most reliable tools of the administrator are diplomacy and persuasion.

—**Donald E. Walker** (1921–),
President, Idaho State University;
President, Southeastern Massachusetts
University; Chancellor, Grossmont-
Cuyamaca Community College District

Trustees

1838, lecture at the American Institute of Instruction, August, quoted in Richard Hofstadter and Wilson Smith (eds.), *American Higher Education: A Documentary History, Volume I,* 1961, p. 320.

No college in this country has permanently flourished, in which the trustees have not been willing to concede to the faculty, the rank, dignity, honor and influence, which belong essentially to their station.

—**Jasper Adam** (1793–1841),
President, Charleston College

1913, "Reminiscences of Columbia University in the last quarter of the last century," *Columbia University Quarterly,* September, p. 321.

The finest thing which civilization has yet produced is a great American university upon a private foundation. A company of gentlemen associate themselves and assume the obligation of providing the means for, and the organization of, an institution for the highest culture . . . without any pecuniary compensation to themselves, . . . and a body of scholars, selected by this original association, who, sacrificing at the outset the prospect of worldly gain, devote

themselves zealously and enthusiastically to the discovery of truth and its dissemination and to the making of character—such in brief outline, is this great product of human evolution. No other nation on the earth has brought the like of it forth. It is the peculiar offspring of American conscience and American liberty. To have had an honorable part in the creation of such an institution is a privilege of the highest order.

—**John W. Burgess** (1844–1931),
Dean, Columbia College

1918, *The Higher Learning in America,* Chapter 2.

[T]hese governing boards of businessmen commonly are quite useless at the university for any businesslike purpose. Indeed, except for a stubborn prejudice to the contrary, the fact should readily be seen that the boards are of no material use in any connection; their sole effectual function being to interfere with the academic management in matters that are not in the nature of business, and that lie outside their competence and outside the range of their habitual interest.

Chapter 2.

Business success is by common consent, and quite uncritically, taken to be conclusive evidence of wisdom even in matters that have no relation to business affairs. . . . Such is the outcome, to the present date, of the recent and current secularization of the governing boards. The final discretion in the affairs of the seats of learning is entrusted to men who have proved only their capacity for work that has nothing in common with the higher learning.

Chapter 2.

Plato's classic scheme of folly, which would have the philosophers take over the management of affairs, has been turned on its head; the men of affairs have taken over the direction of the pursuit of knowledge.

—**Thorstein Veblen** (1857–1929),
U.S. sociologist

1920, "The relation between faculties and governing boards," *At War With Academic Traditions in America,* 1934, p. 286.

Teaching in all its grades is a public service, and the administration of every public service must comprise both expert and lay elements. Without the former, it would be ineffectual; without the latter it will become in time narrow, rigid, or out of harmony with its public object. . . . From this flows the cardinal principle, popularly little known but of well-nigh universal application, that experts should not be members of a non-professional body that supervises experts.

—**Abbott Lawrence Lowell**
(1856–1943), President,
Harvard University

1936, *The Higher Learning in America,* p. 23.

[A] university that is run by its trustees will be badly run.

—**Robert Maynard Hutchins**
(1899–1977), President,
University of Chicago

c. 1948, attributed in Myron F. Wicke, *Handbook for Trustees,* 1963, p. 31.

Every time the board of trustees meets, the agenda paper should contain but two items. The first ought always to be, "Shall we fire the president today?" If the answer is "Yes," then item two on the agenda paper should be, "Who shall serve on the committee to select a new president?" The board should then adjourn. But if the decision on the first question is, "We shall

not fire the president today," number two should be, "What can we do to support the administration?"

—**Isaiah Bowman** (1878–1950),
President, Johns Hopkins University

1956, "How to be a good Fellow," *Harvard Alumni Bulletin,* February, quoted in Clark Kerr and Marian L. Gade, *The Guardians,* 1989, p. ii.

[T]he job of a lay member of a governing board . . . boils down to this: Do your best to see that the organization is good, that it is well manned, and that it runs smoothly—but don't try to run it.

—**Charles A. Coolidge** (1894–1987),
senior fellow, Harvard Corporation

1959, *Academic Procession,* p. 44.

[S]omeone asked me to state explicitly what I wanted from a trustee. My response was "work, wealth, and wisdom, preferably all three, but at least two of the three."

—**Henry M. Wriston** (1889–1978)
President, Lawrence College;
President, Brown University

1959, *The American College President,* pp. 71–72.

Education is not an exact science. Its experts can profit from the criticisms and suggestions of intelligent laymen and from the necessity, as experts, to describe their activities and to formulate their own views clearly and convincingly. Lay boards can help presidents and faculties to interpret education.

p. 72.

The board of trustees is a brooding force, present in spirit even when not present in body, frequently exerting influence informally more effectively than by formal resolutions.

p. 81.

Trustees, whether as a board or as individual members, more easily see a record in the tangibles of buildings and facilities than in the intangibles of education. This fact is likely to determine the foci of their interests.

—**Harold W. Stoke** (1903–1982),
President, University of New Hampshire;
President, Louisiana State University;
President, Queens College

1960, speech to the joint meeting of Philippine and U.S. Chambers of Commerce, 17 June, quoted in James B. Simpson, *Simpson's Contemporary Quotations,* 1988.

Some years ago I became president of Columbia University and learned within 24 hours to speak at the drop of a hat, and I learned something more, the *trustees* were expected to speak at the *passing* of the hat.

—**Dwight D. Eisenhower** (1890–1969),
President, Columbia University;
President of the United States

1965, "The new conditions of autonomy," in Logan Wilson, *Emerging Patterns in American Higher Education,* 1965, p. 14.

The triad of university faculty, administration, and lay board of trustees representing the public interest represents a powerful and leathery combination that has provided a remarkably tough and durable buffer between the individual faculty member and those who would prevent his freedom of speech or word. As a matter of fact, we too little appreciate the enormous contribution of the lay trustee as a decisive link in this chain. . . . The informed lay trustee who says, "Stop, it is I who represents the public's interest in this matter," is perhaps

one of the greatest contributors to our free academic communities.

—**James A. Perkins** (1911–1998),
President, Cornell University

1973, *Who Rules the Universities?,* p. 35, quoted in Clark Kerr and Marian L. Gade, *The Guardian,* 1989, p. 27.

[T]rustees are part of the ruling class: an identifiable group of men who control the major institutions in our society, from the corporations to the universities, and who benefit from the continued existence of corporate capitalism and the oppressive social relations capitalism generates and requires.

—**David N. Smith** (1952–), associate professor of sociology, University of Kansas

1975, "The liberal arts college trustee's next 25 years," *AGB Reports,* May/June, p. 40.

I can visualize choosing a very limited number of trustees for wealth alone, but . . . the person who is willing to contribute no more than money is of marginal worth.

—**Atherton Bean** (1910–1998),
trustee, Carleton College

1992, *Imposters in the Temple,* 1992, p. 198.

The composition of our boards of trustees is a recipe for disaster, a witch's brew of incompetence, timidity, and neglect. Because the trustees are remiss—guilty of a dereliction of responsibility on a grand scale—today's colleges and universities are a worker's paradise where the workers, the professors and administration, are in effect the management. . . .

—**Martin Anderson** (1936–),
senior fellow, Hoover Institution,
Stanford University

1992, *How Professors Play the Cat Guarding the Cream,* pp. 116–17.

Most trustees and presidents get along very well together because they never lie to each other. The trustees tell the president what a great job he or she is doing. The president praises the board for the helpful reports submitted by its committees, especially the committee on grounds and buildings for its recent recommendation to save money by bulk purchases. With that in mind, and too often very little else, many trustees can be marked "present" with the rubber stamp of their mumbled "ayes."

—**Richard M. Huber** (1922–), Dean of General Studies, Hunter College

Chapter 10

Management

Accountability and Assessment

1878, *American Colleges: Their Students and Their Work,* p. 99.

A father . . . debating where to educate his son, would get a clearer idea of the type of moral and intellectual character which a college forms in her students from a year's file of their fortnightly paper than from her annual catalog or the private letters of her professors.

—**Charles F. Thwing** (1853–1937), President, Adelbert College; President, Western Reserve University

c. 1900, quoted in Jacques Barzun, 1944, *Teacher in America,* p. 13.

Madam, we guarantee results—or we return the boy!

—**Francis L. Patton** (1843–1932), President, Princeton University

1902, "University building," *Popular Science Monthly,* August, p. 334.

Institutions can not be graded by the number in attendance. This is the most frequent and most vulgar gauge of relative standing. The rank of an institution is determined no more by the number of its students than by the number of rocks on its campus.

—**David Starr Jordan** (1851–1931), President, Stanford University

1906, *Launching of a University,* p. 41.

[The] glory of the university should rest on the character of the teachers and scholars here brought together, and not upon their number, nor upon the buildings constructed for their use. . . .

—**Daniel Coit Gilman** (1831–1908), President, Johns Hopkins University

1930, address, trustee-faculty dinner, 8 January, quoted in Henry A. Ashmore, *Unseasonable Truth,* 1989, p. 83.

We can derive little satisfaction from the thought that our faculty is getting larger each year. The university with the longest list of courses is not necessarily the greatest.

—**Robert Maynard Hutchins** (1899–1977), President, University of Chicago

1955, *Report of the Educational Survey, The First Year,* 30 June, quoted in Theodore Caplow and Reese J. McGee, *The Academic Marketplace,* 1958, p. 25.

A university is an institution which applies systematic research to almost everything under the sun—except itself.

—University of Pennsylvania

1965, "Government and the universities" in Logan Wilson, *Emerging Patterns in American Higher Education,* 1965, p. 287.

Just as the government agency tends to tighten the defining conditions of the relationship, so university people seek to loosen them. . . . The ideal relationship as far as the university man is concerned would be one entirely without any complicating context, which is to say without any context at all, money passed in the dead of night from a donor who would never know the object of his largesse to a recipient who would never know who gave the money or why. Some government observers refer to this as the "leave it on a stump" approach.

—John W. Gardner (1912–2002), educational statesman; professor of public service, Stanford University

1968, *The Academic Revolution,* p. 125.

Those who look askance at testing should not . . . rest their case on the simple notion that tests are "unfair to the poor." Life is unfair to the poor. Tests merely measure the results.

—Christopher Jencks (1936–), professor of social policy, Harvard University; **David Riesman** (1909–2002), professor of sociology, Harvard University

1968, "Trees grew in Brooklyn: Robert M. Hutchins interviewed by Frank K. Kelly," *The Center Magazine,* November, p. 21, quoted in J. B. Lon Hefferlin, *Dynamics of Educational Reform,* 1969, p. xv.

The whole business about a university and about education can be summed up in a question: Has the institution vitality? Is anything going on? Is there anything exciting about it? This is the only test of a good university.

—Robert Maynard Hutchins (1899–1977), President, University of Chicago

1973, *Governance of Higher Education: Six Priority Problems,* p. 22.

No Holy Writ gives higher education a right to reasonable independence for institutional actions. No natural law confers upon it escape from public surveillance. The case for reasonable independence must be made with reasonable arguments.

—Carnegie Commission on Higher Education

1975, "The art of planning," *Educational Record,* Summer, pp. 172–73.

The value of a truly educated person is no more to be weighed and measured than is a sonnet or a smile. The true values we seek in higher education are, at bottom, matters of faith. Why pretend that the teaching-learning enterprise lends itself to simplistic analysis?

—Harold L. Enarson (1919–), President, Ohio State University

1975, "The public and private lives of higher education," *Daedalus,* 104, p. 123.

A good deal of what has made great universities really creative has been a function of bad data collection. Much of the best as well as the worst of higher education has flourished in a decent obscurity.

> —**Martin A. Trow** (1926–),
> professor of sociology,
> University of California, Berkeley

1977, *Investment in Learning,* p. 22.

[T]he call for accountability cannot be satisfied if all the results of higher education must be reduced to neat quantitative terms, preferably with dollar signs attached. Higher education is concerned with matters of intellect, personality, and value that simply cannot be rigorously quantified or aggregated by adding up dollar amounts or computing rates of return.

> —**Howard R. Bowen** (1908–1989),
> economist; President, Grinnell College;
> President, University of Iowa;
> Chancellor, Claremont University Center

1978, "In praise of inefficiency," *AGB Reports,* January/February, p. 47.

The danger of measurement, however, is that we will believe it and that we will regard it as the truth instead of as evidence. In universities this could be catastrophic. It is particularly important to remember that universities are institutions almost as preposterous and improbable as the human race itself, and this of course is what makes them so delightful.

> —**Kenneth E. Boulding** (1910–1993),
> U.S. economist; professor of economics,
> University of Colorado

1979, *Measuring the Outcomes of Colleges,* 1979, p. 114.

[A]mong all the major institutions in our society, it may well be that colleges and universities have been the most thoroughly and repeatedly studied—more so than hospitals or prisons, government bureaus or military organizations, business or industrial organizations, churches or charitable organizations. . . .

> —**C. Robert Pace** (1912–), professor of
> higher education, UCLA

1980, "Quality and accountability: Are we destroying what we want to preserve?," *Change,* October, p. 9.

As state boards and other state and federal agencies reach into institutions and transfer decision-making to higher levels, they disperse the authority and accountability they have sought to foster. When no one is in charge, no one is fully accountable. I could once say decisively, "the buck stops here." Now it never stops.

> —**Harold L. Enarson** (1919–),
> President, Ohio State University

1981, address given at the University of Texas, quoted in Howard R. Bowen, *The State of the Nation and the Agenda for Higher Education,* 1982, p. 11.

Our state of ignorance about the outcomes of higher education is not bliss.

> —**Alexander Astin** (1932–), professor
> of higher education, University of
> California, Los Angeles

1983, "Quality—indefinable but not unattainable," *Educational Record,* Winter, p. 8.

[I] thought about the input and output jargon and concluded it is nonsense. It is bush-league economics. It is zeal for quantification carried to its inherent and logical absurdity. . . . [T]here is no substitute for individual judgment, the power of informed and thoughtful minds, observation drawn from experience; no substitute for that most uncommon quality that, by curious distortion, we call *common sense.* . . . Quality I knew in my bones, even though I had not at various times the courage to live up to its many imperatives.

—**Harold L. Enarson** (1919–),
President, Ohio State University

1986, *Higher Learning,* p. 3.

[N]o one knows a great deal about how much students learn in colleges and universities, and it is very difficult to find out.

—**Derek Bok** (1930–), President,
Harvard University

Corporatization

1888, Inaugural Address, 20 June, quoted in Henry W. Bragdon, *Woodrow Wilson: The Academic Years,* 1967, p. 203.

College administration is a business in which trustees are partners, professors the salesmen and students the customers.

—**Francis L. Patton** (1843–1932),
President, Princeton University

1906, "The university presidency,"
Atlantic Monthly, XCVII, p. 36.

Of course the university cannot become a business corporation, with a business corporation's ordinary implications. Such a corporation is without what is being called *spiritual aim,* is without moral methods. Universities are to unlock the truth and turn out the best and the greatest men and women. . . . A university cannot become such a [business] corporation without ceasing to be a university.

—**Andrew S. Draper** (1848–1913),
President, University of Illinois

1909, "The Harvard classics and Harvard," *Science,* XXX, p. 440.

The men who control Harvard to-day are very little else than business men, running a large department store which dispenses education to the millions. Their endeavor

is to make it the *largest* establishment of the kind in America.

—**John Jay Chapman** (1862–1933),
U.S. essayist and poet

1913, "The administrative peril in education," in J. McKeen Cattell, *University Control,* p. 322.

No single thing has done more harm in higher education in America during the past quarter century than the steady aggrandizement of the presidential office and the modeling of university administration upon the methods and ideals of the factory and the department store.

—**Joseph Jastrow** (1863–1944),
professor of psychology,
University of Wisconsin

1914, commencement address, 6 December, quoted in Joseph N. Crowley, *No Equal in the World,* 1994, p. 76.

Nothing would be more unfortunate for the office of university president than to cease to be an educational post and to become merely a business occupation.

—**Nicholas Murray Butler**
(1862–1947), president,
Columbia University

1918, *The Higher Learning in America,* Chapter 3.

Men dilate on the high necessity of a businesslike organization and control of the university, its equipment, personnel and routine. What is had in mind in this insistence on an efficient system is that these corporations of learning shall set their affairs in order after the patterns of a well-conducted business concern. In this view the university is conceived as a business house dealing in merchantable knowledge, placed under the governing hand of a captain of erudition, whose office it is to turn the means in hand to account in the largest feasible output.

Chapter 8.

[T]he intrusion of business principles in universities goes to weaken and retard the pursuit of learning, and therefore to defeat the ends for which a university is maintained. This result follows, primarily, from the substitution of impersonal, mechanical relations, standards and tests, in the place of personal conference, guidance and association between teachers and students. . . .

—**Thorstein Veblen** (1857–1929),
U.S. sociologist

1927, Life and the Student, pp. 180–81.

It is a peculiarity of American universities, incident to their expansion, that much of their activity resembles that of aggressive business. The administrative officers who have this activity in charge receive higher pay than the scholars, and in some cases appear more imbued by the commercial spirit than the academic. Their lives may or may not offer to the student any argument to change the ideals of success he has brought with him from the world outside. The scholars may even seem like a kind of caged and subdued animals whose exotic attractions are proclaimed and exploited by their keepers.

—**Charles Horton Cooley** (1864–1929),
professor of sociology,
University of Michigan

1944, Teacher in America, p. 177.

Nothing so strikes the foreign observer with surprise as the size and power of American collegiate administration. The best offices in the best building, the rows and rows of filing cabinets, the serried rank of secretaries and stenographers, make the European feel that he has wandered by

mistake into some annex of a large business concern. The thick carpets, the hush and polish of the surroundings, cannot form part of an academy. The foreigner is used to a distinctive shabbiness, to hollowed steps and an inky smell, without which no school, college, or university seems genuine, be the place England, Germany, Italy, or France.

—**Jacques Barzun** (1907–),
Dean of Faculties and Provost,
Columbia University

1988, A Free and Ordered Space, p. 41.

[U]niversities that ten years ago were run in a collegial fashion [are] now completely structured to look from the outside as if they were manufacturing or banking firms, with tables of organization replete with executive vice-presidents, vice-presidents, lawyers; all the appurtenances of a major profitmaking corporation. This has been thought on the whole to be a wonderful thing. I do not necessarily think it is a wonderful thing at all. . . .

—**A. Bartlett Giamatti** (1938–1989),
President, Yale University

1990, Killing the Spirit, p. 13.

Since universities sold their souls some time ago, when they began accepting enormous federal grants to do work for the military-industrial complex, the corporate connection in the biotechnology-computer realm was a natural and probably inevitable next step. Let us pray that one consequence will be that we will hear no more pious pronouncements about the universities' being engaged in the "pursuit of truth." What they are clearly pursuing with far more dedication than the truth is big bucks.

—**Page Smith** (1917–1995), historian;
Provost, University of California
at Santa Cruz

2001, "It's lowly at the top: What became of the great college presidents?," *Washington Post,* 10 June, p. B01.

The universities that once were lean enclaves of science and philosophy, windows into the future, now look like huge tubs of money, fed by middle-class parents who will pay anything to enroll their children. They are not colleges any more, but corporations. Their presidents follow the modern CEO practice of keeping Wall Street and boards of directors happy.

—**Jay Mathews** (1945–), U.S. journalist

2001, "Leading higher education in an era of rapid change," 48th Annual Meeting of the State Higher Education Executive Officers, 30 July.

Like the boards of directors of publicly-held corporations, the university's governing board should consist of members selected for their expertise and experience. They should govern the university in [a] way that serves the interests of its various constituencies. This, of course, means that the board should function with a structure and a process that reflect the best practices of corporate boards.

—**James J. Duderstadt** (1942–),
President, University of Michigan

Decision Making

1908, *Microcosmographia Academica,* reprinted in *Two Papers on Academic Change,* 1972, p. 9.

A principle is a rule of inaction, which states a valid general reason for not doing in any particular case what, to unprincipled instincts, would appear to be right.

p. 11.

Other democracies have reached this peak of excellence; but the academic democracy is superior in having no organised parties. We thus avoid all the responsibilities of party leadership (there are leaders, but no one follows them), and the degradations of part compromise. It is clear, moreover, that twenty independent persons, each of whom has a different reason for not doing a certain thing, and no one of whom will compromise with any other, constitute a most effective check upon the rashness of individuals.

p. 12.

The *Principle of the Dangerous Precedent* is that you should not now do an admittedly right action for fear you, or your equally timid successors, should not have the courage to do right in some future case, which *ex hypothesi,* is essentially different, but superficially resembles the present one. Every public action which is not customary, either is wrong, or, if it is right, is a dangerous precedent. It follows that nothing should ever be done for the first time.

p. 12.

Even a little knowledge of ethical theory will suffice to convince you that all important questions are so complicated, and the results of any course of action are so difficult to foresee, that certainty, or even probability, is seldom, if ever, attainable. It follows at once that the only justifiable attitude of mind is suspense of judgment; and this attitude, besides being peculiarly congenial to the academic temperament, has the advantage of being relatively easy to attain.

—**F. M. Cornford** (1874–1943),
professor of ancient philosophy,
Cambridge University

1955, "The administrator: Leader or officeholder?," *Freedom, Education, and the Fund,* 1956, pp. 171–72.

The administrator who is willing to be an administrator and not merely an officeholder will find that the strain is chiefly upon his character, rather than his mind.

... I do not minimize the intellectual difficulties involved in reaching an important practical decision. I merely say that these difficulties are of such a nature that previous formal instruction will do little to assist in their solution, and that, compared with the strain on the character that administration of the means carries with it, the strain on the mind is insignificant.

—**Robert Maynard Hutchins**
(1899–1977), President,
University of Chicago

1964, "The scientist as university president," Eric Compton Memorial Lecture, Washington University, St. Louis, 13 May, quoted in Clark Kerr and Marian L. Gade, *The Many Lives of Academic Presidents,* 1986, pp. 202–3.

[C]ollective decision-making without leadership encourages a drift toward mediocrity.

—**Eric Ashby** (1904–1992), botanist;
Vice-chancellor, Cambridge University

1965, "The new conditions of autonomy," in Logan Wilson, *Emerging Patterns in American Higher Education,* 1965, p. 10.

[I]t takes a courageous dean and fearless president to deal firmly with budgetary requests from a specialty they can neither pronounce nor spell. And when they dare to intervene, they must rely heavily on past training in the proper interpretation of voice inflection and iris dilation as useful guides for executive decision making. But, of course, this is the stock in trade of all administrators, be they deans, presidents, company officers, or public officials.

—**James A. Perkins** (1911–1998),
President, Cornell University

1974, *Leadership and Ambiguity,* p. 33.

In a university anarchy each individual in the university is seen as making autonomous decisions. Teachers decide if, and when, and what to teach. Students decide if, when, and what to learn. Legislators and donors decide if, when, and what to support. . . . Resources are allocated by whatever process emerges but without explicit accommodation and without explicit reference to some superordinate goal. The "decisions" of the system are a consequence produced by the system but intended by no one and decisively controlled by no one.

—**Michael D. Cohen** (1945–), professor of complex systems, information, and public policy, University of Michigan; **James G. March** (1928–), professor of international management, political science, and sociology, Stanford University

1982, " 'The Uses of the University' two decades later: Postscript 1982," *Change,* October, p. 30.

[T]he status quo is the only solution that cannot be vetoed.

—**Clark Kerr** (1911–2003), Chancellor, University of California, Berkeley; President, University of California

1983, *Academic Strategy,* p. 86.

Universities love to explore processes and methodology but hate to make decisions. . . . Decisions in a university often get made randomly—by deans, legislators, a financial officer, the president.

—**George C. Keller** (1928–),
higher education writer and analyst

1990, *The University: An Owner's Manual,* p. 33.

We have a system of governance that permits non-consensual and unpopular decisions to be made when necessary. We have learned that not everything is improved by making it more democratic.

—**Henry Rosovsky** (1927–), Dean of the Faculty of Arts and Sciences, Harvard University

Efficiency

1914, *Report for 1913–14,* quoted in Edward C. Elliott (ed.), *The Rise of a University, Vol. II,* 1937, pp. 23–24.

Nothing is more irrational than to measure the effectiveness of a university and the success of its work by the standards that are so easily applicable to mechanical processes, or even to a business conducted for gain. A university is precluded from being efficient in the mechanical or business sense by its essential character and by its necessary policies. . . . The man with the measuring rod, the tape line, and the impertinently inquisitive questionnaire is as great a nuisance about a university as a contagious disease would be.

—**Nicholas Murray Butler** (1862–1947), President, Columbia University

1921, *The Frontier in American History,* pp. 292–93.

The university has to deal with both the soil and sifted seed in the agriculture of the human spirit. Its efficiency is not the efficiency which the business engineer is fitted to appraise. If it is a training ship, it is a training ship bound on a voyage of discovery, seeking new horizons. The economy of the university's consumption can only be rightly measured by the later times which shall possess these new realms of the spirit which its voyage shall reveal. If the ships of Columbus had engaged in a profitable coast-wise traffic between Palos and Cadiz they might have saved sail cloth,

but their keels would never have grated on the shores of a New World.

—**Frederick Jackson Turner** (1861–1932), professor of history, University of Wisconsin

1930, *Universities: American English German,* p. 186.

Efficiency in administration and fertility in the realm of ideas have in fact nothing to do with the other—except, perhaps, to hamper and destroy each other.

—**Abraham Flexner** (1866–1959), U.S. educator

1973, "Combatting the efficiency cultists," *Change,* June, p. 9.

Our supreme function is not to improve managerial efficiency in education. . . . [O]ur supreme obligation is to remind ourselves and our public and private benefactors that a partially unquantifiable and inherently untidy system of higher education must routinely make legitimate demands upon the treasuries of the purse in order to nourish the treasuries of the mind and spirit. For freedom is the condition of nobility, and knowledge is the condition of freedom.

—**Stephen K. Bailey** (1916–1982), professor of education, Harvard University; Vice President, American Council on Education

1976, *The States and Higher Education,* p. 17.

[W]e caution that the external search for small efficiencies and improvements in the short run may kill the spirit of initiative, the self-reliance, and the self-responsibility of higher education in the long run and thus, also, lead to major inefficiencies and deterioration.

—**Carnegie Foundation for the Advancement of Teaching**

1978, "In praise of inefficiency," *AGB Reports,* January/February, p. 45.

Some of the redundancies and inefficiencies of universities are part of that ultimate product of human activity which is the reason for living at all. These redundancies are also an extremely important reserve of high-quality ability in time of crisis. To make universities narrowly efficient might well be the greatest disservice we offer society.

—**Kenneth E. Boulding** (1910–1993), U.S. economist; professor of economics, University of Colorado

1989, "The role of faculty in campus governance," in Jack Schuster et al., *Governing Tomorrow's Campus,* p. 117.

Higher education's present love affair with data gathering is in some instances approaching numerology. Signs of data wallowing are everywhere.

—**Patricia R. Plante** (1932–), president, University of Southern Maine

2001, "Higher education and those 'out-of-control costs'," in Philip Altbach et al., *In Defense of American Higher Education,* p. 166.

What is unique [to higher education]— and what invites the constant barrage of charges of wrong priorities—is the absence of a common, undisputed, easy-to-measure, and unambiguous metric such as contribution to profit. A business only has to apply the single metric of profit to each of its products. A university cannot do this—not because it does not want to or know how to but because *it cannot be done.*

—**D. Bruce Johnstone** (1941–), President, Buffalo State College; Chancellor, State University of New York

Finance

1955, *Report of the Educational Survey, The First Year,* 30 June, quoted in Theodore Caplow and Reese J. McGee, *The Academic Marketplace,* 1958, p. 25.

The tendency is strong in most universities to expand in more directions than available finances make wise. The resulting poverty is shared by all.

—**University of Pennsylvania**

1956, *Freedom, Education, and the Fund,* p. 165.

There is a good deal of evidence, I think, that the educational system as a whole needs less money rather than more. The reduction of its income would force it to reconsider its expenditures. The expectation that steadily increasing funds will be forthcoming justifies the maintenance of activities that ought to be abandoned; it justifies waste.

—**Robert Maynard Hutchins** (1899–1977), President, University of Chicago

1965, "Basic premises for a national policy in higher education," in Logan Wilson, *Emerging Patterns in American Higher Education,* 1965, p. 268–69.

Higher education will be financed adequately only when costs are regarded as investments rather than expenditures.... Nearly everybody knows that ordinary capital investments in labor-saving machinery more than pay for themselves. What more people must learn is that the dividends from investments in education are even greater.

—**Logan Wilson** (1907–1990), President, University of Texas at Austin; President, American Council on Education

1967, "Basic research and financial crisis in the universities," *Science,* 4 August, pp. 519–20.

The simple facts are that we sell our research, we sell our educational functions, we sell our social service to the community—everything—at a loss.

> **—George Pake** (1924–),
> Executive Vice-chancellor,
> Washington University, St. Louis

c. 1973, "Terman's Law," attributed in Thomas L. Martin, Jr., *Malice in Blunderland,* 1973, p. 57.

There is no direct relationship between the quality of an educational program and its cost.

> **—Frederick E. Terman** (1900–1982),
> Provost, Stanford University

c. 1973, "Bowker's Corollary to Terman's Law," attributed in Thomas L. Martin, Jr., *Malice in Blunderland,* 1973, p. 57.

An awful lot of money is being wasted on every college campus.

> **—Albert H. Bowker** (1919–),
> Chancellor, City University of New York;
> Chancellor, University of California,
> Berkeley

1973, *Higher Education: Who Pays? Who Benefits? Who Should Pay?,* p. vii.

Benefits from higher education flow to all, or nearly all, persons in the United States directly or indirectly, and the costs of higher education are assessed against all, or nearly all, adults directly or indirectly. Few Americans are denied any benefits and few adults escape any costs. The benefits take many forms and are delivered in quite unequal amounts; the costs, likewise, are assessed in many ways and in quite diverse sums.

> **—Carnegie Commission
> on Higher Education**

1978, attributed by Ann Landers in her column, 26 March, quoted in Howard Bowen, *Investment in Learning,* 1977, p. 3.

If you think education is expensive, try ignorance.

> **—Derek Bok** (1930–), President,
> Harvard University

1980, *The Costs of Higher Education,* pp. 19–20.

The "Laws" of Higher Education Costs. 1. The dominant goals of institutions are educational excellence, prestige, and influence. . . . 2. In quest of excellence, prestige, and influence, there is virtually no limit to the amount of money an institution could spend for seemingly fruitful educational ends. . . . 3. Each institution raises all the money it can. . . . 4. Each institution spends all it raises. . . . 5. The cumulative effect of the preceding four laws is toward ever increasing expenditure.

> **—Howard R. Bowen** (1908–1989),
> economist; President, Grinnell College;
> President, University of Iowa;
> Chancellor, Claremont University Center

1986, *Christian Science Monitor,* 25 November, p. 21.

The university's characteristic state may be summarized by the words of the lady who said "I have enough money to last me the rest of my life, unless I buy something."

> **—Hanna Holborn Gray** (1930–),
> historian; President,
> University of Chicago

1988, "Pure knowledge, impure profit" (editorial), 19 September, p. 22.

Oscar Wilde could resist everything except temptation. University presidents, it seems, can resist everything except money.

> **—New York Times**

1998, *Creating Entrepreneurial Universities,* p. xiii.

Governments expect universities to do much more for society in solving economic and social problems, but at the same time they back and fill in their financial support and become unreliable patrons.

—**Burton R. Clark** (1921–), professor of sociology, University of California, Los Angeles

2003, *Universities in the Marketplace: The Commercialization of Higher Education,* p. 9.

Universities share one characteristic with compulsive gamblers and exiled royalty: there is never enough money to satisfy their desires.

p. 185.

The prospect of new revenue is a powerful temptation that can easily lead decent people into unwise compromises. . . .

—**Derek Bok** (1930–), President, Harvard University

Fund-Raising

1643, *New England's First Fruits,* quoted in Richard Hofstadter and Wilson Smith (eds.), *American Higher Education: A Documentary History, Volume I,* 1961, p. 6.

And as wee were thinking and consulting how to effect this great Work; it pleased God to stir up the heart of one Mr. *Harvard* (a godly Gentleman, and a lover of Learning, there living amongst us) to give the one halfe of his Estate (it being in all about 1700.l.) towards the erecting of a colledge; and all his Library: after him another gave 300.l. others after them cast in more, and the publique hand of the State added the rest; the Colledge was, by common consent, appointed to be at *Cambridge,* (a place very pleasant and accommodate) and

is called (according to the name of the first founder) *Harvard Colledge.*

—**Author Unknown**

1858, "Parson Turell's legacy," quoted at <http://209.11.144.65/eldritchpress/owh/parson.html>.

God bless you, Gentlemen! Learn to give
Money to colleges while you live.
Don't be silly and think you'll try
To bother the colleges, when you die,
With codicil this, and codicil that,
That Knowledge may starve while Law grows fat;
For there never was pitcher that wouldn't spill,
And there's always a flaw in a donkey's will!

—**Oliver Wendell Holmes, Sr.** (1809–1894), U.S. writer; professor of anatomy, Harvard Medical School

1869, Inaugural Address, quoted in Edgar W. Knight, *What College Presidents Say,* 1940, p. 33.

And what is the cry that comes up from every college large and small in the land, but "money! money!! money!!!" The religious press rings with appeals for gifts and endowments, alumni of colleges pour in large offerings of love and gratitude, noble men and women dying, bequeath rich legacies to favorite institutions, but still the cry is "money, money, money! . . ."

—**William W. Folwell** (1833–1929), President, University of Minnesota

no date, quoted in John S. Brubacher and Willis Rudy, *Higher Education in Transition,* 1958, p. 303.

No donor has any right before God or man to interfere with the teaching officers appointed to give instruction in a university.

—**William Rainey Harper** (1856–1906), President, University of Chicago

1902, "Concerning the American university," in *Popular Science Monthly,* June, p. 180.

The president and trustees as they now exist have their chief justification in financial conditions. We know that the lack of money is the root of all evil.

—**J. McKeen Cattell** (1860–1944),
professor of psychology,
Columbia University

1906, quoted in Frederick Rudolph, *The American College and University: A History,* 1962, p. 352.

It [the University of Chicago] is the best investment I ever made in my life.

—**John D. Rockefeller** (1839–1937),
U.S. industrialist

1910, *Great American Universities,* p. 360.

All college presidents find it easier to get new buildings than to get professors to use them or janitors to clean them.

—**Edwin E. Slosson** (1865–1929),
chemist; U.S. writer

1936, *The Higher Learning in America,* p. 4.

It is sad but true that when an institution determines to do something in order to get money it must lose its soul, and frequently does not get the money.

—**Robert Maynard Hutchins**
(1899–1977), President,
University of Chicago

1952, "Education and independent thought," *Freedom, Education, and the Fund,* 1956, p. 164.

The principal duty of the chief executive of a university is to produce a university

that deserves support. His secondary duty is to raise the money to support it.

—**Robert Maynard Hutchins**
(1899–1977), President,
University of Chicago

1959, *The American College President,* p. 54.

If Aesop were writing his fables today, he would not choose pouring water in a basket as a symbol of futility; he would choose a college president trying to find enough money for his institution.

pp. 58–59.

No matter how he tries to organize himself or his institution, the college president cannot fully escape the money-raising job. "To beg like a college president" has become a well-understood simile.

—**Harold W. Stoke** (1903–1982),
President, University of New Hampshire;
President, Louisiana State University;
President, Queens College

1967, "The job of a college president," *Educational Record,* Winter, p. 70.

Money is a claim on society's resources. When a university seeks money—that is, seeks authorization to make that claim—it will be, and ought to be, successful only if it can make as persuasive a case for itself as is made by innumerable other would-be claimants: colleges, psychiatric clinics, symphony orchestras, city parks, food for India, and bird sanctuaries. To say that a president is a fund-raiser is to say that he is an interpreter to society of the goals of the college.

—**Herbert A. Simon** (1916–), Professor
of Computer Sciences and Psychology,
Carnegie Institute of Technology

1980, *The Costs of Higher Education,* p. 20.

No college or university ever admits to having enough money and all try to increase their resources without limit.

—**Howard R. Bowen** (1908–1989), economist; President, Grinnell College; President, University of Iowa; Chancellor, Claremont University Center

1982, "What's a college president? Not what he thought it was," *New York Times,* 10 January, p. 63.

No sooner had I been inaugurated than I found that attempts on my part to actively participate in these professorial activities was regarded with the same favor as a tap-dancer at a funeral. The first role of a university president, I was informed in no uncertain terms, is to bring the school to the attention of people with money in their pockets.

—**Stephen Joel Trachtenberg** (1937–), President, George Washington University

2003, *Universities in the Marketplace: The Commercialization of Higher Education,* p. x.

Was everything in the university for sale if the price was right?

—**Derek Bok** (1930–), President, Harvard University

Management and Planning

1869, Inaugural Address, 19 October, in *A Turning Point in Higher Education,* 1969, p. 54.

When it comes to hiring learning, and inspiration and personal weight, the law of supply and demand breaks down altogether. A university cannot be managed like a railroad or a cotton mill.

—**Charles William Eliot** (1834–1926), President, Harvard University

1910, *Academic and Industrial Efficiency,* p. 7.

There are very few, if any, of the broader principles of management which obtain generally in the commercial world which are not, more or less, applicable in the college field, and as far as was discovered, no one of them is now generally observed.

—**Morris Llewellyn Cooke** (1872–1960), mechanical engineer employed by the Carnegie Foundation for the Advancement of Teaching

1910, *Report for 1909–10,* quoted in Edward C. Elliott (ed.), *The Rise of a University, Vol. II,* 1937, p. 426.

There is a strong temptation in a large university to multiply unnecessarily formal business, to institute boards and committees for all sorts of purposes, and even to carry on by elaborate correspondence with officers in adjoining rooms or under the same roof, business that could be disposed of in a moment's conversation.

—**Nicholas Murray Butler** (1862–1947), President, Columbia University

1912, letter to D. Francis Greenwood Peabody, 12 February, in Henry James, *Charles W. Eliot,* 1930, volume II, pp. 224–25.

The direction and growth of a live American university is determined by the new needs of our democratic community seen and understood by some farsighted persons in the active administration. The growth is not initiative but responsive. Even in regard to the layout of grounds and buildings it has proved impossible at Harvard and every other growing university to make a layout for years to come and adhere to it.

—**Charles William Eliot** (1834–1926), President, Harvard University

1929, *The Aims of Education and Other Essays,* Chapter Seven.

The faculty should be a band of scholars, stimulating each other, and freely determining their various activities. You can secure certain formal requirements, that lectures are given at stated times and that instructors and students are in attendance. But the heart of the matter lies beyond all regulation.

—**Alfred North Whitehead** (1861–1947), English philosopher and mathematician; professor of philosophy, Harvard University

1938, *What a College President Has Learned,* p. 21.

[O]ne cannot both do things and take credit for them.

—**Abbot Lawrence Lowell** (1856–1943), President, Harvard University

1967, "The job of the college president," *Educational Record,* Winter, p. 69.

Comparing colleges with other organizations in our society, one sees that their most striking peculiarity is not their product, but the extent to which they are operated by amateurs. They are institutions run by amateurs to train professionals.

—**Herbert A. Simon** (1916–), professor of computer sciences and psychology, Carnegie Institute of Technology

1973, "Combatting the efficiency cultists," *Change,* June, p. 8.

Efficiency is what we render unto Caesar, and we hardly need reminding that Caesar has his legions. But . . . there are limits to accountability, limits to efficiency, limits to slide-rule definitions of educational productivity. Surely the ultimate philistinism of our culture would be totally to impose management science upon the educational process.

p. 8.

We have heard it all before: If we could just run our universities as General Motors is managed, most of our educational problems would vanish.

—**Stephen K. Bailey** (1916–1982), professor of education, Harvard University; Vice President, American Council on Education

1973, *The Purposes and the Performance of Higher Education in the United States,* p. 71.

The campus is primarily an academic institution. We consider it a contradiction when the campus takes on functions which are at odds with the inherent nature of academic life. We also consider it inefficient when an academic institution takes on nonacademic operations which can be performed as well or better by other institutions.

—**Carnegie Commission on Higher Education**

1974, *Leadership and Ambiguity,* p. 114.

[A]cademic plans seem to suffer from two conspicuous administrative problems: (1) they often had no connection to any decisions that anyone might be called upon to make; and (2) they rejected the idea of scarcity. At best, they were lists of what the various academic departments wished Santa Claus would bring them. At worst, they were fantasies, neither believed in nor intended to be believable.

—**Michael D. Cohen** (1945–), professor of complex systems, information, and public policy, University of Michigan; **James G. March** (1928–), professor of international management, political science, and sociology, Stanford University

1975, "The liberal arts college trustee's next 25 years," *AGB Reports,* May/June.

[I]f a certain conglomerate of faculty, students, and administration denominated a "college" is to turn in a first-rate performance, it requires its own special style. . . . This "running things like a business" theme is a dead horse, and commentators on and within the academic scene should stop beating it.

—**Atherton Bean** (1910–1998),
trustee, Carleton College

1975, "The art of planning," *Educational Record,* Summer, p. 174.

Planning is inseparable from management, and both involve those elements we associate with art—intuition, creativity, discernment, command of the work tools and materials, and appreciation of the interaction of form and function.

—**Harold L. Enarson** (1919–),
President, Ohio State University

1976, "Where numbers fail," in Dyckman W. Vermilye (ed.), *Individualizing the System: Current Issues in Higher Education,* p. 9.

Some [planning] enthusiasts . . . argue that the financial problems of higher education would be resolved if only it would adopt sound, hard-headed, and rational business management procedures. This claim surely exaggerates the potential returns from any conceivable managerial technique.

p. 12.

A good college or university, like a good family, is largely a work of art. The principles of production are only vaguely known except through tradition, intuition, and judgment.

pp. 12–13.

In view of our monumental ignorance, one must ask whether academic planning is possible at all in the strict sense of measuring the means and the ends.

—**Howard R. Bowen** (1908–1989),
economist; President, Grinnell College;
President, University of Iowa;
Chancellor, Claremont University Center

1976, *The Unconscious Conspiracy,* p. 20

[B]ennis's First Law of Academic Pseudodynamics, to wit: Routine work drives out nonroutine work, or: how to smother to death all creative planning, all fundamental change in the university—or *any* institution.

p. 22.

[B]ennis's Second Law of Academic Pseudodynamics: Make whatever grand plans you will, you may be sure the unexpected or the trivial will disturb and disrupt them.

—**Warren G. Bennis** (1925–),
psychologist; President,
University of Cincinnati

1980, "How we talk and how we act: Administrative theory and administrative life," *Values, Leadership and Quality: The Administration of Higher Education,* 1990, p. 47.

Management may be extremely important even though managers are indistinguishable. It is hard to tell the difference between two different light bulbs also; but if you take all light bulbs away, it is difficult to read in the dark.

—**James G. March** (1928–), professor of sociology, political science, and management, Stanford University

1983, *Academic Strategy,* p. 5.

American colleges and universities . . . constitute one of the largest industries in the nation but are among the least businesslike and well-managed of all organizations.

—**George C. Keller** (1928–),
higher education writer and analyst

1983, "Squeezing the firm's midriff bulge," *Wall Street Journal,* 25 March, p. 14, quoted in Paul F. Sharp, "American college presidents since World War II," *Educational Record,* 1984, Spring, p. 12.

The inflation in management titles has been even more severe these last 30 years than the inflation of money. In the liberal art college of 1950, for instance, five secretaries did the same work now being done by seven or eight deans and assistant vice presidents—and did it very well.

—**Peter Drucker** (1909–),
U.S. management consultant and writer

1987, "Deaning," *Harvard Magazine,* January-February 1987, p. 36.

The technical skills of the executive are trivialities compared with the understanding of the fundamental nature of the university. And this has to come from experience acquired by long hours in library, laboratory, and with students.

—**Henry Rosovsky** (1927–),
Dean of the Faculty of Arts and Sciences, Harvard University

1988, *How Colleges Work,* p. 4.

[I]t might be that at least to some extent our colleges and universities are successful *because* they are poorly managed, at least as *management* is often defined in other complex organizations. If this is true, then attempts to "improve" management processes might actually diminish rather than enhance organizational effectiveness in institutions of higher education.

—**Robert Birnbaum** (1936–),
Chancellor, University of
Wisconsin-Oshkosh

1988, Josef Martin (pseudonym), *To Rise above Principle,* p. 156.

Wise men don't need to plan, because they know what to do.

—**Henry H. Bauer** (1931–), Dean of
Arts and Sciences, Virginia Polytechnic
Institute and State University

1995, *Once Upon a Campus,* p. xix.

Sailing a ship cross the Pacific is no different from organizing a college or university for performance improvement. In both instances, it is immensely helpful if we can come to some agreement on which way to aim the pointy end.

—**Daniel Seymour** (1947–),
education and management consultant

Section Four

Educational Roles

Chapter 11

The Faculty

Faculty Appointment

1902, "Concerning the American university," in *Popular Science Monthly,* June, p. 177.

It is more important to find a good man than to fill a vacant position.

—**J. McKeen Cattell** (1860–1944),
professor of psychology,
Columbia University

1915, "Declaration of principles on academic freedom and academic tenure," *Policy Documents and Reports, Ninth Edition,* 2001, p. 294.

If education is the cornerstone of the structure of society and if progress in scientific knowledge is essential to civilization, few things can be more important than to enhance the dignity of the scholar's profession, with a view to attracting into its ranks men of the highest ability, of sound learning, and of strong and independent character.

—**American Association
of University Professors**

1920, *The State University and the New South,* pp. 32–33.

To appoint to the instructing staff only persons with a Ph.D. degree saves some trouble to the appointing power, and provides at least a minimum security. It looks well in the catalogue, and requires no apology. But as a fetish, it is like any other fetish,— more awe-inspiring when not too closely investigated.

—**Abbot Lawrence Lowell** (1856–1943),
President, Harvard University

1931, *Life and the Student,* pp. 184–85.

It is strange that we have so few men of genius on our faculties; we are always trying to get them. Of course, they must have undergone the regular academic training (say ten years in graduate study and subordinate positions) and be gentlemanly, dependable, pleasant to live with, and not apt to make trouble by urging eccentric ideas. . . .

—**Charles Horton Cooley** (1864–1929),
professor of sociology,
University of Michigan

1939, *Report on Some Problems of Personnel in the Faculty of Arts and Sciences,* quoted in Derek Bok, *Beyond the Ivory Tower,* 1982, p. 119.

Personal characteristics should not be considered as primary criteria [for faculty appointment]. A faculty made up wholly of amiable and attractive men, or even of saints, would not as such serve the purposes of a college or university.

—**Harvard University Committee**

1945, letter to the *New York Times,* August 13, p. 18.

There is only one proved method of assisting in the advancement of pure science—that of picking men of genius, backing them heavily, and leaving them to direct themselves. There is only one proved method for getting results in applied science—picking men of genius, backing them heavily, and keeping their aim on the target chosen.

—**James Bryant Conant** (1893–1978), President, Harvard University

1958, *The Academic Marketplace,* pp. 113–14.

When we examine the specific procedures of hiring in the American university, they turn out to be almost unbelievably elaborate. The average salary of an assistant professor is approximately that of a bakery truck driver, and his occupancy of a job is likely to be less permanent. Yet it may require a large part of the time of twenty highly-skilled men for a full year to hire him.

—**Theodore Caplow** (1920–), professor of sociology, University of Virginia; **Reese J. McGee** (1929–), professor of sociology, Purdue University

1960, "What every Yale freshman should know," *Saturday Review,* 23 January, p. 13.

Children whose curiosity survives parental discipline and who manage to grow up before they blow up are invited to join the Yale faculty. Within the university they go on asking their questions and trying to find the answers ... it is a place where the world's hostility to curiosity can be defied.

—**Edmund S. Morgan** (1916–), professor of history, Yale University

1977, *Why Professors Can't Teach,* p. 92.

Universities hire professors the way some men choose wives—they want the ones that others will admire.

—**Morris Kline** (1908–1992), professor of mathematics, New York University

1986, speech at the University of California, Berkeley, 27 March, quoted in Henry Rosovsky, *The University: An Owners Manual,* 1990, p. 207.

Faculty control of appointments *can* sometimes be a means to self-perpetuating quality. It can more especially be a means to self-perpetuating mediocrity. And in a world of change, it can be a powerful tendency to academic obsolescence.

—**John Kenneth Galbraith** (1908–), U.S. statesman and professor of economics, Harvard University

Faculty Compensation

1776, *The Wealth of Nations,* Book One, Chapter X.

Before the invention of the art of printing, a scholar and a beggar seem to have been terms very nearly synonymous. The different governors of the universities before that time appear to have often granted licenses to their scholars to beg.

Book Five, Chapter I.

In some universities the salary makes but a part, and frequently but a small part, of the emoluments of the teacher, of which the greater part arises from the honoraries or fees of his pupils. The necessity of application, though always more or less diminished, is not in this case entirely taken away. . . . In other universities the teacher is prohibited from receiving any honorary or fee from his pupils, and his salary constitutes the whole of the revenue which he derives from his office. His interest is, in this case, set as directly in opposition to his duty as it is possible to set it. It is the interest of every man to live as much at his ease as he can; and if his emoluments are to be precisely the same, whether he does or does not perform some very laborious duty, it is certainly his interest . . . either to neglect it altogether, or, if he is subject to some authority which will not suffer him to do this, to perform it in as careless and slovenly a manner as that authority will permit.

—**Adam Smith** (1723–1790),
Scottish philosopher and economist

1824, "The plan of studies at the University of Virginia," quoted in Richard Hofstadter and Wilson Smith (eds.), *American Higher Education: A Documentary History, Volume I,* 1961, p. 231.

The collegiate duties of a professor, if discharged conscientiously, with industry and zeal, being sufficient to engross all his hours of business, he shall engage in no other pursuits of emolument unconnected with the service of the University without the consent of the Visitors. . . .

—**University of Virginia,
Board of Visitors**

1837, Commencement Address, quoted in Richard Hofstadter and Wilson Smith (eds.), *American Higher Education: A Documentary History, Volume I,* 1961, p. 247.

The office of president and professor is universally looked up to as the highest and most respected which can be obtained by aspiring candidates for honourable rank in society. No political or professional station takes precedence of these. Nor would the head of any distinguished or opulent family be ambitious of more creditable vocation or post of honor for a favourite and talented son, than that of a college professorship.

—**Philip Lindsley** (1786–1855),
President, University of Nashville

1842, *Thoughts on the Present Collegiate System in the United States,* quoted in Richard Hofstadter and Wilson Smith (eds.), *American Higher Education: A Documentary History, Volume I,* 1961, p. 362.

[I] believe the instructors of Colleges in this country, are remunerated, at a lower rate than almost any other profession. That this is the case, is manifest from the fact that few young men with fair prospects before them can be ever induced to leave their profession for any office that a College can offer. . . .

—**Francis Wayland** (1796–1865),
President, Brown University

1869, letter to George Brush, 24 June, quoted in Henry James, *Charles W. Eliot,* 1930, volume I, p. 250.

I want to do everything I can towards improving the position of a College professor. It is essential to command the services of young men of the best ability. Meat three times a week does not attract such.

—**Charles William Eliot** (1834–1926),
President, Harvard University

1869, Inaugural Address, 19 October, in *A Turning Point in Higher Education,* 1969, p. 48.

The poverty of scholars is of inestimable worth in this money-getting nation. It maintains the true standards of virtue and honor. The poor friars, not the bishops, saved the church. The poor scholars and preachers of duty defend the modern community against its own material prosperity. Luxury and learning are ill bedfellows.

p. 53.

It is very hard to find competent professors for the University. A very few Americans of eminent ability are attracted to this profession. The pay has been too low, and there has been no gradual rise out of drudgery, such as may reasonably be expected in other learned callings.

—**Charles William Eliot** (1834–1926),
President, Harvard University

1874, *German Universities: A Narrative of Personal Experience,* p. 345.

It is difficult to understand why [American] professors, who are men of ability and culture, who devote themselves unselfishly to the best interests of the nation, should not be paid as liberally as our best lawyers and physicians, why the guardians of the spiritual interests of men should fare worse than those who look merely after their bodies and estates.

—**James Morgan Hart** (1839–1916),
professor of rhetoric and English philology, Cornell University

1889, "The universities and colleges," in *The American Commonwealth,* Volume II.

The [American] professors seem to be always among the social aristocracy of the city in which they live, although usually unable, from the smallness of their incomes, to enjoy social life as the corre-sponding class does in Scotland, or even in England.

—**James Bryce** (1875–1938),
professor of civil law, Oxford University

1923, *The Goose-Step,* Chapter 77.

There are few more pitiful proletarians in America than the underpaid, overworked, and contemptuously ignored rank and file college teacher. Everyone has more than he—trustees and presidents, coaches and trainers, merchants and tailors, architects and building contractors, sometimes even masons and carpenters.

—**Upton Sinclair** (1878–1968),
U.S. author

1930, speech to the Common Wealth Club of San Francisco, 25 July, quoted in George A. Pettitt, *Twenty-eight Years in the Life of a University President,* 1966, p. 60.

If the stream of our civilization is not to be dried up at the source, we must pay salaries in education that will attract first-class men in competition with business and other professions.

—**Robert G. Sproul** (1891–1975),
President, University of California

1962, "Economic pressure and the professor," in Nevitt Sanford, *The American College,* 1962, p. 447.

[M]ost teachers are poor. The Hollywood stereotype of the professor as a man in worn and tasteless clothes, driving a decrepit car from a home in need of repairs to give an address to the well-kept elders of the town is not inaccurate in the physical image it presents. It is only wrong in its suggestion that the professor, through some ivory-towered preoccupation with ideas, is indifferent to the things of this world. If he is ill-dressed, ill-housed, ill-transported, and otherwise ill, it is because he cannot afford good clothes, good house-keeping, a good car, or even very elaborate medical attention.

> —**Anthony Ostroff** (1923–1978),
> professor of rhetoric, University of
> California, Berkeley

1980, *Free to Choose,* quoted in Eugene Ehrlich and Marshall DeBruhl, *The International Thesaurus of Quotations,* 1996, p. 599.

The esteem or approval of fellow scholars serves very much the same function that monetary reward does in the economic market.

> —**Milton Friedman** (1912–), professor
> of economics, University of Chicago;
> **Rose Friedman** (1912?–), economist

1992, *Imposters in the Temple,* 1992, p. 38.

No longer poor, threadbare idealists who seemed to care little for the material bene-fits of this world as they strove for truth and knowledge, today's academic intellec-tuals have perhaps the best combination of working conditions and pay of any large occupational group in America. In the multibillion-dollar industry that is higher education, the captains of that industry go first-class.

> —**Martin Anderson** (1936–),
> senior fellow, Hoover Institution,
> Stanford University

Faculty Culture

1858, *The Idea of a University,* Discourse V.

This I conceive to be the advantage of a seat of universal learning, considered as a place of education. An assemblage of learned men, zealous for their own sci-ences, and rivals of each other, are brought by familiar intercourse and for the sake of intellectual peace, to adjust together the claims and relations of their respective subjects of investigation. They learn to re-spect, to consult, to aid each other. Thus is created a pure and clear atmosphere of thought, which the student also breathes, though in his own case he only pursues a few sciences out of the multitude.

> —**John Henry (Cardinal) Newman**
> (1801–1890), Rector,
> Catholic University of Ireland

1863, *Reminiscences of Amherst College,* pp. 316–17.

A college Faculty are looked upon by many as an aristocratic, arbitrary and ty-rannical set, whom every humane man is bound to oppose. . . .

> —**Edward Hitchcock** (1793–1864),
> President, Amherst College

1910, *Great American Universities,* p. 217.

[T]he university of the future will be com-posed of three classes: men who have the genius for discovering truth, men who are especially adapted to imparting it to oth-ers, and men who are successful in show-ing how it may be applied to the problems of life. It is unfortunately rare to find these three forms of ability equally developed in the same individual, so the next best thing is to bring them together in the same fac-ulty, where they may mutually strengthen each other and give the institution as a whole an unprecedented power in the com-munity.

p. 455.

Even in small and isolated colleges each man works in his separate star and de-scends to meet his colleagues, talking triv-ialities with them instead of giving them the best of his thought. The confusion of Babel has lasted long enough. It is time for those who are working side by side in the erection of the Temple of Wisdom to learn each other's language.

—**Edwin E. Slosson** (1865–1929), chemist; U.S. writer

1912, "The administrative peril in education," in J. McKeen Cattell, *University Control,* 1913, p. 324.

Truly the academic animal is a queer beast. If he cannot have something at which he can growl and snarl, he will growl and snarl at nothing at all.

—**Joseph Jastrow** (1863–1944), professor of psychology, University of Wisconsin

1918, *The Higher Learning in America,* Chapter 1.

No man whose energies are not habitually bent on increasing and proving up the domain of learning belongs legitimately on the university staff. The university man is, properly, a student, not a schoolmaster.

—**Thorstein Veblen** (1857–1929), U.S. sociologist

1946, *Adventures of a Biographer,* p. 79.

The professors laugh at themselves, they laugh at life; they long ago abjured the bitch-goddess Success, and the best of them will fight for his scholastic ideals with a courage and persistence that would shame a soldier. The professor is not afraid of words like *truth;* in fact, he is not afraid of words at all.

—**Catherine Drinker Bowen** (1897–1973), U.S. author

c. 1948, comment at faculty meeting with Columbia President Dwight D. Eisenhower, attributed in George Dennis O'Brien, *All the Essential Half-Truths about Higher Education,* 1998, p. 15.

Sir, the faculty are not the *employees* of Columbia University, the faculty *is* Columbia University.

—**I. I. Rabi** (1898–1988), professor of physics, Columbia University

1958, *The Academic Marketplace,* p. 85.

Formerly, it was possible to make a career either in the university *or* in the discipline, and the man who chose a local career sustained himself through service to the institution and personal relationships in the faculty. The campus elder statesman is still a familiar figure on American university campuses, but it would seem that, as the present elders retire, there will not be many of a younger generation to take their places.

p. 221.

It is only a slight exaggeration to say that academic success is likely to come to the man who has learned to neglect his assigned duties in order to have more time and energy to pursue his private professional interests.

—**Theodore Caplow** (1920–), professor of sociology, University of Virginia; **Reese J. McGee** (1929–), professor of sociology, Purdue University

1958, "A president's perspective," in Frank C. Abbot, *Faculty-Administrative Relationships,* p. 7.

Any sizable enterprise is likely to have in its membership some maladjusted individuals who simply cannot function amicably and effectively in any kind of normal environment. Since a college or university chooses its professional employees largely on the basis of technical competence and often pays scant attention to personality traits, it is perhaps to be suggested that there is sometimes a fairly high proportion of "screwballs."

—**Logan Wilson** (1907–1990),
President, University of Texas at Austin;
President, American Council
on Education

1963, Grover Sale, Jr., "The scholar and the loyalty oath," *San Francisco Chronicle,* 8 December, quoted in Henry Rosovsky, *The University: An Owner's Manual,* 1990, p. 164.

There are three professions which are entitled to wear the gown: the judge, the priest and the scholar. This garment stands for its bearer's maturity of mind, his independence of judgment, and his direct responsibility to his conscience and his god.

—**Ernest K. Kantorowicz** (1895–1963),
professor of history, University of
California, Berkeley

1967, "Metaphors for the university," *Educational Record,* Winter, p. 25.

If the university is thought of as a zoo, then the center of interest is the exhibits, the professors, rather than the head keeper, the president. In this zoo, specimens from far and near are brought together to have their uniqueness observed by curious spectators. Some specimens burrow into the ground to discover its secrets while others contemplate the mystery of the heavens or investigate the nature of the trees or the earth or the other specimens or, sometimes, the spectators. A few preen themselves all day, admiring their own beauty while deprecating the others' deficiencies, and some constantly make loud noises, prompting the spectators to say: "I'm glad he is caged in there where he can do no harm." Each specimen is proud of his uniqueness and displays it colorfully at least once a year, usually in June.

—**Charles H. Monson, Jr.** (1924–1974),
Academic Vice President,
University of Utah

1968, *The Academic Revolution,* p. 14.

[L]arge numbers of Ph.D.s now regard themselves almost as independent professionals like doctors or lawyers, responsible primarily to themselves and their colleagues rather than their employers, and committed to the advancement of knowledge rather than of any particular institution.

—**Christopher Jencks** (1936–),
professor of social policy, Harvard
University; **David Riesman** (1909–2002)
professor of sociology,
Harvard University

1971, *Malice in Blunderland,* p. 56.

Martin's Laws of Academia: (1) The faculty expands its activity to fit whatever space is available, so that more space is always required. (2) Faculty purchases of equipment and supplies always increase to match the funds available, so these funds are never adequate. (3) The professional quality of the faculty tends to be inversely proportional to the importance it attaches to space and equipment.

—**Thomas L. Martin, Jr.** (1921–),
President, Illinois Institute of Technology

no date, attributed in Donald E. Walker, *The Effective Administrator,* 1986, pp. 172–73.

[S]ome of those brilliant [faculty] minds are encased in some of the most miserable human beings on earth.

—**Deane W. Malott** (1898–1996),
Chancellor, University of Kansas;
President, Cornell University

1980, *Being Lucky,* p. 124.

There are likely to be many people with unusual behavior in any large faculty—eccentric by ordinary standards—simply because the man who prepares for the life of scholarship and teaching is by the very nature of his vocation a person who likes independence of thought and action. He is the very antithesis of the organization man, the Madison Avenue type, the gray-flannel suit kind of person, and he exhibits this difference frequently by his informal style of dress, his individuality, his behavior in many respects.

—**Herman B Wells** (1902–2000),
President, Indiana University

1983, *The Academic Ethic,* p. 3.

The discovery and transmission of truth is the distinctive task of the academic profession, just as the care of the health of the patient is the distinctive task of the medical profession, and the protection, within the law, of the client's rights and interests is the distinctive task of the legal profession.... That truth has a value in itself, apart from any use to which it is put, is a postulate of the activities of the university.

p. 10.

The obligations of the academic profession are inherent in the custodianship of the pursuit, acquisition, assessment, and transmission of knowledge through systematic study, in accordance with methodical procedures including observational techniques, rules of evidence and principles of logical reasoning. The obligation to adhere to these norms is entailed in the acceptance of this custodianship. The commitment to rigorous methods of inquiry and of assessment of the results of inquiry is inherent in the decision to pursue an academic career.

—**Edward Shils** (1910–1995), professor
of sociology, University of Chicago

1986, "The academic ethos," *Minerva 24,* pp. 393, 395.

[T]he social role of a university teacher . . . [is] that of a permanently appointed man of [disciplined] leisure. . . . Leisure as a situation of action without any direct purpose, leisure as time that does not have to be accounted for, is . . . an essential for the effectiveness of the university and the university teacher.

—**Walter Rüegg** (?–?), Rector,
University of Frankfurt

no date, confirmed by William F. Buckley, Jr., personal communication.

The academic community has in it the biggest concentration of alarmists, cranks and extremists this side of the giggle house.

—**William F. Buckley, Jr.** (1925–),
U.S. journalist and author

1988, *A Free and Ordered Space,* p. 43.

University professors never think of themselves as employees; they think of themselves as the heart of the place, as the texture of the place, as the essence of the place. And they are right.

—**A. Bartlett Giamatti** (1938–1989),
President, Yale University

1990, *A Primer for University Presidents,* pp. 8–9.

From time to time, the president will be waited on by groups of faculty who will gravely inform him or her that "faculty morale is at an all-time low." Indeed, the president may have already read that distressing news in the campus newspaper. Orations in the faculty senate may have deplored the low state of faculty morale. Be not overly concerned, Mr./Madam president. Faculty morale is always "at an all-time low."

—**Peter T. Flawn** (1926–), President, University of Texas, San Antonio; President, University of Texas, Austin

1991, "The professor's life," *Dartmouth Alumni Magazine,* February, p. 14.

Because the search for knowledge is open-ended, there can be no point of conscientious rest.

—**James O. Freedman** (1935–), President, University of Iowa; President, Dartmouth College

1992, "Introduction," *Sex, Art, and American Culture,* p. ix.

[O]ur major universities are now stuck with an army of pedestrian, toadying careerists, Fifties types who wave around Sixties banners to conceal their record of ruthless, beaverlike tunneling to the top.

—**Camille Paglia** (1947–), professor of humanities, University of the Arts

1994, *There's No Such Thing as Free Speech, and It's a Good Thing, Too,* pp. 276, 278.

If one listens to academics, one might make the mistake of thinking they would like their complaints to be remedied; but in fact the complaints of academics are their treasures, and were you to remove them, you would find either that they had been instantly replenished or that you were now their object. The reason academics want and need their complaints is that it is important to them to feel oppressed, for in the psychic economy of the academy, oppression is the sign of virtue. . . . The essence of it all is . . . *Academics like to eat shit, and in a pinch, they don't care whose shit they eat.*

—**Stanley E. Fish** (1938–), Dean, College of Liberal Arts and Sciences, University of Illinois at Chicago

1996, *The University in Ruins,* p. 180.

Anyone who has spent any time at all in a University knows that it is not a model community, that few communities are more petty and vicious than University faculties. . . .

—**Bill Readings** (1960–1994), associate professor of comparative literature, University of Montreal

1997, *Straight Man,* p. 204.

My colleagues are academics. They indulge paranoid fantasies for the same reason dogs lick their own testicles.

—**Richard Russo** (1949–), U.S. novelist

1999, *The Dons,* p. 5.

[A don] was a teacher and a fellow of an Oxford or Cambridge college; a teacher who stood in a peculiar relation to his pupils in that they came to his rooms individually each week and were taught by him personally. And since these were men of his own college, his first allegiance was not to the university but to his college—to the close-knit society whose members had elected him. To the other fellows he was bound by ties of special loyalty and affection—sometimes, of course, by no less binding ties of enmity and loathing which led to feuds and vendettas within the society.

—**Noel Annan** (1916–2000), Vice-chancellor, University of London

Faculty Meetings

c. 1850, attributed in W. H. Cowley, *Presidents, Professors and Trustees,* 1980, p. 81.

I remember having one [faculty meeting] once, some thirty-six years ago, but I never wish to have another.

> —**Eliphalet Nott** (1773–1866), President, Union College

no date, quoted in William James, *Eliot,* 1930, vol. 1, p. 305.

[The faculty] is a ruminating animal; chewing a cud a long time, slowly bringing it into a digestible condition.

> —**Charles William Eliot** (1834–1926), president, Harvard University

1908, *Microcosmographia Academica,* reprinted in *Two Papers on Academic Change,* 1972, p. 13.

When other methods of obstruction fail, you should have recourse to *Wasting Time.* . . . The simplest method is *Boring.* Talk slowly and indistinctly, at a little distance from the point. No academic person is ever voted into the chair until he has reached an age at which he has forgotten the meaning of the word 'irrelevant'; and you will be allowed to go on, until everyone in the room will vote with you sooner than hear your voice another minute. . . .

> —**F. M. Cornford** (1874–1943), professor of ancient philosophy, Cambridge University

1910, *Great American Universities,* pp. 520–21.

[T]he deliberative bodies of universities, small and large, have substantially the same method of procedure, and I suggest that if the following rules were framed and hung on the wall of the faculty room, it would save time now wasted in discussing the proper order:—

Order of Business at Faculty Meetings
1. Present motion. 2. Pass it. 3. Discuss it. 4. Reconsider it. 5. Amend it. 6. Amend the amendment. 7. Discuss it. 8. Move to lay on the table. 9. Discuss it. 10. Refer to a committee with power to act. 11. Discuss it. 12. Adjourn. 13. Discuss it.

> —**Edwin E. Slosson** (1865–1929), chemist; U.S. writer

1927, *Life and the Student,* p. 169.

One of the most depressing things I do is go to faculty meeting [sic]. How much more edifying are students than professors!

> —**Charles Horton Cooley** (1864–1929), professor of sociology, University of Michigan

1959, *The American College President,* p. 121.

When Henry Adams wanted to indicate his contempt for the small-mindedness of congressional debates he said that they were as bad as a Harvard faculty meeting.

> —**Harold W. Stoke** (1903–1982), President, University of New Hampshire; President, Louisiana State University; President, Queens College

1991, "Letter from academia," *Chronicles,* September, p. 48.

There is nothing on this earth as boring, as stupefying, as a typical departmental or faculty meeting. The intensity of discussion and debate is inversely proportional to the importance of the topic, and since academic meetings almost always dwell on trivial issues, the boredom is intense.

> —**Murray N. Rothbard** (1926–1995), professor of economics, University of Nevada, Las Vegas

Professor

1764–1799, *Aphorisms,* quoted in Keith Allan Noble, *The International Education Quotations Encyclopaedia,* 1995.

People who have taken no intellectual food for ten years, except a few tiny crumbs from the journals, are found among professors; they aren't rare at all.

—**George C. Lichtenberg** (1742–1799), German physicist

no date, attributed in William Cole and Louis Phillips (eds.), *The Random House Treasury of Humorous Quotations,* 1996, p. 1.

There was an old cannibal whose stomach suffered from so many disorders that he could only digest animals with no spines. Thus for years, he subsisted only on university professors.

—**Louis Phillips** (1860–1904), Russian writer, dramatist

1911, *A Thousand and One Epigrams.*

Now, owls are not really wise—they only look that way. The owl is a sort of college professor.

—**Elbert Hubbard** (1856–1915), U.S. writer and publisher

1917, "Political Parties in Russia and the Tasks of the Proletariat" (pamphlet), July, in *Collected Works,* vol. 24, 1964, p. 99.

[T]he experience of all revolutions has shown that the cause of popular freedom is lost when it is entrusted to professors.

—**Vladimir Ilich Lenin** (1870–1924), Russian revolutionary leader

1919, "Criticism of criticism of criticism," in *Prejudices: First Series,* p. 12.

[A] professor must have a theory, as a dog must have fleas.

—**H. L. Mencken** (1880–1956), U.S. editor and writer

1922, "The dismal science," in *Prejudices: A Selection,* 1958, p. 149.

The professor must be an obscurantist or he is nothing; he has a special and unmatchable talent for dullness; his central aim is not to expose the truth clearly but to exhibit his profundity, his esotericity— in brief, to stagger the sophomores and other professors.

—**H. L. Mencken** (1880–1956), U.S. editor and writer

1923, *College Days,* p. 105.

The professor easily falls into little ways and mannerisms of his own. In the deference of the classroom they go unchallenged and uncorrected. With the passage of the years they wear into his mind like ruts.

—**Stephen Butler Leacock** (1869–1944), professor of political economy, McGill University

1927, *Life and the Student,* p. 185.

It is true in university life as elsewhere that early success, as distinguished from eventual fame, usually implies an opportunism scarcely compatible with genius.

—**Charles Horton Cooley** (1864–1929), professor of sociology, University of Michigan

no date, attributed at <http://philosophy-shop.com/may200.htm>.

The three sexes are men, women, and professors.

—**Joel E. Spingarn** (1875–1939), social reformer; professor of English, Columbia University

1938, *Here Are My Lectures,* p. 245.

[I] am what is called a *professor emeritus*—from the Latin *e,* for 'out', and *meritus,* 'so he ought to be'.

—**Stephen Butler Leacock** (1869–1944), professor of political economy, McGill University

1940, "The species professor Americanus and some natural enemies," *Association of American Colleges Bulletin,* November, p. 405.

Why is it, I have been asking myself, that in Europe an ordinary mortal, when he sees a professor, tips his hat, whereas in these United States he taps his forehead? Why is it that in Europe the professor is the jewel of the salon while in the United States he is the skeleton at the feast? Why is it that in Europe a professor is a lion who is diligently hunted by the arbiters of society, while in the United States he is a lone ass braying in the desert?

—**Marten ten Hoor** (1890–1967), Dean, College of Arts and Sciences, Tulane University

no date, quoted in Vincent Fitzpatrick, *H. L. Mencken,* 1989, p. 3, at <http://www.io.com/gibbonsb/mencken/megaquotes.html>.

Some boys go to college and eventually succeed in getting out. Others go to college and never succeed in getting out. The latter are called professors.

—**H. L. Mencken** (1880–1956), U.S. editor and writer

1942, *The Academic Man,* p. 4.

[A] professor in this country may be many things besides a member of a college or university faculty. He may be a secondary school teacher, an instructor in a barbering college or a business school, a quack 'psychologist,' a circus barker, or even a piano player in a house of prostitution.

—**Logan Wilson** (1907–1990), President, University of Texas at Austin; President, American Council on Education

1943, *Cornell University: Founders and the Founding,* quoted in Richard Hofstadter and Wilson Smith (eds.), *American Higher Education: A Documentary History, Volume II,* 1961, p. 809.

A professor . . . is a man who thinks otherwise.

—**Carl Becker** (1873–1945), professor of history, Cornell University

1949, *The Need for Roots,* quoted in Tony Augarde, *The Oxford Dictionary of Modern Quotations,* 1991, p. 224.

Culture is an instrument wielded by professors, to manufacture professors, who when their turn comes will manufacture professors.

—**Simone Weil** (1909–1943), French philosophical writer

no date, attributed in Keith Allan Noble, *The International Education Quotations Encyclopaedia,* 1995.

A professor is one who talks in someone else's sleep.

—**W. H. Auden** (1907–1973), U.S. poet

no date, attributed in Keith Allan Noble, *The International Education Quotations Encyclopaedia,* 1995.

Every advance in education is made over the dead bodies of 10,000 resisting professors.

> —**Robert Maynard Hutchins**
> (1899–1977), President,
> University of Chicago

1967, quoted by Theodore H. White, "In the halls of power," *Life,* 9 June, p. 57.

No one should tell a professor what to think about. A good professor is a bastard perverse enough to think what *he* thinks is important, not what government thinks is important.

> —**Edward C. Banfield** (1916–1999),
> professor of government,
> Harvard University

1973, *This Beats Working for a Living,* p. 11.

I have met few professors whom I would hire to run a peanut stand, let alone be the guardian of wisdom and Western civilization.

> —**Professor X** (pseudonym)

1984, at his retirement, attributed at <http://www.ag.wastholm.net/aphorism/ A-1384>.

It is time I stepped aside for a less experienced and less able man.

> —**Scott Elledge** (1914–1997), professor
> of English, Cornell University

1988, *ProfScam,* p. 4.

Almost single-handedly, the professors— working steadily and systematically—have destroyed the university as a center of learning and have desolated higher edu-

cation, which no longer is higher or much of an education. The story of the collapse of American higher education is the story of the rise of the professoriate.

p. 7.

The modern university—insatiable, opportunistic, and implacably anti-intellectual— is created in the image of the *Professorus Americanus.* Today, the professor is the university.

> —**Charles J. Sykes** (1954–),
> U.S. journalist

1990, *The University: An Owner's Manual,* p. 161.

The essence of academic life is the opportunity—indeed, the demand—for continual investment in oneself. It is a unique chance for a lifetime of building and renewing intellectual capital.

p. 202.

We seek the best scholar-teachers, and if they happen to have abominable personalities, why then we claim joyfully to suffer in the name of learning.

p. 204.

There are occasional geniuses whom one would want to have on a faculty even if their customary mode of communication took the form of grunts and mumbles.

> —**Henry Rosovsky** (1927–), Dean of
> the Faculty of Arts and Sciences,
> Harvard University

1992, *Imposters in the Temple,* p. 125.

There is a wide streak of snobbery in almost everyone who considers himself or herself an academic intellectual. . . . It is not all their fault. Academic intellectuals are the only large group in our society that is certified smart, whose intelligence has the equivalent of the Good Housekeeping Seal of Approval.

—**Martin Anderson** (1936–),
senior fellow, Hoover Institution,
Stanford University

1993, *Alma Mater: A College Homecoming,* p. 8.

I remember my Kenyon professors, not my courses. Who keeps college notebooks, all these years of stenography, context fading, handwriting indecipherable, memories and morals turning into mulch? Likewise those big-ticket textbooks gather dust, those pages of underlining, exclamation marks, and marginal notes that remind you of an earlier self, some too confident hunter roaming through print with a ballpoint pen, marking, gotcha, gotcha, gotcha. You remember the professors.

—**P. F. Kluge** (1942–), U.S. author

Tenure

1902, "Concerning the American university," in *Popular Science Monthly,* June, p. 178.

It is better that an occasional man should be retained who is not quite up to the standard, rather than that all professors should feel that their chairs are insecure, subject to the automatic law of supply and demand, or up to the possible caprice of an individual.

—**J. McKeen Cattell** (1860–1944),
professor of psychology,
Columbia University

1902, *The President's Report, July 1892–July 1902,* quoted in Edgar W. Knight, *What College Presidents Say,* 1940, p. 225.

If an officer on permanent appointment abuses his privilege as a professor, the University must suffer and it is proper that it should suffer. This is only the direct and inevitable consequence of the lack of foresight and wisdom involved in the original appointment.

—**William Rainey Harper** (1856–1906),
President, University of Chicago

1907, "Academic freedom," *Science,* July, quoted in W. H. Cowley, *Presidents, Professors, and Trustees,* 1980, p. 98.

A long tenure of office is well nigh indispensable, if a just academic freedom is to be insured for them. . . . Teachers . . . , when once their capacity and character have been demonstrated, should hold their offices without express limitation of time, and should be subject to removal only for inadequate performance of duty or for misconduct publicly proved.

—**Charles William Eliot** (1834–1926),
president, Harvard University

1912, *Report for 1911–12,* quoted in Edward C. Elliott (ed.), *The Rise of a University, Vol. II,* 1937, pp. 170–71.

There is, unfortunately, no public opinion, either within a university or in the community at large, which will sustain the displacement of a teacher simply because he cannot teach. If he is a person of good moral character, of reasonable industry and of inoffensive personality, his place is perfectly secure no matter what havoc he may make in the classroom. It is this inequitable security of tenure, the like of which is not to be found in any other calling, that attracts to the teaching profession and holds in it, despite its modest pecuniary rewards, so much mediocrity.

—**Nicholas Murray Butler**
(1862–1947), President,
Columbia University

1913, *University Control,* pp. 38–39.

A university which dismisses professors when the president thinks they are inefficient or lacking in loyalty to him . . . will in the end obtain a faculty consisting of a few adventurers, a few sycophants and a crowd of mediocrities.

> —**J. McKeen Cattell** (1860–1944), professor of psychology, Columbia University

1917, *Report for 1916–17,* quoted in Edward C. Elliott (ed.), *The Rise of a University, Vol. II,* 1937, p. 395.

Security of tenure is desirable, but competence and loyalty are more desired still, and a secure tenure purchased at the price of incompetence and disloyalty must sound a death-knell to every educational system or institution where it prevails.

> —**Nicholas Murray Butler** (1862–1947), President, Columbia University

1920, "The relation between faculties and governing boards," *At War with Academic Traditions in America,* 1934, p. 288.

Permanence of tenure lies at the base of the difference between a society of scholars in a university and the employees in an industrial concern. . . . [I]n the university the usefulness of the scholar depends largely upon his sense of security, upon the fact that he can work for an object that may be remote and whose value may not be easily demonstrated.

> —**Abbott Lawrence Lowell** (1856–1943), President, Harvard University

1940, "Statement of principles on academic freedom and tenure," *Policy Documents and Reports, Ninth Edition,* 2001, p. 3.

Tenure is a means to certain ends; specifically 1) freedom of teaching and research and of extramural activities, and 2) a sufficient degree of economic security to make the profession attractive to men and women of ability. Freedom and economic security, hence tenure, are indispensable to the success of an institution in fulfilling its obligations to students and to society.

> —**American Association of University Professors**

1952, "Education and independent thought," *Freedom, Education, and the Fund,* 1956, p. 156.

[M]istakes cannot be avoided in the appointment of professors to permanent tenure. Some men may incorrectly be suspected of the ability to think; others may stop thinking when they have arrived at life tenure. This is the price that is paid for the independence of professors, which is another way of saying that it is part of the price that is paid for the greatness of a university.

> —**Robert Maynard Hutchins** (1899–1977), President, University of Chicago

1966, "The university," *The New Republic,* May 28, pp. 18–19.

The selection and the tenure of the members of the community of scholars is subject to the criterion that scholars shall be free of any control except a stern duty to bear faithful allegiance to the truth they are appointed to seek. A judgment as to whether a scholar has been faithful is one that only his peers can render. The supreme sin of a scholar, *qua* scholar, is to lie, not about where he spent the previous weekend, but about whether two and two make four.

> —**Walter Lippman** (1889–1974), U.S. editor and author

1968, "A different way to restructure the university," *New York Times Magazine,* 18 December, p. 50.

They [faculty] may even admit that the presence of tenured faculty is one of the reasons that the university has been—with the possible exception of the post office—the least inventive (or even adaptive) of our social institutions since the end of World War II.

> —**Irving Kristol** (1920–), U.S. editor

1985, "The sorcerers and the 7½ hour week," *Milwaukee Magazine,* October, quoted in Charles J. Sykes, *ProfScam,* 1988, p. 60.

If a tenured professor decapitated the chancellor and raped his wife, he would have the right to 36 hearings over six years before university committees, retaining his tenure while his colleagues debated endlessly definitions and procedures. Fire a tenured professor for gross teaching incompetence? Forget it.

> —**Jay G. Sykes** (1922–1985), professor of mass communications, University of Wisconsin, Milwaukee

1988, *ProfScam,* p. 258.

Tenure corrupts, enervates, and dulls higher education.

> —**Charles J. Sykes** (1954–), U.S. journalist

1990, *The University: An Owner's Manual,* p. 184.

[T]enure carries the implication of joining an extended family; that is the social contract. Each side can seek a divorce: the university only in the most extraordinary circumstances, and the professor as easily as a male under Islamic law.

p. 186.

It is fashionable for outstanding and well-known younger scholars to say that they do not care and never worried about tenure, particularly after they have attained that status.

> —**Henry Rosovsky** (1927–), Dean of the Faculty of Arts and Sciences, Harvard University

1990, *Killing the Spirit,* p. 114.

[T]enure and its partner in crime, the Ph.D., have inflicted what may turn out to be fatal wounds on higher education.

> —**Page Smith** (1917–1995), historian; Provost, University of California at Santa Cruz

1991, *Consciousness Explained,* p. 171.

The juvenile sea squirt wanders through the sea searching for a suitable rock or hunk of coral to cling to and make its home for life. For this task, it has a rudimentary nervous system. When it finds its spot and takes root, it doesn't need its brain anymore, so it eats it! (It's rather like getting tenure).

> —**Daniel Clement Dennett** (1941–), professor of philosophy, Tufts University

1992, *An Aristocracy of Everyone,* p. 196.

No one was ever tenured at a major college or university on the basis of great teaching alone; and no one with great record of research and publication was ever denied tenure because of a poor teaching record. Teaching is the gravy, but research is the meat and potatoes.

> —**Benjamin R. Barber** (1939–), professor of political science, Rutgers University

1992, *Imposters in the Temple,* 1992, p. 121.

Tenure is corrupting; it gives academic intellectuals almost unlimited license to do as they please with no fear of consequences. Its major effect is to encourage sloth. In a nutshell, professors who are good don't need tenure, and those who need tenure usually aren't very good.

—**Martin Anderson** (1936–),
senior fellow, Hoover Institution,
Stanford University

1993, *Inside American Education,* p. 228.

Anyone who has been through this experience is likely to find it a horror not to be repeated. Those who must try two or three institutions before finally achieving tenure can spend the better part of a decade in limbo, without as much job security as a factory worker in a viable business.

—**Thomas Sowell** (1930–),
U.S. economist

1996, "Tenure today: Happening and why?," remarks at the American Association for the Advancement of Science meeting on Scientific Freedom, Responsibility, and Tenure, 24 September, quoted in Richard P. Chait, *The Questions of Tenure,* 2002, p. 10.

[T]enure is the worst of personnel systems save for all the others.

—**Robert O'Neil** (1934–), President,
University of Wisconsin System;
President, University of Virginia

Chapter 12

The Students

Admissions

1642–1650, Laws of Harvard College, quoted in John S. Brubacher and Willis Rudy, *Higher Education in Transition,* 1958, p. 12.

When any Schollar is able to read Tully [Cicero] or such like classicall Latine Authour ex temporare, and make and speake true Latin verse and prose Suo (ut aiunt) Marte [by one's own skill], and decline perfectly the paradigmes of Nounes and verbes in the Greek tounge, then may hee bee admitted into the Colledge, nor shall any claim admission before such qualifications. . . .

—**Harvard College**

1869, Inaugural Address, 19 October, in *A Turning Point in Higher Education,* 1969, p. 38.

The rigorous examination for admission has got one good effect throughout the college courses; it prevents a waste of instruction upon incompetent persons.

—**Charles William Eliot** (1834–1926), President, Harvard University

1904, letter to Charles Francis Adams, 9 June, in Henry James, *Charles W. Eliot,* 1930, volume II, pp. 150–51.

I want to have the College open equally to men with much money, little money, or no money, provided they all have brains. . . . I care for the young men whose families have so little money that it would make a real difference to them whether Harvard tuition fees were $150 or $225. . . . To my thinking, they constitute the very best part of Harvard College.

—**Charles William Eliot** (1834–1926), President, Harvard University

1910, *Great American Universities,* p. 294.

A State university is obliged to keep in touch with all parts of its territory. Its attitude is very different from that of a private university. One aims to be inclusive and the other to be exclusive. The private university is always saying to itself: "How high can we raise our standards of admission without losing students?" The State university says: "How low can we place our standards of admission without losing prestige?"

—**Edwin E. Slosson** (1865–1929), chemist; U.S. writer

1927, "Ideals for the development of Rollins College, *School and Society,* 6 August, p. 155.

[I] would admit to Rollins [College] any student above the intelligence of a moron, and mature enough to carry on college work, provided only that he show capacity for improvement.

—**Hamilton Holt** (1872–1951),
President, Rollins College

1933, *Bulletin of the American Association of Collegiate Registrars,* July, p. 336.

Instead of admitting students on the basis of years in school, grades acquired, courses taken, and credits accumulated, I should prefer to admit to the University of Chicago any student who can read and write and who is recommended by somebody who knows something about him as a person who deserves a chance at a collegiate experience.

—**Robert Maynard Hutchins**
(1899–1977), President,
University of Chicago

1938, *Saturday Evening Post,* 22 January, p. 16.

College is the greatest place in the world for those who ought to go to college and who go for the right reasons. For those who ought not to go to college or who go for the wrong reasons, college is a waste of time and money.

p. 16.

[T]he following persons should not go to college: Children whose parents have no other reason for sending them other than that they can afford to. Children whose parents have no other reason for sending them than to get them off their hands for four years. Children whose characters are bad and whose parents believe that college will change them for the better. Children who have had no other reason for going to college than to avoid work or have a good time for four years. Children who have no other reason for going to college than to have a stadium in which to demonstrate their athletic ability. Children who have no other reason for going to college than the notion that it will help them achieve social or financial success in later life.

—**Robert Maynard Hutchins**
(1899–1977), President,
University of Chicago

1955, *Time,* 29 August, p. 44.

The scramble to get into college is going to be so terrible in the next few years that students are going to put up with almost anything, even an education.

—**Barnaby C. Keeney** (1914–1980),
President, Brown University

1966, "Implications for education and for adjustment of curricula to individual students," in Earl J. McGrath, *Universal Higher Education,* 1966, p. 44.

A model for us as a society might be what the British aristocracy of a century ago did as a class. . . . [S]tupidity was no bar to a university education—not when the parents of the stupid young man controlled the universities and regarded their prime function to be doing something for their young people. Every young aristocrat was to be taught something that was useful to him, in the sense that it enabled him to enjoy life and to participate as a full member of his class. If he could not be taught to enjoy books then he could be taught riding; in any case he could be taught how to speak, and what to say on most occasions, and thus to take his place in society.

—**Nevitt R. Sanford** (1909–1995),
professor of psychology and education,
Stanford University

1970, *The Campus and the Racial Crisis,* p. 135.

[T]he typical admissions officer today functions more like a handicapper; he tries merely to pick the winners. . . . The problem here is that an educational institution is supposed to function less like a handicapper and more like a jockey or trainer: it has a responsibility to *improve the performance* of the individual, not just to identify those with the greatest potential.

—**Alexander Astin** (1932–), professor of higher education, University of California, Los Angeles

1973, *Up the University,* p. 81.

College is not a privilege, much less a right. It is a blessing, a golden moment in life in which the life of the mind and the spirit can be explored to the fullest. Many students fresh out of high school are not ready for such a "blessing." . . . We suggest that most seventeen-year-olds be *discouraged* from going straight to college.

—**Robert Solomon** (1942–), professor of philosophy and business, University of Texas; **Jon Solomon** (1950–), associate professor of classics, University of Arizona

1974, quoted in Carol Tavris, " 'What does a college education do for a person?' 'Frankly, very little,' " *Psychology Today,* September, p. 73.

So much of what colleges are supposed to do is predetermined by the kinds of people who are admitted in the first place.

—**Theodore Newcomb** (1903–1984), professor of sociology and psychology, University of Michigan

1986, quoted in Colin Campbell, "The Harvard factor," *New York Times Magazine,* 20 July, p. 21.

Harvard admissions is an exercise in social engineering.

—**Henry Rosovsky** (1927–), Dean of the Faculty of Arts and Sciences, Harvard University

1994, *A Different Shade of Crimson,* p. 60.

For generations, bright young students have wandered through Harvard Square in the first few weeks feeling like frauds. We are convinced that the admissions office must have made a dreadful mistake. This is Harvard, we tell ourselves. The school of Emerson, Thoreau, and Kennedy. What am I doing here?

—**Ruben Navarrette, Jr.** (?–), U.S. journalist and writer

2001, "College admissions: Why selectivity matters," *Chronicle of Higher Education,* 29 June.

Any discussion of selective colleges taps into a deep American uneasiness about social class or status. But that uneasiness has no more legitimate a role in discussions of college admissions than it does in discussions of how the Cleveland Orchestra selects its members.

—**William C. Dowling** (1944–), professor of English, Rutgers University

Alumni

1910, *Great American Universities,* p. vii.

The alumnus who returns for the decennial reunion finds his Alma Mater greatly changed. Usually he is inclined to think that the change has not been altogether for the better in spite of the new buildings and crowds of students. He can, in fact, name the date when his Alma Mater began to decline and to lose the real old college spirit. It was ten years ago, when was graduated what is universally conceded by all its members to be the brightest class that ever came forth from its walls.

—**Edwin E. Slosson** (1865–1929),
chemist; U.S. writer

1923, *The Goose-Step,* p. 363.

I asked one of the most eminent of American scientists, a man who has lived most of his life in universities, what is the matter with these institutions, and his answer came in an explosion: "It is the semisimian mob of the alumni! They have been to college for the sake of their social position; they have gone out utterly ignorant, and made what they call a success in the world, and they come back once a year in a solid phalanx of philistinism, to dominate the college and bully the trustees and the president."

—**Upton Sinclair** (1878–1968),
U.S. author

1926, *Which Way Parnassus?,* p. 107.

If the alumni could only be taught to give money when asked and to keep their mouths firmly shut, the colleges would make astonishing progress. . . .

—**Percy Marks** (1891–1956),
U.S. writer and instructor of English

1934, "The sentimental alumnus," commencement address at Oberlin College, *No Friendly Voice,* 1936, p. 87.

All alumni are dangerous. They see their Alma Mater through a rosy haze that gets thicker with the years. They do not know what the college was really like. They do not want to know what it is like now. They want to imagine that it is like what they think it was like in their time. Therefore they oppose all change.

—**Robert Maynard Hutchins**
(1899–1977), President,
University of Chicago

1942, "The past instructs," *American Scholar,* Winter, 1941–42, p. 4.

Anyone who has opportunity to meet and study in large numbers the alumni of the American colleges is likely to have attacks of depression. In spite of the vast investment of money and energy in these institutions, it is only too clear that in a great many cases education has failed to "take," or the infection has been so slight that few traces are to be perceived after five or ten years of the wear and tear of American life.

—**W. A. Neilson** (1869–1946),
President, Smith College

1962, *The American College,* p. 10.

The trouble with students, the saying goes, is that they turn into alumni. Indeed, a close look at the college-educated people in the United States is enough to dispel any notion that our institutions of higher education are doing a good job of liberal education.

—**Nevitt R. Sanford** (1909–1995),
professor of psychology and education,
Stanford University

Athletics: Football

1891, letter to coach Amos Alonzo Stagg, quoted in John S. Brubacher and Willis Rudy, *Higher Education in Transition,* 1958, p. 128.

I want you to develop teams which we can send around the country and knock out all the colleges. We will give them a palace car and a vacation too.

—**William Rainey Harper** (1856–1906),
President, University of Chicago

1901, "The ethical functions of football," *North American Review,* November, quoted in Edgar W. Knight, *What College Presidents Say,* 1940, p. 168.

The gridiron is a small ethical world, marked all over with the white lines of moral distinctions . . . it is in ethics what the Socratic thinking shop was supposed to be—a training of the individual. It thus helps to make the finest type of gentleman.

—**Charles F. Thwing** (1853–1937), President, Adelbert College; President, Western Reserve University

1904, *College Life,* p. 10.

Training for football means early hours, clean life, constant occupation for body and mind. Breach of training means ostracism. That this game tides many a Freshman over a great danger, by keeping him healthily occupied, I have come firmly to believe. . . . [I]t affords an outlet for the reckless courage of young manhood,—the same reckless courage that in idle days drives young men headlong into vice.

—**LeBaron Russell Briggs** (1855–1934), Dean, Harvard College

1905, "The future of football," *Colliers Weekly,* 9 December, p. 19, quoted in Ernest L. Boyer, *College: The Undergraduate Experience in America,* 1987, pp. 183–84.

Let the football team become frankly professional. Cast off all the deception. Get the best professional coach. Pay him well and let him have the best men the town and the alumni will pay for. Let the teams struggle in perfectly honest warfare, known for what it is and with no masquerade of amateurism or academic ideas. The evil in current football rests not in the hired men, but in academic lying and in the falsifica-

tion of our own standards as associations of scholars and men of honor.

—**David Starr Jordan** (1851–1931), President, Stanford University

1906, *Reports of the President and Treasurer of Harvard College, 1905–06,* quoted in Edgar W. Knight, *What College Presidents Say,* 1940, p. 173.

No game is fit for college uses in which men are so often knocked or crushed into insensibility or immobility that it is a question whether by the application of water and stimulants they can be brought to and enabled to go on playing. . . . From an educational point of view, the value of any sport is to be tested by the number of persons who habitually take part in it for pleasure during the educational period and enjoy it in after life. Tried by this test, football is the least valuable of all college sports.

—**Charles William Eliot** (1834–1926), President, Harvard University

1910, *Great American Universities,* p. 505.

There is only one new rule needed to reform football and only one that will do it; that is, the abolition of the grand stand. Let the students play football as much as they like and stop when they get tired, according to any rules or none. If there is nobody watching them, they will not injure themselves much and others not at all. The evil of a prize fight lies not in the fight, but in the prize.

—**Edwin E. Slosson** (1865–1929), chemist; U.S. writer

1910, *A History of Education in the United States Since the Civil War,* pp. 138–39.

Football, the most significant of all college games, can be defended on the ground of being a training for the brain, a training for the heart, and a training for the will. With all that may be said against athletics—and much may be said—much more, very much more, may be said in their favor. The credit arising from athletics, to be placed to the advantage of the American college, is great.

—**Charles F. Thwing** (1853–1937), President, Adelbert College; President, Western Reserve University

1911, *The Devil's Dictionary.*

ACADEME, n. An ancient school where morality and philosophy were taught. ACADEMY, n. [from ACADEME] A modern school where football is taught.

—**Ambrose G. Bierce** (1842?–1914?), U.S. journalist

1911, *A Thousand and One Epigrams.*

Football occupies the same relationship to education that a bullfight does to farming.

—**Elbert Hubbard** (1856–1915), U.S. writer and publisher

1923, 24 November, quoted in "Yale football glossary" at <http://www.yale.edu/athletic/Showcase/Football/glossary.htm>.

Gentlemen, you are now going out to play football against Harvard. Never again in your whole life will you do anything so important.

—**TAD Jones** (1887–1957), football coach, Yale University

1924, *New York Tribune,* 19 October, quoted at <http://lamb.archives.nd.edu/rockne/rice.html>.

Outlined against a blue-gray October sky, the Four Horsemen rode again. In dramatic lore they are known as Famine, Pestilence, Destruction and Death. These are only ali-

ases. Their real names are Stuhldreher, Miller, Crowley and Layden. They formed the crest of the South Bend cyclone before which another fighting Army football team was swept away over the precipice at the Polo Grounds yesterday afternoon as 55,000 spectators peered down on the bewildering panorama spread on the green plain below.

—**Grantland Rice** (1880–1954), U.S. sportswriter

1926, quoted in David J. Loftus, *The Unofficial Book of Harvard Trivia,* 1985, p. 88.

Harvard will be willing to trade President Lowell, President Emeritus Eliot and three heads of departments for a good running backfield and no questions asked. [N.B.—proposition defeated by vote of 1,324 to 1,227].

—**Harvard *Crimson* reader's poll**

1927, *Life and the Student,* p. 177.

There is a function of a quasi religious nature performed by a few experts but followed in spirit by the whole university world, serving indeed as a symbol to arouse in the students and in the alumni certain congregate and hieratic emotions. I refer, of course, to football.

—**Charles Horton Cooley** (1864–1929), professor of sociology, University of Michigan

1929, "Preface," in Howard J. Savage, *American College Athletics,* p. xiv.

Once in college the student who goes in for competitive sports, and in particular for football, finds himself under a pressure, hard to resist, to give his whole time and thought to his athletic career. No college boy training for a major team can have much time for thought or study.

—**Henry S. Pritchett** (1857–1939), President, Carnegie Foundation for the Advancement of Teaching

c. 1930s, attributed in John Thelin, *The Cultivation of Ivy,* 1976, p. 46.

> It's general knowledge that many a
>   college
> That's not very socially smart
> Has teams that can crush dear old
>   Harvard to mush
> And take Yale and Princeton apart
> But gridiron heroes exclusively hail
> (in stories) from Harvard, or Princeton
>   or Yale!

—**Berton Braley** (1882–1966), U.S. poet

1940, half-time speech, in the MGM film *Knute Rockne—All American.*

Well, boys . . . I haven't a thing to say. Played a great game . . . all of you. Great game. I guess we just can't expect to win 'em all. I'm going to tell you something I've kept to myself for years—. None of you ever knew George Gipp. It was long before your time. But you know what a tradition he is at Notre Dame . . . And the last thing he said to me—"Rock," he said,—"sometime, when the team is up against it—and the breaks are beating the boys—tell them to go out there with all they got and win just one for the Gipper . . . I don't know where I'll be then, Rock," he said—"but I'll know about it—and I'll be happy."

—**Knute Rockne** (1888–1931) [Pat O'Brien], football coach, Notre Dame

1940, in Robin D. Lester, *The Rise, Decline and Fall of Intercollegiate*

Football at the University of Chicago, 1890–1940, unpublished dissertation, University of Chicago, 1974, p. 266, quoted in Henry A. Ashmore, *Unseasonable Truth,* 1989, p. 201.

Since we cannot hope to win against our present competition and since we cannot profitably change our competition, only two courses are open to us; to subsidize players or to discontinue intercollegiate football. We cannot subsidize players or encourage our alumni to do so without departing from our principles and losing our self-respect. We must therefore discontinue the game.

—**Robert Maynard Hutchins** (1899–1977), President, University of Chicago

1943, *Barefoot Boy with Cheek,* p. 42.

Four years ago he was an unknown boy roaming around the North Woods precariously keeping body and soul together by stealing bait from bear traps. Then a Minnesota football scout saw him, lassoed him, put shoes on him, taught him to sign his name, and brought him to the university to play football. And last year Eino was All-American! All American!

—**Max Shulman** (1919–1988), U.S. writer

1948, "Morals, religion, and higher education," *Freedom, Education, and the Fund,* 1956, p. 90.

My class never saw Yale win a big game, and it was said of the coach of that time that he had conferred one inestimable moral benefit upon the student body: he had taught them not to bet—or at least not to bet on Yale. I do not depreciate this contribution; for temperance and prudence would seem to forbid gambling. But this contribution, important as it is, seems to me negligible in contrast to the enormous expenditure of time, money, effort, and interest that went into the acquisition of it.

—**Robert Maynard Hutchins**
(1899–1977), President,
University of Chicago

1950, testimony to the Oklahoma State Legislature, *Presidents Can't Punt,* 1977, p. 145.

I would like to build a university of which our football team can be proud.

—**George Lynn Cross** (1905–1998),
President, University of Oklahoma

1951, "The democratic dilemma," *Freedom, Education, and the Fund,* 1956, p. 115.

There is not a college or university president in America who would not get rid of what is called big-time intercollegiate football if he felt that it was safe to do so. The howls of the alumni and the public, who have come to rely on his institution to supply them with entertainment on Saturday afternoons in the autumn, ring in his ears as he considers such a decision, and he concludes that it would not be safe.

—**Robert Maynard Hutchins**
(1899–1977), President,
University of Chicago

no date, attributed in *Your Ultimate Success Quotation Library* (software program) at <http://www.cybernation. com/>.

An atheist is a man who watches a Notre Dame–Southern Methodist University game and doesn't care who wins.

—**Dwight D. Eisenhower** (1890–1969),
President, Columbia University;
President of the United States

1954, "The sheepskin myth," *Journal of Higher Education,* December, p. 487.

The familiar symbol of the lamp of learning whose flame enlightens the mind of men, and the common motto of *"Lux et Libertas,"* might, I suggest, more appropriately be replaced by the figure of a fullback *couchant* before the goal posts *rampant.*

—**Martin Staples Shockley** (1908–),
professor of English,
North Texas State College

no date, attributed in Mervin D. Hyman and Gordon S. White, Jr., *Big Ten Football, Its Life and Times, Great Coaches, Players, and Games,* 1977, p. 130.

If it meant the betterment of Michigan State, our football team would play any eleven gorillas from Barnum and Bailey any Saturday.

—**John A. Hannah** (1902–1991),
President, Michigan State University

1956, Note no. 186, in *Minority Report: H. L. Mencken's Notebooks,* p. 135.

College football would be much more interesting if the faculty played instead of the students, and even more interesting if the trustees played. There would be a great increase in broken arms, legs and necks, and simultaneously an appreciable diminution in the loss to humanity.

—**H. L. Mencken** (1880–1956),
U.S. editor and writer

1963, *Left-Handed Dictionary,* p. 235.

University—a college with a stadium seating over 40,000.

—**Leonard L. Levinson** (1904–1974),
U.S. author

no date, attributed in <www.creative quotations.com>.

A school without football is in danger of deteriorating into a medieval study hall.

—**Frank Leahy** (1908–1973),
U.S. football coach

no date, attributed in Mervin D. Hyman and Gordon S. White, Jr., *Big Ten Football, Its Life and Times, Great Coaches, Players, and Games,* 1977, p. 140.

Our grants-in-aid are based on academic achievement and need. By academic achievement, we mean can the boy read and write. By need—well, we don't take a boy unless we need him.

—**Hugh Duffy Dougherty** (1915–1987),
football coach, Michigan State University

1973, *Sports Illustrated,* 12 November, p. 24.

It was like a heart transplant. We tried to implant college in him [a football player] but his head rejected it.

—**Barry Switzer** (1937–),
football coach, University of Oklahoma

1975, Paul W. Bryant and John Underwood, *Bear: The Hard Life and Good Times of Alabama's Coach Bear Bryant,* p. 325.

I used to go along with the idea that football players on scholarship were "student athletes," which is what the NCAA calls them. Meaning a student first, an athlete second. We were kidding ourselves, trying to make it more palatable to the academicians. We don't have to say that, and we shouldn't. At the level we play the boy is really an athlete first and a student second.

—**Paul W. ("Bear") Bryant**
(1913–1983), football coach,
University of Alabama

1977, *Curriculum,* pp. 288–89.

The lore of college and university athletics would have us locate in athletic teams and coaching staffs the ultimate locus of value training. Yet four of the last five presidents of the United States were college football players, and any survey of the wreckage of these years would have to ask whether peace, justice, and liberty would not have been better served if our presidents had instead been ballet dancers.

—**Frederick Rudolph** (1920–),
professor of history, Williams College

1978, Dan Hruby, "Football degree may be next," *San Jose Mercury-News,* 25 June, quoted in John R. Thelin, *Higher Education and Its Useful Past,* 1982, p. 119.

[A] person who's a woodworker and who is in school to learn to carve isn't interested in the guy working on computers in the engineering department. And the saxophone player who wants to become a music teacher couldn't care less about the law classes. If a kid wants to play football, with the idea of turning professional, then he ought to be allowed to earn a degree in football.

—**John Majors** (1935–),
U.S. football coach

1978, "A few words in praise of the red-swine cult," *Los Angeles Times,* 1 January, quoted in John R. Thelin, *Higher Education and Its Useful Past,* 1982, p. 123.

As for the sheer, vulgar spectacle of the thing, cheerleaders, pom-pom girls, marching band, imprisoned mascot and all, I find it exhilarating. We might well be living in medieval London.

—**Gene Lyons** (?–?), U.S. sportswriter

1993, *International Herald Tribune,* 6 October, quoted in Keith Allan Noble, *The International Education Quotations Encyclopaedia,* 1995.

Big-time American football, for which the brittle human body is unsuited, flourishes on campuses, where it is inappropriate.

—**George F. Will** (1941–),
U.S. editor and political columnist

1999, "The business of college sports and the high cost of winning," *Milken Institute Review* (third quarter), p. 28.

No university generates a large enough surplus to justify the capital expenditures necessary to field a football team.

—**Roger G. Noll** (1940–), professor of public policy, Stanford University

2001, *Chronicle of Higher Education,* 6 July, p. A35.

In football, we are not educating half of the young men we're responsible for. The things we're supposed to do, we're not doing.

—**Theodore M. Hesburgh, C.S.C.**
(1917–), President,
University of Notre Dame

2001, *A Call to Action,* p. 16.

There are students on our football team this year who will graduate when both faculty and students know they cannot read or write.

—**Knight Foundation Commission on Intercollegiate Athletics**

Athletics: General

1858, *The Idea of a University,* Discourse V.

There is . . . a great variety of intellectual exercises, which are not technically called "liberal;" on the other hand . . . there are exercises of the body which do receive that appellation. Such, for instance, was the palaestra, in ancient times; such the Olympic games, in which strength and dexterity of body as well as of mind gained the prize. . . . Many games, or games of skill, or military prowess, though bodily, are, it seems, accounted liberal. . . .

—**John Henry (Cardinal) Newman**
(1801–1890), Rector,
Catholic University of Ireland

1860, *The Report of the President of Harvard College, 1859–1860,* quoted in Edgar W. Knight, *What College Presidents Say,* 1940, p. 163.

The wise men of antiquity . . . drew the line firmly between gymnastic exercise, for the cultivation of vigor and beauty, as curative processes and gentlemenlike accomplishments, as part of the education of the boy and the daily recreation of the man, on the one hand, and the training of the athletes on the other. The former they regarded as essential to a sound mind in a sound body; the latter as mischievous and immoral.

—**Cornelius C. Felton** (1807–1862),
President, Harvard College

1888, *Report for 1887–1888,* quoted in William F. Russell (ed.), *The Rise of a University, Vol. I,* 1937, p. 205.

As these [athletic] contests approach, there is more or less distractions of the minds of the students from their proper pursuits, and, for the time being, a more or less serious neglect of study. This is an evil inevitable while the present system is maintained, and is of sufficient magnitude to justify . . . an absolute prohibition of intercollegiate games altogether.

—**Frederick A. P. Barnard**
(1809–1889), President,
Columbia University

1892–93, Annual Report, cited in Howard J. Savage, *American College Athletics,* 1929, p. 294.

Athletic sports have infused into boys and young men a greater respect for bodily excellence and a desire to attain it; they have supplied a new and effective motive for resisting all sins which weaken or corrupt the body; they have quickened admiration for such manly qualities as courage, fortitude, and presence of mind in emergencies and under difficulties; they have cultivated in a few the habit of command, and in many the habit of quick obedience and intelligent subordination; and finally they have set before young men prizes and distinctions which are uncontaminated by any commercial value, and which no one can win who does not possess much patience, perseverance, and self-control in addition to rare bodily endowments.

—**Charles William Eliot** (1834–1926),
President, Harvard University

1903, "University tendencies," *Popular Science Monthly,* June, p. 147.

[T]he value of athletic games is lost when outside gladiators are hired to play them. . . . If an institution makes one rule for the ordinary student and another for the athlete it is party to a fraud.

—**David Starr Jordan** (1851–1931),
President, Stanford University

1912, *Proceedings of the National Collegiate Athletic Association,* quoted in Paul R. Lawrence, *Unsportsmanlike Conduct,* 1987, p. 22.

An amateur in athletics is one who enters and takes part in athletic contests purely in obedience to the play impulse or for the satisfaction of purely play motives and for the exercise, training, and social pleasures derived. The natural or primary attitude of mind and motives in play determines amateurism. A professional in athletics is one

who enters or takes part in athletic contests for any other motive than the satisfaction of purely play impulses or for the exercise, training, and social pleasures derived, or one who desires and secures from his skill or who accepts of spectators, partisan, or other interest, any material or economic advantage or reward.

—**NCAA Committee on Amateurism**

1923, *The Goose-Step,* Chapter 54.

[W]hat college athletics really means is that two per cent of the students, or in small colleges probably ten per cent, get an excessive amount of exercise, sometimes to the permanent injury of their vital organs; while the great bulk of students are surrendered to the mob-excitements of a series of gladiatorial combats and sporting events, which provide exercise only for the vocal cords and the gambling instincts. College athletics, under the spur of commercialism, has become a monstrous cancer, which is rapidly eating out the moral and intellectual life of our educational institutions. . . .

—**Upton Sinclair** (1878–1968),
U.S. author

1929, "Preface," in Howard J. Savage, *American College Athletics,* p. xvi.

In no other nation of the world will a college boy find his photograph in the metropolitan paper because he plays on a college team. . . . Into this game of publicity the university of the present day enters eagerly. It desires for itself the publicity that the newspapers can supply. It wants students, it wants popularity, but above all it wants money and always more money. The athlete is the most available publicity material the college has. A great scientific discovery will make good press material for a few days, but nothing to compare to that of the performance of a first-class athlete. Thousands are interested in athletics all the time, while the scientist is at best only a passing show.

p. xxi.

[I]t requires no tabulation of statistics to prove that the young athlete who gives himself for months, body and soul, to training under a professional coach for a grueling contest, staged to focus the attention of thousands of people, and upon which many thousands of dollars will be staked, will find no time or energy for any serious intellectual effort. The compromises that have to be made to keep such students in the college and to pass them through to a degree give an air of insincerity to the whole university-college regime.

> —**Henry S. Pritchett** (1857–1939),
> President, Carnegie Foundation for the
> Advancement of Teaching

1929, *American College Athletics,* p. 82.

[T]he fundamental purpose of intercollegiate contests ought to be the diversion or development of undergraduates, alumni, other members of the college family, and their guests. As matters now stand, their fundamental purpose is financial and commercial.

p. 128.

The moral qualities that participation in college athletics is widely supposed to engender—courage, obedience, unselfishness, persistence, and the rest—have formed the theme of countless eulogies of athletics and athletes. No attempt to measure them has yielded unmistakable results.

p. 240.

The recruiting of American college athletes, be it active or passive, professional or non-professional has reached the proportions of nationwide commerce. . . . [I]ts effect upon the character of the school boy

has been profoundly deleterious. Its influence upon the nature and quality of American higher education has been no less noxious.

p. 297.

The fact is that the subsidized athlete of to-day connives at disreputable and shameful practices for the sake of material returns and for honors falsely achieved. Arguments in support of such practices are specious, calculated to mislead, and fundamentally insincere. Viewed in the light of common honesty, this fabric of organized deceit constitutes the darkest single blot upon American college sport.

p. 306.

The fundamental causes of the defects of American college athletics are two: commercialism, and a negligent attitude toward the educational opportunity for which the college exists.

pp. 307–8.

[A]t no point in the educational process has commercialism in college athletics wrought more mischief than in its effect upon the American undergraduate. And the distressing fact is that the college, the Fostering Mother, has permitted and even encouraged it to do these things in the name of education.

> —**Howard J. Savage** (1886–1973),
> staff member, Carnegie Foundation
> for the Advancement of Teaching

1930, *Universities: American English German,* p. 65.

There is not a college or university in America which has the courage to place athletics where every one perfectly well knows they belong.

> —**Abraham Flexner** (1866–1959),
> U.S. educator

1934, "The search for values through character development," *Bulletin of the Association of American Colleges,* March, p. 10.

Where better than in games can they learn fair play, team-work, self-control, and the necessity of playing hard if they are to win? And are not these as important as anything else learned in the classroom?

—**Edmund D. Soper** (1876–1961), President, Ohio Wesleyan University

1938, quoted in *New York Times* upon his death, 8 July, p. 17.

[W]e teach subjects as thoroughly as the athletic rules will allow us.

—**Robert. E. Blackwell** (1854–1938), President, Randolph-Macon College

1954, *Sports Illustrated,* 27 September, p. 16.

The fundamental difference between inter-collegiate and professional athletics is that in college the players are supposed to be students first and foremost. This does not mean that they should all be Phi Beta Kappas or physics majors, but neither should they be subnormal students majoring in Ping-Pong.

—**Theodore M. Hesburgh, C.S.C.** (1917–), President, University of Notre Dame

no date, attributed in Keith Allen Noble, *The International Education Quotations Encyclopaedia,* p. 127.

With one or two exceptions, colleges expect their players of games to be reasonably literate.

—**Maurice Bowra** (1898–1971), English classical scholar; Warden of Wadham College

1959, *The American College President,* p. 101.

In a great many institutions, it [athletics] ceases to be student recreation, which is normally and naturally a part of student life, and becomes public entertainment, an activity which has little to do with education. This transformation takes place whenever specialized coaches are selected, and when players are chosen in order to win games rather than to play them. It is this shift of emphasis which draws a line between the student and the athlete. The interest of the college in the student lies in what it can do for him; its interest in the athlete lies in what he can do for it.

—**Harold W. Stoke** (1903–1982), President, University of New Hampshire; President, Louisiana State University; President, Queens College

no date, attributed in Keith Allan Noble, *The International Education Quotations Encyclopaedia,* 1995.

A college which is interested in producing professional athletes is not an educational institution.

—**Robert Maynard Hutchins** (1899–1977), President, University of Chicago

1974, "The full court press for women in athletics," in Barbara J. Hoepner (ed.), *Women's Athletics: Coping with Controversy,* p. 92.

The athletic model designed and perpetuated by men pervades schools and society, and it is, in part, a repellent one. Women cannot, in good conscience, enter a struggle for the prize of brutality, authority, or the exploitation of young athletes. But women have never believed that sport necessitated such things, nor would they foster them in their programs. Men have excluded women from sport because they recognized that it would be changed by them.

—**Jan Felshin** (1931–),
professor of physical education,
East Stroudsburg University

1974, *Like It Is,* p. 238.

The last thing in the world a college or university should be concerned with is being number one in football or basketball if the price one pays for that is the corruption of character and the undermining of true student morale on campus. And believe me, that is the price.

—**Howard Cosell** (1918–1995),
U.S. sports broadcaster

1988, *A Free and Ordered Space,* p. 166.

I believe athletics is part of an education of a young person, as the Greeks and the English schoolmaster believed; and I believe athletics is part of an education because athletics teaches lessons valuable to the individual by stretching the human spirit in ways that nothing else can.

—**A. Bartlett Giamatti** (1938–1989),
president, Yale University

1999, "The business of college sports and the high cost of winning," *Milken Institute Review* (third quarter), p. 24.

[I]ntercollegiate sports chronically generate serious controversy that leave college administrators cringing behind their desks. . . . To the rest of the world, American intercollegiate athletics seem like pagan rituals.

p. 32.

For an athlete who has no interest in the educational aspects of being a college athlete, the part of a scholarship that covers academics has no value. If attending college were regarded as more or less a full-time job, the student-athlete could do

better working an equivalent number of hours at a fast-food restaurant. The problem from the athlete's perspective is that McDonalds does not field a football team.

—**Roger G. Noll** (1940–), professor of
public policy, Stanford University

2001, *Intercollegiate Athletics and the American University,* p. 146.

The mad race for fame and profits through intercollegiate athletics is clearly a fool's quest.

—**James J. Duderstadt** (1942–),
President, University of Michigan

Commencement

1952, "Commencement at the large university," *Journal of Higher Education,* February, p. 93.

[C]ommencement chairmen now concentrate on staging a ceremony with sweep and pageantry. Colorful processions, great masses of black-gowned candidates, acres of spectators, and a stately, traditional ritual create an impressive and often exciting spectacle. Such a ceremony . . . may well be termed "the greatest academic show on earth."

—**Garff B. Wilson** (1909–1998),
professor of rhetoric and drama,
University of California, Berkeley

1960, *Time,* 27 June, p. 42.

The commencement speaker represents the continuation of a barbaric custom that has no basis in logic. If the spate of oratory that inundates our educational institutions during the month of June could be transformed into rain for southern California, we should all be happily awash or waterlogged.

—**Samuel B. Gould** (1916–1997),
President, Antioch College; Chancellor,
University of California, Santa Barbara;
Chancellor, State University of New York

1984, Commencement Address, Bard College, 26 May, quoted in James B. Simpson, *Simpson's Contemporary Quotations,* 1988.

My job is to bore you and let the hardness of your seat and the warmth of your robe prepare you for what is to come.

> —**William H. McNeill** (1917–),
> professor of history,
> University of Chicago

no date, Commencement Address, Dixie College, attributed in Alan Ross (ed.), *Speaking of Graduating . . . ,* 2001, p. 14.

Graduation is where a commencement speaker tells rows and rows of graduates, all dressed exactly the same, that individuality is what makes the world tick.

> —**Orrin Hatch** (1934–), U.S. Senator

no date, attributed in Alan Ross (ed.), *Speaking of Graduating . . . ,* 2001, p. 18.

Commencement speeches were invented largely in the belief that outgoing college students should never be released into the world until they have been properly sedated.

> —**Garry Trudeau** (1948–),
> U.S. cartoonist

1995, Commencement Address, University of Massachusetts, Amherst, quoted in <www.famous-quotations. com>.

I will try to follow the advice that a university president once gave a prospective commencement speaker. "Think of yourself as the body at an Irish wake" he said. "They need you in order to have the party, but no one expects you to say very much."

> —**Anthony Lake** (1939–), professor of international relations, Amherst College;
> National Security Advisor

Minority Students

1834, letter, 15 December, quoted in Richard Hofstadter and Wilson Smith (eds.), *American Higher Education: A Documentary History, Volume I,* 1961, p. 391.

I desire you, at the first meeting of the Trustees, to secure the passage of the following resolution, to-wit: 'Resolved, That students shall be received into this Institution irrespective of color,' This should be passed because it is a right principle, and God will bless us in doing right. . . . Indeed, if our Board would violate right so as to reject youth of talent and piety because they were *black,* I would have *no heart* to labor for the upbuilding of our Seminary, believing that the curse of God would come upon us. . . .

> —**Mr. [?] Shipherd** (?–?),
> principal financial agent,
> Oberlin Collegiate Institute

1848, response to protests against admission of a black student to Harvard, quoted in David Loftus, *The Unofficial Book of Harvard Trivia,* 1985, p. 43.

If this [black] boy passes the examinations he will be admitted; and if the white students choose to withdraw, all the income of the college will be devoted to his education.

> —**Edward Everett** (1794–1865),
> President, Harvard University

1903, "The talented tenth," in *The Negro Problem: A Series of Articles by Representative American Negroes of Today.*

The Negro race, like all races, is going to be saved by its exceptional men. The problem of education, then, among Negroes must first of all deal with the Talented Tenth; it is the problem of developing the Best of this race that they may guide the

Mass away from the contamination and death of the Worst, in their own and other races. . . . The Talented Tenth of the Negro race must be made leaders of thought and missionaries of culture among their people. No others can do this work and Negro colleges must train men for it. The Negro race, like all other races, is going to be saved by its exceptional men.

—**W. E. B. Du Bois** (1868–1963), civil rights leader; professor of sociology, Atlanta University

1928, "How it feels to be colored me," in *The World Tomorrow,* May, p. 216, quoted in Barbara Miller Solomon, *In the Company of Educated Women,* 1985, p. 163.

Beside the waters of the Hudson, I feel my race.

—**Zora Neale Hurston** (1891–1960), U.S. writer [student at Barnard College]

1959, "Theme for English B," *Selected Poems of Langston Hughes,* quoted in *Columbia World of Quotations,* 1996.

[H]ere
to this college on the hill above Harlem
I am the only colored student in my
  class.

—**Langston Hughes** (1902–1967), U.S. poet

1969, "The road to the top is through higher education—not black studies," *New York Times,* 11 May, sec. 6, p. 52.

Blacks in America are inevitably and perpetually a minority. This means that in all administrative and leadership positions we are going to be outnumbered by white folks, and we will have to compete with them not on our terms but on theirs. The only way to win this game is to know them so thoroughly that we can outpace them. For us to turn our back on this opportunity,

by insisting on mingling only with other black students in college, is folly of the highest order.

—**W. Arthur Lewis** (1915–1991), professor of economics, Princeton University

c. 1980, talk to graduates, quoted in Stephen James Nelson, *Leaders in the Crucible,* 2000, p. 135.

[Y]our children must know that there were legions of quiet heroes, many of whom through their strength and courage, brought you to this college graduation. . . . Your children must not forget that the diploma which buys their ease was bought with hundreds of years of gnarled fingers from gripping shovels and picks in ditches, miles too long and in ground too rocky and hard.

—**Elias Blake, Jr.** (1929–), President, Clark Atlanta University

1989, in Brian Lanker, *I Dream a World,* quoted in Rosalie Maggio, *The Beacon Book of Quotations by Women,* 1992, p. 97.

We have what I would call educational genocide. . . . [W]hen I see more black students in the laboratories than I see on the football field, I'll be happy.

—**Jewell Plummer Cobb** (1924–), biologist; President, California State University at Fullerton

Student Life

c. thirteenth century, "Morale scholarium of John of Garland," quoted in A. C. Spectorsky, *College Years,* 1958, pp. 31–32.

Be not a fornicator, O student, a robber, a murderer, a deceitful merchant, a champion at dice. . . . Avoid drunkards, those who indulge in secret sin, those who like to beat and strike, those who love lewdness, evil games, and quarrels. . . . Avoid insincere speeches. Unless you wish to be considered a fool learn to keep your mouth shut in season.

> —**John of Garland** (?–?), professor,
> University of Paris

1800, Thomas N. Hoover, *The History of Ohio University,* 1954, pp. 15–16, quoted in Frederick Rudolph, *The American College and University,* 1962, p. 99.

Chambers in colleges are too often made the nurseries of every vice and cages of unclean birds.

> —**Manasseh Cutler** (1742–1823),
> U.S. Congressman;
> founder of Ohio University

1805, letter, 23 November, quoted in Ned Sherrin, *The Oxford Dictionary of Humorous Quotations,* 1995, p. 102.

This place [Cambridge University] is the Devil, or at least his principal residence, they call it the University, but any other appellation would have suited it much better, for study is the last pursuit of the society; the Master eats, drinks, and sleeps, the Fellows drink, dispute, and pun, the employments of the undergraduates you will probably conjecture without any description.

> —**Lord Byron** (1788–1824), British poet

1848, quoted in Frederick Rudolph, *The American College and University,* 1962, p. 90.

This is certain: that parents need never look to a college for any miraculous moral regeneration or transformation of character.

> —**Philip Lindsley** (1786–1855),
> President, University of Nashville

1869, Inaugural Address, 19 October, in *A Turning Point in Higher Education,* 1969, p. 44.

[T]here is no place so safe as a good college during the critical passage from boyhood to manhood. The security of the college commonwealth is largely due to its exuberant activity. Its public opinion, though easily led astray, is still high in the main. Its scholarly tastes and habits, its eager friendships and quick hatreds, its keen debates, its frank discussions of character and of deep political and religious questions, all are safeguards against sloth, vulgarity, and depravity. Its society and, not less, its solitudes are full of teaching.

> —**Charles William Eliot** (1834–1926),
> President, Harvard University

1870, "Analysis of some statistics of collegiate education," 3 January, p. 28.

It seems to be thought that college authorities have it in their power to protect young men against the moral dangers to which youth are exposed, very much as a father of a family can watch over his own children beneath his own roof. Surely no impression can be more mistaken than this. There is no situation in the world in which an individual is more completely removed from all effectual straint [sic], whether the restraint of direct authority or that of public opinion, than within the walls of an American college.

> —**Frederick A. P. Barnard**
> (1809–1889), President,
> Columbia University

no date, quoted in Waitman Barbe, *Going to College,* 1899, p. 51.

There are no other places where between eighteen and twenty two she [a young woman] is so likely to have a genuine good time. Merely for good times, for romance, for society, college life offers unequaled opportunities.

—**Alice Freeman Parker** (1855–1902),
President, Wellesley College

no date, quoted in Waitman Barbe,
Going to College, 1899, p. 48.

The good of a college is to be had from the fellows who are there and your associations with them. I do not belive [sic] that any life outside of a college has been found that will in general do so much for a man in helping for this business of living.

—**Edward Everett Hale** (1822–1909),
U.S. minister; author

1898, *Educational Reform,* p. 148.

Let no one imagine that a young man is in peculiar moral danger at an active and interesting university. Far from it. Such a university is the safest place in the world for young men who have anything in them—far safer than counting-room, shop, factory, farm, barrack, forecastle, or ranch. The student lives in a bracing atmosphere; books engage him; good companionships invite him; good occupations defend him; helpful friends surround him; pure ideals are held up before him; ambition spurs him; honor beckons him.

—**Charles William Eliot** (1834–1926),
President, Harvard University

1909, "What is a college for?,"
Scribner's Magazine, October, p. 576.

The sideshows are so numerous, so diverting—so important, if you will—that they have swallowed up the circus, and those who perform in the main tent must often whistle for their audiences, discouraged and humiliated.

—**Woodrow Wilson** (1856–1924),
President, Princeton University;
President of the United States

1920, *The Liberal College,* pp. 32–33.

The college is a good place for making friends; it gives excellent experience in getting on with men; it has exceptional advantages as an athletic club; it is a relatively safe place for a boy when he first leaves home; on the whole, it may improve a student's manners; it gives acquaintance with lofty ideas of character, preaches the doctrine of social service, exalts the virtues and duties of citizenship. All these conceptions seem to the teacher to hide or to obscure the fact that the college is fundamentally a place of the mind, a time for thinking, an opportunity for knowing.

—**Alexander Meiklejohn** (1872–1964),
president, Amherst College

1927, "What college did to me," in *The Early Worm.*

My college education was no haphazard affair. My courses were all selected with a very definitive aim in view, with a serious purpose in mind—no classes before eleven in the morning or after two-thirty in the afternoon, and nothing on Saturdays at all. That was my slogan. On that rock was my education built.

—**Robert Benchley** (1899–1945),
U.S. author and humorist

1944, *Teacher in America,* p. 237.

To run newspapers and fraternity houses, hold debates and give plays, manage lecture series on social problems, form leagues and represent the country's political parties on the campus—to play at being grown-up, in short—is a normal wish. It is likewise excellent training in a variety of standard accomplishments as well as in dealing with one's fellows. For to learn to read the man sitting next to you in class is as important as learning to read the book before your eyes.

—**Jacques Barzun** (1907–),
Dean of Faculties and Provost,
Columbia University

1962, "Motivational factors in college entrance," in Nevitt Sanford, *The American College,* p. 209.

[C]ollege and travel are alternatives to a more open interest in sexuality.

—**Elizabeth Douvan** (1926–2002),
research associate, University of
Michigan; **Carol Kaye** (?–?), instructor
in psychiatry, Boston University

1968, "A plea for student freedom,"
Time, 12 July, p. 40.

Colleges are not churches, clinics, or even parents. Whether or not a student burns a draft card, participates in a civil-rights march, engages in premarital or extramarital sexual activity, becomes pregnant, attends church, sleeps all day or drinks all night, is not really the concern of an educational institution.

—**Lewis B. Mayhew** (1916–), professor
of education, Stanford University

1978, in the film *Animal House.*

Toga! Toga! Toga!

—**John (Bluto) Blutarsky,** fictional
character, Delta Tau Chi fraternity,
Faber College

1978, in the film *Animal House.*

[A]s of this moment, they're [Delta Tau Chi fraternity] on double secret probation.

—**Vernon Wormer,** fictional character,
Dean, Faber College

1980, *Being Lucky,* pp. 128–29.

In the best of all possible worlds student regulations would consist only of those that David Starr Jordan issued when he was president of Indiana University. He is alleged to have done away with all student rules except two: students were not permitted to shoot the faculty or to burn any buildings.

p. 144.

It is the ambition of each student editor to reform the university, so thank God that their terms are short and that when the next one comes he will have a different program.

—**Herman B Wells** (1902–2000),
President, Indiana University

1989, *The Lost Continent,* p. 72.

In my day, the principal concerns of university students were sex, smoking dope, rioting and learning. Learning was something you did only when the first three weren't available, but at least you did it.

—**Bill Bryson** (1951–), U.S. writer

no date, attributed in
<www.houseofquotes.com>.

I think sleeping was my problem in school. If school had started at 4:00 in the afternoon, I'd be a college graduate today.

—**George Foreman** (1949–),
U.S. boxer and entrepreneur

Students

1865, *Sketches from Cambridge, By a Don,* pp. 8–9.

What a blessed place this would be if there were no undergraduates! ... [N]one of your noisy boys to make night hideous and to waste good brains in cramming bad ones.

—**Leslie Stephen** (1832–1904),
English author and critic

1874, *German Universities: A Narrative of Personal Experience,* p. 303.

The idler of Germany, I am confident, has forgotten twice as much as the idler of America, the industrious student knows twice as much as the industrious undergraduate, and the future scholar of Germany is a man of whom we in America have no conception. He is a man who could not exist under our system, he would be choked by recitations and grades. What he studies, he studies with the devotion of a poet and the trained skill of a scientist.

> —**James Morgan Hart** (1839–1916), professor of rhetoric and English philology, Cornell University

1905, speech, New York, quoted in Bergen Evans, *Dictionary of Quotations,* 1968, p. 123.

The most conservative persons I ever met are college undergraduates.

> —**Woodrow Wilson** (1856–1924), President, Princeton University; President of the United States

1906, *A History of Higher Education in America,* quoted in W. H. Cowley, *Presidents, Professors, and Trustees,* 1980, p. 99.

The College Student is not a class, he is a race, and he is a race which is the same, apparently, in all countries as in all climes.

> —**Charles F. Thwing** (1853–1937), President, Adelbert College; President, Western Reserve University

1923, *The Rise of the Universities,* p. 59.

"A University," it has more than once been remarked by professors, "would be a comfortable place if it were not for the students."

> —**Charles Homer Haskins** (1870–1937), professor of history, Harvard University

1927, *Life and the Student,* p. 171.

It was a formidable criticism when a student said, "They do not know I am here." In fact no teacher or official does, in most cases, become aware of the student as a human whole; he is known only by detached and artificial functions.

p. 173.

On certain mornings the lecturer, watching the faces flow past, may think, "This is God; the real thing, no myth; in these individuals and this humanity is the passing current of that continuing and inscrutable life."

> —**Charles Horton Cooley** (1864–1929), professor of sociology, University of Michigan

1930, "Self-education in college," *Journal of Higher Education,* January, p. 66.

[A]ll true education in college is self-education; and, therefore, the student must be induced to desire to make an effort, and a strenuous effort.

> —**Abbot Lawrence Lowell** (1856–1943), President, Harvard University

1930, *Universities: American English German,* p. 69.

It is no exaggeration to say that most college students look upon college as a means of getting ahead in life; for them the college is largely a social and athletic affair. Intellectual concentration would take too much time; it would restrict the student's social contacts. Besides, it doesn't really matter.

> —**Abraham Flexner** (1866–1959), U.S. educator

1944, *Teacher in America,* p. 238.

[A] young man who is not a radical about something is a very poor risk for education.

—**Jacques Barzun** (1907–),
Dean of Faculties and Provost,
Columbia University

1956, News Summaries, 3 September, quoted in James B. Simpson, *Simpson's Contemporary Quotations,* 1988.

A student is not a professional athlete. . . . He is not a little politician or junior senator looking for angles . . . an amateur promoter, a glad-hander, embryo Rotarian, café-society leader, quiz kid or man about town. A student is a person who is learning to fulfill his powers and to find ways of using them in the service of mankind.

—**Harold Taylor** (1914–1993),
President, Sarah Lawrence College

1959, *The American College President,* p. 144.

Colleges and universities do not "live for students"; they can do little for their students unless those students are enlisted in the same cause which the institutions serve, and unless the students submit themselves to the same discipline. Colleges and universities exist not to serve students but to wage war against ignorance; what army was ever organized merely to serve its recruits?

—**Harold W. Stoke** (1903–1982),
President, University of New Hampshire;
President, Louisiana State University;
President, Queens College

1972, *Where Has All the Ivy Gone?,* p. 261.

What I often forget about students, especially undergraduates, is that surface appearances are misleading. Most of them are at base as conventional as Presbyterian deacons.

—**Muriel Beadle** (1915–1994),
U.S. author and community organizer

1973, *LA Examiner,* 8 April, quoted in James B. Simpson, *Simpson's Contemporary Quotations,* 1988.

How anybody dresses is indicative of his self-concept. If students are dirty and ragged, it indicates they are not interested in tidying up their intellects either.

—**S. I. Hayakawa** (1906–1992),
U.S. Senator; President,
San Francisco State College

1976, "Who needs college?," *Newsweek,* 26 April, pp. 64–65.

Teenagers go to college to be with their boyfriends and girlfriends; they go because they can't think of anything else to do; they go because their parents want them to and sometimes because their parents don't want them to; they go to find themselves, or to find a husband, or to get away from home, and sometimes even to find out about the world in which they live.

—**Harold Howe II** (1918–),
U.S. Commissioner of Education

1990, *The University: An Owner's Manual,* p. 43.

As dean, it is hard to see students or faculty at their best since nearly everyone wants something. Students are generally pleasant in classrooms or during extracurricular activities, or at the dinner table. Unfortunately, as politicians they grow up much too fast: argumentative, verbose, self-righteous, self-important, condescending, and deeply suspicious of institutions and elders.

—**Henry Rosovsky** (1927–), Dean of
the Faculty of Arts and Sciences,
Harvard University

Chapter 13

The President

Presidential Criticism

1780, petition to President Samuel Langford, quoted in Frederick Rudolph, *The American College and University: A History,* 1962, p. 39.

As a man of genius and knowledge we respect you; as a man of piety and virtue we venerate you, as President we despise you.

—**Harvard students**

1897–1898, *Report of the United States Commissioner of Education,* cited in Howard J. Savage, *American College Athletics,* 1929, p. 23.

The powerlessness of our educational leaders to originate, and their failure to adopt, effectual measures for evolving order out of the athletic and gymnastic chaos over which they nominally preside, constitutes one of the marvels of our time.

—**Edward Mussey Hartwell** (1850–1922), statistician

1913, *University Control,* p. 31.

In the academic jungle, the president is my black beast.

—**J. McKeen Cattell** (1860–1944), professor of psychology, Columbia University

1913, "The college presidency," *Science,* 2 May, p. 654.

[I]f my observations are correct, two college presidents out of every three are regarded as failures.... A majority of college and university presidents in the United States have failed, on the whole, to perform, to the satisfaction of those most intimately concerned, the various duties now assigned to that office. If I were to class as failures those who have proved unequal to one or more obligations usually attached to the office, there would remain in the successful group scarcely a score.

—**William T. Foster** (1879–1950), President, Reed College

1916, address at the inauguration of H. M. Brooks, President, Alma College, quoted in Edgar W. Knight, *What College Presidents Say,* 1940, p. 35.

If there is a danger of America being absorbed in money getting for its own sake, there is also a danger that college presidents may catch the same disease.

—**Henry N. MacCracken** (1880–1970), President, Lafayette College

1948, "Last words of a college president," *American Mercury,* August, p. 163.

> I walked and sat erect for thirty years,
> A proud merchant of correct ideas,
> Cold gladness and unsullied decorum,
> I fashioned cautious men without souls
> And brittle women with measured
>   passion.
> Behold a traitor
> To his Creator.

> —**Charles Angoff** (1902–1979),
> U.S. writer

1959, *The American College President,* p. 3.

Two opposing views of college presidents prevail. Some see them as fervent, dedicated men. . . . Others see these same presidents as furious promoters, hucksters of the educational world, timid or pompous as the occasion requires, and with no real appreciation for the work of scholars and teachers. To paraphrase the remarks of Thomas Paine about George Washington (and perhaps with no greater justification), they profess to be puzzled as to whether the college president has abandoned good principles, or never had any.

> —**Harold W. Stoke** (1903–1982),
> President, University of New Hampshire;
> President, Louisiana State University;
> President, Queens College

1965, *How College Presidents Are Chosen,* p. 1.

Anyone who is even casually familiar with the affairs of American higher education is aware that in the presidents' chairs of many institutions sit persons of great distinction. Nor is it a secret that, on some campuses, the presidencies are occupied by singularly undistinguished men.

> —**Frederick deW. Bolman**
> (1912–1985), President,
> Franklin and Marshall College

no date, attributed in August Kerber, *Quotable Quotes on Education,* 1968, p. 225.

Too often our institutions of higher learning and their chief executive officers can be characterized as the "bland leading the bland."

> —**Ewald B. Nyquist** (1914–1987),
> commissioner of education,
> State of New York

1977, *The Academic President: Educator or Caretaker?,* p. 121.

[P]residents are too inclined to withhold information when keeping a matter confidential is of no great importance and when disclosure would increase understanding and inspire confidence.

> —**Harold W. Dodds** (1889–1980),
> President, Princeton University

1996, *The University in Ruins,* p. 55.

In the University of Excellence . . . the president is a bureaucratic administrator who moves effortlessly from the lecture hall, to the sports stadium, to the executive lounge. From judge, to synthesizer, to executive and fund-raiser, without publicly expressing any opinions or passing any judgments whatsoever.

> —**Bill Readings** (1960–1994), associate
> professor of comparative literature,
> University of Montreal

Presidential Exit

1855, quoted in Walter C. Bronson, *The History of Brown University,* 1914, p. 302.

No one can conceive the unspeakable relief and freedom which I feel at this moment to hear that bell ring, and to know, for the first time in nearly twenty-nine years, that it calls me to no duty.

> —**Francis Wayland** (1796–1865),
> President, Brown University

1955, "The administrator: Leader or officeholder?," *Freedom, Education, and the Fund,* 1956, p. 171.

The pressure upon a university administrator to become an officeholder is enormous. But there is an easy way of avoiding these troubles, and that is not to take the job. No man of mature years who accepts an administrative position in a university can claim that he did not know what his troubles would be. If there is such a man, he still has a way out; he can resign.

—**Robert Maynard Hutchins** (1899–1977), President, University of Chicago

1959, *The American College President,* p. 33.

After the college president leaves his position, whether he retires, resigns, or is fired, life can be something of an anticlimax. No position less exacting can fully engage him. He is ill at ease as a teacher again, yet he is so conditioned to campus life that he feels himself a stranger elsewhere. He is a general who, after the excitement of campaigns, finds peace dull, an explorer who has visited lands his associates have only read about.

—**Harold W. Stoke** (1903–1982), President, University of New Hampshire; President, Louisiana State University; President, Queens College

1967, Clark Kerr, *The Blue and the Gold,* volume 2, 2003, p. 309.

[I] had left the presidency of the university as I had entered it: "fired with enthusiasm"; my own on the way in, that of certain others on my way out.

—**Clark Kerr** (1911–2003), Chancellor, University of California, Berkeley; President, University of California

1980, *Being Lucky,* p. 146.

If you don't like to be president, resign; many others would like a crack at it.

p. 149.

Quit while you are ahead. Try to incite some irate taxpayer to take a gun in hand and make you a martyr; remember history's treatment of Lincoln. But, if you aren't shot, you can always resign when you're ahead.

—**Herman B Wells** (1902–2000), President, Indiana University

1986, *The Many Lives of Academic Presidents,* p. 44.

The presidency is like a berry patch surrounded by netting—some of the birds on the inside are trying desperately to get out and many birds on the outside are trying desperately to get in.

—**Clark Kerr** (1911–2003), Chancellor, University of California, Berkeley; President, University of California; **Marian L. Gade** (1934–), research associate, University of California, Berkeley

Presidential Influence

no date, L. A. Tollemache, *Benjamin Jowett,* 1895, quoted by W. H. Cowley, *Presidents, Professors, and Trustees,* 1980, p. 59.

Never retract, never explain. Get it done and let them howl.

—**Benjamin Jowett** (1817–1893), Master, Balliol College; Vice-chancellor, Oxford University

1888, The Inauguration of President Patton, Princeton University, 20 June, quoted in Edgar W. Knight, *What College Presidents Say,* 1940, p. 2.

The presidents of our American colleges have from the beginning been men of noble mark, the very elect in their callings, leaders in the Church, not seldom leaders in both Church and State. No other class of men have done more than they to build up our American civilization. . . .

—**James O. Murray** (1827–1899),
Dean, Princeton University

p. 103.

A close study of the situation will show that when all has been said, the limitations of the college president, even when he has the greatest freedom of action, are very great. In all business matters he is the servant of the trustees or corporation; and his views will prevail in that body only in so far as they approve themselves to their good judgment. In educational policy he must be in accord with his colleagues. If he cannot persuade them to adopt his views, he must go with them. It is absurd to suppose that any president, however strong or willful he may be, can force a faculty, made up of leaders of thought, to do his will.

p. 103.

If there is one institution in which the president has too much power, there are ten in which he has too little.

—**William Rainey Harper** (1856–1906),
President, University of Chicago

1913, *University Control,* p. 33.

The prestige of the president is due to the growth of the university, not conversely. He is like the icon carried with the Russian army and credited with its victories.

—**J. McKeen Cattell** (1860–1944),
professor of psychology,
Columbia University

1922, "College education: An inquest, II," *The Freeman,* New York, 1 March, p. 584.

[T]he university president presides over a tropical jungle. . . . The jungle is full of queer animals, old, young, and middle-aged. Some run about, seeking whom they may devour. Others sit quietly in corners, shrinking from observation, searching curiously for unknown things. There are all kinds of customs, laws, compacts, understandings, agreements, promises, and obligations, created by years of conscious, unconscious and subconscious operations. It is a vast, magnificent, and historic tangle. About all that the mighty gentleman who presides over it can do, is to stand on a height above it and squirt perfume on the ensemble.

—**Somnia Vana** (pseudonym)

1925, presentation at the 59th annual dinner, Harvard Club of New York, 23 July, quoted in Henry A. Yoemans, *Abbott Lawrence Lowell,* 1948, p. 300.

What then are the powers of the President? They are very easily defined. He has a right to be informed of what is going on; he has a right to be consulted; he has a right to advise; and he has a right to persuade, if he can.

—**Abbot Lawrence Lowell** (1856–1943),
President, Harvard University

no date, attributed in Harold W. Dodds, *The Academic President: Educator or Caretaker?,* 1977, p. 48.

If the faculty accepts my idea without objection or hesitation—I know I am at least ten years too late.

—**Ray Lyman Wilbur** (1875–1949),
President, Stanford University

1955, "The administrator: Leader or officeholder?," *Freedom, Education, and the Fund,* 1956, p. 185.

It is one thing to get things done. It is another to make them last.

—**Robert Maynard Hutchins**
(1899–1977), President,
University of Chicago

1959, *Academic Procession,* p. 128.

A president cannot "boss" a faculty these days. It is rare indeed when he can lead it. But he can stimulate it, and he should. Such activity will not make him the benign or the well-beloved; but the object of holding office is educational progress, not popularity.

> —**Henry M. Wriston** (1889–1978), President, Lawrence College; President, Brown University

1959, *The American College President,* p. 20.

One thing is clear: colleges must have presidents and it makes a great difference who they are.

p. 22.

It is a wonderful paradox that the more power, the less freedom; that the man who theoretically should be able to say whatever comes into his mind actually has the least freedom of speech of all. The college president begins to understand Rousseau: one thinks himself the master of others, yet remains a greater slave than they.

> —**Harold W. Stoke** (1903–1982), President, University of New Hampshire; President, Louisiana State University; President, Queens College

1963, *The Uses of the University,* p. 33.

Instead of the Captain of Erudition . . . there is the Captain of the Bureaucracy who is sometimes a galley slave on his own ship. . . .

> —**Clark Kerr** (1911–2003), Chancellor, University of California, Berkeley; President, University of California

1964, *Letters to College Presidents,* p. 30.

It is said that one military man remarked soon after his election as president of a

university: "What kind of a place is this? I give an order and nothing happens. People pay no attention to what I say, or reply that they will take it under advisement. I ask for an opinion on how to proceed, and I get fifty different opinions. I propose what I think is a capital idea, and it produces a faculty wrangle. How does a man get things done in a place like this?"

> —**Thomas Elsa Jones** (1888–1973), President, Fisk University; President, Earlham College

1964, "The scientist as university president," Eric Compton Memorial Lecture, Washington University, St. Louis, 13 May, quoted in Clark Kerr and Marian L. Gade, *The Many Lives of Academic Presidents,* 1986, p. 203.

If a British university president has a bright idea . . . it would be the height of ineptitude to publish it to his faculty, and fatal to issue a directive about it. He must unobtrusively—if possible, anonymously—feed it into the organization, at quite a low level, informally over lunch, and watch it percolate slowly upwards. With luck it will come on to his desk months later for approval, and he must greet it with the pleased surprise which parents exhibit when their children show them what Santa Claus has brought them for Christmas.

> —**Eric Ashby** (1904–1992), botanist; Vice-chancellor, Cambridge University

1971, *An Uncertain Glory,* p. 8.

Presidential success or failure is, I fear, largely a matter of luck. . . . The college president is almost always in a war, and whether he wins or loses bears only a marginal relation to his foresight, his knowledge, his wisdom, his charm, his blood pressure, his . . . and I could go on.

p. 45.

For decades now—ever since the decline and fall of the old presidential monarchic system—the campus head has been so increasingly powerless that the various recent utterances by politicians and pundits on his ineffectuality seem almost redundant.

p. 149.

It was said of his [presidential] predecessor that he was a man of no small talent: after all, not every one could have taken a third-rate institution and turned it into a fourth-rate one in only a few short years.

> —**Frederic W. Ness** (1914–1998),
> President, Fresno State College

1974, *Leadership and Ambiguity,* p. 2.

The presidency is an illusion. Important aspects of the role seem to disappear on close examination. . . . Compared to the heroic expectations he and others might have, the president has modest control over the events of college life. The contributions he makes can easily be swamped by outside events or the diffuse qualities of university decision making.

p. 79.

The status of a president is apparently less dependent on the quality of his tenure as president than it is on the quality of his school. Colleges make presidents, not the reverse.

p. 151.

The college president is an executive who does not know exactly what he should be doing and does not have much confidence that he can do anything important anyway.

p. 203.

It is probably a mistake for a college president to imagine that what he does in office affects significantly either the long-run position of the institution or his reputation as a president. So long as he does not violate some rather obvious restrictions on his behavior, his reputation and his term of office are more likely to be affected by broad social events or by the unpredictable vicissitudes of official responsibilities than by his actions.

> —**Michael D. Cohen** (1945–), professor
> of complex systems, information, and
> public policy, University of Michigan;
> **James G. March** (1928–), professor
> of international management,
> political science, and sociology,
> Stanford University

1977, *The Academic President: Educator or Caretaker?,* p. 32.

Let no man assume that his office does not make a difference.

> —**Harold W. Dodds** (1889–1980),
> President, Princeton University

1978, memorandum, *A Free and Ordered Space,* 1988, p. 18.

To the members of the University Community: In order to repair what Milton called the ruin of our grand parents, I wish to announce that henceforth, as a matter of University policy, evil is abolished and paradise is restored. I trust all of us will do whatever is possible to achieve this policy objective.

> —**A. Bartlett Giamatti** (1938–1989),
> President, Yale University

1986, *The Effective Administrator,* p. 118.

[C]ampuses simply do not change permanently in response to the decisions and the will of a single person.

> —**Donald E. Walker** (1921–),
> President, Idaho State University;
> President, Southeastern Massachusetts
> University; Chancellor, Grossmont-
> Cuyamaca Community College District

1986, *The Many Lives of Academic Presidents,* p. 4.

Institutions of higher education are seldom the "lengthened shadow of one man" to the extent they once were—and some were; yet the president may still cast more of shadow than anyone else—and most do— and their shadows take many forms.

p. 4.

Some institutions will have survived because of their presidents while a few will have failed for the same reason; some institutions will have improved marginally, while others will have declined, again marginally, due to their efforts. Occasionally an institution will have been moved clearly ahead; and, rarely, some segment of higher education—or even all of higher education—will have been clearly advantaged because of some president's contributions. These are the ultimate tests of performance that very few ever pass.

—**Clark Kerr** (1911–2003), Chancellor, University of California, Berkeley; President, University of California; **Marian L. Gade** (1934–), research associate, University of California, Berkeley

1992, *How Academic Leadership Works,* pp. 195–96.

Presidents may be important in some situations, but the performance of colleges may usually be less dependent upon presidential leadership than most of us care to believe. Most college presidents do the right things, and do things right, most of the time. It is possible that college leaders can become marginally more effective. But those who seek major changes in the way presidents behave, or believe that such changes will make major differences in

our campuses, are likely to be disappointed.

—**Robert Birnbaum** (1936–), Chancellor, University of Wisconsin-Oshkosh

1992, *How Professors Play the Cat Guarding the Cream,* p. 18.

The less prestigious the university, the more powerful the president. In their drive to make their university a national research center, presidents collect about them forceful faculty with doctorates earned at distinguished institutions. The irony is that the degree to which presidents succeed in putting their institution on the academic map is the degree to which the power of the presidency in relation to the faculty is diminished.

—**Richard M. Huber** (1922–), Dean of General Studies, Hunter College

Presidential Learning

1918, *The Higher Learning in America,* Chapter 8.

[T]he university executive, who by pressure of competitive enterprise comes to be all things to all audiences, will come also to take on the colour of his own philandropic [sic] pronouncements: to believe, more or less conveniently, in his own blameless utterances.

—**Thorstein Veblen** (1857–1929), U.S. sociologist

1923, *The Goose-Step,* Chapter 76.

The president of a college or university is the great reconciler of irreconcilabilities; he is the chemist who mixes oil and water, the high priest who makes peace between God and Mammon, the circus-rider who stands on two horses going in opposite directions; and all these things not by choice, but ex-officio and of inescapable necessity. . . . How does he do it? I am moved to be blunt, and say in plain English that he does it by being the most universal faker and the most variegated prevaricator that has yet appeared in the civilized world. He does it by making his entire being a conglomeration of hypocrisies and stultifications, so that by the time he has been in office a year or two he has told so many different kinds of falsehoods and made so many different kinds of pretenses to so many different people, that he has lost all understanding of what truth is, or how a man could speak it.

—**Upton Sinclair** (1878–1968), U.S. author

1974, *Leadership and Ambiguity,* p. 41.

The modern college president does not suffer from lack of advice. Presidents, ex-presidents, and would-be presidents provide a steady stream of prescriptions. Universities are filled with and surrounded by persons who believe they know how to manage a university, have access to a publisher, and have time on their hands.

—**Michael D. Cohen** (1945–), professor of complex systems, information, and public policy, University of Michigan; **James G. March** (1928–), professor of international management, political science, and sociology, Stanford University

1977, *The Academic President: Educator or Caretaker?,* p. 26.

[N]o president completely escapes grubby details. What he must watch is that he is not confusing sheer activity with a sense of accomplishment.

—**Harold W. Dodds** (1889–1980), President, Princeton University

1980, *Being Lucky,* p. 147.

Strive to avoid the deadly occupational disease of omniscience and omnipotence.

Only the physician, surrounded by nurses and frightened families, is as tempted as is a president to be omniscient and omnipotent.

—**Herman B Wells** (1902–2000), President, Indiana University

1984, *Power of the Presidency,* p. 2.

Presidents know how important the office is, but are at first ignorant of its price, and later unsure they are willing to pay it.

—**James L. Fisher** (1931–), President, Towson State University

Presidential Problems

1769, on his deathbed, attributed in Samuel Eliot Morison, *Three Centuries of Harvard, 1636–1936,* p. 99.

If any man wishes to be humbled and mortified, let him become president of Harvard College.

—**Edward Holyoke** (1689–1769), President, Harvard College

1777, *The Literary Diary of Ezra Stiles, Vol. 2* [1901], p. 209, quoted in W. H. Cowley, *Presidents, Professors, and Trustees,* 1980, p. 53.

At best the Diadem of a President is a Crown of Thorns.

—**Ezra Stiles** (1727–1795), President, Yale University

1832, letter to his sister, quoted in Francis Wayland and H. L. Wayland (eds.), *A Memoir of the Life and Labors of Francis Wayland, Vol. 1,* p. 357.

I am . . . a perfect drayhorse. I am in harness from morning to night, and from one year to another. I am never turned out for recreation.

—**Francis Wayland** (1796–1865), President, Brown University

c. 1860–1862, quoted in Samuel Eliot Morison, *Three Centuries of Harvard, 1636–1936,* 1936, p. 301.

[T]here is no more comparison between the pleasure of being professor and president in this college than there is between heaven and hell.

—**Cornelius C. Felton** (1807–1862),
President, Harvard College

1872, quoted in Walter P. Rogers, *Andrew D. White and the Modern University,* 1942, p. 170.

This [the presidency] is a dog's life. . . . [N]o chance at the reputation I have most coveted—no cessation of duties which have always been most irksome. . . . [There are] rebuffs—the cold shoulder—unsuccessful pleading and unheeded begging—and such very green pastures in other directions.

—**Andrew D. White** (1832–1918),
President, Cornell University

c. 1900, "The college president" (unpublished), quoted in Richard J. Storr, *Harper's University,* 1966, pp. 103–4.

The college presidency means the giving up of many things, and, not the least among these, one's most intimate friendships. Moreover, this feeling of separation, of isolation, increases with each recurring year, and in spite of the most vigorous effort, it comes to be a thing of permanence. This is inevitable, and it is as sad as it is inevitable.

—**William Rainey Harper** (1856–1906),
President, University of Chicago

1913, *University Control,* p. 31.

Of course, the president is by nature as truthful, honorable and kind as the rest of us, and is likely to have more ability or enterprise, or both. But he really finds himself in an impossible situation. His despotism is only tempered by resignation;

and in the meantime he must act as though he were a statue of himself erected by public subscription.

—**J. McKeen Cattell** (1860–1944),
professor of psychology,
Columbia University

1922, "College education: An inquest, II," *The Freeman,* New York, 1 March, p. 585.

By constantly mediating among contending academic interests, and adjusting contests between the trustees and the scholastic body, he [the president] is in mortal peril of losing his soul, if by the time he is elected by the board of trustees, he has one left to lose. Years of this business give him, inevitably, a talent for manipulation that must leave its marks upon his benign countenance.

—**Somnia Vana** (pseudonym)

1930, *Universities: American English German,* p. 183.

One of the wisest of American philanthropists, head of a great business organization, long a trustee of a prominent university, once remarked to me: "A man may be president of a transcontinental railroad, an international banking corporation, a far-flung business; but the presidency of a great university is an impossible post."

—**Abraham Flexner** (1866–1959),
U.S. educator

1936, "The grand plan—the president's chief preoccupation," *The Management of Universities,* 1953, p 69.

It is easy to bury a president—although occasionally some members of the institution do not think it is easy enough.

—**Samuel P. Capen** (1878–1956),
director, American Council
on Education; President,
University of Buffalo

1940, *What College Presidents Say,* p. 362.

Not all presidents have been productive scholars. Those who have had a flair for research have been irked by administration—as was President David Starr Jordan, of Leland Stanford Junior University, who is reported to have complained that every time he learned the name of a student he forgot the name of a fish.

—**Edgar W. Knight** (1885–1953), professor of education history, University of North Carolina

1948, Spring, quoted in Travis Beal Jacobs, *Eisenhower at Columbia,* 2001, p. 87.

In a moment of weakness I listened to the blandishments of a couple of your trustees and here find myself with this gigantic organization on my hands, and I don't know a goddam thing about it.

—**Dwight D. Eisenhower** (1890–1969), President, Columbia University; President of the United States

1949, "What should a college president be?," address delivered at Texas Technological College, quoted in Joseph N. Crowley, *No Equal in the World,* 1994, p. 114.

[A college president] is one of the most burdened, . . . harassed, . . . put-upon people in American life. He is a hewer of wood and a drawer of water, a dray horse, a galley slave, a bellhop, a hack and a nursemaid all wrapped in one.

—**W. H. Cowley** (1899–1978), President, Hamilton College

1959, *The American College President,* p. 20.

Exciting, exacting, exhausting—it is probably these very characteristics of the college presidency which attract those who are eager to try it. But the position is full of paradoxes—those who enjoy it are not very successful, and those who are successful are not very happy. The explanation is hidden somewhere in the philosophy of power. Those who enjoy exercising power shouldn't have it, and those who should exercise it are not likely to enjoy it.

p. 23.

[The president] is a man of many acquaintances but few friends. The reason is simple: friendship is possible only between equals, and a college or university has only one president. . . . The loss of natural friendship with close associates is a grim price but it must be paid. The first responsibility of good administration is justice, and the requirements of justice and of friendship are incompatible.

p. 102.

Every president of an athletics-minded college knows that he stands on an active volcano.

—**Harold W. Stoke** (1903–1982), President, University of New Hampshire; President, Louisiana State University; President, Queens College

1967, "The job of the college president," *Educational Record,* Winter, p. 78.

A college president who tries to make education professional should not expect a unanimous vote of thanks from his faculty, or even his students. If a man's first aim in life were to be comfortable and to be liked, he would choose an easier occupation than college president.

—**Herbert A. Simon** (1916–), Professor of Computer Sciences and Psychology, Carnegie Institute of Technology

1970, "Presidential discontent," in David C. Nichols (ed.), *Perspectives on Campus Tensions,* 1970, p. 151.

Trouble rises to the level of the presidency and falls to the level of the presidency. The president is the institutional lightning rod. In a time of troubles, the president will be in trouble.

—**Clark Kerr** (1911–2003), Chancellor, University of California, Berkeley; President, University of California

1971, *Born to Rebel: An Autobiography,* p. 196.

To be president of a college and white is no bed of roses. To be president of a college and black is almost a bed of thorns.

—**Benjamin E. Mays** (1895–1984), President, Morehouse College

1976, *The Unconscious Conspiracy,* p. 106.

Much is made of that final responsibility "the buck stops here." However, a president is often lucky if he can find the buck at all, learn where it stopped, or discover who stopped it before it reached him. I wish I could get some genuine "bucks" on my desk, rather than the myriad of frittering detail that does get dumped there so that (what I have phrased as Bennis's law) routine work drives out the important.

—**Warren G. Bennis** (1925–), psychologist; President, University of Cincinnati

1976, "The reeling presidency," *Educational Record,* Spring, p. 78.

What is it like to be a college president in these times? If you speak with enough administrators, especially those who have resigned in times of crisis, it may sound as though it is nothing so much as dodging shrapnel in a pressure cooker dropping through space upside down with bells ring-

ing and horns blowing in three dimensional living color.

—**Charles C. Cole, Jr.** (1922–), President, Wilson College

1986, *The Many Lives of Academic Presidents,* p. 97.

A president tied down by Lilliputians becomes more like a Lilliputian himself.

—**Clark Kerr** (1911–2003), Chancellor, University of California, Berkeley; President, University of California; **Marian L. Gade** (1934–), research associate, University of California, Berkeley

1988, *A Free and Ordered Space,* p. 17.

Being president of a university is no way for an adult to make a living. Which is why so few adults actually attempt to do it. It is to hold a mid-nineteenth-century ecclesiastical position on top of a late-twentieth-century corporation.

—**A. Bartlett Giamatti** (1938–1989), President, Yale University

1991, "Wanted: Miracle workers," *Newsweek,* 8 April, pp. 48–49.

[These days, running a university is] a combination of being a CEO and an elected politician—without the powers of command of a CEO and without the steady constituency of the politician. It's about the hardest job in the United States.

—**Robert M. Rosenzweig** (1931–), President, Association of American Universities

1998, "The art of the presidency," *The President,* Spring, p. 17.

Overburdened university presidents do not *suffer* burnout; they *create* it, inflicting it upon themselves by their lack of responsible work habits. The campus is unlikely to prosper if its leader is so worn down by the burdens of office that he or she conveys a sense of joyless routine and weary resignation.

—**Frank H. T. Rhodes** (1926–),
President, Cornell University

Presidential Qualifications

c. 1875, quoted in Henry James, *Charles W. Eliot,* 1930, volume I, p. 309–10.

To a questioner who asked him [Charles W. Eliot], after he had been at the head of Harvard for a few years, to name the quality most essential to a college president, he answered, "The capacity to inflict pain."

—**Charles William Eliot** (1834–1926),
President, Harvard University

1876, letter to Daniel Coit Gilman, quoted in Lawrence R. Veysey, *The Emergence of the American University,* 1965, p. 328.

Candor and frankness are after all the most necessary qualities in a college president.

—**Charles William Eliot** (1834–1926),
President, Harvard University

c. nineteenth century, attributed to Frank H. T. Rhodes, as quoted in Clark Kerr and Marian L. Gade, *The Many Lives of Academic Presidents,* 1986, p. 234.

When Yale University was searching for a president in the 19th century, one of its board members characterized the search for the individual—assumed, in those days, as inevitably a man—as follows: He had to be a leader, a magnificent speaker, a great writer, a good public relations man, a man of iron health and stamina, married to a paragon of virtue. His wife, in fact, had to be a mixture of Queen Victoria, Florence Nightingale, and the best-dressed

woman of the year. We saw our choice as having to be a man of the world, but an individual with great spiritual qualities; an experienced administrator, but able to delegate; a Yale man, and a great scholar; a social philosopher, who though he had the solutions to the world's problems, had still not lost the common touch. After lengthy deliberation, we concluded that there was only one such person. But then a dark thought crossed our minds. We had to ask—*is God a Yale man?*

—**Unknown Yale Trustee**

1902, "Concerning the American university," in *Popular Science Monthly,* June, p. 176.

There is no other office so fit for a past President of the United States as the presidency of a university.

—**J. McKeen Cattell** (1860–1944),
professor of psychology,
Columbia University

1912, "The administrative peril in education," in J. McKeen Cattell, *University Control,* 1913, p. 337.

[T]he only type of man safely to be entrusted with the prerogatives of the presidency is one whose principles would require him to decline the office.

—**Joseph Jastrow** (1863–1944),
professor of psychology,
University of Wisconsin

1955, "The administrator: Leader or officeholder?," *Freedom, Education, and the Fund,* 1956, p. 169.

The minimum qualifications of an administrator in his dealing with the means are four. They are courage, fortitude, justice, and prudence or practical wisdom. . . . When I say that the administrator should have courage, fortitude, justice, and prudence, I am only saying that he should be a good man.

p. 176.

[T]he administrator must be a troublemaker; for every change in education is a change in the habits of some members of the faculty.

—Robert Maynard Hutchins
(1899–1977), President,
University of Chicago

1956, "Introduction: Education,"
Freedom, Education, and The Fund,
p. 73.

The only kind of man who can cheerfully administer a large university is one who is not interested in education. A man who is interested will find himself constantly frustrated.

—Robert Maynard Hutchins
(1899–1977), President,
University of Chicago

1959, *Academic Procession,* p. 16.

I cannot deny that ministers, lawyers, military officers, bankers, business men, and others have occasionally done well. But the sound rule is that the president should be a scholar; all the other essential attributes should be present, but secondary.

—Henry M. Wriston (1889–1978),
President, Lawrence College;
President, Brown University

1963, *The Uses of the University,*
pp. 29–30.

The university president in the United States is expected to be a friend to the students, a colleague of the faculty, a good fellow with the alumni, a sound administrator with the trustees, a good speaker with the public, an astute bargainer with

the foundations and the federal agencies, a politician with the state legislature, a friend of industry, labor, and agriculture, a persuasive diplomat with donors, a champion of education generally, a supporter of the professions (particularly law and medicine), a spokesman to the press, a scholar in his own right, a public servant at the state and national levels, a devotee of opera and football equally, a decent human being, a good husband and father, an active member of a church. Above all, he must enjoy traveling in airplanes, eating his meals in public, and attending public ceremonies. No one can be all of these things. Some succeed at being none.

—Clark Kerr (1911–2003), Chancellor,
University of California, Berkeley;
President, University of California

1964, *Los Angeles Times* column, 8
November, quoted in Milton S. Mayer,
Robert Maynard Hutchins: A Memoir,
1993, pp. 396–97.

[G]ood men become college presidents only because they do not know any better. . . . If a man knows what it is like to be a university president and still wants to be one, he is not qualified for the job.

—Robert Maynard Hutchins
(1899–1977), President,
University of Chicago

1965, *How College Presidents are Chosen,* pp. 1–2.

A president who might have been an institution's savior, twenty years ago, may bring about its ruin today. Or a man who would be ideal at the helm of one college or university might nearly cause a shipwreck at another.

—Frederick deW. Bolman
(1912–1985), President,
Franklin and Marshall College

1967, *Power, Presidents, and Professors,* p. 61.

Boards of trustees search for supermen. They appoint human beings.

> —**Nicholas J. Demerath** (1913–1996), professor of sociology, Washington University

1974, *Leadership and Ambiguity,* p. 193.

Although becoming a president typically requires ambition, ambition is badly served by the presidency—and the presidency is badly served by ambition.

> —**Michael D. Cohen** (1945–), professor of complex systems, information, and public policy, University of Michigan; **James G. March** (1928–), professor of international management, political science, and sociology, Stanford University

1975, "Casting about for a president," *Chronicle of Higher Education,* 18 February, p. 32.

The faculty does not want a leader in curriculum reform; the trustees do not want better management if it threatens such pet programs as intercollegiate athletics, as it must; and the students do not want to be straightened out by the president—which is what the alumni want him to do. . . . A search committee that accepts the logic of this argument has its job immeasurably simplified: hire an actor as president. It allows everyone to focus on the qualities which are *really* sought in a president—the capacity to speak sincerely and with conviction about many things, the ability to give consistently good performances on tour while, above all, looking and dressing like a president.

> —**Paul A. Lacey** (1934–), Provost, Earlham College

1980, *Being Lucky,* p. 143.

My first maxim [for the young college president] is: Be lucky.

p. 147.

Be born with the physical charm of a Greek athlete, the cunning of Machiavelli, the wisdom of Solomon, the courage of a lion, if possible; but in any case be born with the stomach of a goat.

> —**Herman B Wells** (1902–2000), President, Indiana University

1984, "American college presidents since World War II," *Educational Record,* Spring, p. 12.

The towering presidents of the late nineteenth century proudly displayed sonorous, three-worded names [e.g., William Rainey Harper, Daniel Coit Gilman, David Starr Jordan, Andrew Sloan Draper, Andrew Dickson White] that possessed majesty and commanded a respect lacking in the ordinary household names of mid-twentieth century presidents. Can a college president today aspire to greatness with only two names?

> —**Paul F. Sharp** (1918–), President, University of Oklahoma; President, Drake University; Chancellor, University of North Carolina, Chapel Hill; President, Hiram College.

1988, *How Colleges Work,* p. 24.

The old joke states the qualifications for college president as "white hair for that look of experience and hemorrhoids for that look of concern." As is true of many jokes, there is an important core of reality in this one that suggests that the effects of leadership may rely as much on our preconceptions and biases as on the observed outcomes that are clearly the consequences of leadership behavior.

—**Robert Birnbaum** (1936–), Chancellor, University of Wisconsin-Oshkosh

Presidential Rewards

c. 1900, "The college president" (unpublished), cited in Richard J. Storr, *Harper's University,* 1966, p. 105.

The life of a university officer is in many respects the most ideal that exists. The minister meets everywhere sorrow and sickness and death. The lawyer struggles against dishonesty, dissipation and fraud. The physician is almost wholly occupied with want and pain and suffering. With the college professor and the college president it is essentially different. They have to deal with all that is uplifting in life, with the constructive and not the destructive forces of life. The satisfaction which this brings no man can describe.

—**William Rainey Harper** (1856–1906), President, University of Chicago

1923, *The Goose-Step,* Chapter 76.

The college president has acquired enormous prestige in American capitalist society; he is a priest of the new god of science, and newspapers and purveyors of "public opinion" unite in exalting him. He receives the salary of a plutocrat, and arrogates to himself the prestige and precedence that go with it. He lives on terms of equality with business emperors and financial dukes, and conveys their will to mankind, and perpetuates their ideals and prejudices to the coming generation.

—**Upton Sinclair** (1878–1968), U.S. author

1955, "The administrator: Leader or officeholder?," *Freedom, Education, and the Fund,* 1956, p. 171.

Administration is unpleasant, as anything that requires the exercise of the virtues I have named must be. It is doubtful whether even these virtues can be exercised without divine aid. And the happiness which they give is not, I fear, a happiness in this life.

—**Robert Maynard Hutchins** (1899–1977), President, University of Chicago

1959, *The American College President,* p. 20.

[T]here are obscure impulses in human nature which possess channel swimmers and mountain climbers and, perhaps, the men who become college presidents, impulses to adventure and danger. Danger offers exhilaration; risks and rewards are usually equated. John Erskine once remarked that being a college president was like a small boy walking a high picket fence—thrilled, but in constant danger of being impaled.

—**Harold W. Stoke** (1903–1982), President, University of New Hampshire; President, Louisiana State University; President, Queens College

1969, "The job of the president," *Liberal Education,* October, p. 387.

Certainly the duties are so heavy, the burdens so onerous, that extensive service as a university president may well deserve at least beatification if not canonization.

—**Francis H. Horn** (1908–1999), President, Pratt Institute; President, University of Rhode Island; President, Albertus Magnus College

1979, "The college presidency: Life between a rock and a hard place," *Change,* May-June, p. 44.

Presidents, like all human beings, enjoy an occasional pat on the back. But it is far more realistic to expect numerous kicks in another part of your anatomy when you make a mistake. Criticism is a far greater part of presidential life than plaudits or gratitude.

—**Theodore M. Hesburgh, C.S.C.**
(1917–), President,
University of Notre Dame

1979, "The university president," *The Hesburgh Papers,* pp. 12–13.

We might as well admit that willy-nilly, the president will always be between the rock and the hard place. Having admitted this, let us also admit that there is no better association in the world than a good academic relationship where civility rules disagreement—and comradeship is very real in an endeavor as fundamentally exalted as higher education.

—**Theodore M. Hesburgh, C.S.C.**
(1917–), President,
University of Notre Dame

Presidential Role

c. 1900, "The college president" (unpublished), quoted in Richard J. Storr, *Harper's University,* 1966, p. 105.

One should never himself do what he can in any way find someone else to do. . . . Further, the president should never do today what by any possible means he can postpone until tomorrow. Premature action is the source of many more mistakes than procrastination.

—**William Rainey Harper** (1856–1906),
President, University of Chicago

1904, "The college president," *Educational Record,* April 1938, p. 180.

The college presidency is a profession in which a large percentage of one's time and energy is occupied in saying "no."

—**William Rainey Harper** (1856–1906),
President, University of Chicago

1913, "The college presidency," *Science,* 2 May, p. 654.

What do we expect of the American college president? From my observations, I am inclined to sum it up by saying that he must be all things to all men at all times and under all circumstances.

—**William T. Foster** (1879–1950),
President, Reed College

1918, *The Higher Learning in America,* Chapter 8.

[B]y tradition the president of the university is the senior member of the faculty, its confidential spokesman in official and corporate concerns, and the "moderator" of its town-meetinglike deliberative assemblies. . . . As spokesman for the faculty he is, by tradition, presumed to be a scholar of such erudition, breadth, and maturity as may fairly command something of filial respect and affection from his associates in the corporation of learning. . . .

—**Thorstein Veblen** (1857–1929),
U.S. sociologist

1922, "College education: An inquest, II," *The Freeman,* New York, 1 March, p. 585.

Whenever the president is called into an academic fray, it is to adjust a row between departments in which he suffers defeat, no matter which side wins.

—**Somnia Vana** (pseudonym)

no date, attributed in Harold W. Stoke, *The American College President,* 1959, p. 34.

[A] college president is like a hunter who spends ninety-five per cent of his time swatting at mosquitoes, while remembering that he is where he is in order to get a shot at a moose.

—**Lotus D. Coffman** (1875–1938),
President, University of Minnesota

1926, *The College President,* p. 234.

A college presidency is not a profession. . . . It is an art. It consists in doing.

—**Charles F. Thwing** (1853–1937),
President, Adelbert College; President,
Western Reserve University

1931, "The boon of culture," in *A Mencken Chrestomathy,* 1949, p. 313.

Every American college president, it appears, is in duty bound to write and utter at least one book upon the nature, aims and usufructs [benefits] of the Higher Education. . . . As a rule, he puts it off to his later Autumn days when the hemlock of senility has begun to dull the edge of his troubles, but he seldom dodges it altogether. . . . But I must add in all honesty that I have yet to find, in any such tome, anything properly describable as wisdom.

—**H. L. Mencken** (1880–1956),
U.S. editor and writer

1936, "The grand plan—The president's chief preoccupation," in *The Management of Universities,* 1953, pp. 67–68.

The college presidency is not a profession. What is it then? It is an opportunist's job. The job consists principally of dealing with the unforeseen and the unforeseeable, the irregular and the irrelevant, the unknown and the unknowable; and often making the best of a bad business. Nobody learns it by going to school. There is no school. . . . Like other opportunist's jobs one learns only by trying it. And some very promising neophytes fail.

—**Samuel P. Capen** (1878–1956),
director, American Council
on Education; President,
University of Buffalo

1939, "Hutchins of Chicago," in *Harper's Monthly Magazine,* March, p. 344.

A university president is supposed to go downtown and get the money. He is not supposed to have ideas on public affairs; that is what the trustees are for. He is not supposed to have ideas on education; that is what the faculty are for. He is supposed to go downtown and get the money.

—**Milton S. Mayer** (1908–1986),
U.S. journalist

no date, poem in "The Conning Tower," *New York Tribune,* attributed in a June 1953 unpublished lecture by W. H. Cowley, "Conflicts in the college presidency," quoted by Robert F. Wert, "Leadership: The integrative factor," in Terry F. Lunsford (ed.), *The Study of Academic Administration,* 1963, pp. 92–93.

(To the tune of the Major-General song in Gilbert and Sullivan's *The Pirates of Penzance*)

I am the very pattern of a modern
    college president,
I'm always on the job, though nearly
    always a non-resident.
I tour about the country to assemblies
    gastronomical
And make all sorts of speeches from
    sublime to broadly comical.
I keep the trustees calm and the alumni
    all benevolent,

Restrain all signs of riot and publicity
  malevolent,
I know the market value of each wage-
  slave professorial,
And how much less he'll take for
  honorarium tutorial,
I'm on to all the low intrigues and
  rivalries divisional,
And on the budget how I field my
  fountain pen excisional!
So though I pile up mileage being
  generally non-resident
I am the very model of a modern
  college president!

I mix with all the business kings—the
  Lions and the Rotary.
Of Heiresses and oil tycoons I am
  hopeful votary. . . .
I use the phrase "distinguished guest"
  at every opportunity,
I welcome all alumni to my parlor
  every June at tea. . . .
I've shaken every human hand that's
  manicured and squeezable,
I pass the hat among the rich, the buck
  wherever feasible!
So though I pile up mileage being
  generally non-resident,
I am the very model of a modern
  college president!

—FPA [Franklin Pierce Adams]
(1881–1960), U.S. columnist and author

1946, "The administrator," *Journal of
Higher Education,* November, p. 396.

[I] regard patience as a delusion and a
snare and I think that administrators have
far too much of it rather than too little.

p. 400.

The temptation to bury oneself in routine
is tremendous. There are so many reports,
so many meetings, so many signatures, so
many people to see—all that have some
value to the institution that you can con-

scientiously draw your salary and never
administer at all.

—Robert Maynard Hutchins
(1899–1977), President,
University of Chicago

1959, *The American College President,*
pp. 23–24.

Robbed of his freedom of speech and left
with acquaintances in lieu of friends, a college president, however gregarious out-
wardly, is a lonely man. Since, as Aristotle
said, men, to live alone, must be gods or
beasts, presidents escape their dilemma
largely by forming their warming friendships outside academic relationships or by
seeking the company of their fellow presidents. College presidents form a tight
club, not because they wish to be deliber-
ately exclusive, but because they cannot or
are not allowed to be comfortable members of any club other than their own.

p. 117.

It is the president's job to interpret and defend the academic life to those who understand it less well. If, accustomed himself to
more definable tasks than those of the faculty, he becomes occasionally impatient
with what seems to him their slipshod and
leisurely operations, let him remember that
his kind of schedule and responsibilities
can never produce either good scholarship
or good teaching.

—Harold W. Stoke (1903–1982),
President, University of New Hampshire;
President, Louisiana State University;
President, Queens College

p. 29.

It is sometimes said that the American
multiversity president is a two-faced character. This is not so. If he were, he could
not survive. He is a many-faced character,
in the sense that he must face in many directions at once, while contriving to turn
his back on no important group.

p. 30.

He [the president] should sound like a mouse at home and look like a lion abroad.

p. 36.

The president in the multiversity is leader, educator, initiator, wielder of power, pump; he is also officeholder, caretaker, inheritor, consensus-seeker, persuader, bottleneck. But he is mostly a mediator.

—**Clark Kerr** (1911–2003), Chancellor, University of California, Berkeley; President, University of California

1964, "The scientist as university president," Eric Compton Memorial Lecture, Washington University, St. Louis, 13 May, quoted in Clark Kerr and Marian L. Gade, *The Many Lives of Academic Presidents,* 1986, p. 203.

His [the president's] skill is to balance the centrifugal forces of individuality which tend to pull the institution apart, against centripetal forces—largely generated by himself—which tend to preserve the integrity of the institution.

—**Eric Ashby** (1904–1992), botanist; Vice-chancellor, Cambridge University

1967, *Power, Presidents, and Professors,* p. 41.

Part creature and part creator of the organization in which he works, the university president, like other chief executives, is expected to maintain the organizational structure and to give leadership to the making of general policy decisions.

—**Nicholas J. Demerath** (1913–1996), professor of sociology, Washington University

c. 1970, quoted in Steven B. Sample, *The Contrarian's Guide to Leadership,* 2002, p. 160.

[M]any men want to *be* president, but very few want to *do* president.

—**Vernon Newhouse** (1928–), professor of electrical engineering, Purdue University

1974, *Leadership and Ambiguity,* p. 57.

One can make numerous statements about what the presidency should be with which few will disagree. The difficulty is in finding propositions with some concrete relevance, propositions that actually exclude some possibilities and evoke some substantial agreement. There are many things that presidents should do or be, but none that most presidents, or most of any other group, see as taking clear priority. What priorities there are seem very likely to be unstable over time.

—**Michael D. Cohen** (1945–), professor of complex systems, information, and public policy, University of Michigan; **James G. March** (1928–), professor of international management, political science, and sociology, Stanford University

1977, *The Academic President: Educator or Caretaker?,* p. 57.

When asked how often a president could make the same speech, Woodrow Wilson is said to have replied, "I don't know; I'm still making the same one."

p. 75.

There is a great deal to be done. If I could do it myself it would, of course, be done better than by anyone else. But since I can't do it all, for there are only 24 hours in a day, I must delegate. Even if the work is not done as well as I should do it, it will be done relatively well. In any event, it is more apt to be done than if I tried to do it. Probably it will be done better.

—**Harold W. Dodds** (1889–1980),
President, Princeton University

1980, *Presidents, Professors, and Trustees,* p. 67.

In his *Autobiography,* William Lyon Phelps (1939) described the difference between the old-time college president and his modern successor. When he went as a young man to the office of President Noah Porter of Yale, Phelps usually found him reading Kant. When he later went to see Porter's successor, Timothy Dwight, he almost always found him reading the balance sheet.

—**W. H. Cowley** (1899–1978),
President, Hamilton College

1984, *Presidents Make a Difference,* p. 89.

Few presidents can be much better than their boards; none can be much worse—at least not for very long.

—**Commission on Strengthening Presidential Leadership**

Subject Heading Index

Author Index

About the Author

ROBERT BIRNBAUM is Emeritus Professor of Higher Education at the University of Maryland, College Park, and was formerly Professor and Chair of the Department of Higher and Adult Education at Teachers College, Columbia University. Prior to his faculty career, Birnbaum held administrative appointments as Vice-chancellor of the City University of New York. More recently he served for two years as Founding Vice President and Dean of Faculty of Miyazaki International College in Japan. Birnbaum is author, co-author, or editor of nine books and numerous articles in scholarly and professional journals related to higher education leadership and organization, and the role of higher education in society.